The Petersburg Regiment in the Civil War

A History of the 12th Virginia Infantry from
John Brown's Hanging to Appomattox, 1859–1865

John Horn

Savas Beatie
California

Library of Congress Cataloging-in-Publication Data

Names: Horn, John, 1951- author.
Title: The Petersburg Regiment in the Civil War: A History of the 12th Virginia Infantry from John Brown's Hanging to Appomattox, 1859–1865, by John Horn.
Description: California: Savas Beatie, [2018]|Includes bibliographical references and index.
Identifiers: LCCN 2018052408|ISBN 9781611214369
(hbk.: alk. paper) |ISBN 9781611214376 (ebk)
Subjects: LCSH: Confederate States of America. Army. Virginia Infantry Regiment, 12th.
United States—History—Civil War, 1861–1865—Campaigns.
United States—History—Civil War, 1861–1865—Regimental histories
Classification: LCC E581.5 12th .H67 2018|DDC 973.7/455—dc23
LC record available at https://lccn.loc.gov/2018052408

First Edition, First Printing

SB

Published by
Savas Beatie LLC
989 Governor Drive, Suite 102
El Dorado Hills, CA 95762

Phone: 916-941-6896
(web) www.savasbeatie.com
(E-mail) sales@savasbeatie.com

Our titles are available at special discounts for bulk purchases in the United States. Contact the publisher for details.

To my wife, law partner, and inspiration, H. Elizabeth Kelley,

descendant of two of the regiment's soldiers.

Table of Contents

Table of Contents (continued)

List of Diagrams and Maps

List of Diagrams and Maps (continued)

List of Diagrams and Maps (continued)

Foreword:
A Golden Age of Civil War Studies

A century and a half after the Civil War's conclusion, scholars and readers find themselves at an unexpected, but very welcome, point: The long tradition of studying and interpreting the conflict has been rejuvenated, resulting in a richer, more honest and far broader appreciation of those who fought in the ranks or led from the front, all but a few of whom had faded into the shadows cast by the titans. More than ever before, we have an appreciation of the complex humanity of the common men who did such uncommon things.

Ours is a golden age of Civil War studies.

Although some enlisted veterans produced admirable memoirs, for over a century the written word focused on the famed men of high rank, first with the score-settling reminiscences by generals gray and blue who bickered among themselves all the way to their graves, then with the shameless romanticizing of the great by partisan historians—who robbed their subjects of their true humanity—and on to the popular "overview" histories in which those below the rank of general rarely earned a mention.

Over the last several decades, though, another strain of historical writing began to have an impact, a democratic approach, in which the average soldier's importance and vitality gained recognition. Hand-written memoirs emerged from chests in attics; letters bound with faded ribbons escaped from old tin boxes; and ever more scholars asked themselves "What was it like for the men in the ranks or for the junior officers at war?"

Regimental histories, in particular, evolved from bare-bones recitations of events with rosters appended to richly detailed accounts of how flesh-and-blood men experienced four years of carnage, heartbreak, loneliness, fury, boredom, hunger, sweat, frostbite, wounds, disease, glory and petty grudges, the thrill and ache of mail from home amid camp life's sour drudgery, the profound, rough-handed camaraderie and, not least, the experience of battle.

John Horn's splendid history of the 12th Virginia will stand among the classics of the discipline.

Long years of research and patient crafting allowed the author to deliver an account as detailed and precise, as honest and clear, as any regimental accounting we'll ever see. Following the men of Petersburg and its environs from the naïve enthusiasm of the war's initial months through near-disaster amid the gore at Crampton's Gap, and on through a series of tough stands in the Chancellorsville campaign to the blunt savagery of the war's last year, this chronicle of one hard-used, heroic regiment is a true soldier's book— and that is a great compliment. John Horn takes us as close as words on a page can bring us to the soldier's experience. From merry snowball fights between entire brigades, to the final, bitter defense of their home city, the men of the 12th Virginia leap to life.

Horn's reliance on first-hand accounts reminds us of how casual death became—as well as how hungry those men in gray became as early as the winter of 1863, when at least a few acquaintances of the regiment found rat meat a tasty supplement to their rations.

Simple pleasures and harsh punishments, battlefield confusion and clashes of character . . . informal truces on the picket line and the shock of finding your powder wet as the enemy approaches . . . so often, it's the telling detail, the tidbit ignored by the proponents of grand history, that really bring those Civil War soldiers to life again. And Horn is the master of such details.

Above all, though, this book is a labor of love. And that's key to grasping how this new golden age of Civil War studies occurred. Men and women of serious mien and mind have dedicated their lives to uncovering the conflict's mundane, illuminating details and its neglected actors, what the French historian, Fernand Braudel, called "the structures of everyday life." And those researchers and authors are not doing this expecting financial gain; quite the contrary, they know that book sales rarely bring more than a meager return on their enormous investments of time, energy and lifelong financial outlays. They do this work because of a sense of mission, a sense of duty to those who transformed our nation. And so we gain books such as the volume you hold in your hands. No well-intentioned ceremonies, however large and colorful, honor the dead as mightily as such works.

Another factor contributing to this new golden age is that untamed beast, the internet. Scholars scorn it publicly, but use it privately. Yes, the internet, with its lack of editorial controls and discrimination, can be the domain of extravagant lies and insidious self-deception, of cruel shaming and hard-hearted revenge, but for all that it also enables historians and savvy amateurs to trace and contact descendants of those who fought, to locate never-published documentation, to broaden their research immensely, and to track down obscure newspaper articles, genealogies and public records, even photographs that kin thought lost. For the historian, the internet replaced nothing, but enhanced a great deal. The archives still demand that he or she be present for duty in those glorious prisons for long stretches—there's no substitute for classic, relentless research. But exploited by those of knowledge, judgment and character, the internet is a massively powerful tool.

But the ultimate value of all means of research is that they coalesce to result in a book as fine as this one. Horn's extraordinary work does well by the dead and living alike. The infantrymen of the 12th Virginia will no doubt dip their flags to the author as their ghosts march by.

Ralph Peters (Col., ret)

Introduction

Dr. Richard J. Sommers, dean of Petersburg scholars, set the standard for scholarship about the city's siege in *Richmond Redeemed* by consulting practically everything in print on his subject. I chose to write a unit history to narrow the scope of research to where an amateur such as myself might approach that standard.

Every student of the Civil War should write a unit history. Knowing a unit's history provides a tuning fork with which to test the accuracy of more general works on the Civil War.

To make worthwhile the efforts of an author of such a history, the soldiers of the unit must have left a substantial amount of literature. Otherwise the author can only deduce the unit's activities and experience from more general works and detailed histories of similar units. The author of the history of an articulate unit gives voice to mute units.

The soldiers of the Petersburg Regiment left volumes of diaries, letters, memoirs and articles. These men—and some of their wives and children—wrote the regiment's history. I have tried to use their terminology whenever possible to put the reader in their shoes.

Otherwise, I just tried to stay out of their way.

John Horn

Prologue: A Sad Homecoming

Mrs. Charles E. Waddell lay in the darkness, listening to shells burst around her house on Bollingbrook Street. Just before one in the morning on June 18, 1864, a shell exploded so near that its flash startled her. The crash shook her. A shell fragment struck her back porch, terrifying her sister. The two women hurriedly dressed. With a pair of slaves, they scurried into a neighbor's basement, huddling there for the rest of the night as shells burst outside.

After sunrise, Mrs. Waddell's sister and their mother packed and left for Raleigh, North Carolina. Short on food, low on money and weak from a recent illness, Mrs. Waddell remained home.

She knew that at any moment a cannonball might kill her. She could not imagine what would become of her if the Yankees succeeded in storming her city. Until she learned the fate of her husband in the terrible campaign that had opened in northern Virginia a month and a half earlier, though, she refused to leave. She and the rest of the city expected his unit to arrive momentarily.

At four o'clock that bright, hot afternoon, Mrs. Waddell sat down to dinner. Amid her meal, the sound of approaching fifes and drums rose above the cannon fire and musketry. She ran to the front door.

The Petersburg Regiment had come home. "Sure enough," she recorded that evening, "our own gallant 12th Va. Regiment" led the column turning into the street. She could scarcely recognize the dusty, ragged veterans as the impeccably dressed recruits who had gone off to war more than three years earlier. "It made one's heart ache to look at them," wrote Mrs. Waddell, "and oh! how many familiar faces we missed. . . ." The 12th consisted mainly of men from Petersburg. Hardly a family in the city lacked a relative or friend in the regiment's ranks. Fathers and mothers, sisters and sweethearts rushed out of their houses to greet their dear ones as the 12th passed. Down the street from Mrs. Waddell's house, a mother and daughter ran up a Confederate flag in honor of the regiment's return. The tired soldiers cheered feebly.

The column swung up Bollingbrook Street. Mrs. Waddell saw a poor, thin figure step out of the ranks and wave his battered hat to her. Despite his dust, rags and emaciation, she recognized her husband, Capt. Charles E. Waddell, commander of the 12th's Company A, the Petersburg City Guard. "For a moment I felt frantic with joy to know him that near me and safe; and then overwhelmed with grief to see him in such a sad plight, and to know he was then marching towards death and danger," she recorded.[1] He passed so quickly that "Fan," as he called her, could not get through the crowd to him, but their slave Becky found an unobstructed route.[2] Rushing into the ranks, Becky seized the captain's hand and cheered him with news of home and loved ones.

The regiment turned left onto Sycamore Street. Friends and relatives of the 12th's soldiers almost blocked this street. Private George Bernard of the 12th's Company E, the Petersburg Riflemen, noted finding it "difficult to realize that we were within 2 miles of the enemy's shells & that we were preparing to take position in line of battle."[3] The numerous ladies greeting the troops made them feel as if they were going to take part in some festivity.

Near Sycamore's intersection with Tabb Street, the column passed between the courthouse, with its four-faced clock tower on the eastern side of Sycamore, and the Iron Front Building opposite. From the Iron Front Building's windows, people threw plugs of tobacco to the veterans. The owner of one home farther south on Sycamore brought to his front gate a bucket of water and two gourds for the soldiers. Another homeowner allowed the 12th's men

---

1 Mrs. Charles E. Waddell Diary, June 18, 1864, Papers of Miss Georgia Hicks, Collection of the United Daughters of the Confederacy, North Carolina Division, North Carolina Department of Archives and History, Raleigh, North Carolina. Punctuation, capitalization, emphasis and spelling in quotations have been left alone whenever possible.

2 Charles E. Waddell Diary, August 8, 1863, American Civil War Museum (ACWM), Richmond, Virginia.

3 George S. Bernard Diary, June 19, 1864, George S. Bernard Papers, Alderman Library, University of Virginia (UVA), Charlottesville, Virginia. This collection also includes all Bernard's letters cited herein.

James Eldred Phillips. *Elise Phillips Atkins, Arlington Heights, IL*

to fill their canteens with warm coffee out of a hogshead in one of his wagons.

The ecstatic greeting accorded the Petersburg soldiers awakened pangs of sadness and bitterness in one of the regiment's men from enemy-occupied Norfolk. Sergeant John Sale of the 12th's Company H, the Norfolk Juniors, recorded, "These attentions (which of course were to be expected) made me feel how easily our home was given up to the enemy."[4] On the way to Petersburg, the 12th's soldiers had heard a rumor that the invaders were in possession of the heights southeast of the city. "I, and I reckon most of the command, fully expected to charge the Federals on the heights," recalled the Riflemen's Pvt. Putnam Stith. When the regiment reached Marshall Street, about half a mile south of Bollingbrook, the men saw riding toward them Lt. Col. Gilbert Moxley Sorrel of the staff of Anderson's Corps. The soldiers called out: "Lead us, Sorrel! Lead us as you did in the Wilderness!"[5] Sorrel doffed his hat and bowed low. Remarking that nothing would please him better than to lead them in another charge, he told them they would do no fighting that evening. They had only to go out a short distance from the city, form a line and rest.

At 5 p.m., the troops bivouacked in a pine grove near the Wilcox farm, known as Walnut Hill, two miles south of Petersburg. Many looked among the trees for a place to sleep after their tramp of nearly 30 miles, which had begun at four o'clock that morning. "I saw a pile of small brush . . . so I

4 John F. Sale Diary, June 18, 1864, John F. Sale Papers, Library of Virginia (LV), Richmond, Virginia. This collection also includes all Sale's letters cited herein.

5 John R. Turner, "The Battle of the Wilderness: The Part Taken by Mahone's Brigade; an Address Delivered by Comrade John R. Turner Before A. P. Hill Camp of Confederate Veterans, of Petersburg, VA, on the Evening of March 3rd, 1892," in George S. Bernard, ed., *War Talks of Confederate Veterans* (Petersburg, 1892), 95.

used it as a mattress by putting my blanket on it and I got on it and it was a nice spring mattress sure enough," recalled First Lt. James Phillips of the 12th's Company G, the Richmond Grays. "I slept on it . . . as comfortable as could expect."[6] Soldiers remaining awake enjoyed a barrel of coffee and copious crackers sent by the townspeople. "Our ration of late has been so good & abundant I rather think we live quite as well as the citizens," remembered Bernard.[7]

Roused in the middle of the night along with the rest of Weisiger's brigade, the 12th's men staggered into the fortifications on the right of Anderson's Corps at 2 a.m. Weisiger's brigade belonged to Mahone's division, which was manning Petersburg's earthworks between Jerusalem Plank Road and the Petersburg & Weldon Railroad.

Since the war's beginning, the 12th, its brigade and its division had not consistently distinguished themselves. In the months of fighting that remained, while many of the regiment's men literally fought for their homes, the 12th, Weisiger's brigade and Mahone's division would become some of the Army of Northern Virginia's most renowned shock troops.[8]

6 James Eldred Phillips, "Sixth Corporal" ("Journal of James E. Phillips"), James Eldred Phillips Papers, Virginia Historical Society (VHS), Richmond, Virginia, 57-58.

7 Bernard Diary, June 19, 1864.

8 Douglas Southall Freeman, *Lee's Lieutenants: A Study in Command*, 3 vols. (New York, 1942–1944), 3:38.

CHAPTER 1

Judgment Day

The regiment's core, known as the Petersburg Battalion and officially designated the 4th Battalion, Virginia State Militia, left Petersburg on April 20, 1861. According to John Herbert Claiborne, a physician educated at Randolph-Macon College, the University of Virginia and Philadelphia's Jefferson Medical College, this day acquired the name "Judgment Day" because "it was not believed that any day other than the Judgment could ever be ushered in with such overwhelming and stupendous excitement in any class of people, high or low, white or colored."[1]

The battalion consisted of one battery, the Petersburg Artillery, and five infantry companies: A, the Petersburg City Guard; B, the Petersburg Old or 'A' Grays; C, the Petersburg New or 'B' Grays; D, the Lafayette Guards; and E, the Petersburg Riflemen. Only the Old Grays and the City Guard had drilled on a regular basis before John Brown's October 1859 raid on Harpers Ferry, Virginia. Organized as the Petersburg Grays in 1828, the Old Grays went through the Mexican War under Capt. Fletcher H. Archer, a lawyer. Captain John Pegram May, another attorney, raised the City Guard in 1852. These two companies formed part of the 39th Regiment, Virginia State Militia, at the time of Brown's raid. The 39th's eight remaining companies existed only on paper. The Grays and the City Guard served in the security detail at Charles Town, Virginia, for Brown's hanging on December 2, 1859.

---

1 John H. Claiborne, *Seventy-Five Years in Old Virginia* (New York, 1904), 192.

Dr. John Herbert Claiborne. *Virginia Historical Society*

In response to the threat of slave insurrections raised by other Yankee abolitionists, active militia companies multiplied throughout the South. Before the end of 1859, three more began drilling regularly in Petersburg. Captain Thomas Holton Bond, a railroad station agent, raised a second company of the Petersburg Grays, called the New or 'B' Grays as the first company became the Old or 'A' Grays. Captain William H. Jarvis, a grocer, organized the Lafayette Guards. Captain Daniel Dodson, a bookkeeper, recruited the Petersburg Riflemen.

George Smith Bernard joined the Riflemen as a private December 1, 1859. Born in Orange County and educated at the University of Virginia, he was practicing law in Petersburg. "Let another such attempt as John Brown's be made, and the question will be settled at the point of the bayonet," Bernard recorded.[2] In 1860, Virginia made its first attempt to combine the five active infantry companies in Petersburg with the Petersburg Artillery into the 4th Battalion, Virginia State Militia. Major David Addison Weisiger, a wholesaler who had served as Archer's adjutant during the Mexican War, commanded the battalion. The Old and New Grays declined to join.[3] These two companies and the inactive militia companies in Petersburg remained in the 39th Regiment, Virginia State Militia, under Col. Edgar Longden Brockett, a storeowner.

The Republican presidential candidate's victory on November 6, 1860, led the seven Deep Southern states of South Carolina, Georgia, Florida, Alabama, Mississippi, Louisiana and Texas to secede from the Union to preserve and expand slavery. On February 8, 1861, they formed the Confederate States of America.

2 Bernard Diary, December 21, 1859.

3 Lee A. Wallace, Jr., *A Guide to Virginia Military Organizations 1861–1865* (Lynchburg, VA, 1986), 242.

David Addison Weisiger, early in the war.
Virginia Historical Society

In the Upper South, pro-slavery forces did not predominate. Not until February 13, 1861, did Virginia's secession convention meet in Richmond, the state capital. Most delegates favored remaining in the Union—including Petersburg's delegate, Thomas Branch, who reflected the wishes of most of Petersburg's citizens. As late as April 4, the convention voted 88-55 against secession. Bernard recorded the perplexity he shared with many other Virginians, "What is to be done? Should we 'coerce' the seceding States? No. Shall we endeavor to persuade them to return? No. This would be impossible."[4]

On April 12, Confederate forces under Brig. Gen. Pierre Gustave Toutant "Gus" Beauregard opened fire on Fort Sumter in the harbor of Charleston, South Carolina. The fort surrendered next day. On April 15, President of the United States Abraham Lincoln called for 75,000 troops to suppress the rebellion. This demand met with resounding disapproval in the Upper South. Of the eight states of that region, only Maryland and Delaware signified even a qualified willingness to comply. The other six—Virginia, North Carolina, Kentucky, Tennessee, Missouri and Arkansas—refused to furnish their quotas. Virginia reacted the most violently, seceding April 17. Over the next two months, Arkansas, North Carolina and Tennessee followed her out of the Union.

On April 19, responding to Governor John "Honest John" Letcher, the 4th Battalion and both companies of Grays encamped on Poplar Lawn, a city-owned tract on South Sycamore Street used as their mustering place and drill ground. The Old Grays, now under Capt. John Lyon, a lawyer, finally joined the 4th Battalion, as did the New Grays. The battalion's soldiers enlisted for one year in the state army. Many others joined that day. The failure of Virginia's authorities to insist that the troops enlist for three years

4 Bernard Diary, January 14, 1861.

or for the duration betrayed an underestimate of the struggle they faced. This mistake would later have serious consequences.

On the morning of "Judgment Day," Weisiger's men were still scrambling to set their affairs in order. A letter from Bernard indicated the swiftness with which events had overtaken Virginians. Apologizing for leaving his finances "in so embarrassed a state," he described his hurried precautions to spare family and friends any problem arising in case of his death. "I can not now better my condition," he concluded. "These troubled times have frustrated my plans."[5]

The battalion had present about 375 of 509 members.[6] Orders came to move. Everyone knew the battalion's destination—Gosport Navy Yard at Portsmouth, Virginia, just across Elizabeth River from Norfolk. This installation contained warships, facilities to construct and repair ships, enormous quantities of naval supplies and more than 1,000 cannon. Its capture would enable Virginia to build, arm and maintain her own navy and stud her coastlines with shore batteries.

Letcher assigned the Virginia State Militia's Maj. Gen. William Booth Taliaferro to seize intact the shipyard and the warships anchored there. The City Guard and Old Grays knew Taliaferro well. He had held command at Charles Town for John Brown's hanging. Taliaferro arrived in Norfolk on April 18, 1861, to find 600 militia from Norfolk and Portsmouth sinking merchant vessels in Elizabeth River's ship channel to isolate the Yankee sailors and marines at the Navy Yard. Needing reinforcements, he telegraphed Letcher, who dispatched Weisiger's battalion.

The battalion hiked down Sycamore from Poplar Lawn. Passing Courthouse Square, the troops turned right on Bollingbrook, heading for the Norfolk & Petersburg Railroad's depot. There they found a train, remembered Claiborne, serving as a private in the Riflemen, "the engine fired up and puffing steam, as if awaiting, with the same impatience as the men, the order to start."[7] An avid Secessionist, Claiborne had just resigned his seat in Virginia's State Senate, where he represented Petersburg.

5 George S. Bernard to Father, April 20, 1861.

6 George S. Bernard Notebook, George S. Bernard Papers, Duke University, Durham, North Carolina, 3.

7 Claiborne, *Seventy-Five Years in Old Virginia*, 191.

The occasion's gravity weighed on all. The troops faced the prospect of death. Petersburg's civilians confronted the possibility of losing loved ones. Excitement reached a previously unimagined level. Laughing, crying, cheering and praying, the townspeople mobbed the depot. Reverend William H. Platt, Rector of Petersburg's St. Paul's Church, a Mexican War veteran who had just finished drilling volunteers on Poplar Lawn, made a short speech, praying that "God would cover the heads of the boys in the day of battle."[8]

Weisiger drew up his battalion in double order, with the rear and front ranks facing one another. The civilians passed between the lines to bid their farewells. Mothers, wives and sisters blessed and kissed their soldiers. The troops embraced their dear ones. Everyone wondered which soldiers would return and when. The locomotive's whistle blew. The troops filed into the cars. The train chugged away at 2.30 p.m. The crowd and the departing soldiers cheered.

About three hours later, a courier from Taliaferro halted the locomotive at the bridge over Elizabeth River's South Branch, three miles from the Navy Yard. Assuming the messenger bore orders for an immediate attack on the installation, Weisiger had his men detrain, form line parallel to the tracks and prepare for action. Instead, the courier told Weisiger to deploy his soldiers to meet any attempt by the Federals in the shipyard to ascend the river and destroy the bridge.

Buckling on their equipment, the Virginians loaded their weapons. "I realized, as I had not done before, that war was upon us, and that an unpleasant duty was ours," Claiborne remembered. This feeling intensified when Dodson cautioned the Riflemen to remain steady, look along the line of their muskets and "fire low."[9]

No Federals appeared. Weisiger's men got back on the cars. Their train passed within gunnery range of the warships in the harbor. The soldiers feared a broadside but none came. The train reached the Norfolk depot at sundown.

The Virginians disembarked. Their companies formed and tramped up Main Street. "As the battalion marched along with solemn and decided step," Bernard recorded, "scores of ladies waved their handkerchiefs to us and cheer after cheer was given us by the men & boys along the street."[10]

8 Ibid.; Psalms 140:7.

9 Claiborne, *Seventy-Five Years in Old Virginia*, 193.

10 Bernard Notebook, 4.

Daniel Dodson. *Petersburg Siege Museum*

Orders came to bed down for the night, pleasing the tired soldiers. The staff quartered at the National Hotel. The rank and file found themselves in an empty hotel behind Main Street. The men lay 40 or 50 to a room, "like so many logs side by side with the blankets under and over them, their heads on their knapsacks, guns & accoutrements lying helter-skelter in piles," noted Bernard, whose company drew the dining room and bar on the first story.[11] Despite their fatigue, few of the Riflemen slept. "A few humorous fellows by their talk made it quite impossible," Bernard observed.[12]

At 10.30 p.m., Weisiger received an order to prepare to move at a moment's notice. Weariness with false alarms was setting in among his troops. Not all of them donned their equipment. The skeptics proved correct. No movement followed.

Quiet prevailed, but not for long. A thunderous sound like cannon fire reached them from Portsmouth. The Northerners had set the Navy Yard ablaze. Commodore Charles McCauley had fallen prey to a ruse.

Without enough men to assault the shipyard despite the arrival of Weisiger's battalion, Taliaferro had bluffed the Unionists into abandoning the place. The idea came from William Mahone, president of the Norfolk & Petersburg and colonel of the 6th Regiment Virginia Volunteers. Mahone had empty trains pull in and out of the depot. Taliaferro positioned troops there with instructions to cheer each arrival as if it brought reinforcements. This convinced McCauley that he faced an enormous host. Hours before Weisiger's battalion arrived at the bridge over Elizabeth River's South Branch, McCauley directed his 600 sailors and 100 marines to scuttle all

11 George S. Bernard to Mrs. Mary Jones, April 21, 1861.

12 Bernard Notebook, 4.

William Mahone, Former President of the Norfolk & Petersburg Railroad. *National Archives*

but one of the ships in the harbor to prevent them from falling into the Virginians' hands.

After dark, with a light swinging at every porthole, the ten-gunned steam sloop-of-war USS *Pawnee* threaded her way through the obstructions in Elizabeth River. At 8 p.m., half an hour after the Petersburg lads reached Norfolk, *Pawnee* arrived at the Navy Yard and disembarked 370 Massachusetts militia and another 100 marines. Informed by McCauley that the Virginians vastly outnumbered their forces, the captain of *Pawnee* did not believe that he could hold the installation long. He therefore fired the shipyard and the scuttled vessels.

Many of Weisiger's soldiers walked up to their hotel's top story to see the conflagration. Others went down to the river. All observed the Navy Yard and several abandoned vessels ablaze. Cannon exploded as the fires burned downward. Early on April 21, by the burning shipyard's light, Weisiger's troops saw *Pawnee* inching down Elizabeth River toward Fort Monroe with USS *Cumberland* in tow. After gawking at the burning Navy Yard, the men returned to their rooms and fell asleep. "Here at this hotel was the first blood lost by the Virginia troops," remembered Pvt. Robert Nixon Northen of the Old or 'A' Grays. "One of the 'A' Grays went to sleep in the window and fell out on his nose, causing it to bleed."[13]

The destruction of the Navy Yard and the 11 other vessels berthed there dealt a heavy blow to the Secessionists' hopes, though many of the captured cannon armed Southern forts from Virginia to Arkansas.[14] The Federals had denied the Confederates a small fleet. Blockading it would have required Union vessels needed elsewhere.

13 Robert N. Northen, "The Raw Confederate of April 1861," in *Southern Historical Society Papers* (hereinafter *SHSP*), (1893), 21:347.

14 "Burning of Gosport Navy-Yard," New York *Times*, April 24, 1861, p. 1, cols. 4-5.

CHAPTER 2

Garrisoning Norfolk

"I began to realize what camp life is, when I washed my face & hands in a horse bucket and wiped them in my handkerchief," Bernard recorded at 7 a.m. April 21. Seated on his knapsack, he waited for his squad of 10 to march to breakfast. They had "a most sumptuous" repast at the Atlantic Hotel.[1] Afterward, some read their Bibles, wrote letters, or patronized neighboring barbershops. Others smoked or chatted. Sergeants led off to churches squads of those wishing to attend services.

A call to fall in dressed in fighting trim reached the battalion. The men hurried to their rooms, pulled off their dress coats and donned their blue uniform shirts, their overcoats and the rest of their combat equipment. They left behind their knapsacks, haversacks and other impediments. Nobody knew their destination. The soldiers felt eager for a fight.

Forming line, they trotted back to their rooms and retrieved their baggage. The commotion betokened not a battle but a mere change of quarters. The men plodded a mile and a half to Norfolk's Fair Grounds. The Old Grays, New Grays and Riflemen drew accommodations in a bowling alley. "Soon we were relieved of our heavy knapsacks, which had quite broken us down, and a few minutes thereafter we might have been seen lolling about in the pleasant grove which surrounds our quarters," Bernard noted.[2] Taliaferro

---

1 Bernard Notebook, 5-6.

2 Ibid., 7.

detached the Petersburg Artillery from the rest of Weisiger's battalion. The paths of its infantry and the artillery would not cross again for more than a year.

The Riflemen drew picket duty at sunset. A rumor arose that the enemy would land a few miles above Norfolk and march to the city's powder magazine, near the battalion's camp. The Riflemen expected the landing to occur when the moon set, shortly after midnight. They split into two platoons at the forks of a road near the Fair Grounds.

Dodson led the first platoon down one fork. Second Lieutenant Robert R. Banks led the second platoon down the other. Before the two formations put 100 yards between them, Dodson's platoon saw troops a short distance ahead. His men discerned that they faced both cavalry and infantry. The cavalry charged. Dodson's platoon fixed bayonets and braced to receive the horsemen. Private Leroy Summerfield Edwards, a graduate of Randolph-Macon College in Banks' platoon, wrote home, "There was some excitement, but every man stood his ground and I think every man was really happy that the time had come but the cavalcade, some twenty-five or thirty in number, proved friends. . . ."[3]

Banks' platoon found quarters at the cottage of Edmund Ferby, an elderly free black, about a mile from the Fair Grounds. Dividing the platoon into three squads, Banks sent his first squad down the road toward Elizabeth River. Bernard, among those who remained at Ferby's cottage, noted "the elegant coffee served out to us by old Edmund Ferby and his lady, which has made us all feel like different men."[4] Banks' second and third squads stood picket in their turns, straining their eyes toward the river, but no Yanks appeared.

Next day, the battalion established a regular encampment at the Fair Grounds. Tearing down several 100 yards of fences took a few minutes. The messes then erected their kitchens, which ideally consisted of a plank shed about six feet in height, length and breadth protecting a few bricks assembled upon three sides of a square. "Various inventive geniuses improved upon, or fell short of this model," observed Bernard.[5] The troops pitched tents

3 Leroy S. Edwards to Father, April 22, 1861, Leroy Summerfield Edwards Letters, Hargrett Rare Book and Manuscript Library, The University of Georgia, Athens, Georgia. All Edwards' letters cited herein come from this collection unless otherwise specified.

4 Bernard Notebook, 8.

5 Ibid., 9.

or improvised other shelters. Bernard recorded that his party "very soon metamorphosed an old sail and a few sapling poles into a canvas house of very respectable dimensions, sufficiently large to accommodate . . . twenty odd in number."[6] After sunset, the battalion's campfires blazed. The first meal the soldiers prepared since leaving home met with an enthusiastic reception. They slept on the ground, many for the first time in their lives. They had not changed clothes since leaving Petersburg.

At the Fair Grounds, Weisiger held drill two hours every morning and two hours every afternoon. Dress parade followed. Every day, citizens of Petersburg visited. Civilians who traveled to Norfolk included Reverend Platt, who had the companies drawn up in line before him and delivered what Bernard termed "some very appropriate little addresses."[7] Prayer services took place every morning and night. The troops frequently received boxes from home containing ham, bacon, biscuits, cakes and puddings.

Major General Robert E. Lee, commander of the Virginia State Forces, relieved Taliaferro for failing to seize the Navy Yard intact. Brigadier General Walter Gwynn replaced Taliaferro. An engineer, Gwynn had participated in the capture of Fort Sumter. He continued the work begun by Taliaferro on the Norfolk defenses. Though the Federals had destroyed much of the Navy Yard's contents on April 20, the Confederates had salvaged enough to comprise an arsenal worth defending, and Unionist ships could scarcely venture up James River so long as Norfolk remained in Secessionist hands.

Virginia assembled her infantry and cavalry companies into regiments. Weisiger's unit formed the nucleus for an infantry regiment. Orders assigned his battalion to the 12th Regiment Virginia Volunteers in the Virginia State Forces. Word reached the 12th's officers in late April that Letcher was considering for their commander Maj. Thomas Jonathan Jackson, a professor from Virginia Military Institute.[8]

"Who is this Thomas J. Jackson?" asked members of Virginia's legislature upon his nomination as colonel.

6 Ibid.

7 George S. Bernard to Father, April 28, 1861.

8 The Somerset (OH) *Press*, February 12, 1875, p. 2, col. 2; Clarksville (TN) *Chronicle*, February 27, 1875, p. 4, col. 2.

"I can tell you who he is," replied Hon. Samuel McDowell Moore of Rockbridge. "If you put him in command at Norfolk, he will never leave it alive, unless you order him to do so."[9]

Considered a crack regiment, the 12th represented a plum assignment, but Jackson's reputation as an officer of "an eccentric and ascetic disposition" torpedoed the appointment. The regiment's officers protested so strongly that Letcher assigned Jackson elsewhere.[10]

Gwynn attached infantry companies to the 12th from the same part of the state as Petersburg, including the Archer Rifles and Lee's Life Guard, both from Petersburg, the Hargrave Blues from adjacent Dinwiddie County, the Huger Grays from slightly more distant Brunswick and Greensville Counties and the Richmond Grays from the City of Richmond. Soldiers referred to the command as "the Petersburg Regiment."[11]

Less than a week after the battalion's arrival in Norfolk, the inadequacies of the camp at the Fair Grounds became apparent. Claiborne, the battalion's acting surgeon, advised a change of quarters because of the water's scarcity and poor quality. At dress parade on April 26, Weisiger directed his men to prepare to relocate. "At this we were all highly delighted and with light hearts set to work packing our knapsacks," Bernard recorded.[12] Later, instructions came for the soldiers to hold themselves ready to move at a moment's notice. They slept on their arms. Tension left nerves frayed.

Nothing happened. The men slumbered until reveille at 4.30 a.m. Within two hours they headed for Norfolk, carrying most of their luggage on their backs. After a tiring three-hour march, they arrived at their new quarters—the Marine Hospital at Ferry Point. The Riflemen drew two spacious rooms, a wide passage and a long corridor on the first floor. The

---

9 Jennings C. Wise, *The Military History of the Virginia Military Institute from 1839 to 1865* (Lynchburg, VA, 1915), 143.

10 Somerset (OH) *Press*, Feb. 12, 1875; Clarksville (TN) *Chronicle*, Feb. 27, 1875; G. F. R. Henderson, *Stonewall Jackson and the American Civil War*, 2 vols. (London, 1897), 1:86; James I. Robertson, Jr., *Stonewall Jackson* (NY, 1997), 219. New Grays' Lt. Louis L. Marks studied at VMI under Jackson. William Henderson, *12th Virginia Infantry* (Lynchburg, 1984), 140.

11 William Mahone to Francis H. Smith, May 8, 1861, Preston Library, Virginia Military Institute (VMI), Lexington, Virginia; James E. Whitehorne to Sister, June 9, 1861, James E. Whitehorne Papers, LV; "Casualties In The *Petersburg Regiment*, Correspondence of the Petersburg *Express*, 'On the Wing,' Below Richmond, June 2d, 1862," Bird Family Papers, VHS.

12 Bernard Notebook, 10.

City Guard received the rooms above the Riflemen. The other companies found quarters in neighboring houses.

The residents of Ferry Point treated the soldiers kindly. The Riflemen experienced this hospitality to an extraordinary degree. They set up a picket post at the drawbridge across the river to Norfolk. Near the bridge stood a brick mansion. Its proprietor had relatives in Petersburg. Every day he furnished the guard of eight or ten with their meals. Every night he put a bed in his house at the disposal of those not on duty.

Camp life began in earnest at the Marine Hospital. "Sweeping up and wheeling out the dirt, getting wood and water, forming regular messes, cooking, and doing guard and picket duty, now employed us," Pvt. Robert Nixon Northen recalled.[13] The first time it fell to his lot to cook, he received instructions to get two pans and a bag and to take to the commissary a slip of paper with the number of men in his mess. "Off I went, thinking I was now an officer, with power to give orders, if it were only to say, 'march to dinner,'" he remembered.[14] He found the butchers carving up a bullock. Seeking a good cut of meat, he sidled up to the chief butcher, a slight acquaintance, and addressed him by his first name. The man looked up, surprised at such familiarity. "I knew not the pomp of rank," Northen recollected. "Three years after, under the same circumstances, I would have addressed him as General."[15]

Northen had a long wait before drawing rations for his mess. He received a decent piece of meat, 10 pounds of rice, 20 pounds of flour and some potatoes. Returning to his kitchen, he started his fire and cleaned his pot, pan and tripod or spider. After making biscuits and bringing his water to a boil, he threw in his rice. "It seemed that with a little sugar, one man could eat it all," he recalled. A few minutes later, the big pot boiled over, puzzling him. He dipped out about half the rice. "In three minutes" the pot boiled over again. "At 12 o'clock I had enough boiled rice to feed the regiment," he recollected. "Every vessel in the mess was full, also all we could borrow, and five gallons in the ashes. . . ."[16] Before his mess finished dinner, its members voted unanimously to employ a genuine cook.

---

13 Northen, "The Raw Confederate of April 1861," 347.

14 Ibid.

15 Ibid.

16 Ibid., 349.

Picket duty too gave rise to its share of misadventures. On a foggy night soon after Weisiger's men had established themselves at the Marine Hospital, the New Grays' Pvt. Philip Francis Brown stood sentry outside the dwelling of a suspected spy. The former clerk of the Bollingbrook Hotel felt a shock when he saw something crouching close to the house wall and apparently creeping up on him. He ported his musket. "Who comes there?" he cried. No reply followed. "Who comes there?" he again demanded. Again, his challenge met with silence. "I was about to draw bead," he remembered, "when a large Newfoundland dog gave a vigorous shake, as if to assure me that he meant no harm."[17]

Ordinarily, nothing occurred more startling than occasional splashes from big fish chasing their prey, but pickets learned to appreciate these disturbances. The clock's monotonous strokes and the hiss of the tide creeping up the beach conspired against wakefulness. A sleeping sentinel merited a penalty of death.

The soldiers heard rumor after rumor, alarm after alarm. Few received confirmation. By May 6, the troops had slept on their arms for the fourth time. "What the occasion, have not heard," Bernard recorded, and he commented, "It seems very difficult for us privates & subordinates to hear anything authentic."[18] In their off-duty hours the men visited Norfolk and Portsmouth. Some went down to the wharves to view ferry boats and schooners. Others peered through the spyglass atop the signal tower, observing enemy vessels off Fort Monroe and Yankee soldiers at Newport News. The troops chafed under petty constraints. "Very annoying to be required to ask permission of our officers to do this or that little thing," Bernard noted.[19]

The Southerners erected fortifications and shore batteries in case the Federals attempted to recover the Navy Yard. By May 8, orders detailed 20 men from each of the battalion's companies to fatigue duty at St. Helena, opposite the installation. The soldiers spent two days clearing up the site, then built breastworks to guard against an attack on the shipyard from the southeast.

The time when the Northerners could easily recapture the Navy Yard had almost passed. When completed, the shore batteries and breastworks

---

17 Philip F. Brown, *Reminiscences of the War of 1861–1865* (Richmond, 1917), 11.

18 Bernard Notebook, 11,

19 Ibid., 12.

would safeguard against attack by water. The Southerners expected the enemy to attempt the shipyard's recapture before May 23, the day of Virginia's referendum on ratifying the ordinance of secession. The Yankees supposedly reasoned that Virginia really opposed secession and that an invasion of her territory would embolden Union men to vote secession down. Every evening a Virginian steamer went out as far as Craney Island at the mouth of Elizabeth River to give the alarm if the enemy vessels in Hampton Roads did anything suspicious. Every night, Southern sentinels received directions to watch out for signal rockets presaging a Federal landing.

Throughout the afternoon of May 18, Weisiger's troops heard a cannon fire every 15 minutes. Before evening, a rumor arose that Federal gunboats had obliterated the Confederate battery at Sewell's Point, about 10 miles down Elizabeth River from Norfolk.

Soon after breakfast next day, the men received orders to prepare to march. Rumor had them trekking to a farm nine miles downriver to guard the road leading to Norfolk. Comfortable at the well located Marine Hospital, they did not relish the prospect of leaving, but no cannon fire resounded that afternoon and no marching orders came during daylight hours.

At nine o'clock that rainy night, they heard the long roll instead of tattoo and received instructions to move. "What's the matter?" asked officer and private alike.[20] Nobody knew. A rumor circulated that *Pawnee* had run past Craney Island and threatened to descend upon Norfolk. Forming line, the troops headed for Norfolk and passed Craney Island without seeing *Pawnee*. Another rumor arose that the enemy had landed at Sewell's Point. When the men arrived there, they found everything quiet, disgusting those eager for a fight.

An engagement had occurred, but combat had again eluded Weisiger's troops. After two days of fighting, the Confederate batteries at Boush's Bluff and Sewell's Point had driven off a pair of Unionist gunboats earlier that evening. Weisiger's men rested at Sewell's Point for less than two hours. They began the long hike back to the Marine Hospital wet and hungry, arriving at noon next day, less than 13 hours after departing, exhausted. "The only casualty was one of the 'A's' men falling into a creek and being fished out with a bayonet," recalled Northen.[21]

20 Northen, "The Raw Confederate of April 1861," 349.

21 Ibid., 349-350.

The referendum on Virginia's ordinance of secession went as expected. The voters ratified the ordinance. Virginia officially seceded. On the same day, Lee relieved Gwynn of command. Lee had become dissatisfied with Gwynn's failure to complete the Norfolk defenses, his immersion in detail and his constant calls for more troops. Brigadier General Benjamin Huger replaced Gwynn. Like Lee, Huger had distinguished himself during the Mexican War. Gwynn returned to the Engineer Corps.

On June 7, the residents of Ferry Point prepared for the battalion a sumptuous dinner which the soldiers greatly enjoyed. The dinner impressed them more than their mustering into Confederate service next day. When the time came a few days later for the men to leave their quarters at the Marine Hospital, the dinner and the other kindnesses shown them by Ferry Point's residents heightened their regret.

"We only played soldiers, and tried to pass away the time, as only men can do without the presence of ladies, playing all sorts of pranks and jokes on our comrades," recalled Northen.[22] The New Grays' Pvt. John Dunlop, born in Great Britain and nicknamed "English John" because of his accent, became the butt of such a joke. Uncomfortable sleeping on the floor of the room that his mess of five had rented near the Marine Hospital, Dunlop had an inflatable rubber mattress sent to him from Petersburg. Nearby, on hard mattresses, lay Brown and a fellow New Gray—Pvt. Donald McKenzie "Doncey" Dunlop, John's cousin and the son of a prominent Petersburg tobacco merchant.

"Phil, I am going to play a prank on John, as soon as he is sound asleep," Doncey whispered to Brown.

When John started snoring, Doncey crept over and opened the valve that let the air escape John's mattress. Watching John sink, Brown remembered, "it was all we could do to withhold our risibles." Finally, the hard floor woke John.

"This blasted thing has sprung a leak," he roared.[23]

The Old Grays and Lafayette Guards left the Marine Hospital first, on June 11, the day after the engagement at Big Bethel on the York-James Peninsula. They pitched their tents in a cornfield on the Harrison farm, several miles east of Norfolk, near the junction of the roads to Willoughby

22 Ibid., 351.

23 Brown, *Reminiscences of the War*, 10.

Point in the north and the Atlantic beaches farther east. The New Grays departed on June 14, as a rumor of a fight at Philippi in western Virginia arrived. By that time, the Harrison farm had become known as the Entrenched Camp. As of June 16, the 12th mustered 47 officers and 816 men present.[24]

The City Guard and the Riflemen departed the Marine Hospital at 1 p.m., June 17. The cornfield assigned to these soldiers displeased them. By June 19, they had laid off and leveled the grounds, dug ditches, finished the street between the rows of tents and laid floors. They then viewed the Entrenched Camp in a different light. "These tents," Bernard observed, "each occupied by five or six men, I have no doubt we will soon prefer to quarters of any other kind—certainly until winter sets in. . . ."[25] Supplied with coffee, sugar, molasses, vinegar, light bread and Virginia bacon, the soldiers lived luxuriously. Messes sent men to the market each morning to supplement this plenty. Four cents bought as many potatoes as a mess could eat. Fifty cents bought a good dinner. The troops also continued receiving boxes of delicacies from home.

A consensus formed that the war would not last long. Many thought peace resolutions recently passed by some Northern legislatures indicated that public sentiment in the North would soon stop the war. Those holding a different opinion included Bernard. Realizing that Northerners regarded the war as one to suppress a rebellion, he recorded, "there is but little doubt that the people of that section having now fully entered into the enterprise will resort to every device to carry it through."[26]

On July 1, Weisiger became the 12th's colonel.[27] Fielding Lewis Taylor of Norfolk, who resided in Gloucester County and had attended Washington College, joined the regiment as lieutenant colonel. Brockett became the 12th's major. John Claiborne remained surgeon and received a major's commission. Another Claiborne—Pvt. James William Claiborne, also of the Riflemen but no relation to John—became assistant surgeon with a captain's

---

24 John H. Claiborne to David Camden DeLeon, June 16, 1861, John Claiborne Papers, VHS. Claiborne mentioned 40 others, neither "command" nor "enrolled men," as "entitled to medicine." Ibid. They probably represented a combination of hired men and body servants.

25 Bernard Notebook, 23,

26 Ibid., 24.

27 Henderson, 12VI, 164.

commission.[28] A native of Richmond, James had studied medicine at the University of Pennsylvania and practiced in California during the Gold Rush.

On July 12, Huger designated the companies that would constitute the 12th Regiment Virginia Infantry in Confederate service. The Petersburg Battalion furnished the first five companies. The City Guard became Company A, the Old Grays B, the New Grays C, the Lafayette Guards D and the Riflemen E.

The Huger Grays formed Company F. Captain Everard Meade Feild, a Greensville County farmer and former captain of the City Guard, raised the Grays in Greensville and Brunswick Counties. They were quartering at Norfolk Academy.

The Richmond Grays, formed in 1844, became Company G. They, like the Old Grays, had served in the Mexican War. Like the City Guard and Old Grays, the Richmond Grays had served in the security detail for John Brown's hanging. John Wilkes Booth charmed the Grays on the train ride up to Charles Town. He stood as a supernumerary in the company's ranks at the hanging, about thirty feet from the gallows. Around the same height as Booth, the Grays' Pvt. Philip Whitlock stood next to him. "When the drop fell, I noticed that he got very pale, and I called his attention to it," remembered Whitlock, a native of Poland and a clerk in civilian life. "He said that he felt very faint and that he would give anything for a good drink of whiskey."[29]

The Grays, remembered Pvt. Miles Turpin Phillips of that company, a paper hanger and upholsterer, "were considered the best drilled and equipped of any company in the state."[30] Detached from the 1st Virginia and dispatched to Norfolk under Capt. Wyatt Moseley Elliott, a Virginia Military Institute graduate and the Richmond *Whig*'s publisher, they were quartering with the Huger Grays at Norfolk Academy.

A company that had not belonged to the 12th in state service joined the regiment, becoming its Company H. Formed in 1802, the Norfolk

28 Major Claiborne mentions Captain Claiborne but not that the two were related. Claiborne, *Seventy-Five Years in Old Virginia*, 195.

29 Phillip Whitlock, "The Life of Phillip Whitlock, Written by Himself," Beth Ahabah Museum and Archives Trust, Richmond, Virginia. http://www.jewish-history.com/civilwar/philip_whitlock.html

30 Grand Army of the Republic, Massachusetts Department, Post No. 15, John A. Andrew, *The Old Stars and Stripes of the Richmond Grays, and the 'Grays' in the Confederate Army* (Boston, 1887), 8.

The Richmond Grays at John Brown's hanging, including Philip Whitlock (in kepi at upper far right) and (possibly) John Wilkes Booth (just behind and to the left of the man in the upper middle). *Virginia Historical Society*

Finlay F. Ferguson. *Petersburg Siege Museum*

Juniors constituted the oldest militia company in Norfolk. In state service, they belonged to the 6th Regiment Virginia Volunteers. Captain Finlay F. Ferguson, a former Norfolk mayor, led the Juniors, who had participated in the siege of Gosport Navy Yard and the battle of Sewell's Point and were supporting the battery at Boush's Bluff.

The Hargrave Blues formed Company I. Captain Arthur M. Goodwyn recruited them in Dinwiddie County during June 1861. When they reached Norfolk later that month, they joined the Juniors at Boush's Bluff.

The Archer Rifles became Company K. The Rifles' Cpl. George Douglas Chappell, a bartender, said the company had representatives of nearly every class of men, "from a Methodist preacher down to a horse thief."[31] Fletcher Archer recruited the Rifles in Petersburg after the departure of Weisiger's battalion for Norfolk, then resigned, leaving them under Capt. John Richard Lewellen, another Mexican War veteran who had helped Archer organize the company.[32] The Rifles found quarters on Craney Island upon arriving in Norfolk in May.

Lee's Life Guard, recruited in Petersburg in May of 1861 and led by Capt. James Read Branch, also quartered on Craney Island. This company, part of the 12th in state service, did not join the regiment in Confederate service. Instead, it became Company K, 16th Regiment Virginia Infantry.

Weisiger's regiment constituted a regiment only on paper. The Petersburg Battalion's five companies had united at the Entrenched Camp, but the Huger Grays and Richmond Grays remained at Norfolk Academy, the

---

31 George S. Bernard Papers, Southern Historical Collection (SHC), University of North Carolina at Chapel Hill, Chapel Hill, North Carolina.

32 "Death of Col. Lewellen," The Daily Asheville *Citizen* (NC), December 8, 1886, p. 4, col. 3.

Norfolk Juniors and the Hargrave Blues still garrisoned Boush's Bluff and the Archer Rifles stayed on Craney Island.

Other Confederate forces won the first battle of Manassas on July 21, where the Thomas Jonathan Jackson whom the 12th had rejected as its colonel became known as Stonewall Jackson.[33] Two days later, Bernard wrote after failing to wrap up his law practice, "We are tired of our inactive life behind the breastworks at Harrison's Farm."[34] The men wanted to go to Manassas, where more fighting seemed imminent, but the only members of the 12th to depart Norfolk did so through disease, discharge, detail, detachment, transfer, or leave. Within two months, Bernard became ill with a fever resulting in his medical discharge.

All the regiment's companies had gathered at the Entrenched Camp by mid-September, except for the Hargrave Blues and the Archer Rifles. The Blues shifted from Boush's Bluff to Tanner's Creek Battery. The Rifles stayed at Craney Island.

Living remained easy. The men daily drew as much beef, coffee and sugar as they wanted. Once a week they received a day's worth of bacon, rice and molasses. Boxes of delicacies from home such as eggs and pound cake still supplemented their rations. "We have fried ham & eggs every day for dinner," wrote the Huger Grays' First Sgt. James Edward "Eddie" Whitehorne, a farmer's son from Pleasant Shade in Greeneville County.[35] They also employed Norfolk washer women and black cooks.

The Old Grays' Cpl. Alexander Whitworth Archer, a Petersburg native, had worked as a store clerk in New York City at the war's outbreak. On April 19, the sight of Yankee troops marching down Broadway on the way to fight his people inspired him to return to Virginia, where he enlisted. "York" became his nickname. "We had good fly tents, straw beds, plenty to eat, good clothes, elegant Bone Jack & Kilikiwick smoking tobacco & last but by no means least, *a wee wee drap of the crather*," he recalled of service in Norfolk. "Indeed were we a kid glove set. . . ."[36]

---

33 The Somerset (OH) *Press*, February 12, 1875, p. 2, col. 1. "[A]nd the Twelfth Virginia kept very quiet about a certain little matter." Ibid.

34 George S. Bernard to Father, July 23, 1861.

35 James E. Whitehorne to Sister, October 15, 1861. Whitehorne was Orderly Sergeant—First Sergeant.

36 Alexander Whitworth Archer, "Recollections of a Private Soldier—1861," Papers of R. E. Lee Camp, United Confederate Veterans, VHS.

On October 15, Huger organized his command into two brigades, one east of Elizabeth River, the other west. Mahone received command of the brigade east of Elizabeth River and a promotion to brigadier general the following month. His brigade included the 3rd Alabama and the 12th Virginia as well as his own 6th Virginia.

Born in 1826 in Southampton County, southeast of Petersburg, Mahone entered Virginia Military Institute in 1844. Graduating as adjutant of the Corps of Cadets, he worked as a teacher at Rappahannock Academy in Caroline County and later as a civil engineer. In 1849, the Orange & Alexandria Railroad employed him as a surveyor. Next year, he served as chief engineer of Orange Plank Road, which ran from Fredericksburg to Orange Court House. In 1855, he became the Norfolk & Petersburg's chief engineer, rising to become its president and general superintendent as well in 1858.

The City Guard's Pvt. Westwood A. Todd, a Norfolk lawyer educated at Norfolk Academy and the college of William and Mary, knew Mahone personally before the war. "He is about five feet, six inches (possibly seven) high, has a well shaped head, very thin, sallow face, and dark blue eyes, which light up finely under excitement, being his best feature," wrote Todd, who did not believe Mahone ever weighed as much as 100 pounds.[37] Like Weisiger, Mahone emphasized discipline. His men had brigade drill every morning for two hours, battalion drill for two hours every afternoon and dress parade every evening.

The Confederate forces around Norfolk prepared for winter. Huger ordered his soldiers to equip themselves with flannel shirts. On October 25, Weisiger detailed some of the 12th's 41 carpenters to construct winter quarters for the regiment at the Entrenched Camp, which became known as the Cockade Barracks. The designation came from a nickname for Petersburg, "the Cockade City," which arose from the exploits of a company of soldiers from Petersburg during the War of 1812. Cockades, or rosettes, ornamented their hats. They fought so gallantly at the siege of Fort Meigs in Ohio that they earned for Petersburg the sobriquet of "the Cockade City of the Union."

While his command built winter quarters, Huger suspended drilling. This led to indifference to duty among his soldiers. The Archer Rifles on Craney Island, where idlers often hid, finished and resumed drills by November

37 Westwood A. Todd, "Reminiscences of the War Between the States April 1861-July 1865," SHC, 54.

25. The Hargrave Blues proceeded without incident at Tanner's Creek Battery. Progress on the Cockade Barracks at Harrison's farm lagged. When December began, some of the companies there had not even begun. "If we don't get into quarters soon, we will all freeze," Whitehorne complained on December 3, while the previous night's "sharp snow" still lay on the ground.[38] Others kept matters in perspective. "It is true we are exposed a good deal to the bleak winds from the north and the hard ships of camp life yet under the circumstances we are blest [compared] to some now in the field," wrote the Hargrave Blues' First Lt. Archibald B. Goodwyn on December 18. "When I read of western Virginia the hardships the soldiers undergo it gives me [consolation] to know that we ought to be satisfied until we can do better."[39]

Major Claiborne exited the regiment. Without seeking office, he won reelection to his former seat in Virginia's State Senate, requiring him to resign his commission, but he wanted to serve as a physician rather than as a legislator. Resigning from the state Senate again, he received orders assigning him to command of all the military hospitals in Petersburg. Captain Claiborne became the 12th's surgeon. The City Guard's Pvt. Philip B. Baker, who had studied medicine at the University of Virginia, replaced Captain Claiborne as the regiment's assistant surgeon.

Shortly before Christmas, the Confederates at Norfolk braced for an attack by a Yankee force assembled at Annapolis—the Coastal Division of Brig. Gen. Ambrose E. Burnside. Huger suspended the furloughs that helped make garrison duty tolerable. "The reason for slashing the furloughs is we expect to have a battle on the river somewhere but we cannot tell where it will be," wrote Goodwyn. "The probability is that it will be in the hampton rivers."[40] The troops could not attend Christmas parties because the state of alert prohibited absence from camp after tattoo. Private John Francis Sale of Norfolk, who studied architecture in Williamsburg before enlisting in the Juniors in May, thought the Christmas season "a very dull one."[41] Almost

38 James E. Whitehorne to Sister, December 3, 1861.

39 Archibald B. Goodwyn to Dr. Crawford, December 18, 1861, Private Collection of John Horn, Oak Forest, Illinois.

40 Ibid.

41 John F. Sale to Aunt, December 28, 1862.

the whole regiment got drunk on Christmas Day. "The Guard house was ramed & cramed with its victims," wrote Whitehorne.[42]

As 1861 ended, the men who remained with the colors were becoming used to military life. "I was a full fledged soldier, up to all manner of tricks and rascality, not contrary to the 975,000 Articles of War," York Archer recalled.[43]

The regiment was changing though it had not yet fought. One company, the Juniors, had replaced another, Lee's Life Guard, during the transition from State to Confederate service. About 1,068 men had flooded into the ranks and at least 127 soldiers had trickled out—"separated," cutting their ties with the 12th.[44]

An ancient philosopher reportedly pronounced it impossible to step into the same river twice.[45] The constant flow of waters made the river a different entity at any given moment. Though some men would join the 12th more than once, none of them stepped twice into quite the same regiment. The personnel changed as constantly as the waters in a river. Enlistment, conscription, substitution, transfers and returns from details, detached duty or convalescence added to the ranks. Disease, discharges, desertion, details, detachments, transfers, resignations and battle casualties depleted the 12th's strength.

The nature of the 12th's personnel manifested itself in the number of its men who served as officers before the war's end. Of 1,538 soldiers who finished the war in the regiment or became permanently separated from the service while on the rolls, 134 served as commissioned officers.[46] Seven others served as surgeons or assistant surgeons. Three more served as chaplains.

The 12th contained a high proportion of educated men. At least forty soldiers had attended institutions of higher learning. Many others had

42 James E. Whitehorne to Sister, January 10, 1862.

43 Archer, "Recollections of a Private Soldier—1861."

44 Rolls 514-534, Compiled Service Records of Confederate Soldiers Who Served in Organizations From the State of Virginia, M324, Record Group 109 (Rolls 514-534, M324, Record Group 109), National Archives (NA); Confederate Service Records of Virginia Soldiers 1861-1865, Confederate Rosters, 2:1-56, LV; Henderson, *12VI*, 106-167. I include in the 12th from Lee's Life Guard only those who separated while their company belonged to the 12th in state service.

45 Heraclitus of Ephesus, c. 535-c. 475 B.C.

46 Henderson, *12VI*, 106-167; Rolls 514-534, M324, Record Group 109; Confederate Rosters, 2:1-56.

attended private secondary schools. Only 57 illiterates joined the regiment, 29 of them from the portion of the 12th recruited in rural areas.

The 12th displayed its predominantly urban character not only in the extent of its education and literacy, but in the skills possessed by its soldiers who lacked college and postgraduate degrees. These skills became apparent in the details, detachments and special discharges their possessors received.

All the regiment's soldiers probably went on detail or detached service at some time. Details that did not take men far from the line of fire, such as fatigue duty, went unrecorded, but at least 332 members of the 12th went on details or detached service that removed them from the regiment's battle line long enough to warrant entries on their service records. More than 100 of these men probably never returned to the 12th from such duty. A dozen others had such important skills that they received special discharges.

One hundred and sixty-two of the regiment's men listed clerk as their occupation when joining the 12th. They may not have had the wealth, education, temperament or connections necessary for a commission, but their administrative and clerical skills made them desirable for rear echelon work. Other members of the regiment had mechanical skills that made them too valuable to risk on the battlefield. Some assignments—as a courier, in a division pioneer battalion or in a brigade sharpshooter battalion—took men into the forefront of battle. Most details, detachments and special discharges put men in the rear.

Not all the 12th's soldiers with soft spots in the rear remained there. Otherwise the regiment would have put far fewer men on its battlefields. Detailed or detached soldiers often returned to the ranks voluntarily and subsequently suffered death, wounds, or captivity. Several of these men left accounts of why they returned. They included Brown, who began a series of details in the Ordnance Department and on a brigadier general's headquarters staff shortly after the Petersburg Battalion arrived in Norfolk. At first, Brown recalled, he felt "quite elated to be removed from the hardships of camp life to a nice office in the custom house."[47] Nonetheless, he left the comfortable environment of his detail to spend Sundays with his comrades on Harrison's farm. In May of 1862, after the evacuation of Norfolk, Brown's detail took him to Richmond. After the battle of Seven Pines, he met many of his former comrades, some of them wounded. He decided to return to

---

47 Brown, *Reminiscences of the War*, 13.

the ranks. "My determination to do so, came about after thinking seriously over what my record would be when the war closed, and I could only show a 'bomb-proof position.'" he explained.[48]

Men returned to the ranks or refused to leave them for the same reasons that they overcame their natural fear of death and fought instead of running. Corporal James Eldred Phillips, a master tinsmith who had enlisted as a private in the Richmond Grays, recalled:

> Honor is all that convinced me in the war. If I had not belonged to a soldier Co., Richmond Grays, I don't know whether I would have gone in at all or not, as I had nothing to fight for. Did not own anything, not even a negro's toe nail. Was not mad with anyone. Did not want war like very many others of the best men. Was opposed to secession.[49]

Some shunned bomb-proof details and detached duty because they loved the thrill of fighting. "There is something so indescribably glorious in a hot fight that camp life afterwards seems unbearable," the New Grays' Pvt. Henry Van Leuvenigh "Birdie" Bird, a former clerk in a Petersburg dry goods store, wrote after returning to the ranks from a Malvern Hill wound and a bout of typhoid to serve with the color guard and the sharpshooter battalion—both hazardous duty for picked men. "The roar of artillery, the rattle of musketry, and the ringing cheer of the charges makes the blood bound through the veins like lightning, braces the nerves and makes a common individual like myself accord with my youthful idea of a soldier."[50]

Only one untested man who failed to return to the ranks from details and discharges recorded his thoughts. He felt none of the embarrassment anticipated by Brown. Despairing of becoming an officer and of the Confederate cause's success, Whitlock sought release from service by providing a substitute, but found the price of obtaining one too dear. Ill during 1862's fighting, he went on detached duty in the Quartermaster Department for the war's remainder. "As far as I was concerned, I was not very anxious to go to the front, as they called it," remembered Whitlock. "While I realized that I was a soldier whose business it was to fight if that was his profession, I

---

48   Ibid., 14.

49   Phillips, "Sixth Corporal," 41.

50   Henry Van Leuvenigh Bird to Margaret Randolph, September 8, 1864, Bird Family Papers. All Bird's letters cited herein come from this collection unless otherwise specified.

knew that that was not mine."[51] Whitlock did not lack initiative and courage altogether, just martial initiative and courage. During early 1863, he left his bomb-proof position for a foray through enemy lines and back, spending a week in New York City purchasing luxury goods that he hoped to sell for a big profit in Richmond. The venture only broke even and from then until hostilities ceased he stayed in the Quartermaster Department.[52]

Some combat veterans went on detached duty with relief and at the same time with regret at leaving comrades with whom they had shared the "dangers, hardships and pleasures" of the ranks. After a Second Manassas wound, Todd would accept an opportunity to go on detached duty as a brigade ordnance officer, he recalled, as "I had no insurmountable repugnance to leaving the ranks (I suppose no man ever had who tried it well) and was not thirsting for glory, and inasmuch as I had 'seen the elephant' from the tip of his trunk to the end of his tail, and was sufficiently amused therewith…"[53] Though Todd would not return to the ranks from his new position, it would not entirely remove him from the line of fire.

---

51 Whitlock, "The Life of Phillip Whitlock, Written by Himself."

52 Ibid.

53 Todd, "Reminiscences," 144-145.

CHAPTER 3

The Peninsula Campaign

At the beginning of 1862, Burnside's expedition sailed from Annapolis. Rumor had these Federals bound for Savannah, but their disappearance did not lift Huger's suspension of furloughs in Norfolk.

The Norfolk garrison's morale remained low. "We are not in the volunteer Service, it is more like regular Service," Whitehorne groused. "All of the officers are tyrants & if things are carried on much longer as they are now there will be a Rebellion among our Selves."[1] On January 10, Burnside's expedition rendezvoused and coaled at Fort Monroe. Next day the Yanks headed back out to sea, encountering gales which disorganized their flotilla and sank some ships. The Unionists reached Hatteras Inlet on January 13. Later that month the weather abated enough for them to cross the bar into Pamlico Sound. The Confederates failed to prepare adequately for the impending attack.

Forty-five miles north of Hatteras Inlet, Roanoke Island guarded the back door to Norfolk. The island sat amid the narrows between Pamlico Sound and Albemarle Sound. Once past Roanoke Island, the Unionists would have open to them Albemarle and Currituck Sounds, which afforded many landing places within two or three days' march of Norfolk.

Brigadier General Henry A. Wise, a former Governor of Virginia, commanded at Roanoke Island. He knew that he must obstruct the narrows on either side and construct batteries on the southernmost point. But instead

1 James E. Whitehorne to Sister, January 10, 1862.

of following the advice of his immediate superior, Huger, and improving the island's defenses with the troops at hand, Wise wasted time badgering Huger and Secretary of War Judah P. Benjamin with requests for reinforcements and munitions. Not until February 1 did Wise issue long overdue orders for his command to improve the island's defenses.

On February 7, the enemy fleet steamed past the island's undefended southern half and drove off the Confederate gunboats north of the unfinished pilings. With the Secessionist gunboats gone, Burnside's infantry landed undisturbed on the island's western shore. Next day, the Federals captured the island, its batteries and its garrison. Wise escaped.

"We were very much excited when we recd the news of our defeat at Roanoke Island," declared Whitehorne.[2] The 6th Virginia, also stationed at the Entrenched Camp, departed for Currituck Bridge at midnight. "We expected to be ordered away every moment, but was disappointed," Whitehorne wrote.[3] At 8 a.m., February 9, the 3rd Georgia marched past the Entrenched Camp on its way from Sewell's Point to South Mills to guard the Dismal Swamp Canal's locks. The cold, wet weather that followed eased the frustration the 12th's men felt at remaining behind again.

While the Northerners consolidated, Wise campaigned to shift the blame for Roanoke Island's loss. He pulled all his strings in the newly assembled Confederate Congress, which issued a report absolving him of responsibility for the loss of Roanoke Island and blaming Huger and Benjamin. The misdirected odium from the island's loss led Davis to make Benjamin his Secretary of State and started Huger on the road to oblivion.

The 12th's rank and file despaired of holding Norfolk much longer. The regiment's officers shared this pessimism. "General Mahone's wife is going up to Petersburg tomorrow," May wrote on March 2, watching his superiors send away spouses and baggage. "It seems the Generals are all getting frightened." The continuing suspension of furloughs for the rank and file remained demoralizing. The availability of leave to the officers aggravated matters. May explained why he would not apply for leave: "Apart from the chance of an action taking place during my absence, it has a bad effect upon the men for the officers to be going home so often."[4]

2 James E. Whitehorne to Sister, February 19, 1861.

3 Ibid.

4 John Pegram May to Wife, March 2, 1862, Private Collection of James G. Thayer, Richmond, Virginia.

Garrison duty grated on the Richmond Grays. "It got to be very monotonous as several battles were fought in which we did not participate," recalled Whitlock. "Some of the boys were much dissatisfied and were continually murmuring." The Grays circulated a petition to have themselves transferred back to the 1st Virginia Infantry, which had been fighting the Federals since before First Manassas, but the effort failed. "I was not one of those who were spoiling for a fight," Whitlock remembered. "Considering the circumstances I was willing to remain where we were until the war was over, for . . . the duties were light and we had some diversion as we very often went to Norfolk where we were very kindly received by the people we visited."[5]

As morale sagged and Norfolk seemed doomed, Gosport Navy Yard produced an innovation that inspired the troops and gave the city a new lease on life in the Confederacy. The Yanks had scuttled and burned to the waterline the steam frigate USS *Merrimack* in the shipyard on Judgment Day, but she proved salvageable. During the summer of 1861, the Southerners remodeled her in dry dock as an ironclad to break the wooden-ship blockade of Hampton Roads. Machinists detailed from the Confederate army, including some from the 12th, fitted her with a ram and armored her with iron plates. The brass named her CSS *Virginia*, but the troops called her "Merrimac" or "Marymack."[6] In mid-February *Merrimac* emerged from dry dock. By February 25 she bore 10 cannon.

Early in March, the Confederates brought their James River Squadron down near Mulberry Island. The squadron consisted of five wooden vessels including CSS *Patrick Henry*, which had served as a freight and passenger steamer between Richmond and New York until caught in Southern waters at the beginning of hostilities. The Secessionists armed her with 12 cannon.

On March 7, *Merrimac* and the James River Squadron prepared for action. That night, a rumor *Merrimac* would sortie next day ran through the Department of Norfolk from Sewell's Point to Suffolk, "like an electric shock," recalled the Lafayette Guards' Second Lt. William Evelyn Cameron.

---

5 Whitlock, "The Life of Phillip Whitlock, Written by Himself."

6 James E. Whitehorne to Sister, March 11, 1862; Todd, "Reminiscences," 11; Bernard Notebook, 26; Brown, *Reminiscences of the War*, 13-14; Theophilas Daniel to "my Dear wife," April 3, 1862, Private Collection of John Horn.

"It was one of those secrets which telepathy betrays, and which once abroad take unto themselves the wings of the wind."[7]

Cameron had reached the 12th by a circuitous route. The son of a Petersburg cotton broker, Cameron left in 1858 to attend the Military Institute in Hillsboro, North Carolina, and then St. Louis' Washington College in 1859. In 1860, he studied for West Point entry. Though admitted, he did not attend because of the war. Instead, he joined the Missouri State Guard as a drillmaster. On May 9, 1861, he fell into enemy hands at St. Louis' Camp Jackson when Federal forces attacked that facility. Released soon afterward, he returned to Petersburg and on June 4 enlisted as a private in the City Guard. Ten days later he won election to his lieutenancy.

Before dawn on March 8, Cameron and two comrades went to Pig's Point and hired a boat from which to view the anticipated battle. Other members of the regiment watched from Pig's Point and Sewell's Point. The Archer Rifles observed from Craney Island. *Merrimac* appeared at noon, gliding across the calm waters toward the Federal blockaders. She began the battle by ramming and sinking one wooden blockader while others came to the victim's assistance. Southern reinforcements arrived. "Standing down the long open reach, under full head of steam, right into the pelting storm of missiles, dashed the five wooden vessels of the James River Squadron," recalled Cameron.[8]

Patrick Henry led the squadron, carrying into action the first soldier of the 12th to participate in combat while belonging to the regiment. Like the Huger Grays' Eddie Whitehorne, the Hargrave Blues' Pvt. William W. Spratley hailed from Pleasant Shade in Greensville County. His family ran a store in the hamlet. While Cameron bobbed about off Pig's Point, Spratley helped man one of *Patrick Henry* guns.[9] A shell through her boiler disabled her and scalded to death four of her complement but she soon returned to action. Until darkness ended the fighting, *Merrimac* continued to wreak havoc among the wooden Federal blockaders and the James River Squadron provided supporting fire.

---

7 William E. Cameron, "Historic Waters of Virginia: The Battle in Hampton Roads as Viewed by an Eye Witness, The Achievements of the Virginia; An Interesting Paper— The Improvised Confederate Fleet," *SHSP* (1904), 32:348-349.

8 Ibid., 351.

9 Whitehorne to Sister, March 11, 1862.

In the morning, when *Merrimac* ventured forth to finish off a grounded wooden blockader, the ironclad encountered USS *Monitor*. A drawn battle followed and *Merrimac* retired to dry dock at Gosport Navy Yard. *Patrick Henry* and the rest of the James River Squadron docked at Norfolk next day. Billy Spratley left *Patrick Henry* and proceeded to the Cockade Barracks, where he spent the night with his friends from Pleasant Shade in the Huger Grays.

While *Monitor* and *Merrimac* clashed, the Secessionists evacuated Centreville in northern Virginia. General Joseph E. Johnston, commander of the Southern army there, feared the Yanks would use their command of the sea to land troops in his rear and cut him off from Richmond. He had read the mind of his opponent, Maj. Gen. George B. McClellan, who intended to disembark part of his army on the Middle Peninsula, between Rappahannock and York Rivers.

Johnston's retreat forced McClellan to alter his plan. In mid-March, he began landing his troops at Fort Monroe, at the York-James peninsula's tip. On April 4, his men advanced toward Richmond. The Northerners encountered the Southern earthworks constituting the Yorktown-Warwick River Line. McClellan settled down for a siege.

McClellan's host threatened Norfolk's flank and rear. The Yorktown-Warwick River Line ran from Yorktown on the peninsula's northern side to Jamestown on the southern side. Batteries at Yorktown and Jamestown helped close York and James Rivers to the enemy. If those batteries fell, the Confederate artillery on the rivers' opposite sides could not reliably close them to the Yankees, who might then land forces far in the rear of any Southern units defending the Middle Peninsula or Norfolk.

In March, as McClellan landed, Secessionist reinforcements began arriving at Norfolk. More than 1,000 militiamen from southwest Virginia assembled in a camp at the Fair Grounds. Confederate authorities mistreated these troops, insisting that they remain but refusing to furnish medicine for their sick. Many died of disease aggravated by homesickness. "When they were taken sick many of them seemed to have no powers of resistance," remembered Todd, detailed by Mahone as assistant to the militia camp's commissary. "They seemed to lose all hope, and died from want of will to live." Mahone's brigade supplied the militia with drillmasters. "It was ludicrous to see the awkward squads marching and double-quicking under the command of these young sprigs," recalled Todd. "Their patriotism soon oozed out under the

First Lieutenant Joseph Richard Manson, Early in the War. *Private Collection of Richard Cheatham*

treatment."[10] Any militiaman who had sufficient influence used it to get out of service. Todd doubted if half the militia at the Fair Grounds ever entered the Confederate army.

Reinforcements continued reaching Norfolk. They included one of the soldiers who set foot in the regiment more than once—George Bernard. Recovered from the illness that caused his medical discharge, he started teaching school in Greensville County, a few miles north of Belfield on January 27, 1862. Within two weeks, teaching became oppressive. News of the Confederate disasters at Roanoke Island and Forts Henry and Donelson arrived and Bernard decided he belonged with the army. "Like all ex-privates desiring to return to the service I of course desired to go back in the best capacity possible," he wrote on February 19. He found two opportunities that appealed to him—a sergeancy in "a very good company" to be organized in Belfield three days later, and a lieutenancy in a Petersburg company that had "certain little things objectionable in their character which perhaps will make me hesitate to accept even a very good position. . . ."[11] On February 22, he took the sergeancy in the Meherrin Grays, the infantry company organizing at Belfield that day. Like the Huger Grays, this company came from Brunswick and Greensville Counties. Bernard remembered the rank and file as a "heterogeneous collection of rough country men" recruited by Capt. Richard Watson Jones, a Greensville County landowner's son educated at Randolph-Macon College and the University of Virginia, and First Lt. Joseph Richard Manson, a Brunswick County farmer educated at Randolph-Macon College. Marriage to a relative of Col. Turner Ashby, Jr. made Manson kin to Bernard, whose mother belonged to the Ashby clan. The company also included Second Lt. Edward Pegram Scott, Jr., a graduate

10 Todd, "Reminiscences," 7.

11 George S. Bernard to Father, February 19, 1862.

of Virginia Military Institute and the grandnephew of Lt. Gen. Winfield Scott, the former Petersburg lawyer who had just retired from command of the United States Army.

Jones dismissed the company with orders to report back to Belfield on March 13 prepared to entrain for Petersburg. Bernard prevailed upon the trustees of his school to accept a friend as a substitute teacher and gathered with the rest of the Grays at Belfield on March 13. Jones appointed the company's non-commissioned officers and Bernard became third sergeant. That afternoon, the Grays boarded the Weldon Railroad's freight cars and at Petersburg mustered into Confederate service. After quartering for several days in the city's western suburbs, the Grays removed to Poplar Lawn for provost guard duty along with Petersburg's militia or "milish," as Bernard termed them.[12] The war department assigned the Grays to the 12th.

Reaching Norfolk on April 19, the Grays marched to Harrison's farm. The 12th's other soldiers looked with scorn upon the untrained Meherrin Grays and styled them "the Herrings."[13] Weisiger detailed privates from the other companies as drillmasters for what Todd would have termed the "fresh fish."[14] Bernard found "the other companies of the regiment most comfortably quartered in neatly constructed houses, living almost in luxury." Rations remained abundant. The Norfolk market continued to afford "the extras." Messes still employed cooks and dining room servants. Most of the men could afford to purchase their own provisions and scorn government issue.

In another respect, the 12th had changed for the worse. "There prevailed throughout the regiment a great laxity of discipline compared with that which had previously ruled both officers & men almost to the letter of the army regulations," Bernard remembered.[15] The indiscipline's source lay in "The Bounty and Furlough Act".

The need for the Act arose from the Secessionists' mistaken assumption that the war would prove short. They had enlisted almost all their troops for only 12 months. In December of 1861, as the prospect of a lengthy struggle loomed, the Confederate Congress passed the Bounty and Furlough Act to encourage re-enlistment of the 12-months' volunteers whose terms would

12 Bernard Notebook, 32.

13 Ibid., 33.

14 Todd, "Reminiscences," 319.

15 Bernard Notebook, 34.

expire in the late winter or early spring. The Act disorganized the Confederate states army when the South seemed under Yankee attacks from all directions.

The Act allowed the men to elect their own company and field officers. This pressured commissioned officers to relax discipline to enhance their prospects of reelection. It discouraged non-commissioned officers from enforcing discipline if they aspired to a commission. In the 12th, the rank and file passed in and out of camp whenever they pleased. The officers coddled the men. "If it rains a little at night the Col. calls in the sentinels and does not allow them to be put on until morning," Bernard wrote.[16] Another provision allowed soldiers to change companies or even their arm of the service. Over the war's course, transfers to other branches of the service would deprive the all-important infantry of many able-bodied men. Furloughs of 60 days for all enlisted men and non-commissioned officers who would re-enlist for the war's duration or a maximum of three years threatened to send as much as a third of the army home at the beginning of the 1862 campaign.

Virginia acted more forcefully than the Confederate Congress and through a draft compelled her 12-months' troops to reenlist. On February 8, as Roanoke Island fell, Virginia's General Assembly enrolled in the militia all male citizens between 18 and 45 years. Letcher called 40,000 of these men to active duty on March 10. The troops from southwest Virginia encamped at Norfolk's Fair Grounds and the milish the Herrings found on Poplar Lawn in Petersburg had come in response to this call. Letcher also authorized a draft of militiamen to replace 12-months' troops who did not reenlist. The latter would pass into the militia and service in the militia looked like a big furlough to some of them. The governor banished such notions on April 11 when he ordered volunteers who fell into the militia on failing to re-enlist drafted at once "into the same companies to which they lately belonged."[17]

This measure helped maintain order within Virginia units in Confederate service, but the Virginians who had enlisted for one year felt cheated. The rules had changed in the middle of the game. The troops' resentment

16 George S. Bernard to Father, April 21, 1862.

17 Special Orders, No. 5, April 11, 1862, United States War Department, *The War of the Rebellion: A Compilation of the Official Records of the Union and Confederate Armies* (Washington, D.C.: U.S. Government Printing Office, 1880-1901) (hereinafter *OR*) (128 vols.), Series I (all will be from Series I unless otherwise specified), vol. 51, 2:534.

displayed itself in the number of men who withdrew from the firing line by every means that the law allowed—substitutes, transfers, details, detached duty and discharges—as well as those that it prohibited—absence without leave and desertion. The chickens were coming home to roost for Virginia's failure to insist from the start that her troops enlist for the duration.

Davis wanted the Confederate Congress to enact an identical conscription plan. A bill drawn up at Lee's direction provided for the conscription of all white males between 18 and 45, but the Secessionist legislators grafted to it the Bounty and Furlough Act's most obnoxious provisions, reduced the upper age limit from 45 to 35 and liberally allowed exemptions. On April 16, the bill became law, affecting the 12th in the ways most feared by the administration.

The Herrings arrived as the militiamen from southwest Virginia were assigned to volunteer companies. The 12th drew about 75 of these disgruntled troops, mostly from Patrick County. Nearly all went into the under-recruited Lafayette Guards. The militiamen failed to thrive in the 12th. At least 22 would die of disease during the war, a death rate exceeding that of any other group in the regiment.

Election of company officers occurred May 1. Three officers refused to seek re-election. Thirteen other incumbents lost. First Lt. Charles E. Waddell won election as the Petersburg City Guard's captain. Lyon remained in command of the Petersburg Old Grays. Bond won reelection in the Petersburg New Grays. In the Lafayette Guards, the militiamen from southwest Virginia voted as a block. James P. Critz of Patrick County replaced Jarvis as company commander. Men from Patrick County won two of the three other positions up for election. Only one of the four officers of the Lafayette Guards who sought reelection prevailed. Those who lost included Cameron, but on May 18 he received a commission as a first lieutenant and an appointment as regimental adjutant. In that position, he replaced First Lt. Louis Leoferick Marks, a graduate of Virginia Military Institute and lumber merchant elected captain of the New Grays.

Banks, who replaced Dodson when he resigned in October, won reelection as commander of the Petersburg Riflemen. Feild remained in command of the Huger Grays. First Lt. Jacob Valentine Crawford became captain of the Richmond Grays when Elliott declined to stand for reelection. First Lt. Thomas Flint Owens won election as captain of the Norfolk Juniors. Jones remained captain of the Herrings, who took the place of the Hargrave Blues as the 12th's Company I. Manson remained the Herrings' first lieutenant. In the Archer Rifles, Lewellen won reelection.

Louis Leoferick Marks. *National Parks Service*

The regiment elected field officers two days later. Weisiger and Taylor remained in their positions but May replaced Brockett as the 12th's major. Like the other officers who did not stand for or win reelection—except for Cameron—Brockett left the regiment.

The 12th lost still more members through the Bounty and Furlough Act's transfer provisions. Lee's Life Guards took advantage of the act to reorganize as Branch's Field Artillery on March 18. After the election of officers, 17 of the Petersburg men in the Lafayette Guards transferred to Branch's Field Artillery.

The Bounty and Furlough Act had one virtue which compensated for all its defects. It encouraged enlistments in existing units and further strengthened them with the men who waited for conscription. The Union army, which did not employ conscription until July 1863, suffered until then from a failure to strengthen existing formations. Instead, new units formed while old ones dwindled into insignificance. Without the Bounty and Furlough Act and its successors, the 12th and many other Confederate regiments that remained strong to the war's end would have withered away. The constant strengthening of existing formations gave the Southerners an advantage in combat. Conscripts assigned to veteran outfits learned soldiering more quickly than volunteers forming green units. Conventional wisdom valued one recruit in an experienced formation as highly as three in a new unit. The Bounty and Furlough Act and its successors accounted for much of the edge in fighting efficiency that Secessionist soldiers enjoyed over Unionist troops.[18]

18 For a discussion of these matters, along with sources, see John Horn, *The Petersburg Campaign: The Battles for the Weldon Railroad, August 1864* (El Dorado Hills, CA, 2015), 11-12, n. 11.

On the same day as the regiment elected field officers, Johnston's forces withdrew from the Yorktown-Warwick River Line. With the batteries on the north side of James River in Yankee hands, Norfolk became too risky to defend. An enemy force landing at Suffolk could cut off the entire department. This threat led the Confederates to abandon Norfolk.

On the afternoon of May 7, Weisiger prepared a battalion of the 12th to leave Norfolk. Before sunset, May led the formation through the city to the Norfolk & Petersburg depot. "The streets were filled with ladies, most of whom seemed the picture of despair," recalled Bernard, who marched with May.[19] The battalion brought considerable surplus baggage. "We were a Saratoga trunk regiment," remembered Manson.[20]

The Juniors also marched with May. Before they boarded the train for Petersburg, at least 21 deserted. Five more would desert before the summer's end. Of 153 men who served in the Juniors during the war, 38 would desert—25 percent. This company accounted for nearly 30 percent of the regiment's 127 deserters. Even the 79 soldiers the regiment would ultimately draw from southwest Virginia had a lower proportion of deserters—23 percent, representing 18 men.

None of the Norfolk men explained why he deserted, but a Patrick County soldier gave his reasons—the Lafayette Guards' Pvt. Isaac W. Underwood. Conscripted on March 25, 1862, with most of the other men from Patrick County, Underwood found army life miserable. This small farmer disliked leaving his wife and baby, and the prospects of combat and exposure to the elements daunted him. "Being very weakly, I soon became unable to do any service in camp at all and was nearly always in a hospital," he recalled. "I there had typhoid fever, pneumonia, smallpox, and scrafals, and was a burden to the hospital and myself, and a constant distress to my wife, fearing that I could never return home anymore."[21]

Underwood remained hospitalized from May until November of 1862 and for the same period during 1863. After another hospitalization beginning in February of 1864, he deserted at Fayetteville, West Virginia, in August of that year. Underwood remembered, "I went North and stayed ten months in

19 Bernard Notebook, 35.

20 Joseph R. Manson, "From Ease Of Camp, To Discomfort and Danger of Field," *The Sunny South* (Atlanta, GA) n.d., Joseph R. Manson Papers, Private Collection of Richard Cheatham, Richmond, Virginia.

21 Wille Bruce Underwood, comp., *Isaac W. Underwood: His Ancestors and Descendants* (Baltimore, 1988), 63-64.

the winding up of the rebellion, for I was no war man anyway, and it was slaves that the issue was about, and I had none of them to fight for, and I thought it was wrong for me to fight for other people's property unless they paid me for it."[22]

The train carrying May's battalion reached Petersburg by 10 a.m., May 8. Marching to Poplar Lawn, May's soldiers pitched their tents, awaiting the arrival of the regiment's remainder.

The rest of the 12th, still at the Cockade Barracks, sent away surplus baggage. The evacuation of Norfolk went smoothly until a tugboat captain informed the Yankees about it. Lincoln, then at Fort Monroe, prodded his subordinates into landing troops at Ocean View and advancing from there upon Norfolk on the morning of May 10.

At daybreak that morning, the long roll awakened the battalion at the Cockade Barracks. The men fell in quickly. "I knew by the manner of the Officers, and the great stir and packing up all through camp that something extraordinary had happened," wrote Todd, recently returned from the militia camp and transferred from the City Guard to the Riflemen.[23] The troops formed line. Orders to load at will came.

Word of the enemy landing at Ocean View circulated. Rumor had it that the battalion would meet the Federals as they marched on Norfolk. The battalion took the road toward Norfolk. At James' Corner, it turned right and hiked down the lane to Indian Poll Bridge. The soldiers carried many unnecessary items in their knapsacks. In the heat, the burdens became intolerable. Many men deposited knapsacks and contents in the yards of the neighboring farmers. Crossing Indian Poll Bridge, the troops tramped to Tanner's Creek Cross Roads.

Weisiger drew his soldiers up in line of battle. Every minute they expected the Northerners to appear. "Many a heart beat quickly that morning," recalled Todd.[24] Orders came to countermarch, re-cross the bridge and burn it behind them. As the soldiers retraced their steps, they recovered the items they had abandoned in the farmers' yards. Giving away to people on the road everything but their blankets and a flannel shirt, a pair of socks and a pair of drawers, the men substituted for knapsacks the Confederate equivalent— blanket rolls. They rolled shirt, socks and drawers in their blankets. Tying

22 Ibid., 63.

23 Todd, "Reminiscences," 8.

24 Ibid., 9.

together the blankets' ends formed an oblong hoop which the troops slung over their left shoulders. Todd remembered, "On their first day's experience of actual warfare, they learned a valuable lesson, viz.: always be ready to move in the lightest marching order."[25]

The battalion reached Norfolk. The hearts of the remaining soldiers from that city sank at leaving it in enemy hands without a struggle. "If a few hundred Yankees had been made to bite the dust that morning it would have been some satisfaction," recalled Todd.[26] The formation halted in Market Square. The scene resembled "Judgment Day" in Petersburg, but a far more somber mood prevailed. Citizens passed down the line looking for and taking leave of relatives and friends. A 15-year-old slave belonging to Todd's family approached Todd to say goodbye. The thought crossed Todd's mind to carry off the lad, who would have made a useful mess servant, Todd remembered, "but he had come to me in such a frank and kindly manner that I didn't have the heart to take him."[27]

From Market Square, Weisiger's battalion—the last Confederate soldiers to leave Norfolk—marched to the docks.[28] The troops embarked on a ferry to Portsmouth, then trudged toward Suffolk along a dusty county road. In the blazing heat, the formation disintegrated. Its men reached Suffolk that night in squads, ready to collapse and sleep anywhere.

About 4.30 a.m., they heard the explosion of *Merrimac's* magazines. Because she drew too much water to withdraw up James River, the Confederate Navy destroyed her by running her aground in the bight of Craney Island, landing her crew and setting her afire.[29]

Boarding the Norfolk & Petersburg's cars, Weisiger's battalion arrived at Petersburg before noon. The Richmond Grays quartered in the Iron Front Building on Sycamore Street. The battalion's remainder joined the five companies of May's command on Poplar Lawn.

On May 12, the regiment shifted to Dunn's Hill on the north side of Appomattox River, overlooking Petersburg. The tents pitched on Dunn's

25   Ibid., 8.

26   Ibid., 9.

27   Ibid.

28   "From Virginia," *Enquirer*, Yorkville (SC), May 22, 1862, p. 1, col. 5.

29   "Monitor-Merrimac Fight," *Daily News*, Greensboro (NC), October 27, 1918, p. 12, cols. 1-5.

Hill could not match the Cockade Barracks. "Our hammocks had been left in our quarters in Norfolk," Manson remembered. "We are sleeping on the ground, and the swing of the earth does not lull to gentle slumber."[30]

The regiment said good-bye to the Hargrave Blues. Transferred to the Department of Richmond, the Blues would remain there until November 1863, when they would become second Company H of the 9th Virginia Infantry in Barton's brigade, Pickett's division. The Blues would not serve on the same battlefield as the 12th again until 1864.

On May 14, the Riflemen and the Richmond Grays drew duty guarding obstructions in the Appomattox. A courier rode into the 12th's camp on Poplar Lawn, halting at Weisiger's tent. Moments later the long roll sounded, followed by the order, "Fall in!" This threw the camp into turmoil. Many men of the eight companies there had eaten supper and gone to bed. Now they groped for their equipment. Only Weisiger knew the regiment's destination.

The soldiers boarded the Richmond & Petersburg Railroad's flatcars in a jubilant mood. Departing Petersburg, they sang "A Soldier's Life Is Always Gay:"

> Now let the wide world wag as it will,
> We'll be gay and happy still;
> Gay and happy, gay and happy,
> We'll be gay and happy still.[31]

The train rattled northward. An order came to stop singing and not make any noise. This "caused us to reflect that our campaigning was about to assume a serious phase," recalled Bernard. "It was something new to be so near the enemy as to be under the necessity of preserving silence."[32] The regiment disembarked at Half Way House, named for its position halfway between Richmond and Petersburg. The troops marched up Richmond & Petersburg Turnpike to within a mile or two of Drewry's Bluff. Stacking arms in the road, they halted and went to sleep on the damp ground.

They awoke still sleepy on May 15. The day remained quiet until about 8 a.m., when the men heard several discharges of heavy cannon. The troops

30 Manson, "From Ease of Camp, to Discomfort and Danger of Field."

31 Ibid; George S. Bernard Papers, SHC; Francis Trevelyan Miller and Richard Sampson Lanier, eds., *Poetry and eloquence of Blue and Gray* (New York, 1911), 348-349.

32 Bernard Notebook, 36.

paid little attention until a huge shell hurtled toward them over the woods and snapped off the top of a big tree within 100 yards of the regiment's left. "I had no idea that a shell made such a terrible noise," Bernard wrote. "It is more of a rattling noise than like any other, and has been very aptly compared to the noise we might suppose a keg of nails would make if hurled through the air."[33] The 12th had come under enemy fire for the first time. A shell that big meant enemy ships. The soldiers cheered. Minutes later, Weisiger called them to attention. With the rest of Mahone's brigade, they tramped toward Drewry's Bluff.

"It was anything but pleasant to have the ponderous shells hurled from the gunboats crashing among the trees to our left as we filed along the edge of the woods," recalled Bernard."[34] Soon the 12th passed the Confederate earthwork atop Drewry's Bluff—Fort Drewry. From inside the fort, batteries including a few guns from *Patrick Henry* serviced by her crew, and other cannon manned by artillerists from *Merrimac*, fired down at the Unionist flotilla consisting of *Monitor*, two more ironclads and two wooden gunboats.[35] Mahone posted Weisiger's regiment and the 3rd Alabama under the cover of a hill between the fort and the ships to guard against any land force the invaders might disembark to assault the fort. The brigadier ordered the 6th Virginia to line the banks of James River and snipe at the vessels' crews.

The 12th remained under the hill's cover for the rest of the action. "Here we had a fine opportunity of learning & being familiarized to the hum of the shell," Bernard wrote.[36] Intervening trees prevented the men from seeing the fort. The hill hid the ships. The regiment's soldiers marked the flotilla's position by the smoke from the guns and the sound of the shells. They often heard the crash of a projectile as it struck the ships.

The regiment suffered no casualties, but other Confederate units lost several wounded. The 12th's men had their first sight of the results of enemy missiles. A shell took off one unlucky fellow's leg above the knee. The 12th also had its initial encounter with skulkers and their wild rumors

33 George S. Bernard to Father, May 16, 1862.

34 Bernard Notebook, 37.

35 R. Thomas Campbell, *Academy on the James: The Confederate Naval School* (Shippensburg, PA, 1998), 53; R. Thomas Campbell and Alan B. Flanders, *Confederate Phoenix: The CSS Virginia* (Shippensburg, PA, 2001), 219.

36 George S. Bernard to Father, May 16, 1862.

of defeat. Two men on the way to the rear reported the fort demolished and the Yankees heading up James River toward Richmond.

Firing ceased minutes later. A glimpse of masts and smokestacks going downriver as the ships passed a bend confirmed that the Confederates had won. The 12th had participated in one of the most important actions of the war's Eastern theater. The first battle of Drewry's Bluff set the upper limit of Federal naval power on the James. Had the Northern ships successfully run Fort Drewry, Richmond might have fallen as ignominiously as New Orleans the previous month.

The regiment bivouacked in woods about a mile behind the fort. The Riflemen and the Richmond Grays joined the rest of the 12th next day. The regiment had 1,100 men present and absent.[37] It remained near Drewry's Bluff for about a week. "We could not get any eatables and suffered more than we had done before," recalled Phillips, recently promoted to sergeant.[38] Finally receiving rations, the regiment moved to Charkley's Hill near the turnpike, about a mile and a quarter from Drewry's Bluff. The soldiers pitched a regular camp, with drills, dress parades and inspections varied by an occasional stroll into the countryside.

37 Henry Van Leuvenigh Bird to Margaret Randolph, August 29, 1864.

38 Phillips, "Sixth Corporal," 5.

CHAPTER 4

Seven Pines

By late May, McClellan had arrived within 10 miles of Richmond. His army straddled Chickahominy River, with three corps on the north bank and two more entrenched on the south side by a crossroads called Seven Pines, near Fair Oaks Station on the Richmond & York River Railroad. Another enemy corps advancing southward from Fredericksburg threatened to link up with McClellan's forces, which would render the Confederate capital's situation desperate.

On the night of May 28, the 12th's men struck their tents. Johnston had determined to employ Mahone's brigade and the rest of Huger's division—the "Norfolk Division"—in an attack on McClellan's right, north of the Chickahominy, to drive it away from the corps approaching from Fredericksburg.[1] By 10 p.m., the regiment's soldiers were groping their way from Drewry's Bluff to Half Way House. There, on the morning of May 29, Mahone's brigade boarded a train for Richmond. Detachment of the 2nd North Carolina and the 6th and 16th Virginia reduced the brigade to the 3rd Alabama and the 12th and 41st Virginia.

Arriving at Richmond, the 12th formed on Grace Street, between 6th and 7th Streets. The "Kid Glove Boys," as the troops of Mahone's brigade styled themselves, then marched to Capitol Square.[2] The neat appearance of

---

1 Andrew, *The Old Stars and Stripes of The Richmond Grays, and The Grays in The Confederate Army*, 8.

2 Alexander Whitworth Archer to George S. Bernard, November 29, 1893, George S. Bernard Papers, SHC. The brigade may have acquired the name from the 6th Virginia's

the men from Norfolk contrasted with the raggedness of the veterans from the York-James Peninsula and Northern Virginia. Todd recalled that "as we passed through the streets, we created quite a sensation, for we were without doubt the best drilled and the best dressed troops in the Confederacy."[3] The veterans laughed at the garrison soldiers' fine uniforms, but others called Mahone's brigade "General Lee's Regulars."[4] The 12th remained at Capitol Square for several hours. Late that evening the regiment trekked to the Williams farm, about two miles east of the city. There the men halted and remained for the night.

The troops tramped northward on the morning of May 30. Crossing the York River Railroad, they halted on Randolph's Hill, near Oakwood Cemetery. Stacking arms, they at once set to work to protect themselves against an impending tempest. That afternoon a severe storm blew up, with thunder and lightning every few seconds. Many of the Richmond Grays went into their hometown to spend the night. The men who remained on the hillside had no shelter from the driving rain but pup tents and small cedar brakes. The water coursed down the hillside.

"God damn it, York, there is a river running down my back!" cried the Riflemen's Pvt. Littleberry E. Stainback, a clerk in civilian life, who shared a tent with Archer.[5]

The torrent routed them. Like many other soldiers, they slept no more that night.

In the morning the men built fires, dried their clothes and breakfasted. They received orders to hold themselves in readiness to march. Breaking camp, they plodded not north but south.

Johnston had changed plans. Intelligence reached him on May 28 that the enemy corps proceeding southward from Fredericksburg had turned back. The recent thrust northward in the Shenandoah Valley by Stonewall Jackson, now a major general, aroused fears for the safety of Washington. To guard against Jackson, orders halted the Unionist corps marching southward from Fredericksburg. On the night of the storm, Johnston decided to shift

---

Company G, known also as the "Kid Glove Regiment." Michael Cavanaugh, *6th Virginia Infantry* (Lynchburg, VA, 1988), 5.

3 Todd, "Reminiscences,," 12.

4 J. Watts de Peyster, "A Military Memoir of William Mahone, Major General In The Confederate Army," *The Historical Magazine* VII, Second Series (1870), 394.

5 Archer to Bernard, November 29, 1893.

his attack to the weaker Yankee left, south of the Chickahominy. Success seemed more likely there than north of the river.

The new battle plan called for Huger's division to relieve Rodes' brigade of D. H. Hill's division near White's Tavern on Charles City Road as early as possible on May 31. Rodes' brigade would join the rest of its division in front of the Federals at Seven Pines on Williamsburg Road about 8 a.m. A signal gun would then open the battle. The three divisions of the Confederate army's right wing, under Maj. Gen. James Longstreet, would attack toward Seven Pines in three columns. Longstreet's own division would strike along Nine Mile Road. Farther right, D. H. Hill's division would charge down Williamsburg Road. Still farther right, surging forward from Charles City Road, Huger's division would turn the Yankee left. The Secessionist army's left wing and reserve would support Longstreet's attack down Nine Mile Road. Johnston hoped this onslaught would annihilate the invaders south of the Chickahominy.

The plan miscarried from the start. Longstreet deviated from it by leading his division toward Williamsburg Road instead of along Nine Mile Road. Reaching Blakey's Mill on rain-swollen Gillies Creek before Huger, Longstreet began crossing his soldiers single file on an improvised bridge. When the Norfolk Division arrived, he refused to allow Huger's men to pass before his own division had finished crossing. Longstreet's departure from Johnston's plan severely impeded the Norfolk Division. The 12th's men did not cross Gillies Creek until 10.30 a.m. They hiked south for a mile past the Williams farm, then turned east into muddy Williamsburg Road. Half a mile's sloshing took them to the Tudor house, where they halted and rested. Johnston's plan fell further behind schedule.

After noon, cannonading began several miles eastward and continued steadily. Major General Daniel Harvey Hill had on his own initiative ordered Rodes' brigade to join him before Huger's division relieved the brigade. Before Rodes' brigade arrived, Hill attacked. Afterward, about 1 p.m., the 12th returned to Williamsburg Road and headed toward the firing. "The men were fresh, eager, and in light marching trim," recalled Cameron.[6] The Virginians could hear small arms fire as well as artillery. They met

---

6 Gustavus W. Smith, "Two Days of Battle at Seven Pines," in Robert U. Johnson and Clarence C. Buel, eds., *Battles and Leaders of the Civil War*, 4 vols. (New York, 1884, 1888), 2:229.

wounded coming back from the battle ahead. The inexperienced troops found the sight discouraging.

Mahone's brigade and the rest of Huger's division turned off Williamsburg Road half a mile east of the Tudor house. Longstreet had directed Huger to march on Charles City Road three miles southwest of Seven Pines and wait there for further orders. The Virginians trudged down the road, halting just beyond the Jordan farm, about a mile short of White's Tavern. The brigade formed line of battle across the road. While the battle raged three miles northeastward, Huger's division remained idle awaiting orders from Longstreet. At sunset Mahone's brigade bivouacked in the woods. The 12th's soldiers received instructions to make as little noise as possible and to build no fires despite the evening's damp and chill. Distant musketry reminded them that they would soon face the foe. "Pieces of white linen are given us to tie around our hats or caps to distinguish us in battle from the enemy," Bernard remembered.[7]

The regiment's men did not know what was happening. Whitehorne recalled, "A private soldier has no idea of future events, can always have lots of rumors to keep his imagination busy and excited, but he never knows what is about to happen, till events tread upon his heels. . . ."[8] The Confederates had driven a division of the enemy IV Corps from an unfinished redoubt, capturing prisoners, cannon and colors, but also suffering heavy casualties. These included Johnston himself, wounded as he reconnoitered. The army's control devolved on Maj. Gen. Gustavus W. Smith, commander of its left wing, which had attacked unsuccessfully down Nine Mile Road. With enemy reinforcements crossing the swollen Chickahominy, little chance remained of destroying the Yankee left as Johnston had planned. Of 29,500 men in the three divisions under Longstreet's command, the man whom Lee would one day call his "Old War Horse" got only 12,500 into the fight. Longstreet proved much better at public relations than at attacking the Federals. That evening Richmond buzzed with the rumor that Huger was responsible for the attack's failure.

While Richmond gossiped, Huger ordered Mahone to advance to Seven Pines and report to Hill. At 2 a.m., Mahone and his men rubbed the sleep from their eyes. Tottering out of their bedrolls, they trudged back up Charles

7 Bernard Notebook, 39.

8 Fletcher L. Elmore, comp., *Diary of J. E. Whitehorne, 1st Sergt., Co. "F," 12th VA Infantry, A. P. Hill's Corps, A. N. Va.* (Utica, KY, 1995), 19.

City Road and turned eastward on Williamsburg Road. Both highways lay in terrible condition, ribbons of mud and water. The sun rose. The troops could hear fighting ahead. On both sides of Williamsburg Road stood many soldiers. The 12th's men supposed these troops had fought in the previous day's action. The regiment also saw hundreds of skulkers coming from the battlefield, many carrying booty. One sat on a captured cannon which a detachment of artillerists was removing from the field. He seemed in ecstasy as he devoured a piece of fruit.

"Hurry up boys, there are lots of oranges & lemons, sugar & coffee, and every sort of good thing ahead of you," he shouted.[9]

Another man walking toward the rear held up his musket to show the passing troops that a minnie had perforated its stock.

"Nobody needn't say the Yankees don't know how to shoot," he cried, pointing to the hole. "See here, what they did for me."[10]

The green Virginians bought his bluster. "This fellow, in my own mind, I voted at once a hero," Bernard recalled. "We had not then the experience of after years to whisper the damaging suspicion that such as he had never— But perhaps I do injustice."[11]

The 12th's soldiers got their first glimpse of a man killed in battle. "How strange our feelings are as we look at this corpse!" remembered Bernard.[12] Mahone's troops passed through dense, swampy woods, gleaning whortleberries from abundant bushes. Soon they emerged into an open field where camps, breastworks and twin houses stood. The breastworks, known as Casey's Redoubt, had fallen to Hill's division the previous day. The bodies of men and horses, lying as they had fallen on the trampled ground, bespoke a terrible struggle.

Mahone called a halt. His brigade filed off to the road's right and formed line of battle west of Casey's Redoubt, facing southeastward. The 12th, the brigade's first regiment, constituted the van in the line of march and the right in the line of battle. The 3rd Alabama stood in the center, the 41st Virginia on the left. The brigade held its proper position in Huger's division. As the division's second brigade, Mahone's brigade followed Armistead's

---

9 Bernard Notebook, 40.

10 Ibid.

11 Ibid.

12 Ibid.

brigade, which formed the division's right. Brigadier General James E. B. "Jeb" Stuart guided Mahone to Hill's headquarters. Mahone saluted Hill.

"You are late in getting here," observed Hill, whose dyspepsia and diseased spine soured his disposition.

While his fellow dyspeptic Mahone seethed at Hill's remark, a courier rode up.

"The enemy are coming right there," he said, pointing to the woods north of Williamsburg Road.

"Take your brigade in there, General Mahone," said Hill.[13]

Mahone ordered his brigade into the woods north of the road, on the left of Armistead's brigade. This required Mahone's brigade to go into reverse. The 41st Virginia became the lead regiment and formed line of battle facing north, with the 3rd Alabama next in line on the 41st's right. Mahone expected the 12th Virginia to bring up the rear and form on the 3rd Alabama's right, but Hill detached the 12th from the rest of the brigade. The regiment remained in the open near Casey's Redoubt while the other two regiments charged into the woods and slammed into French's and Howard's brigades of Richardson's division in the enemy II Corps—Federal reinforcements that had crossed the Chickahominy the previous evening. This ignited a confused fight in which the 53rd Virginia, separated from Armistead's brigade, briefly joined Mahone's men in the timber and exchanged fire with the 41st Virginia.[14] Eventually the weight of numbers told. By eight o'clock, the eight regiments of the two Unionist brigades had driven the three Confederate units back to the woods' southern edge.

Near Casey's Redoubt, the 12th stood at order arms. The first sergeants had just begun to call the roll. Heavy musketry erupted from the woods to the northeast. Several of the regiment's soldiers were wounded. The troops looked toward the firing and the twin houses that stood just east of the redoubt. Dozens of skulkers had collected around the houses to pick up plunder. At the sound of the musketry they skedaddled.

In column of fours, the regiment double-quicked northeastward toward the woods. Men continued to fall wounded, including York Archer. Near the

13 William Mahone to James Longstreet, January 25, 1887, James Longstreet Papers, SHC; George S. Bernard, "War Recollections: From Drewry's Bluff to Seven Pines, the Engagement with the Federal Gunboats May 15, 1862, and the Battle of June 1, 1862," Petersburg *Index-Appeal*, June 14, 1903.

14 *OR* 11, 1:774, 785.

abandoned Unionist camp of Naglee's brigade and its surrounding abatis, the 12th went from column of fours to company front, then into line of battle facing the firing. The troops took pride in carrying out these maneuvers as precisely as on the drill field at Harrison's farm.

Behind the parade ground appearance lay a strictly choreographed formation, born of much instruction and drill. Each company stood in two ranks. Thirteen inches separated the rear rank's breasts from the backs of the men in front. The line thus formed divided right and left into two equal parts, the first and second platoons. Each platoon likewise broke down right and left into two sections. Corporals posted themselves on the right and left of the front rank of the two platoons according to height. The tallest corporal and the tallest man formed the first file, standing one behind the other on the right. The next two tallest men constituted the second file, and so on to the last file, on the left—the shortest corporal and the shortest man. The captain stood on the front rank's right. The first sergeant took position on the rear rank's right, directly behind the captain, and served as

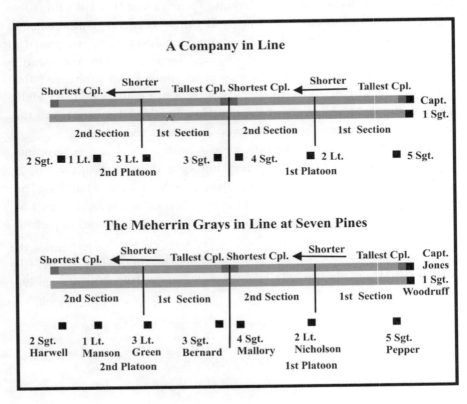

A Company in Line

The Meherrin Grays in Line at Seven Pines

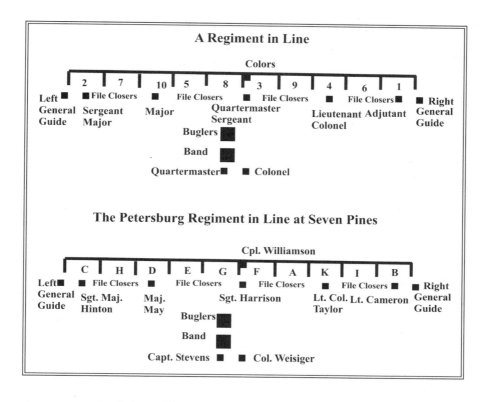

A Regiment in Line

The Petersburg Regiment in Line at Seven Pines

the company's right guide. The second sergeant stood behind the second file from the left and served as the left guide, though in the regiment's left company he posted himself on the front rank's left. The remaining officers and sergeants served as file closers, two paces behind the rear rank.

The regiment's 10 companies stood from right to left in the following order, according to the rank of their captains—first, sixth, fourth, ninth, third, eighth, fifth, tenth, seventh and second.[15] The Old Grays stood on the 12th's right. Then, moving left, came the Herrings, the Archer Rifles, the City Guard, the Huger Grays, the Richmond Grays, the Riflemen, the Lafayette Guards, the Juniors and finally the New Grays. The first five companies constituted the regiment's right wing, the next five its left wing.

Unlike company officers, most of the field officers entered battle mounted. Only Cameron, the adjutant, remained on foot. Weisiger sat his horse 30 paces

---

15 William H. Hardee, *Rifle and Light Infantry Tactics, for the Exercise and Manoevres of Troups when Acting as Light Infantry or Riflemen* (Philadelphia: Lippincott, Crawford & Co., 1855, 2 vols.), 1:5.

behind the file closers in the regiment's center. A dozen paces behind the file closers, Taylor rode in alignment with the right wing's center. May sat his horse the same distance behind the left wing's center. Eight paces behind the file closers, Cameron and Sgt. Maj. William Edward Hinton stood aligned with the regiment's right and left, respectively. Captain Samuel Stevens the quartermaster, Claiborne the surgeon, and other staff officers rode in one rank on Weisiger's left and three paces behind him. The 12th's buglers stood in four ranks, twelve paces behind the file closers, with their left behind the Lafayette Guards' center. Quartermaster Sergeant Benjamin Harrison took post two paces to the right of the buglers' front rank. The regimental band, with one of the principal musicians at its head, formed five paces behind the buglers.

Eight corporals distinguished for regularity and precision in maneuver composed the color guard, taking position on the Huger Grays' left. In the center of the guard's front rank stood Color Sgt. James Williamson. Weisiger had selected him to bear the regiment's flag based on how he carried himself under arms and his accuracy in marching. The guard's two ranking corporals took position respectively on Williamson's right and left. The three corporals next in seniority formed the guard's second rank. Behind them stood the three remaining corporals, in the line of file closers.

Two general guides almost completed a textbook picture of a regiment drawn up in line of battle. These sergeants stood in the line of file closers, one behind the right flank and the other behind the left. Weisiger had chosen them from among the sergeants other than the first sergeants according to the same criteria employed in the color bearer's selection. They had as important a role in keeping the 12th properly aligned.[16]

The regiment's deployment fell short of perfect in only one way. Weisiger had failed to throw out skirmishers.[17] For this omission the 12th would pay dearly.

Taylor rode down the line of battle.

"I thank God, I do not see a blanched cheek in this regiment," he said.[18]

Todd saw plenty of blanched cheeks.

---

16 Ibid., 1:5-10.

17 Hampton Newsome, John Horn and John Selby, eds., *Civil War Talks: Further Reminiscences of George S. Bernard & His Fellow Veterans* (Charlottesville, Va., 2012), 63.

18 Todd, "Reminiscences," 13.

The First Flag of the Petersburg Regiment. *Petersburg National Battlefield Park*

"Forward, guide center, march!" Weisiger shouted a moment later.[19]

His troops strode toward the woods, inclining leftward. A horse burst out of the pines and galloped through the Richmond Grays, briefly disordering them. The animal belonged to Col. Tennent Lomax, the 3rd Alabama's commander, killed seconds before by the invaders.

The 12th passed Mahone.

"Hurry up, boys, the 14th has just captured a battery," he cried. "I want you to capture two for myself."[20] The 14th Virginia belonged to Armistead's brigade, engaged to the 12th's right.

Another 100 yards brought the regiment to the pines' edge. The troops plunged into the thick undergrowth, still inclining leftward and edging across a white sand lane. Enemy balls kept taking their toll. Cameron recalled that he "heard the zip-zip of bullets, but had not realized what they were in the slightest degree." He saw a man in the battle line sink into a brook's bed and thought the fellow was skulking. "I approached him with up-lifted sword and an imprecation," Cameron recalled. "I shall never forget the remorse I felt when the poor fellow turned his face up to me for answer and I saw the blood pouring from a ghastly wound under the left eye."[21]

19 Ibid.

20 E. Leslie Spence to George S. Bernard, December 1, 1893, George S. Bernard Papers, SHC.

21 Newsome, Horn, Selby, eds., *Civil War Talks*, 63.

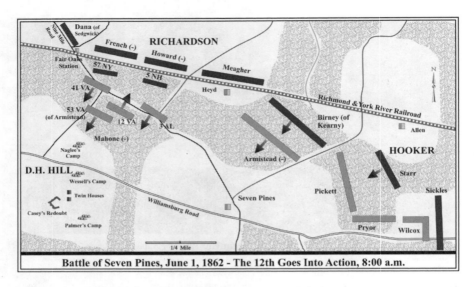

Battle of Seven Pines, June 1, 1862 - The 12th Goes Into Action, 8:00 a.m.

The pines and brambles gave way to a swamp. The men floundered through the mud and creepers. Their line grew ragged. Fifty yards beyond the woods' edge, the 12th suffered the consequences of Weisiger's negligence. With no skirmishers to screen its front, the regiment stumbled into the enemy. The brush ahead seemed to explode. The Virginians took a volley from the 5th New Hampshire—the skirmish line of Howard's brigade—concealed on the swamp's other side.[22] The Federals fired while lying behind tents and small bushes as little as 40 yards away.

The blast checked the 12th's advance and threw part of its line into confusion. The field officers shouted conflicting orders. The color bearer wavered. The rank and file returned fire. Standing in mud and water knee deep, they blazed away at the gun flashes of an enemy made otherwise invisible by the undergrowth. Bullets flew around their heads "thick as hail," wrote Whitehorne.[23] Solid shot also struck among the Virginians. The other regiments of Howard's brigade pitched in to support the Granite Staters.

22 William A. Child, *History Of The Fifth Regiment New Hampshire Volunteers in the American Civil War 1861-65.* (Bristol, NH, 1893), 82-84; Gilbert Frederick, *The Story Of A Regiment, Being A Record Of The Military Services Of The Fifty-Seventh New York State Volunteer Infantry In The War Of The Rebellion 1861-1865* (Chicago, 1895), 53-54, 61; *OR* 11, 1:771.

23 James E. Whitehorne to Father, June 2, 1862.

The mounted officers provided inviting targets. Mahone had his mare, Sally Lubbock, killed under him. The soldiers of Howard's brigade wounded Weisiger's horse. The animal threw Weisiger and bolted. Even Dr. Claiborne had his sorrel mare shot from under him.

An unforeseeable factor afflicted Weisiger's command. Regimental musicians doubled as stretcher-bearers, but the stretcher-bearer's role required the bravest and strongest men in each company. The musicians did not promptly carry off the wounded for medical attention. Demoralization spread to the unhurt.

The firefight lasted no more than 15 minutes. Yanks from Birney's brigade of Kearny's division ended the struggle. Driving Armistead's brigade from the woods to the right of Mahone's brigade, these Unionists halted at a crest and enfiladed Mahone's men, who suffered so badly from this fire that Mahone ordered them to fall back out of the swamp and reform their line.[24] Some of the 12th's companies retreated in good order, but others disintegrated. Some men ran.[25]

Reforming near Naglee's Camp, Mahone's brigade retired toward the twin houses. The Virginians lay down behind the embankment of Williamsburg Road near the abandoned Yankee camp of Wessel's brigade. Taylor, who took Williamson's hesitation for want of courage, summarily deprived him of the colors and demoted him from his position as color bearer.

The Northerners advanced a cannon to a position several hundred yards in front of the 12th's left. The gun began shelling the regiment. One of its round shot, barely missing the embankment, whizzed overhead and struck the body of a dead Northerner near one of the tents a few feet behind the 12th. The shot hurled the body several feet in the air.

"That Yankee went nearer Heaven just now than he will ever go again," a soldier remarked.[26]

A small Confederate force advancing from the cannon's right forced its gunners to limber up and retreat. A North Carolina regiment from Colston's brigade of Longstreet's division began filing past the 12th's left on the way to the pines from which Mahone's brigade had withdrawn. Hill arrived and promptly infuriated the 12th.

24 Mahone to Longstreet, January 25, 1887.

25 Newsome, Horn and Selby, eds., *Civil War Talks*, 65.

26 Ibid., 49; Bernard Notebook, 42.

"Go in North Carolinians and show Virginians that you can fight," said Hill. "Here is a whole brigade that ran."[27]

"It's a lie," a Virginian shouted.[28]

"Are they Hatteras and Roanoke Island heroes?" sneered other members of the 12th.

Approaching Hill, Taylor said he considered himself a brave man, he knew the regiment had not left the woods before he had left and the 12th had not left until ordered. Hill replied that he had only intended his words as an encouragement to the troops headed for battle. Taylor called down the line for Mahone.

"Your men are being slandered on the field of battle," Taylor said when Mahone arrived. Taylor then reported Hill's remark.

Mahone rode over to Hill.

"You are a God damn liar, and I will hold you personally responsible for this hereafter," Mahone said. "I ordered my men out of the woods."

A courier dashed up to Hill.

"General Pickett says his right flank is exposed and asks for reinforcements," the courier said. Brigadier General George E. Pickett commanded a brigade of Longstreet's division engaged farther east on Williamsburg Road, to the right of where Armistead's brigade had fought. The Yankees were threatening to drive Pickett's men from the field.

"I have no troops but these," Hill said, referring to Mahone's brigade. "You can use them."

Hill gave Mahone directions to the threatened point.

"Attention!" shouted Mahone, when Hill had finished.

Mahone's troops rose to their feet at once. "Every man in the brigade would have charged a 10-gun battery alone, if ordered, as they were all so mad that such a stigma had been put on them on their first battlefield," recalled the Richmond Grays' Pvt. Emmett Leslie Spence.[29] Weisiger marched his regiment half a mile eastward. Pausing at a captured Federal camp near the Seven Pines crossroads, his men found an abundance of spoils as well as Northern dead and wounded in the tents and on the swampy ground.

---

27 Spence to Bernard, December 1, 1893; Newsome, Horn and Selby, eds., *Civil War Talks*, 49.

28 Bernard Notebook, 43.

29 Spence to Bernard, December 1, 1893; Newsome, Horn and Selby, eds., *Civil War Talks*, 49.

Weisiger did not intend to suffer surprise again. As soon as the 12th reached the camp, he sent forward the Riflemen and the Richmond Grays as skirmishers. Behind them, the rest of the regiment formed line of battle and lay down. The skirmishers deployed and advanced into some woods firing at an enemy scarcely visible among the trees. Bullets whizzed over the regiment's battle line, which remained prone.

The colonel soon withdrew the skirmishers. They took their places in the battle line. A few minutes later, his troops heard a heavy volley several hundred yards in their left rear. The crest from which Birney's brigade had fired upon them hid from view the musketry's origin. The 12th's men wondered what the volley meant and felt uneasy, but soon a cannon roared from that direction. Unable to see it, but recognizing it as theirs, they listened to the rattle of the cannister it flung at the foe. "What a feeling of security it gave us!" Bernard recalled. "We shall always remember the relief we felt at each discharge reverberating among the hills so near us."[30]

Soon after the Confederate artillery had thwarted this enemy counterattack, the 12th withdrew. The regiment halted near Wessel's Camp and the twin houses. The battle had ended. Johnston's attempt to smash the Federal left had failed. Mahone's men spent the day's remainder sitting around and discussing the morning's events, roaming the battlefield and picking up plunder, or helping the wounded.

The contents of Wessel's Camp impressed even Confederate soldiers from the bountiful Department of Norfolk. Many of the 12th's men gathered rubber cloths for sleeping on the damp ground. The Confederate Ordnance Department collected wagonloads of muskets and hauled away captured cannon. Scroungers picked and chose among the food, liquor, clothing, ammunition, blankets and tents. Most of the other spoils, from useless linen collars to precious medical supplies, went up in smoke.

After nightfall the regiment's men worried the enemy might attack them in the morning. They contemplated the miserable prospect of again fighting in the woods and swamps. Corpses of men and horses lay near the troops on all sides, some in the ditches from which the living drew water. Too exhausted to dwell for long on their predicament, the soldiers went to sleep, unaware of Johnston's wound or that Lee had taken command.

At 1 a.m. on June 2, the regiment's officers woke the men and warned them to remain as silent as possible. In the darkness the soldiers could dimly see a column within a few yards of them moving towards Richmond.

30 Bernard Notebook, 44.

They soon grasped that their army was withdrawing. The 12th joined the column. Wagons and cannon up to their axles in mud hindered the retreat. Some soldiers fretted that dawn would catch them not yet out of sight of the previous night's camp. "Seeing us retreating, the enemy would rush upon our column so embarrassed by the woods & the swamps as to be unable to resist them successfully," Bernard imagined.[31] Sunrise found the men well on the way to Richmond, with no Yankees in sight. By 11 a.m., Mahone's brigade had returned to its former position on Charles City Road.

Later that day, after sleeping, the regiment's officers and men reflected on their ordeal at Seven Pines. Muddy up to his knees, without a change of clothing, Weisiger wrote, "We have had a very hard time but the sufferings in the way of hardship is nothing to what I have suffered in mind at seeing some of my best men and brave boys shot down before my face. . . ."[32] The 12th lost 44 soldiers. The Northerners had killed nine and wounded 34.[33] Three of the wounded died of their injuries. Only one man ended up a prisoner.[34] Within a few days, the rest of the 75 soldiers initially reported missing returned to the 12th or reported themselves sick.

The results of the regiment's first encounter with enemy infantry mortified the 12th's men. The regiment lost cohesion in the woods. Its color bearer suffered disgrace. The enemy forced the 12th to retire. Parts of the regiment panicked during the withdrawal. Hill humiliated the 12th by accusing it of running. Longstreet put his criticism in writing: "Some of the brigades of Major General Huger's division took part in defending our position on Sunday, but, being fresh at the work, did not show the same steadiness and determination as the troops of Hill's division and my own."[35]

The 12th's men resolved never to let such things happen again.

---

31 Ibid.

32 David A. Weisiger to Wife, June 2, 1862, Weisiger Family Papers, VHS. All Weisiger's letters cited herein come from this collection. Weisiger reported 10 killed, 27 wounded and 75 missing. Ibid.

33 Roll 66, M861, Record Group 109, NA; "Casualties In The *Petersburg Regiment,* Correspondence of the Petersburg *Express*, 'On the Wing,' Below Richmond, June 2d, 1862," Bird Family Papers; Henderson, *12VI,* 18.

34 Ibid., 106-167.

35 *OR* 11, 1:940.

CHAPTER 5

The Seven Days

After the Confederate defeat at Seven Pines, Lee redeployed his forces. McClellan, convinced that the Secessionists outnumbered his army, hesitated in exploiting his victory. On June 3, Lee addressed his troops, declaring an end to retreating and designating the watchword as, "Victory or death."[1] The 12th fended off a reconnaissance by an enemy regiment that afternoon while the Southerners strengthened their position.[2]

At daylight June 4, the 12th trudged northwestward up Charles City Road. After more than a mile, the soldiers formed line of battle across the road in a flat bottom near the Parada farm. The Parada house stood on the road's north side a mile and a half south of Williamsburg Road. Some men spread their rubber cloths on the ground and tried to sleep. Responding to a report of Yankees advancing up the road, a battery unlimbered near the 12th to rake the foe. The artillery made the troops feel secure. A small detachment advanced to burn a house 100 yards from the regiment's line lest it serve as protection for enemy sharpshooters. No Federals appeared. The 12th encamped, remaining there several weeks with its pickets eventually standing on a line about a quarter mile east in a belt of swampy woods between the two armies.

1 "The Fight near Richmond," *Spirit of the Age* (Raleigh, NC), June 9, 1862, p. 2, col. 1.

2 "From the Virginia Army," Memphis Daily *Appeal*, June 4, 1862, p. 2, col. 4.

The soldiers found the place miserable. "It is so wet and muddy that I can't walk three steps without getting my feet really wet & it seems to me that it rains all the time," Whitehorne wrote. "The country for 10 miles around here is nothing but Swamps."[3] The men referred to this base as the "Mud Camp."[4] They had none of the Cockade Barracks' comforts. Rations, cooked far to the rear, cooled or spoiled before reaching them. Not until June 10 did they receive their tent flies, which finally gave them some protection from the elements. The brigade's water supply became a serious problem, aggravated by clouds of flies. The only water the soldiers got came from holes dug about two feet deep. "The men suffer very much from Diarrhoea caused by drinking such mean muddy water," wrote Whitehorne.[5]

Night and day, the 12th engaged in picket skirmishing and, worse, scouting to keep the high command apprised of the enemy's posture and movements. The troops found scouting the war's most unpleasant duty. The experience resembled that of twentieth century soldiers in jungle warfare. The woods and undergrowth in the swamps prevented the men from seeing 20 yards ahead. The advantage lay with the side which set up an ambush, fired from concealment, then retired. "I always felt on those scouts like a man walking through tall grass, infested with snakes, expecting to be bitten any moment," recalled Todd.[6]

Every morning, before daybreak, a company slipped beyond the Confederate picket line to feel the enemy III Corps' sentry line. The Virginians advanced in the dim light without canteens and under orders not to talk above a whisper. Often the Southerners came within a few yards of the Yankee pickets before the invaders discovered them. A quick challenge would issue. A volley from the Federal sentries' rifles would follow. "We seldom had anyone hurt, for they would fire at random, then 'skedaddle,' and we would return to our camp in time to get breakfast," recalled Brown.[7]

Sometimes the 12th's men approached so stealthily that they fired first. On June 15, the Richmond Grays advanced to find the enemy picket line. The Grays had proceeded about two and a half miles when they saw six

---

3 James E. Whitehorne to Sister, June 11, 1862.

4 Bernard, "Notebook," 46.

5 Whitehorne to Sister, June 11, 1862.

6 Todd, "Reminiscences," 18.

7 Brown, *Reminiscences of the War*, 15.

Union sentries. The Grays crept up to within 20 steps of the Northerners. Just as the six saw the Virginians, the Grays fired and killed five.

On other occasions the regiment's scouts collided with Yankees engaged in the same activity. Thirty Juniors had a narrow escape on June 19. Deployed as skirmishers far ahead of the regiment, they met about 300 Unionists who charged them. "We had to get out of that woods in Boston time," wrote Sale, now a sergeant.[8] One of Sale's comrades lost his life.[9]

Late that night the troops received orders to wake up at two in the morning. The brigade advanced at three, then halted waiting for enough daylight to fight. At 4 a.m., the New Grays, Riflemen and Richmond Grays crept forward and cut off the enemy pickets. The Virginians crawled farther forward to a house occupied by Yankee sentries. The Riflemen took to the woods to flank the Federals, who observed the Riflemen and exchanged shots with them. The New Grays charged the Northerners across a field about 300 yards wide. The Riflemen kept the Federals so busy that they did not see the New Grays until they came within 100 yards. The Unionists "broke and ran in fine style, our company going in without firing a shot," wrote Bird.[10] From there the Virginians advanced on another picket line, which fell back without fighting. The soldiers finished at 8 a.m. and returned to camp, going on a similar mission the next day, when another of the Juniors perished.[11]

Night duty proved more terrifying. "Alarms" frequently occurred. The men, Bernard remembered, "were suddenly gotten under arms at different hours of the night & tramped off a half a mile or so in the direction of the enemy, to lurk about in the thickets, watching their approach."[12] For several nights in a row, the Old Grays' Second Lt. Thomas Poindexter Pollard led a 10-man patrol in search of an enemy force firing on the Confederate cavalry's pickets. Finally he located the trouble's source. Pickets of Wright's brigade, which belonged to Huger's division and held a post on the left of Mahone's brigade, had lined up in the woods facing their fellow Secessionists instead of the Yankees.

8 John F. Sale to Aunt, November 11, 1862.

9 Roll 66, M861, Record Group 109, NA.

10 Henry Van Leuvenigh Bird to Margaret Randolph, June 19, 1862.

11 Roll 66, M861, Record Group 109, NA.

12 Bernard Notebook, 46.

By June 23, despite the rigors of scouting and the Mud Camp's squalor, the regiment had 691 officers and men present of 936 present and absent.[13] The ladies of Petersburg gave the 12th a battle flag that had sewn on it letters spelling out "Seven Pines." It replaced the regiment's first banner, which bore a design—the Stars and Bars—retired because it looked too much like the Federal flag. The new ensign had white stars arranged on a blue St. Andrew's cross in a field of red. This design became the definitive Confederate battle flag.

The same rains that made the Mud Camp so miserable prevented McClellan from resuming his advance toward Richmond. His posture remained defensive and his principal movement lay in shifting all but a reinforced corps of his army south of the Chickahominy. The roads became impassable and the swollen Chickahominy washed away its bridges.

In late June the weather cleared. McClellan prepared to strike the Southerners at Old Tavern on Nine Mile Road, about a mile northwest of Fair Oaks Station. Seizing Old Tavern would force the Confederates to retract their left. This would facilitate a junction with the corps at Fredericksburg in case Lincoln allowed it to march down to Richmond. McClellan also viewed the higher ground at Old Tavern as ideal for siege artillery. He wanted his men south of the York River Railroad to join his troops north of the tracks in the attack on Old Tavern. To do this, the Federal forces south of the railroad would first have to drive back the Secessionist picket line on Williamsburg Road.

None of this fit in with Lee's plans. He did not intend to let the Yanks besiege Richmond. With their superior artillery and advantage in numbers, a siege could only result in the city's fall. Lee intended to seize the initiative. His plan called for Jackson to bring down his command from the Valley. Along with the divisions of A. P. Hill, D. H. Hill and Longstreet, Stonewall would strike the Union right, north of the Chickahominy. Pushing back McClellan's right would expose his supply base at White House Landing on Pamunkey River and force him to retreat. The rest of Lee's army, which included Maj. Gen. John B. "Prince John" Magruder's command, Huger's division and Holmes' division, would remain south of the Chickahominy. Led by Magruder, this force would occupy the Northern left by a series of feints deceiving McClellan into thinking an attack imminent there.

13 *OR* 11, 3:615.

Magruder began by pushing the picket line of Huger's division about half a mile farther east after dark on June 24, to the eastern edge of the woods that separated the two armies south of the Chickahominy. The skirmishers of Armistead's brigade struggled forward through the underbrush north of Williamsburg Road. The pickets of Wright's brigade inched through the thickets just south of the road. South of Wright's men, Mahone's skirmishers advanced. Mahone's brigade now consisted of the 6th, 12th, 16th, 41st and 49th Virginia. The 12th's pickets padded through the dense, swampy woods east of Charles City Road with instructions passed on in a whisper from one soldier to another, taking position by twos at intervals of twenty paces. The challenge changed from "Who comes there?" to a low whistle. The countersign became two low whistles. The troops had orders to fire upon anyone who did not give this signal. "It proved a long and weary watch, without incident, save the rushing sound of an immense rocket as it soared on high, throughout the darkened sky, and exploded when nearly out of sight," Brown recalled.[14] His companions feared this signified a Federal attack. Returning to camp, the men learned it came from their own signal corps to communicate with Stonewall.

McClellan knew of Jackson's approach. Deserters from Stonewall's command had stumbled into Unionist lines north of the Chickahominy, but McClellan did not cancel his planned attack on Old Tavern. He hoped to strike before Jackson arrived.

At 10 a.m. on June 25, Yankees of III Corps hit the advanced picket line of Wright's brigade, driving the Confederate sentinels back from King's School House in the middle of the belt of woods west of Seven Pines to French's farm half a mile farther west. There Wright's brigade, reinforced by Ransom's brigade, halted the invaders. Mahone, hearing this struggle to his left, took the 6th, 12th, 41st and 49th Virginia and rushed to the assistance of Wright's brigade. The fighting had ceased by the time the Virginians arrived.

Early that afternoon McClellan visited the front to appraise the situation. He ordered his men forward again, with reinforcements. Mahone prepared to advance some of his men to strike the left of any Unionists attempting to shove Wright's brigade back from French's farmhouse. The force selected for this flank attack consisted of the 49th Virginia, the 41st Virginia and

---

14 Brown, *Reminiscences of the War*, 16.

the second battalion of the 6th Virginia—all under the command of Col. William "Extra Billy" Smith of the 49th. The 12th and the first battalion of the 6th remained on the western edge of French's farm supporting Wright's brigade directly.

At 5 p.m., Kearny's division massed at King's School House to support an advance westward by Hooker's division along Williamsburg Road. From left to right, the Confederate line along the western edge of French's farm consisted of the 1st Louisiana, the 22nd Georgia, the 4th Georgia, the 48th North Carolina, the 12th Virginia, a battalion of the 6th Virginia and Smith's force, which lay in wait for the Yankee left. The 4th Georgia and 48th North Carolina charged across the field of French's farm into the midst of three Federal brigades. The opposing Northerners initially recoiled, but then blasted the Southerners, repelled them and counterattacked in turn. The Yankees stopped in the face of fire from the 12th Virginia and the first battalion of the 6th. Smith charged the extreme Union left—the 20th Indiana from Robinson's brigade of Kearny's division. To the right of the 20th, the 87th New York, also of Robinson's brigade, skedaddled. In danger of envelopment, the Hoosiers also fled, pursued by Smith's Virginians as well as by the 12th and the first battalion of the 6th Virginia, which double-quicked to a worm fence along the edge of a thick growth of small pines near King's School House. The Virginians could not see the Federals, whose bullets knocked chips of bark from the trees.

"Look out to the left!" someone in Smith's force called out after a few minutes. "The Yankees are flanking us!"[15]

The 12th's men could see a mass of the enemy double-quicking westward across the northern edge of French's field toward the Confederate rear, apparently attempting to cut off the Virginians at the fence.

"Fall back!" came the command.[16]

The advanced line of Secessionists retreated to French's farm "in great confusion and disorder," wrote Bird.[17] There it rallied and repulsed the Unionists, who retreated into the woods east of King's School House. Darkness ended the fighting. The 12th returned to the Mud Camp, having suffered 25 wounded, the heaviest casualties in Mahone's brigade. The

15 Ibid.

16 Ibid.

17 Henry Van Leuvenigh Bird to Margaret Randolph, June 26, 1862.

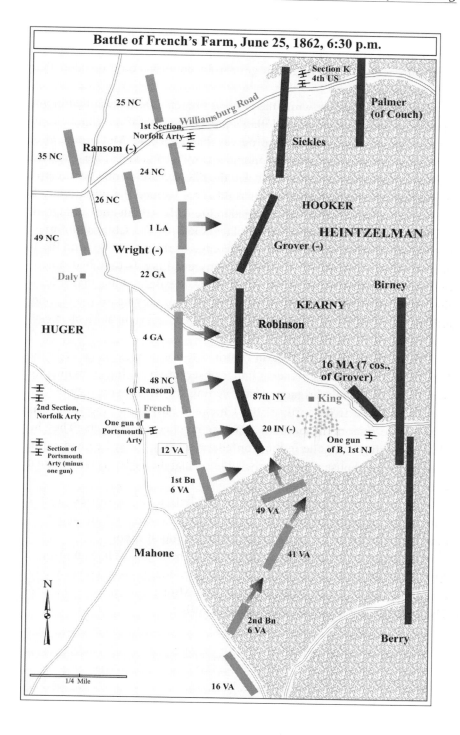

Battle of French's Farm, June 25, 1862, 6:30 p.m.

Section K
4th US

Palmer
(of Couch)

25 NC

Williamsburg Road

1st Section,
Norfolk Arty

Sickles

Ransom (-)

35 NC

24 NC

26 NC

HOOKER

49 NC

1 LA

HEINTZELMAN

Wright (-)

Grover (-)

Daly

22 GA

Birney

KEARNY

Robinson

HUGER

4 GA

16 MA (7 cos.,
of Grover)

48 NC
(of Ransom)

2nd Section,
Norfolk Arty

French

87th NY

King

One gun of
Portsmouth
Arty

Section of
Portsmouth
Arty (minus
one gun)

12 VA

20 IN (-)

One gun
of B, 1st NJ

1st Bn
6 VA

49 VA

Mahone

41 VA

N

2nd Bn
6 VA

Berry

1/4 Mile

16 VA

wounds of four of the regiment's soldiers proved mortal. Another wounded man fell into enemy hands.[18] Smith complimented the 12th on the way it went into action.[19] The regiment gave a far better account of itself than at Seven Pines.

Late that afternoon, while the issue at French's farm remained in doubt, disturbing news required McClellan's presence north of the Chickahominy. Jackson's men had made better progress than expected. McClellan, already convinced that the Southerners outnumbered him, panicked at the exaggerated reports of Jackson's strength, canceled the planned attack on Old Tavern and began bracing for an assault on his right. This yielded the initiative to Lee.

Early on June 26, the 12th returned to French's farm in one of Magruder's feints to keep McClellan's left in place south of the Chickahominy. The regiment's soldiers spent the day in the edge of the woods skirting the field around French's house. In the field enemy dead lay as they had fallen the previous day. The Yankees did not resume the fight. Late that afternoon the Virginians returned to the Mud Camp. There they heard the thunder of artillery far to their left. Lee was attacking the Federal right at Mechanicsville, north of the Chickahominy.

Next day the regiment again returned to the woods' edge at French's farm. The 12th kept the invaders under observation. Things remained quiet in front of Mahone's brigade. That evening the men again listened to the sounds of battle from north of the Chickahominy, this time from Gaines Mill.[20] Wild rumors of Southern victories reached the soldiers. They heard that everything had gone in the Confederates' favor, that Lee had captured McClellan and thousands of enemy soldiers, that the Federals were retreating and that the war's end stood in sight.

The regiment's instructions June 28 belied these stories. The 12th returned yet again to the woods' edge at French's farm. Yet again the troops remained all day and returned to the Mud Camp at night.

On June 29, all stayed quiet for a while. The regiment had an inspection. At 11 a.m., everything changed. The 12th got under arms, then headed down a country road leading eastward from the Mud Camp toward the enemy. The men left without even their blanket rolls.

18 *OR* 11, 2:799; Roll 66, M861, Record Group 109, NA; Henderson, *12VI*, 106-167.

19 Bernard Notebook, 47.

20 Also known as First Cold Harbor.

Events north of the Chickahominy accounted for the alteration. Not everything had gone in the Confederates' favor there, but the Yankees had begun to retreat. With his right pushed back, McClellan abandoned hope of a junction with the corps at Fredericksburg, burned the base at White House Landing and marched to his left across the Chickahominy toward the James. Ascertaining the retreat's direction, Lee determined to head off the Unionists and destroy them. Jackson, with his own command and D. H. Hill's division, would dog the tracks of the enemy army southward from the Chickahominy. Magruder's command would advance eastward along Williamsburg Road to engage and break the Federal column before it reached White Oak Swamp. To intercept the Yankees who made it across the swamp and headed for the James on Long Bridge Road, the rest of Lee's army would march southeastward toward Glendale. From left to right, Huger's division would advance down Charles City Road, Longstreet's and A. P. Hill's divisions down Darbytown Road and Holmes' division down New Market Road. Seizing Glendale—the junction of Charles City Road and Long Bridge Road—these forces would cut the Unionist line of retreat and bag McClellan's army.

The 12th's soldiers crept through the marshy woods they had scouted for the past month. Reaching the enemy's picket line, they found it deserted. The troops picked up and read scraps of newspapers and letters left by Northern pickets. The Federals themselves did not appear. Swinging to its right, the regiment proceeded back toward Charles City Road by another country lane. The 12th's right came within sight of the road. Ahead, the regiment's men heard firing. They halted and prepared for action.

"Those in front of us are our friends!" word came.[21] The 12th's men confronted not the Yankees but the 49th Virginia. The rest of the brigade had stuck to the road. The 49th had mistaken the 12th for the foe.

The 12th filed into the road. Mahone's brigade resumed its southeastward trek. After a mile or two, the 12th met a regiment of cavalry coming from the enemy's direction.

"Where are the Yankees, boys?" the 12th's soldiers asked.

"Not very far—you will see them presently," the horsemen replied.[22]

21 Bernard Notebook, 48.

22 Ibid.

The regiment formed line of battle across the road, preparing to receive Unionist cavalry. The 12th remained in this posture for an hour or two. The position seemed good to the Virginians, who thought they could repulse any enemy attack. The Federals did not accommodate them but continued retreating.

Mahone's brigade resumed its progress. The Virginians advanced a few hundred yards to the Brightwell farm before forming line of battle across the road yet again. The 12th's left exchanged shots with Yankees from Kearny's division of III Corps. The Northerners fired from about 100 yards ahead in the dense pines. "The bullets whistled over our heads and the dry twigs from the pine trees dropped in profusion, but no one was hurt," recalled Brown.[23] To the 12th's left, the inexperienced 16th Virginia broke. Its flight exposed the 12th's left flank. The enemy in front of both regiments did not take advantage of the situation. Blocked from retiring to Glendale along Charles City Road, Kearny's division withdrew across White Oak Swamp via Jordan's Ford and hiked southeastward on New Road, then slipped back across White Oak Swamp by Brackett's Ford and continued retreating via Charles City Road. The 12th's soldiers and the rest of the men of Huger's division slept on their arms five miles from where they had started the day and three miles short of the critical Glendale road junction.

Lee's plan had gone awry. Jackson's lackadaisical pursuit southward from the Chickahominy had allowed the enemy rear guard to fend off Magruder's thrust eastward along Williamsburg Road toward Savage's Station and slip away. The slow march of Huger's division down Charles City Road left open the Glendale crossroads for the Federals to retire southward on Long Bridge Road toward the James.

June 30 began as quietly as the previous day. The Riflemen advanced to feel the enemy and encountered no opposition. Mahone's brigade got moving about 11 a.m., occasionally halting and forming line of battle. At 3 p.m., during one pause, the pioneers of Huger's division advanced with their axes. After a few minutes the column resumed its progress. The Virginians soon saw the reason for employing the pioneers, the equivalent of modern day combat engineers. The enemy—men from Slocum's division of VI Corps—had begun felling trees across the road to impede the progress of Huger's division. Mahone, who should have known better, refused to allow

---

23 Brown, *Reminiscences of the War*, 17.

his men to leave the road to advance. He did not want them to outstrip their accompanying artillery. Huger, to his discredit, failed to overrule Mahone and cut the infantry loose from the batteries. Engaging the enemy would have ended the felling of trees. The Norfolk Division thus engaged in a ludicrous wood-chopping competition with the foe. As fast as the Southern pioneers cleared one tree, the Yankees felled another.

Late that afternoon Huger's division finally approached Glendale. The 12th's soldiers stood less than half a mile northwest of Brackett's Run.

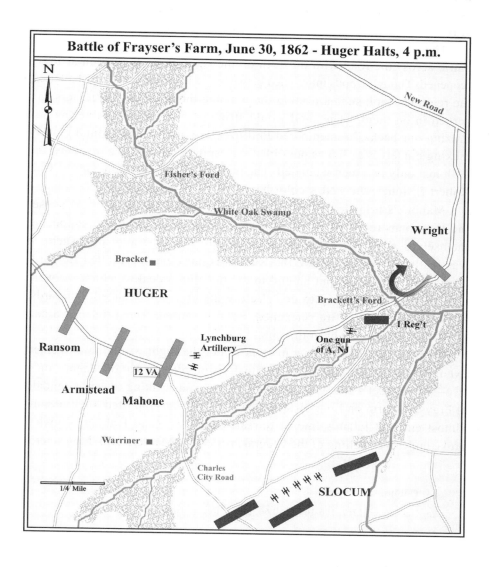

Battle of Frayser's Farm, June 30, 1862 - Huger Halts, 4 p.m.

They heard the report of a piece of artillery in front of them. A solid shot whistled over their heads and struck among the dead pines to their left. Further reports came from the same direction, followed by shot or shell crashing among the trees near the Virginians. The enemy had taken a stand. Mahone ordered his brigade out of the road, allowing Moorman's Virginia battery to advance and engage the enemy artillery. Federal gunners to the front on Charles City Road and to the left, commanding Brackett's Ford of White Oak Swamp, had Mahone's brigade in a crossfire. Projectiles from the enemy battery ahead raked the road. Missiles from the Yankee cannoneers at Brackett's Ford passed mostly in front of the 12th.

The firing stopped in a few minutes. Mahone's brigade formed line of battle across the road with the 12th on the right. Soon the Union artillery reopened. Though woods intervened between the 12th and the enemy batteries, the regiment took such a pasting that its men thought the Northerners had zeroed in on them. "The shell would strike in front and pass over us just grazing our backs," remembered Phillips. "We hugged the ground closely making ourselves as flat as possible."[24] Despite the shellfire's intensity, the 12th lost only two men wounded. The injuries of one—the Old Grays' Cpl. Robert E. Jones, the 12th's color bearer—proved mortal.[25]

Mahone's brigade endured the Yankee barrage for an hour. At sunset the Virginians received orders to advance. The men took heart, supposing themselves about to charge the enemy guns. "Strange as it may seem, it was really a relief to believe that such was our object," recalled Bernard. "Anything that would put an end to the horrible ordeal to which we were subjected we felt willing to do."[26] Before the brigade advanced 100 yards, the enemy batteries' fire slackened. Soon it ceased. The 12th halted and spent that gloomy night in the pines.

Had the men known how matters stood, the night would have seemed even gloomier. Of all the Confederate divisions directed at the enemy, only two—Longstreet's and A. P. Hill's—had attacked, striking toward Glendale at Frayser's farm on Long Bridge Road. Though unsupported, their assault almost cut McClellan's line of retreat. On River Road Holmes' division broke under the shelling of the Federal artillery on Malvern Hill. Magruder's

---

24 Phillips, "Sixth Corporal," 7.

25 Henderson, *12VI*, 106-167; Roll 66, M861, Record Group 109, NA.

26 Bernard Notebook, 50.

command marched and countermarched uselessly between River Road and Glendale in response to conflicting orders. Jackson's force failed to press across White Oak Swamp. Lee's plan to cut off and destroy the Yankee army had failed.

The 12th left camp at nine next morning. About 200 men remained with the colors.[27] The enemy had vanished from the regiment's front. Advancing slowly, Huger's division filled Charles City Road. Soon the 12th passed through the enemy position that had blocked Huger's advance the previous day. At one place dead men lay beside the road. At another stood piles of knapsacks, overcoats and oilcloths. At still another the ground appeared blue with abandoned clothing. Elsewhere muskets, blankets, provisions, tents and anything else that impeded the Federal retreat littered the road. "All appearances of a general stampeed," remembered Phillips.[28] Those who had not scooped up oilcloths and added them to their blanket rolls at Seven Pines had their pick of them now. "They threw away their knapsacks by thousands in order to better make that Grand Strategic move of Mac's," Sale wrote about McClellan's change of base from York River to the James.[29]

Congestion at the junction of Charles City and Long Bridge roads further slowed progress. The 12th halted several times to let other troops pass. Finally the regiment veered southwestward onto Willis Church Road. The 12th tramped through another scene of the previous day's fighting, encountering more dead men, this time in the roadside ditches. Soon the troops passed woods still smoldering from a fire that had swept through them. The column next skirted an open field. Dead men, dead horses and an occasional wounded Northerner lay scattered over the trampled ground. The Virginians wondered why they had not heard the savage struggle that took place here, less than two miles away from their position on Charles City Road.

After a brief pause on this battlefield, the regiment resumed its advance. Its soldiers passed long lines of troops halted in the road. "Weary and dust-covered, sweltering under the hot sun, we could hear the distant booming

---

27 Joseph R. Manson to Wife, July 12, 1862, Private Collection of William T. Zielinski, Haverford, Pennsylvania.

28 Phillips, "Sixth Corporal," 7.

29 Postscript of November 7, 1862, to Letter, John F. Sale to Aunt, November 3, 1862.

of cannon," recalled Brown.[30] The 12th's soldiers made better time than on any other of the Seven Days. At 4 p.m., the regiment debouched into an open field on its left. The men crossed it at right oblique. At its distant edge they passed the still smoking guns and an exploded caisson of a silent battery. Mahone's brigade, now consisting of the 6th, 12th, 16th and 41st Virginia, stopped in front of a crest overlooking a deep ravine. Across the ravine stood the northern slope of Malvern Hill, a strong defensive position occupied by McClellan's rear guard. Ten minutes elapsed. Then a red faced, hot looking, finely dressed officer followed by a gaggle of couriers and aides galloped up to Mahone.

"It's Magruder," the men whispered to one another.[31]

The previous day's delays had proven fatal to Huger's career. Wise had shifted to Huger much of the fault for the fall of Roanoke Island. Longstreet had put on Huger nearly all the blame for the Confederate plan's failure at Seven Pines. Lee rarely sacked a general for one mistake, but he considered Huger's failure on June 30 to seize Glendale his third. Huger now found himself without a command. Lee transferred to Magruder all the Norfolk Division's brigades, including an attached brigade from Holmes' division.

In a loud voice Magruder ordered Mahone to hold his position. Just then a solid shot from a Yankee battery on the hill across the ravine came skipping towards the 12th. The soldiers parted ranks and allowed it to pass through harmlessly. Magruder and his staff rode away but returned after a few minutes. Magruder told Mahone to support Wright's brigade in a charge upon the enemy batteries on Malvern Hill. Mahone directed his men to close on the center, unsling their blanket rolls and prepare to charge. He then sauntered forward to reconnoiter. The killed and wounded of units which had charged the batteries prior to his arrival covered the plateau's slopes.

Returning to his brigade, Mahone led it past others maneuvering for position. The Federal cannon increased their fire. Missiles howled over the heads of his men. Soon the Virginians formed line of battle facing the enemy artillery. Mahone took them into the dense woods at the ravine's bottom. The 12th's soldiers struggled through the forest. "How trying to hear the ponderous missiles whistling over the tops of the trees or crashing among the limbs!" recalled Bernard, now the Herrings' acting second sergeant.

---

30 Brown, *Reminiscences of the War*, 18.

31 Bernard Notebook, 52,

"To be struck by a falling limb would prove as fatal as to be pierced by shot or shell.[32]

The brigade reached a branch with steep banks. The 12th's thirsty soldiers filled their canteens and drank the refreshing water. The ravine sheltered troops repulsed in previous charges on Malvern Hill. In the way beaten soldiers usually expressed themselves, they described themselves as "cut all to pieces."[33] They warned the Virginians that they faced a fearful undertaking and pronounced it safer to follow through after starting to charge than to turn back. While in the ravine, the 12th's chaplain offered up an invocation—Rev. Peter Archibald Peterson had served in the Petersburg Grays under Fletcher Archer during the Mexican War.

Instead of advancing through the broken troops, Mahone's brigade changed directions. It moved by the right flank, skirting Malvern Hill at its base. This course kept the Virginians out of sight of the enemy batteries, which shook the ground that the men crossed. The maneuver exposed them to Yankee fire from a different quarter. In the middle of the move, the 12th's soldiers met a handful of stretcher bearers carrying off a man shot through the neck and taking on the pallor of death.

"Look out, boys, for sharpshooters!" the stretcher bearers cautioned.[34]

Some low grounds extended from the brigade's right to a border of dense woods a quarter mile distant. Marksmen from the 1st United States Sharpshooters hid behind shocks of wheat in the low grounds. They wounded several of the 12th's soldiers.

Mahone decided his men had moved far enough by the right flank. He ordered them to file off to the left. The 12th led the brigade and the Old Grays led the 12th. The Virginians formed line of battle behind Wright's brigade. They lay on their faces several minutes for protection from the sharpshooters.

Wright's brigade charged the Federals atop Malvern Hill. Seizing the colors of one of his brigade's other regiments, Mahone ordered his soldiers forward in support. Yelling at the top of their lungs, the Virginians rushed up the hill. Briars broke their line of battle. Every soldier advanced as best he could. On the brigade's right near the 12th Virginia, with his hat raised

32 Ibid.

33 Todd, "Reminiscences," 21.

34 Bernard Notebook, 53.

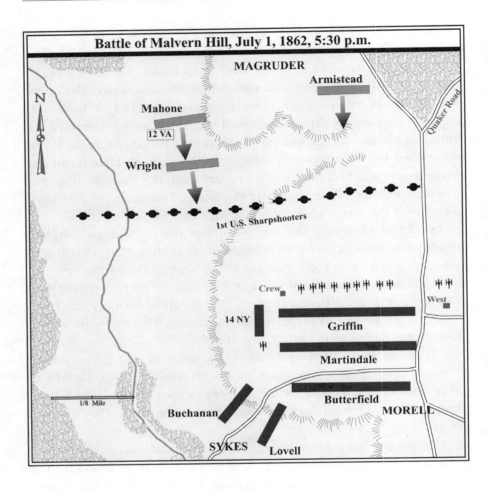

Battle of Malvern Hill, July 1, 1862, 5:30 p.m.

in the air, Mahone cheered on his troops. They followed Wright's brigade so closely that some hallooed, "Go to, Georgia, Old Virginia is at your back."[35] The Virginians reached the plateau's crest, catching a glimpse of an enemy battery dashing away at full speed. The sight elated Mahone's men. "The enemy are flying!" Bernard remembered thinking. "Their artillery & infantry routed! We will have easy work now!"[36]

The Federals—Griffin's brigade of Morell's division—quickly demonstrated Bernard's error. The Virginians got farther up the slope. They saw through

35 Todd, "Reminiscences," 22.

36 Bernard Notebook, 55.

the thick smoke a line of enemy infantry drawn up as if on dress parade 150 yards distant. Behind the infantry stood the Yankee artillery. The foe opened on the Virginians "with terrific fury," recalled Bernard.[37] Shells crashed through the Confederate battle lines. Minie balls rained down upon them. Men fell on all sides. Wright's and Mahone's brigades became intermingled. The staff of the regiment's battle flag shattered in the hands of the City Guard's Color Sgt. George W. Cogbill. He gripped the staff farther up and pressed on, then went down wounded. The banner fell. The Lafayette Guards' redheaded, freckle-faced Pvt. Nicholas Dawson seized the colors and advanced. A bullet killed him instantly. The Riflemen's Pvt. Joseph B. Pollard grasped the flag and continued forward. "By this time our ranks had become so thinned it seemed a forlorn hope to reach the Federal Battery," recalled Todd.[38]

The Riflemen's Pvt. William Arthur Shepard was serving with the color guard that day. Born in Boston, he had worked as an agricultural laboratory assistant while studying at Yale and had taken degrees in chemistry at Virginia's Randolph-Macon College. As he charged near the head of the regiment, a bullet knocked him down, but he rose almost immediately. A flask of sherry in his haversack had stopped the ball. Though a teetotaler, Shepard carried the sherry lest he or a comrade require a reviving stimulant in case of a wound.[39]

Enemy fire drove Wright's and Mahone's brigades back to the protection of the plateau's crest. There they closed ranks. Brigadier General Ambrose R. Wright of the Norfolk Division's Georgia Brigade led the left of the mingled formations in a charge. "His appearance was grand at that moment," Todd remembered. "He was about six feet high, his long flaxen hair and beard flowing in the air, and with his hat in one hand and a sword in the other, he cheered us on."[40] The charge ended like the previous one. Federal fire shattered the Southerners. Wright ordered the remnants of the two brigades to fall back.

"General Mahone has not ordered us back," objected a Virginian.

37 Ibid.

38 Todd, "Reminiscences,," 22.

39 "Prof. Shepard Dead: He was Born in Boston but Cast his Lot in the South," Roanoke *Times*, June 4, 1895, p. 4, col. 3; "Miraculous Escapes," Alexandria *Gazette*, February 1, 1916, p. 3, col. 2; Henderson, *12VI*, 155.

40 Todd, "Reminiscences," 23.

"In the name of General Mahone, I order you back," said Wright. "No men could do more."[41]

Again the Georgians and Virginians returned to the crest. There they halted, lay down and fired at will. "My gun barrel got so hot that it burnt my hand and I had to let it cool," recollected Todd.[42] The enemy artillery's thunder made the small arms fire almost inaudible.

The foe's infantry remained seemingly immovable. "We could scarce believe our eyes," recalled Bernard.[43] Soon the gray clouds of black powder smoke obscured the Yankee foot soldiers. The Virginians would have thought the troops in front of them Confederates who had advanced clear of Mahone's brigade, except that "the crimson looking Federal flag" floated above their line, Bernard remembered.[44]

The 12th kept shooting. The regiment, on the extreme Confederate right, did not receive as hot a return fire as the units to its left. Every few minutes the 12th's men could see a regiment or two in line of battle there charging toward the enemy, loudly yelling. The Northerners would open with heavy musketry. Thick smoke would hide everything from view. Soon a few Southerners would emerge from the cloud and head for the crest's cover. More and more would join them. The unit would rally behind the crest and charge back into the smoke. Shortly afterward, completely shattered, the formation would stream back to the crest. From the crest's protection, like the 12th's men, the survivors would fire at will.

One column charged scarcely 100 yards to the left of the 12th. The men of the column remained visible as they received the Yankee fire. They reeled and fell in droves. "We were reminded of a ten pin alley," Bernard remembered.[45]

His musket and the muskets of many soldiers around him became too heated to load. As Bernard squatted on the slope watching other units charge, the Herrings' Acting First Sgt. Thomas J. Harwell stood on the crest loading and firing.

41 Ibid.

42 Ibid.

43 Bernard Notebook, 55.

44 Ibid.

45 Ibid., 56.

Thomas J. Harwell. *Herbert Coons, Jr., Tallahassee, FL*

"Why are you all not shooting at the enemy?" shouted Harwell, an ordinarily calm Greensville County farmer.

Harwell's "very nature seemed transformed," recalled Bernard. "He was all aglow with the excitement of battle. His face was alight with enthusiasm."

Bernard felt rebuked for lack of enthusiasm.

"Where are the enemy?" he asked.

"Don't you see them?" said Harwell.

He pointed forward, where the slightly near-sighted Bernard could see only billows of smoke and red muzzle flashes.

"Determined that he should not think that I was afraid to go wherever he would go, I went with him over the crest and down the slope of the hill towards the enemy," remembered Bernard.

Still excited, displaying no sense of danger, Harwell pointed towards the smoke and flashes a little to the left of where the two men stood.

"Don't you see 'em there?" he asked. "Don't you see 'em?"

Bernard saw some individuals but not as distinctly as he thought Harwell viewed them.

Harwell fired his musket and immediately fell to the ground. Bernard helped Harwell to his feet, discovered a wound to his arm and assisted him back to the crest. From there Harwell made his way to the rear, where the surgeons amputated his arm.[46] Bernard became the Herrings' acting first sergeant.

At dusk Mahone's brigade crept 75 yards nearer the enemy. The Virginians kept firing. Mahone directed several uncoordinated, ineffectual charges by his brigade. With their commands so intermixed, the Confederates sometimes fired on their own men. Formations suffering casualties from friendly fire

---

46 Newsome, Horn and Selby, eds., *Civil War Talks*, 97.

included Wright's brigade. The elderly colonel of one regiment, told that his men were firing on fellow Secessionists, lost his composure.

"Firing upon our friends!" he raved, brandishing his sword at the bearer of bad tidings. "They are *damned Yankees*. If you say *we are firing upon our friends, God damn* you, I will cut you in two with my sword. *Give it to 'em*, boys! They are nothing but damned Yankees."[47]

"Go it, colonel! I'll stand at your back," exclaimed the Riflemen's Second Lt. John Rice "Pat" Patterson.

"Who is that old officer you are speaking to so familiarly?" Bernard asked.

"Don't know," Pat replied. "I just know he is a colonel."[48]

The Federal artillery continued firing after dark. "The blazing sabot illumined the sky, and shed a weird light over the ghastly field strewn with the dead and dying of the chivalry of the South," recalled Brown.[49] The enemy cannon fell silent shortly before 9 p.m. Their roar had previously drowned out almost all other sounds. Now those who had survived the battle unscathed could hear on all sides the delirious screams of the wounded and dying. Some cried for loved ones in distant homes. Others wailed for water or begged for help. Still others shrieked the names of their regiments. "'Third Alabama!' was uttered by one poor fellow, still rings in my ears," remembered Brown.[50] The cry told Brown that the 3rd, once part of Mahone's brigade, had also bled at Malvern Hill.

The Northerners searched for their dead and wounded. Brown recalled that in the meadow the invaders, "with their lanterns, looked as numerous as lightning bugs."[51] Soldiers from the 12th also ventured onto the battlefield. Ending the evening in the most advanced position of Lee's army made it the regiment's duty to care for wounded of other commands as well as its own. Mahone and Wright detailed numerous men to assist the wounded. Each took as many canteens as he could and filled them from a stream at the

---

47 Bernard Notebook, 56-57.

48 George S. Bernard, "Malvern Hill: Recollections of the Fight by one who was there," *SHSP* (1890), 18:67.

49 Brown, *Reminiscences of the War*, 20.

50 Phillip F. Brown to George S. Bernard, March 22, 1895, in George S. Bernard Papers, SHC.

51 Brown, *Reminiscences of the War*, 20.

hill's base. Whenever they heard a wounded man, they went to him. To all they gave water. Those who complained of feeling cold, they covered with oilcloths or whatever they could get—including the jackets of the dead. "I fixed the cartridge boxes under the heads of several who told me they did not expect to live till morning," remembered Todd, a member of this detail.[52]

With three comrades from the 12th, Brown slipped through the picket line to retrieve a wounded member of the color guard. Brown and his companions ventured within 50 yards of the enemy, whose lanterns cast enough light to permit them to find their friend. Placing him on a rubber cloth, they tried to raise him. This caused the stricken man so much pain that he began to scream, "Put me down!"[53] In subdued tones his friends tried to quiet him. His screams attracted the attention of the Yankee pickets, who opened fire. The Confederate sentries fired back. Brown and his companions lay down beside their wounded friend to avoid the bullets. "For a few minutes," recalled Brown, "it had every appearance of a night battle."[54] The firing died down. The four covered the wounded man with a blanket and crawled back to Confederate lines. As they approached they whispered, "Twelfth Virginia! Twelfth Virginia!"[55] They safely entered the lines with their friend, but his wound proved mortal.

Spurts of picket fire made it seem that fresh troops had arrived. The commands, "Forward! Guide center! Charge!" rang above the groans and screams.[56] The 12th's soldiers realized that these words came from a wounded officer in delirium, shouting the last command he had given before suffering a head wound. Lying among the dead and wounded, the men got little sleep.

Rain began falling. Before daybreak it had soaked the ground. Sunrise found about 300 haggard men from Huger's division huddled near the crest. A fierce-looking line of enemy cavalry confronted them. Soon the stamping of horses and jingling of swords sounded the departure of the Union riders, leaving the Confederates in possession of the battlefield.

52 Todd, "Reminiscences," 24-25.

53 Brown, *Reminiscences of the War*, 21.

54 Ibid.

55 Ibid.

56 Ibid.

The 12th's men scanned the bloodiest landscape they had yet observed. "Gory corpses meet the eye wherever it looks," Bernard wrote.[57] At 10 a.m., the regiment hiked a mile to the rear to make breakfast, stopping near the ravine where their chaplain had led them in prayer. "Many a brave fellow who had heard the good Chaplain's prayer that afternoon was not present to hear the prayer of the next morning," remembered Todd.[58] Drenched, the shivering, hungry survivors stacked arms and broke ranks. They built fires to warm themselves, dry their clothes and cook rations. The many articles abandoned by the Federals enriched the Confederate commissary. Weisiger had the day before ordered a barrel of whiskey from Petersburg. Each soldier now received a gill and many drank whiskey straight for the first time. "It seemed to touch the right spot," Todd recalled.[59]

Lee's army spent the next few days following McClellan's army down to Harrison's Landing, but the Seven Days battles had ended. The Confederates had driven the Unionists from the immediate vicinity of Richmond. The Southerners had failed to destroy Mac's army and they had lost substantially more men than the enemy.

At Malvern Hill the 12th suffered moderate casualties because of its sheltered position on the extreme Confederate right, losing nine killed, 36 wounded and 57 missing. Four of the wounded died of their injuries. Of 57 men listed as missing, none fell into enemy hands.[60] They either quickly found their way back to the colors or insinuated themselves into safe berths in the rear.

By holding the army's most advanced position at the battle's end, the 12th had favorably distinguished itself. The regiment's soldiers prided themselves on this achievement, for which Mahone praised them. They felt they had removed the cloud cast over them at Seven Pines.

57 Bernard Notebook, 57.

58 Todd, "Reminiscences," 27.

59 Ibid.

60 Henderson, *12VI*, 106-167; *OR* 11, 2:981. Roll 66, M861, Record Group 109, NA; "List of Casualties in the 12th Va Regiment, in the Action of July 1st, 1862," Daily Richmond *Enquirer*, July 10, 1862.

CHAPTER 6

Second Manassas

A week after Malvern Hill, Mahone's brigade crossed James River on a pontoon bridge just above Drewry's Bluff. The Virginians had a new division commander, Maj. Gen. Richard Heron Anderson. He had distinguished himself by aggressive leadership during the Peninsula Campaign, acquiring the nickname, "Fighting Dick."[1] The War Department banished Huger to the Trans-Mississippi as that Department's inspector of ordnance.

Mahone's brigade encamped on an airy hill overlooking Falling Creek in Chesterfield County, about a mile from the James. The hill afforded a beautiful view of the neighboring country. "Our brigade will never forget the large and cool spring from which we were supplied with water when we were at Falling Creek," recalled Todd.[2] The spring represented a big improvement over the Mud Camp's shallow, hastily dug wells. Even so, the regiment had "such a disagreeable hot camp," wrote Bird, wounded at Malvern Hill, that he advised his father not to bring anyone to visit him there.[3]

The 12th arrived with fewer than 300 officers and men.[4] The troops who reached Falling Creek had left nearly all their belongings at the Mud

---

1 Joseph Cantey Elliott, *Lieutenant General Richard Heron Anderson: Lee's Noble Soldier* (Dayton, Oh.: 1985), 47.

2 Todd, "Reminiscences," 29.

3 Henry Van Leuvenigh Bird to Margaret Randolph, August 8, 1862.

4 Manson to Wife, July 12, 1862; *OR* 11, 3:615.

Camp. "Everything has been lost and we are as destitute as Adam was in Paradise," Manson complained. "Maybe we are rather better clothed."[5] The men even lacked cooking utensils and mixed their flour in wagon buckets, baking it on smooth rocks collected in the fields. They had a monotonous diet. "We do not get anything but salt bacon and flour," Whitehorne groused. "I would give anything on earth to get some vegetables."[6]

Before July's end, the situation improved for most of the regiment. Commissioned by the City of Petersburg, Capt. Nathaniel Harrison started making trips from Petersburg to Mahone's brigade driving a wagon loaded with "good things for the boys," recalled Bernard.[7] Harrison brought food and clothing from citizens of Petersburg to their friends and relatives in Mahone's brigade, including soldiers who did not belong to Petersburg companies. The townspeople adopted the Norfolk Juniors. Besides any goods that Harrison might bring to individual Norfolk men from friends or relatives in Petersburg, the city sent shipments of food and clothing for the whole company. The Richmond Grays fared at least as well. Less than 10 miles from their hometown, they could expect friends and relatives to deliver packages in person as well as through a commissioner.

Commissioners from Brunswick and Greensville counties also began making trips to the 12th. Greensville County bought an ambulance which shuttled back and forth between Greensville and Falling Creek once a week, keeping the Huger Grays and the Herrings well supplied with vegetables and fresh meat. Manson received more fresh vegetables than he could eat and distributed the surplus to his friends. Enough meat arrived to feed the Herrings for two or three days at a time. "This enables the men to sell their rations which helps out the poor soldier's small pay and enables him to send some home to his family," wrote Manson.[8]

The conscripts from southwest Virginia fared poorly. Distance prevented the commissioners of their counties from frequently visiting these troops. "They look so dejected," Manson wrote. "You can tell one as far as you

5 Joseph R. Manson to Mother, August 9, 1862, The Lewis Leigh Collection—Book 41, U. S. Army Heritage Educational Center (AHEC), Carlisle Barracks, Pennsylvania.

6 James E. Whitehorne to Sister, July 15, 1862.

7 Bernard Notebook, 59.

8 Manson to Mother, August 9, 1862.

can see him. They are so troubled that they become fit subjects for disease and so many of the poor fellows will die in camp...."[9]

The 12th rearmed courtesy of the Union. Success begot success for Lee's army. With each victory, it captured vast quantities of the enemy's superior equipment. Only two of the regiment's companies—the City Guard and the Riflemen—began the war armed with rifled muskets. The men of these two companies had purchased English .577 caliber Enfields at their own expense. These weapons performed effectively at ranges of up to 300 yards and could kill at up to 800 yards. The other eight companies were carrying old .69 caliber smoothbore muskets converted from flintlocks to percussion caps and issued by the State of Virginia. These firearms had an effective range of less than 100 yards. At Falling Creek, the companies armed with smoothbores exchanged them for .58 caliber Springfield rifled muskets captured from the enemy at Seven Pines and during the Seven Days. The brigade's ordnance officer still had to provide the regiment with two calibers of bullets, but the change increased the range of the 12th's firepower.

Despite the improvement in their diet, the troops had difficulty recovering from the Peninsula Campaign. A typhoid epidemic raged within their camp. "This whole country will be covered with fresh graves when this large division of our army goes away," Manson lamented.[10] At least thirteen of the regiment's soldiers died of disease contracted at Falling Creek.[11] The men who went home sick included Bernard and Bird.

Many men took advantage of the provision in the draft law that permitted them to procure substitutes to serve in their stead. "There is a great fever for putting substitutes now and unfortunately every day poor fellows are found who will sell their lives for money," Manson complained. "They are the meanest soldiers in the army."[12] Of the 12th's 52 substitutes, 13, or 25 percent, deserted; and though just over three percent of the regiment, substitutes would provide more than 10 percent of its 127 deserters.[13]

9 Joseph R. Manson to Mother, July 27, 1862, The Lewis Leigh Collection—Book 41, AHEC.

10 Manson to Mother, August 9, 1862.

11 Rolls 514-534, M324, Record Group 109, NA; Confederate Rosters, 2:1-56, LV; Henderson, *12VI*, 106-167.

12 Manson to Mother, August 9, 1862.

13 Rolls 514-534, M324, Record Group 109, NA; Confederate Rosters, 2:1-56, LV; Henderson, *12VI*, 106-167.

On Saturday, August 16, the 12th cooked three days' rations and prepared to move. Rumor had Anderson's division going to guard a ford on Rapidan River. The men cooked everything they had bought for Sunday dinner. Some tried to eat it all, but this proved impossible. The surplus went to the sick who would remain in camp.

In mid-July, the Yankee Army of Virginia under Maj. Gen. John Pope had threatened an advance on Gordonsville. There the Orange and Alexandria Railroad, which ran southwestward, intersected the Virginia Central Railroad, which went west from Richmond. Lee responded to this threat by sending Jackson's wing of the Army of Northern Virginia to confront the enemy. With the army's remainder, Lee kept McClellan's inactive army at Harrison's Landing on James River under observation. Major General Henry W. "Old Brains" Halleck, the Unionist general-in-chief, ordered Mac to withdraw his army from Harrison's Landing and proceed by water to Pope's assistance. McClellan's evacuation of Harrison's Landing permitted the Norfolk Division to leave Falling Creek. Lee planned to use the division to help crush Pope before Mac could come to Pope's rescue. Armed Northerners would not get as close to Richmond again for almost two years.

At noon August 17, the 12th's men struck their tents and plodded five miles toward Richmond through intense heat. Each carried a musket, forty rounds of ammunition, a blanket roll containing a change of underclothes and a haversack. They tramped through Richmond's streets with the regimental band playing "Dixie." That afternoon they boarded a long string of boxcars on the Virginia Central. These boxcars had no seats. The soldiers sat on the floor or stood. The train left Richmond just after 5 p.m. Six and a half uncomfortable hours later, it stopped at Louisa Court House.

Weisiger ordered his men out of the cars and left them to find quarters. Some slept in the village streets, "like hogs," recalled Bernard, who had rejoined the regiment.[14] Others paired off and bedded down on porches, one spreading his rubber cloth on the floor, while the other spread his as a cover. The troops reached Louisa Court House famished. If they had not eaten their rations before leaving Falling Creek, they had consumed them on the train. The commissary wagons had not caught up with the soldiers, who had to scrounge from the village and its environs. Many a stray animal of the local farmers found its way into the men's bellies.

14 Bernard Notebook, 59.

By August 19, the soldiers had slogged to within three and a half miles of Orange Court House. Nearby friends and relatives, learning the 12th was passing through Orange County, flocked to the column bearing baskets of provisions and bottles of buttermilk. Recipients repaired to the roadside and shared with fellow soldiers. Other men, accompanied by their comrades and in search of sustenance, descended upon nearby friends and relatives.

At sunset on August 20, Mahone's brigade arrived within half a mile of Summersville Ford on the Rapidan. Pope had withdrawn from the line of the Rapidan to that of Rappahannock River in time to elude an attempt by Lee to envelop him.

The Virginians forded the Rapidan at 2 p.m. the next day. The congested roads kept the wagon trains far behind. If the troops could not obtain provisions from friends and relatives or scrounge sustenance from the countryside, they would not eat much, if anything. "One day we got bread, and no meat," Todd remembered. "Another day we got meat and no bread."[15] On this day the men received no food at all. Turned loose in a cornfield near Cedar Mountain, they received instructions to take no more roasting ears than necessary. The march took them through a desiccated country. In the 10 miles between the Rapidan and the village of Stevensburg, the soldiers encountered not a single spring. They reached Stevensburg after dark. "The dust had so completely covered us," Brown recalled, "that it was only by the voice that we could recognize one another."[16] Parched with thirst, the men scrambled to find drinking water. The troops ahead had exhausted the wells. The bucket had to remain at the bottom 10 or 15 minutes before drawing. "Then it had a milky color, as seen by the starlight," Brown remembered.[17]

Next morning the 12th hiked in the rain past an enemy spy hanging from a roadside tree. Rumor had it that the Yank had tried to deliver an order that would have led another unit of Lee's army into an ambush. One of the Riflemen appropriated the dead spy's trousers.

The rain turned the roads into quagmires. The mud caused straggling. Every mile soldiers dropped out of the ranks intending to overtake their units in the morning. Scores camped in little groups and built blazing fires.

15 Todd, "Reminiscences," 32.

16 Brown, *Reminiscences of the War*, 25.

17 Ibid.

Around the fires, the men improvised shelters by stretching their rubber clothes on sticks stuck in the ground. While the leaves under the shelters dried, the soldiers sang. They eventually lay down to sleep, snug in beds of dry leaves.

"What brigade, boys?" passing troops asked.

"General Straggler's Brigade!" came the reply.[18]

Hunger tormented the men beyond endurance. "Cornfields have stood no chance where ever we have camped near them," Bernard wrote to his father, whom he had visited as the regiment passed Orange Court House.[19] Discipline declined to where some of the 12th's soldiers plundered the division's commissary store, taking hardtack designated for a Georgia regiment.

The men suffered other hardships as well. The sun blistered the backs of their necks. Rough, unwashed clothing chafed their hides. Heat tortured their feet until they took off their shoes, tied them together, threw them over their muskets and marched barefoot. Walking under the blazing sun, some wag would exclaim, "O, my country, how I bleed for thee!"[20] The troops would take this up and repeat it all along the line.

The regiment picketed a crossing of the Rappahannock on August 25. Lee employed Anderson's division to divert enemy attention while Jackson's wing of the army slipped through Thoroughfare Gap around the Northerners' right and into their rear at Manassas Junction. By August 27, Lee had determined to unite his army at Manassas before the Yankees could concentrate against Stonewall. The rest of Longstreet's wing, to which Anderson's division belonged, was already proceeding toward Thoroughfare Gap. The Norfolk Division departed the Rappahannock that afternoon. At 3:30 p.m., the 12th's soldiers trudged back through Jeffersonton under a light shelling. The turnpike took them through Amissville. They forded Hedgeman's River at daybreak and encamped a mile beyond.

The tramp resumed at noon, with straggling rampant. The regiment passed through the village of Orleans, halting at dark within three miles of Salem after a slog of fifteen miles. The landscape seemed strange to an

18 Bernard Notebook, 62.

19 George S. Bernard to Father, August 25, 1862.

20 Brown, *Reminiscences of the War*, 24.

urban soldier. "Every little spot where there was a Blacksmith shop and a big tree is dubbed a town and is some kind of a ville or a burg," Sale recalled.[21]

In the morning the 12th paraded through Salem and paused half a mile beyond. The villagers' hospitality gave the men a respite from the journey's hardships. They luxuriated in the honey, milk and butter given or sold by the locals. Colonel Robert Buckner Bolling, the owner of Petersburg's Center Hill Mansion, visited the regiment and dispensed refreshments from a little spring wagon drawn by a sleepy gray horse. He had a plantation called Bollingbrook near Upperville in Fauquier County. His son, William N. Bolling, a Princeton graduate, had served in the Riflemen before accepting a lieutenant's commission in the engineers. During this break most of the previous day's stragglers rejoined the command.

At noon the column turned eastward toward Manassas. There Jackson's wing of the army was holding off Pope's entire force. The 12th's men strode through a beautiful countryside, passing over many hills affording magnificent views. They reached Thoroughfare Gap at dark and saw signs of recent fighting. A corpse lay near the railroad tracks the regiment followed through the gap. Almost every minute some man tripped and fell, bruising his knees while his musket barrel struck sparks on the rails and ballast. "Curses loud and deep filled the air," Todd recollected.[22] When the soldiers reached the mountain's eastern side, they filed off into a rocky field on the slope and prepared to encamp. Though they would not have comfortable beds, they hoped to get some rest.

Little repose awaited them. After the regiment stopped and stacked arms, Weisiger called his troops together.

"Men," he announced, "You will be dismissed for the space of two hours, at the expiration of which time the line of march will be resumed."[23]

Throwing themselves down and going to sleep, the men woke at midnight much refreshed but dreading returning to the road. The officers began driving the rank and file toward Manassas. The night's warmth and the scarcity of water fatigued the men. During rare breaks, they sank to the ground for rest. Soon they became so tired they could hardly walk.

21 John F. Sale to Aunt, August 16, 1863.

22 Todd, "Reminiscences.," 36.

23 Bernard Notebook, 66.

At daybreak August 30, Anderson's division reached the battlefield exhausted, halting on a site of the previous day's fighting. Corpses, muskets and equipment lay thick upon the ground. Brown remembered that his comrades "instantly sought rest in a skirt of pines along the roadside; and, I suppose, four-fifths of the men were asleep in three minutes."[24] They did not slumber long but paid for Anderson's failure to send staff officers ahead to reconnoiter. After the soldiers fell asleep, their company officers shook them awake and pointed them to the rear. They had bedded down on the advanced picket line, not fifty yards from masses of the enemy. The Virginians, keeping to the woods and tightly grasping their canteens to prevent noise, retraced their steps about a mile and a half without uttering a word above a whisper, then stacked arms hoping for breakfast.

As Weisiger prepared to order them to break ranks to eat, a courier rode up bearing a dispatch for Mahone. Weisiger's soldiers picked up their arms and walked back toward the enemy, over ground they had already crossed twice. This time they only crossed it halfway. By 9 a.m., their division had deployed in line of battle on a hill at the hinges of the jaws formed by Jackson's wing of the army, north of and parallel to Warrenton Turnpike, which ran from southwest to northeast, and Longstreet's wing, south of and perpendicular to the pike. The Norfolk Division stretched across the turnpike. Mahone's brigade formed the division's right, south of the pike. Artillery stood 400 yards left of the Virginians and north of the pike.

For the next five hours, the 12th's men lay in line of battle under the broiling sun, so tired that many slept half the time. Anderson impressed those who remained awake. He paid little attention to clothes except on the eve of a battle, when he dressed to the nines. That morning he wore his best uniform, a fine hat, a white waistcoat and white gloves, "as if going to a ball," Cameron remembered.[25] Anderson's men would come to say, "Old Dick is dressed up today, and we will catch the Devil."[26]

Lee's headquarters lay in a copse less than 50 yards behind the 12th. Generals, staff officers and couriers constantly came and went. That morning a council of war convened. The regiment's soldiers saw Lee, Longstreet, Jackson and Stuart deliberating. The Yankees, who had spent the previous

---

24 Brown, *Reminiscences of the War*, 26.

25 Bernard, Appendix, *War Talks*, 300.

26 Todd, "Reminiscences," 39.

day assaulting Stonewall's lines, had done nothing so far this day. The four Confederate generals discussed what to do if the enemy attacked or retreated. At the council's end, Lee summoned Anderson. Near the Norfolk Division's hill, they met in the presence of Jackson, who wore a gray homespun suit and a broken-brimmed forage cap. Stonewall sat on the edge of a rock with his face in his hands, apparently pondering some problem.

"Well, General, I suppose your men are a little tired?" Lee said to Anderson, whose division formed the army's reserve.

"Yes, they are a little tired, but I have great confidence in them," said Anderson.

"Give them all the rest you can, we will need them soon."[27]

Jackson returned to his wing of the army, Anderson to his division. Stuart lay on a red blanket, pointing out to Lee roads and positions on a military map spread out before them. At 1 p.m., Bolling arrived in his spring wagon and prevailed upon Lee and his staff to take lunch with him. Afterward, the Federals stirred. A big cloud of dust indicated an enemy force moving toward Stonewall's right.

Turning to Longstreet, Lee said, "These people must be driven back."[28]

Lee summoned Anderson and gestured toward some trees behind the artillery to the Norfolk Division's left.

"Take your men to the woods yonder and refresh them," said Lee. "I may not need you, but these people must be driven back."[29]

About 3 p.m., Mahone's brigade tramped to the rear for rations along Warrenton Turnpike. The men figured they would escape combat that day. They halted in the woods north of the turnpike and 50 yards behind the artillery, stacking arms amid the timber and waiting for the spider wagons to arrive.

Sounds of battle swelled on the right of Jackson's front. The irregular fire of skirmishers in the woods half a mile ahead of Anderson's division signaled the enemy advance. Firing increased as the advance continued. The artillery posted to the division's left rear opened fire on the Northerners at

27 George S. Bernard, "The Maryland Campaign of 1862, A Confederate Soldier's Experiences on a Nine Weeks' Trip—August 17th to October 19th, 1862—An Address Delivered by Mr. George S. Bernard before A. P. Hill Camp of Confederate Veterans, of Petersburg, Va., on the Evening of May 2nd, 1889," in *War Talks*, 17.

28 Bernard Notebook, 67.

29 Bernard, "The Maryland Campaign," *War Talks*, 15-16.

long range. The regiment's soldiers could see Yankee cannonballs strike near the Confederate batteries. The Federal line met Stonewall's men. Musketry and cannonading culminated in a continuous, intense roar.

As the enemy assault on Jackson climaxed, he asked Lee for reinforcements. Lee referred the request to Longstreet. Old Pete knew his enfilading artillery would break up the Unionist attack long before infantry reinforcements reached Stonewall, but Longstreet ordered Anderson's division to Jackson's assistance anyway.

Soon the sound of firing waned. Distant rebel yells proclaimed the assault's repulse. As the Yanks recoiled, Longstreet launched the rest of his wing against their exposed left, south of the turnpike. Still in reserve, the 12th's troops saw their officers' faces assume cheerful looks. The spider wagons finally arrived. The cooks and stewards set out rations. Trays of bread stood in front of each company.

Only now did Longstreet's order to assist Jackson reach Anderson.

The long roll beat.

"Fall in!" came the order.

The famished men left the tantalizing food untouched and grabbed their muskets. Returning to the enemy's side of the artillery, Mahone's brigade crossed an open field. Under the Yankee batteries' fire, the Virginians formed line of battle with their right on the turnpike. They could hear the battle's roar ahead. At 4 p.m., they received instructions to throw off their baggage and go in light. Unslinging their blanket rolls, they advanced eastward behind another battle line which seemed successful in driving the enemy. The Virginians tramped toward some enemy batteries dueling with the Confederate artillery. The men assumed they would charge the Federal cannon. They proceeded until they encountered Anderson. Mounted on a fine black mare, he sat in front of the 12th, which mustered about 220 soldiers.[30] Still under the Unionist batteries' fire, Mahone's brigade halted to dress and reform its battle line. Colonel Walter H. Taylor of Lee's staff dashed up to Anderson, briefly spoke with him, then dashed away.

"Gentlemen, General Jackson says that by the blessing of God his necessities have been relieved," Anderson announced. "So we will go to the right and help Longstreet."[31]

30 Daily Richmond *Dispatch*, September 9, 1862, p. 1, col. 1.

31 Bernard, "The Maryland Campaign," *War Talks*, 15-16.

An hour's fighting had exhausted many of Longstreet's men and disordered most of his formations. He needed the Norfolk Division to give new impetus to his attack.

Relieved at not having to charge the Northern batteries, Mahone's soldiers marched by the right flank toward the enemy left. Their progress took them down the steep north side of the turnpike's cut, then up the opposite side. They swung through the open field south of the turnpike. Wheat stubble and briars broke up their formation. With Federal shells whizzing over their heads, the troops again paused for realignment. The guides began to reposition themselves. An excited staff officer rode up from the front. In his shirtsleeves, wearing a beaver hat, he looked like an old farmer.

"Go on, my boys, and you'll end this war," he yelled, wildly waving his arms. "The Yankees are running like hell."[32]

This apparition disturbed the guides. They paid more attention to him than to holding up their guns and realigning themselves. The men, as distracted as the guides, became still more disordered. Mahone grew incensed.

"Make that damned fool get out of the way," Mahone shouted.[33]

The staff officer quickly departed. The guides realigned themselves. The men reformed their battle line. Mahone's brigade resumed advancing. Its path took it into woods, which disrupted the brigade's alignment yet again. One guide, instead of following a straight line toward the front, followed Cameron, who let the ground's nature govern his progress.

"Damn the adjutant, sir, and damn you, too," roared Taylor, serving despite illness that day. "It's no business of yours where he goes. Why the hell don't you follow your nose?"[34]

Already bewildered, the guide became even more confused. Mahone yet again halted his men to rectify their line. Though suffering casualties, the soldiers dressed line as if on drill. The wounded during this halt included Cameron, struck by a shell fragment.

Emerging from the trees, the Virginians saw ahead of them scores of dead and wounded Federal Zouaves. Their blood red pants made the slope where they lay seem a poppy field. The Virginians rushed over the Zouaves at the double quick. Hunger got the better of some of Mahone's men.

32 Todd, "Reminiscences," 41.

33 Bernard, "The Maryland Campaign," *War Talks*, 17.

34 Bernard, Appendix, *War Talks*, 300.

They broke ranks to rummage for food in the haversacks of the prostrate Unionists. Sale stopped to cut a bag of crackers from an apparent corpse. "Old Zoo" turned over.

"For God's sake, don't kill me," he said.[35]

Mortified, Sale rejoined the ranks without the crackers.

On the slope opposite the brigade opened the mouths of the guns of a battery which the Texas Brigade of Hood's division had captured. The Texans among the cannon cheered the Virginians as they crossed Young's Branch. Soon they passed between the captured guns, stepping over enemy dead and wounded scattered all around. At one piece lay a team of horses shot down in the act of moving the gun, some dead, the others living but bleeding profusely and writhing in agony.

The Virginians reached the top of the hill. Hundreds of Yankee dead and wounded made the field ahead look blue. Men lay here without legs, there without heads. Shells had torn others so that their own mothers would not have recognized them. Many corpses remained in their last living positions, some leaning against trees, one kneeling to shoot. Mahone's brigade double-quicked down the hill, across another branch, then over Chinn Ridge. Mahone proceeded on foot at the head of his men, not far to the 12th's right. The regiment now formed the left of the brigade because of all the marching and countermarching. The Virginians crossed Chinn Branch, then climbed Bald Hill. Yankee cannon of a battery about 400 yards to the left began firing. The shots nearly enfiladed the Virginian line. In front of Mahone's brigade stood a rail fence afire. In a wood to the enemy battery's right, along Manassas-Sudley Road, Southern troops appeared severely engaged. Mahone directed his men around the right of these Confederates. The brigade hopped the burning fence, crossed the road, then swung left, changing front to face north. All eyes stayed on the Union battery, which kept firing.

"Oh, Lordy!" came a shriek from in front of the brigade.[36]

The men turned to see Mahone doubled up in agony. His soldiers had the utmost confidence in him and his injury disheartened them. Command of the brigade devolved upon Weisiger, the senior colonel. May took charge of the 12th because of Taylor's illness. The Virginians reached the woods' edge at Henry House Hill's southern base. There, facing the Federal army's extreme

35   John F. Sale to Aunt, January 31, 1863.

36   Bernard Notebook, 69.

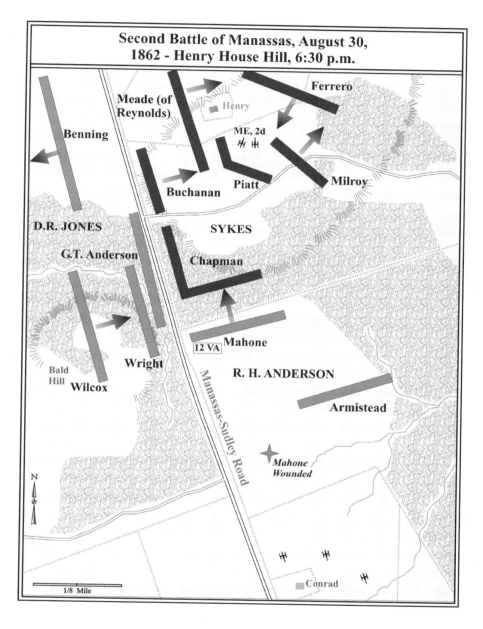

Second Battle of Manassas, August 30, 1862 - Henry House Hill, 6:30 p.m.

Benning

Meade (of Reynolds)

Henry

Ferrero

ME, 2d

D.R. JONES

Buchanan

Piatt

Milroy

SYKES

G.T. Anderson

Chapman

12 VA Mahone

Bald Hill Wright

Wilcox

R. H. ANDERSON

Armistead

Mahone Wounded

N

Conrad

1/8 Mile

left, they halted. A man knocked loose from another command volunteered to act as a scout and entered the woods. Minutes later he dashed out and reported the enemy near. Weisiger ordered his brigade into the trees, then fell wounded by a Yankee bullet.

In the woods, the Virginians confronted Regulars from Chapman's brigade of Sykes' division, V Corps. The Unionists were hurrying into line 50 yards away. Mahone's men fired first. The 12th's soldiers received the deadly enemy musketry while lying down on Henry House Hill's slope. Federal volleys devastated the regiment. The Regulars killed the color bearer, the Richmond Grays' Pvt. George O. Nicholas. Williamson expiated his disgrace at Seven Pines by picking up the flag, then suffering a mortal abdominal wound. Enemy fire also killed Pvt. Marx Myers, another Richmond Gray in the color guard. "The battle flag was always a conspicuous mark at which men fired almost instinctively," recalled Todd.[37] Enemy bullets killed May and wounded the only three captains present, including Lewellen, who suffered a scalp wound.[38] Command of the 12th fell to Manson.

Confusion from losses in the chain of command paralyzed Mahone's brigade and the 12th Virginia. Their fire slackened. The men expected orders to advance that did not come because no one knew who should give them. The number of dead and wounded grew. The latter included Todd. He had fired several rounds when a minnie struck his left hand, taking off the end of one finger, cutting two others and driving lead splinters into his palm. Unable to handle his musket, he lay down and hoped the Regulars would not fire low. "I hugged mother earth as closely, and spread myself as thin as it was possible for a man of my style of architecture to do," he remembered.[39]

Night ended the fight after fifteen minutes. Both the enemy and the Virginians withdrew. The Regulars had saved the day for the Yankees by shooting Mahone's brigade to pieces just when the Virginians threatened to unhinge the Federal position on Henry House Hill, cutting off the Unionist line of retreat. Mahone's brigade had shot the Regulars to pieces as well.

No regimental organization remained in the 12th. Its men groped their way to the rear in squads, marveling at the distance they had covered. It seemed five miles from where they had unslung blanket rolls to where the brigade expended itself. At 9 p.m., they finally reached their commissary wagons, almost too exhausted to consume their rations. Some forewent food; though the task repelled them, necessity compelled them to search the Unionist dead for shoes, clothing and other booty.

---

37 Todd, "Reminiscences," 45.

38 Daily Richmond *Enquirer*, September 5, 1862.

39 Todd, "Reminiscences," 43.

The 12th had suffered nine killed and 73 wounded, more than any other regiment of Anderson's division. Eight of the wounded died of their injuries.[40] The regiment had come a long way from Norfolk to Manassas and not just in terms of miles. In May, one of its men had mocked it as a Saratoga Trunk Regiment. Another had called their brigade Kid Glove Boys. In June at Seven Pines, the 12th had embarrassed itself. At Second Manassas the regiment and its brigade stood toe to toe with the cream of the Union army, Uncle Sam's Regulars, and the Virginians gave as good as they got.

40 Henderson, 12VI, 106-167; Roll 66, M861, Record Group 109., NA.

CHAPTER 7

The Maryland Campaign

Daylight on August 31 revealed enemy dead and wounded lying thickly in the roads and fields. "In several places the limbs and heads had been severed from the body by the artillery wheels, or mashed into a mangled mass by the hoofs of the cavalry trampling over them," Brown recalled.[1] Mahone's brigade reformed at 11 a.m. under the 41st Virginia's Lt. Col. Joseph Powhatan Minetree. Jones took command of the 12th's remainder. The brigade ambled to a position near Centreville and stacked arms. With the rest of Longstreet's wing of the army, the Virginians stayed on the battlefield. The regiment elected major its senior captain, Feild, despite his absence. Lee sent Jackson's wing of the army to cut off the retreating Yankees from the Washington defenses.

Next day Lee ordered Longstreet's wing of the army to Jackson's support. Mahone's brigade, now under the 6th Virginia's Col. George Rogers, plodded north toward Little River Turnpike. Despite rain, the men suffered from lack of water. Rogers rested them frequently. At sundown the tired, thirsty troops reached the turnpike near the border of Prince William and Fairfax counties. There they halted for the night. Jackson's men had fought a Federal flank guard at Chantilly, 10 miles southeast. Stonewall had given up trying to envelop Pope before the fight began. Afterward Pope's army continued its withdrawal into the Washington defenses.

1 Brown, *Reminiscences of the War*, 29.

Mahone's brigade turned southeast onto Little River Turnpike in the morning. The Virginians slogged about three miles toward Fairfax Court House, halting at 11 a.m. A rumor circulated that Lee had received a request for an armistice of 30 days and that the halt would continue while he considered the offer. In fact the pause signified his realization that further pursuit of Pope's army had become futile. Pope had completed his army's withdrawal into the Washington defenses and reinforcements from McClellan's army were arriving.

The halt could not last long. Lee had to move his army. He could not subsist it in the devastation around Manassas. The Confederate commissary could not supply it there. Either he had to lead his men into enemy territory and feed them there, or he had to retreat. Lee characteristically chose the aggressive course. The rumor of an armistice lost its credibility among the 12th's soldiers at 3 p.m. on September 3 when Mahone's brigade marched northwestward.

Mahone's brigade reached Potomac River at White's Ford on September 6. Only the bravest and most rugged waded the river. Headquarters had directed all barefooted men to remain on the south bank. Many took advantage of this order to pull off their shoes and throw them away. Stalwarts disobeyed the order and crossed barefoot. Principle encumbered other soldiers. They had taken up arms only to defend Virginia, not to invade the North. These too declined to cross. After fording the Monocacy River beyond, the remnant of Mahone's brigade halted at 10 p.m. The Virginians encamped near the village of Buckeystown in Frederick County, Maryland.

Next day the soldiers trekked through Buckeystown to just short of Frederick. The people along the way seemed kind and unanimously in the South's favor. Lee aimed to keep them that way, but his orders not to disturb property of any kind made things tough on his troops. "As our wagon train was some distance in the rear, our rations were cut very short," Brown recalled. "Apples and green corn (when it could be had) were our principal diet."[2]

On September 8 and 9, the Virginians remained in the same place two days in a row for the first time in almost two weeks. The soldiers needed the rest. They had marched mostly at night. The commissary wagons often failed to reach them. The torrid temperatures made them jettison everything they had scavenged from dead Northerners at Manassas, except what they

2 Ibid., 31.

could wear. Lack of discipline prevailed. Soldiers who felt tired did not hesitate to drop out, camp for the night and hope they would overtake their commands in the morning. Straggling became the general rule, marching in the ranks the exception.

Many men had no shoes. The sharp pebbles and stones of Maryland's turnpikes caused such pain to feet accustomed to Virginia's soft, sandy lanes that Sale remembered, "Sometimes I would almost curse the hour in which I was born."[3] The footwear available often proved more painful than going barefoot. A pair of stiff, unbreakable Wellingtons acquired the title of "the regimental boots," going from one man to another in the 12th and inflicting misery on all their owners.[4] The men suffered from wearing the same clothes for weeks on end without washing. Many soldiers harbored what Sale termed "a Confederate guard of greybacks."[5]

The respite ended at 2 p.m. on September 10. Mahone's brigade entered Frederick four abreast, with arms on their blanket rolls and elbows extended. The line stretched across the street and gave an exaggerated impression of their strength. Fewer townspeople sympathized with the Secessionists. The Riflemen's Pvt. John E. Crow, a hardware store clerk before the war, limped through Frederick barefoot and dirty, with holes in his jacket's elbows and his cap brim gone. A pause left him in front of a doorway where a beautiful young woman stood wearing an apron fashioned upon the Stars and Stripes. She sneered at him, saying: "You are a nice specimen, you miserable ragamuffin rebel!"[6]

The Virginians turned northwest towards Hagerstown into territory where most people favored the Union. Next day they shambled toward Harpers Ferry behind their army's wagon train. Mahone's brigade encamped at sundown east of the village of Burkettsville, still in the pro-Union area. Lee was leading his army westward to surround the Yankee garrison at Harpers Ferry. Anderson's division formed part of the command of Maj. Gen. Lafayette McLaws, tasked with seizing Maryland Heights on the Potomac's north side. Possession of these heights along with Loudoun Heights on the

3 John F. Sale to Mother and Aunt, October 19, 1862.

4 Bernard, "The Maryland Campaign," *War Talks*, 20-24.

5 John F. Sale to Uncle, November 30, 1862.

6 Bernard, Appendix, *War Talks*, 303.

river's south bank, both of which dominated Harpers Ferry, would force the Union garrison to surrender.

Two days later the Virginians shuffled through Burkettsville, crossing South Mountain just beyond at Brownsville Gap. Half a mile south of the village of Brownsville, they encamped.

On the morning of September 14, Littleberry Stainback approached Patterson.

"Pat, I am tired of marching up and down these damned mountains," said Stainback. "Please detail me to cook today."

Patterson complied, sending Stainback on a detail considered "bomb-proof."[7]

At 3 p.m. that day, the 6th and 12th headed about a mile north to Crampton's Gap, which the 16th was guarding. The 12th marched under Lewellen. He had just recovered from the slight head wound he suffered at Second Manassas. Taylor, still too ill to take charge of the 12th, accompanied the regiment bearing a gold-headed cane. With the 6th and 12th marched the 41st's Col. William Allen Parham, then in command of Mahone's brigade. Cameron called Parham "the bravest of the brave" and "the beau ideal of a dashing soldier."[8] This proud landowner from Sussex County inspired fear even in Mahone, whom most regarded as fearless. Parham obeyed or disobeyed Mahone's orders as Parham pleased and Mahone kept his mouth shut about it. "Bravest man I ever saw," the Old Grays' Pvt. Joseph J. Maclin termed Parham.[9] As a stretcher bearer, Maclin numbered among the bravest of the brave himself.

Stray soldiers from other units took the places of some of the 12th's stragglers. The 13th Virginia Infantry's Pvt. Richard F. Bernard, brother of George Bernard, marched with the 12th that day.

Parham summoned detailed men back to the ranks. Crow and fellow Rifleman Pvt. William E. Douglass were sitting together, both shoeless and

---

7 Statements of John R. Patterson, "The Maryland Campaign," 43n; Appendix, *War Talks*, 302-303.

8 William E. Cameron, "Chancellorsville: A Sketch Of The Battle And Of The Part Taken By Mahone's Brigade, With Incidents And Personal Recollections Of The Campaign, An Address Delivered By Ex-Gov. Wm. E. Cameron Before A. P. Hill Camp Of Confederate Veterans, Of Petersburg, Va., On The Evening Of April 3rd, 1890," in *War Talks*, 49.

9 Statement of Joseph J. Maclin, Notes of St. George Tucker Coalter Bryan, Grinnan Family Papers, VHS.

excused from duty by the regiment's surgeon because of foot problems. As the 12th departed from its camp toward Crampton's Gap, Parham approached the pair.

"What are you boys doing there?" asked Parham.

They explained their situation.

"Boys," said Parham, "the enemy are advancing upon us, there is a stone wall behind which we will fight, and you can shoot them down like squirrels."[10]

The two buckled on their accoutrements and hobbled after the regiment.

The Yankees had found a copy of Lee's orders. McClellan, now in command north of the Potomac River acted with an uncharacteristic energy that alarmed Lee. Mac sent his men to force the passes through South Mountain—Fox's, Turner's and Crampton's Gaps—and fall upon the divided Confederate army. Lee strove to block the passes and compel the surrender of Harpers Ferry. The campaign's crisis had arrived.

The 6th and 12th reached Crampton's Gap 15 minutes after leaving camp. Along the way, Parham commandeered the 10th Georgia of Semmes' brigade, McLaws' division. The Petersburg Regiment, no more than 150 strong, led Parham's column.[11] Waving his sword over his head, Lewellen descended South Mountain a few paces to the 12th's front and right. His men followed him down. They could see converging upon them several dust clouds above the trees. The troops thought the dust came from Yankee cavalry and did not expect much of a fight. By the time the regiment arrived at a fork in the road below the gap, the dust clouds had reached the village of Burkettsville, a mile down the road to the right.

The 16th, picketing below the fork, reverted to Parham's control. He ordered it to contract its line to the right and form behind a stone wall. The 12th deployed on the 16th's left, in front of the fork and behind a worm fence with a stone base that afforded the 12th's soldiers cover. The 6th formed line on the 12th's left behind another worm fence. On the 6th's left lined up eight companies of the 10th Georgia. Parham directed his men to lie down on their faces. Posted eight feet apart to extend their line as far as possible, the 12th's soldiers had enough space between the worm fence and the road to lie down at full length. Despite Parham's orders, many men

10 John E. Crow to George S. Bernard, October 23, 1892, Appendix, *War Talks*, 303.

11 *OR* 19, 1:818, 824. The 12th may have fielded as few as 122. John Michael Priest, *Before Antietam: The Battle for South Mountain* (Shippensburg, Pa., 1992), 278.

remained upright and deployed a few yards west of the road behind trees on the slope of South Mountain.

In front of Parham's troops stretched a plowed field 250 yards wide. His skirmishers advanced to a stone wall on the field's far side. A regiment of cavalry guarded each of the infantry's flanks. A battery of horse artillery unlimbered just below and to the right of Crampton's Gap. A section of the Portsmouth Artillery stood near a meeting house farther down and to the right, where the two remaining 10th Georgia companies deployed.

Parham's soldiers had scarcely gotten into position before the Confederate artillery opened on the advancing Northerners. Shot and shell screamed several hundred feet over the heads of Parham's men. Soon his skirmishers fired a few shots.

Among the Riflemen Paterson noticed that Stainback had joined the company's battle line.

"I thought I had detailed you to cook," said Patterson.

"Oh, hell!" replied Stainback. "I could not stay with that crowd of bummers and wagon-dogs."[12]

The skirmishers retired across the field. The 12th's soldiers raised their heads and saw the enemy deploying behind the stone wall on the field's other side. Flashes of light and puffs of white smoke darted from the muzzles of hundreds of rifles there. The blaze instantly ran down the wall's length.

Bullets kicked up dirt in the field, whistled through the fence's rails and struck trees, stumps, logs and rocks on the side of South Mountain. Despite an order from Parham not to waste ammunition, his troops returned fire. The fusillade lasted for two hours, killing and wounding soldiers on both sides. Chappell, now a second lieutenant, took off his hat and strode up and down the line cursing the enemy "like a wild man," recalled Maclin.[13] Chappell swore that no Yank ever molded lead that could hit him.

Not all the 12th's men could say the same. A ball severely wounded Color Bearer Arthur Williamson "Scrap" Parker of the New Grays. Phillips picked up the colors and gave them to the Old Grays' Pvt. Joseph C. Fowlkes. Another minnie struck Bernard as he lay loading his rifle. He felt a pain in his right leg above the knee, as if a heavy object had hit him a hard blow. A

---

12 Statement of John R. Patterson, Appendix, *War Talks*, 302-303.

13 Statement of Joseph J. Maclin.

glance revealed "an ugly orifice from which the red blood was streaming."[14]
He bound up the wound with his handkerchief, then remembered a leather
strap in his blanket roll that would serve the purpose better. He prevailed
upon the man on his left to stop firing and strap up the leg. "I then lay as
flat as was possible & wondered how long the fight would last, thinking I
would give the wealth of the Indies, if I had it, to be on the other side of
the mountain," Bernard recalled.[15]

The battle's climax came. Major General William B. Franklin commanded
the Union VI Corps. A division of this corps confronted Parham's force.
Franklin, overestimating the Confederates' strength, hesitated to attack.
McClellan deferred to Franklin's judgment. Major General Henry W. Slocum,
who commanded the division facing Parham's troops, assessed the situation
differently and massed his three brigades for an assault. From north to
south, the 32nd, 18th, and 31st New York confronted the 12th Virginia. As
Slocum completed his dispositions, Parham's men ran low on ammunition.
The rail fence in front of the 12th caught fire. The wounded who could,
scuttled away from the flames. The able tried to extinguish the blaze. The
New Yorkers and Pennsylvanians concentrated their musketry on the fire,
wounding several Virginians fighting the flames.

Suddenly the enemy musketry slackened, then ceased.

"Look yonder, boys!" one of the 12th's men cried. "They are coming
across the field."[16]

A massive blue formation surged toward Parham's thin gray line. Southern
fire took its toll. Posted behind a tree behind the stone wall, Sale loaded
his rifle. Taking aim at a big Federal officer leading his men, Sale waited
until the Yankees came within 100 yards, then fired. The officer threw his
arms up in the air and fell. Despite Northern losses, all could see that the
Unionists would quickly reach Parham's men.

"Fix bayonets!" the command ran down the Secessionist line.

The Southerners realized that the blue hordes would overwhelm them.
"Fall back, men," came the cry. "Fall back."[17]

14 Bernard Notebook, 77.

15 Ibid., 78.

16 Ibid., 79.

17 Ibid.

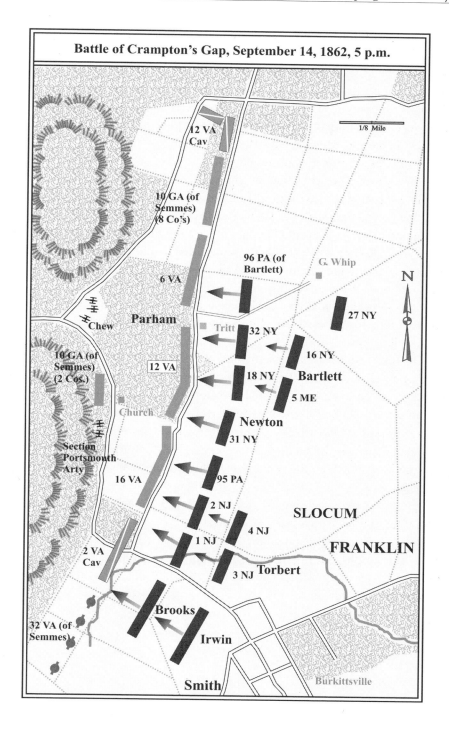

Battle of Crampton's Gap, September 14, 1862, 5 p.m.

The able grabbed their equipment and ran for the rear. Their flight gave the enemy better shots at them. The 12th now suffered most of its killed and wounded that day. Spence went down with a bullet in the neck. When the foe came within 20 yards, Brown took a minnie that broke his left arm. Before the enemy reached the fence, he pulled himself into the road. Taylor fell mortally wounded. Crow saved Taylor's gold-headed cane by sticking it into the barrel of his fouled rifle.

A cry rose that terrified the wounded.

"See yonder, boys!" someone shouted. "Cavalry!"[18]

The terror of the wounded intensified.

"I would be trampled to death by Cavalry!" Bernard recalled thinking. "Or the enemy coming up, would bayonet me!"[19] The blue battle line reached the fence seconds later. The excited Yankees yelled and fired at the Confederates retreating up the mountainside. Maclin carried several wounded to safety, then fell shot in the ankle, hip, calf and side. The Riflemen's Pvt. Joseph Edwin Spottswood picked up Maclin and carried him off on his back. A former clerk for a Petersburg lumber concern, Spottswood had served in the Mexican War.

Dr. Baker, the 12th's assistant surgeon, leapt into the brand-new saddle of his horse, "Bob Lee." Baker galloped southward, then reined up as he met the 16th New York's front line. Dismounting, he shooed Bob and bolted up the slope with bullets ricocheting off the rocks around him.

A short distance up South Mountain, the Confederates rallied and resumed firing on the enemy at the fence. The Union infantrymen thrust their muskets between the fence rails. The muzzles came within inches of the heads of wounded Southerners. "If the enemy did not kill us," Bernard thought, "our own men would, whose bullets I expected every instant to pierce me, one of which I am satisfied did graze my hip...."[20] The Federal artillery's advance also threatened the wounded. Brown lay in the road's wheel rut with his face resting on his blood-covered hand. Yankee cannon rumbled by less than 10 feet to his left. "I could not help thinking of the shocking sights seen after the battle of Manassas, for, should a battery of

---

18 Ibid.

19 Ibid.

20 Ibid., 79-80.

artillery, or a squadron of cavalry, move, I would be ground or trampled to an unrecognizable mass," he recollected.[21]

Retreating up the mountain, Stainback took cover behind the same tree as Shepard. As the Yankees neared, they both fled up the slope again with Shepard rapidly outdistancing the portly Stainback.

"What's your hurry?" the Riflemen's Pvt. Sidney Overton Jones, the son of Bernard's Petersburg landlady, asked as he passed Stainback. "Trying to *catch a train?*"[22]

Manson had gotten so busy tending the wounded that he neglected the chance to escape.

"Be cautious!" he shouted to the enemy. "Don't shoot us. We've wounded men. We've surrendered."[23]

The Yankees ignored him. Bernard removed the white pocket handkerchief from his leg. Manson put it on the end of a ramrod, holding it up in the Federals' faces.

"We surrender!" he yelled.

"Get over the fence then!" shouted the Northerners, still exchanging shots with the Confederates up the mountainside.[24]

A strong, athletic man, Manson seized Bernard and lifted him onto the fence. A Yank helped tumble Bernard over to the other side. Manson then carried his kinsman across the field toward the enemy rear.

The Union infantrymen mounted the fence, charging across the road and up the hill. No longer caught in a crossfire, some of the 12th's wounded got out of the road's ruts. Brown took his shattered left arm in his right and ducked into a cooper's shop near the roadside. Inside, Federals had tapped several barrels of fresh cider. "I passed by them, and seated myself on the back sill still feeling quite faint from the loss of blood," recalled Brown.[25]

Up South Mountain Slocum's men dislodged the remnants of Parham's force, capturing still more of the 12th's men. One Yank got close enough for Sale to hear, "Stop you damned Rebel or I will shoot you."[26] They fired at

21 Brown, *Reminiscences of the War*, 33.

22 Bernard, "The Maryland Campaign," *War Talks*, 43n.

23 Bernard Notebook, 80.

24 Ibid.

25 Brown, *Reminiscences of the War*, 34.

26 John F. Sale to Aunt, November 26, 1862.

one another, missed and Sale kept running. The Northerners drove Parham's men back through Crampton's Gap, overwhelming portions of Cobb's and Semmes' brigades in the process. "We would get in squads, fire and fall back to another squad behind us," remembered Crow.[27] In the retreat Lewellen suffered a severe wound. Command of the 12th fell to Jones. He collected the regiment's survivors in a cornfield at South Mountain's foot, formed line of battle and put the wounded behind the line. The brigade's remnants bedded down in this position.

Brigadier General Howell Cobb rode in among the wounded and ordered them out of his way. Parham, sharing a blanket with another officer, rose and cussed out Cobb.

"Who are you, sir?" Cobb inquired.

Parham's oaths drove Cobb to the rear. Maclin, one of the wounded present, pronounced Parham "expert at swearing."[28]

For the second time in about two weeks, the Unionists had wrecked the regiment's organization. This time they had nearly annihilated its substance. Brigadier General John Paul Semmes of McLaws' division considered the rout of Parham's troops shameful.[29] The casualties refuted Semmes. The 12th lost 86 men, more than 57 percent of its participants, a remarkable loss.[30] The Northerners killed or mortally wounded 11. Forty-five suffered less serious wounds. Twelve of the wounded and thirty unhurt remained in enemy hands, almost twice the number of able-bodied who remained with the colors.[31] Bernard's brother Richard suffered a wound as well. The captives included Stainback.

27 Bernard, Appendix, *War Talks*, 305.

28 Statement of Joseph J. Maclin.

29 Zack C. Waters and James D. Edmonds, *A Small but Spartan Band: The Florida Brigade in Lee's Army of Northern Virginia* (Tuscaloosa, 2010), 144, citing Lafayette McLaws to Captain A. J. McBride, July 3, 1895, Robert K. Krick Collection, Fredericksburg/Spotsylvania National Battlefield Park, Fredericksburg, Virginia.

30 A loss of 40 percent constituted a remarkable loss. William F. Fox, *Regimental Losses in the American Civil War, 1861-1865: A Treatise on the Extent and Nature of the Mortuary Losses in the Union Regiments with Full and Exhaustive Statistics Compiled from the Official Records on File in the State Military Bureaus and at Washington* (Albany, NY, 1889), 556-558. See Table 3.

31 Roll 66, M861, Record Group 109, NA; Henderson, *12VI*, 106-167; Ezra Carman, "The Maryland Campaign," 420, Manuscript Division, Library Of Congress, Washington, D.C.

Few of the 12th's other fights held as much significance for its soldiers. The Archer Rifles' Pvt. Theodoric B. Ruffin, captured at Crampton's Gap, declared the battle one of the brigade's "most glorious achievements."[32] The men of the 6th, 12th and 16th believed they had held off an entire enemy corps for three hours and prevented McClellan from cutting Lee's army in two. While the delay's main source lay in the caution of Mac and Franklin, Crampton's Gap became the Thermopylae of the three regiments in the veterans' memories.

The 12th's soldiers had split into four groups: the stragglers, the wounded from Second Manassas, the prisoners taken at Crampton's Gap and the men who remained with the colors.

The regiment's stragglers probably formed the largest group. It included those who remained in Virginia, as well as those who had fallen out in Maryland.

Ambulances transported the 12th's wounded from Second Manassas over a rough road to Aldie in Loudoun County. There the Confederate Medical Department was supposedly establishing a hospital. The wounded began reaching Aldie on the afternoon of August 31. They found no hospital, no surgeons, no medical supplies and had to rely on the populace's kindness for shelter and medical attention.

Weisiger, exhausted by the long drive and tormented by his wound, found accommodations with a black woman.[33] Before nightfall other citizens of the village and the surrounding country came to the rescue of the wounded. These troops found themselves far better off than if they had landed in a hospital. A gentleman from Upperville in Fauquier County invited to his home Todd and English John Dunlop, who had left the New Grays for a commission as a second lieutenant on the staff of Brig. Gen. Lewis A. Armistead. Todd awaited the arrival of the gentleman's carriage with great anticipation. "The fact is, there were floating in my brain visions of juicy mutton chops, sirloins of beef and the other good things of that land flowing with milk and honey," recalled Todd.[34]

On the morning of September 1, the carriage bore Todd and English John from Aldie to a residence about a mile and a half beyond Upperville. The

32 Bernard, "The Maryland Campaign," *War Talks*, 41.

33 Todd, "Reminiscences," 48.

34 Ibid., 50.

host and his family gave them a warm greeting and a good meal. Over the next few days, a surgeon from Upperville called and dressed their wounds. Dunlop stayed bedridden, but Todd improved rapidly. Many neighbors invited him to their houses. Mounting the pacer at his disposal, his arm in a sling, he rode around the neighborhood visiting almost every day.

He befriended an old gentleman who lived across the road. The "soul of hospitality," this fellow always wanted Todd to dine with him. When Todd did not comply, the man would send his dining room servant with the message, "to hurry over, he had some important news." As Todd would find upon arriving, the "news" amounted to "the ice is melting in the juleps and they'll be ruined if we don't drink them at once."[35]

Mahone found quarters in a private home in Fauquier County. His wound came from a Yankee ball that struck him in the side just above the belt. The bullet hit a button of his jacket and, bearing the impression of the button's Virginia coat of arms, lodged in his boot. But for the button, the ball would probably have inflicted an abdominal wound—almost always fatal because of the absence of antibiotics to combat the peritonitis such a wound caused. The bullet did not break the skin but bruised him so severely that he could not proceed with his brigade.

The wounded from Second Manassas who did not receive invitations to private homes went to the hospital established in Warrenton by the Confederate Medical Department.

Of the prisoners taken from the 12th at Crampton's Gap, the wounded captives met with treatment as kind as that given those who remained in Southern hands. As soon as Manson and Bernard got beyond the stone wall on the field's other side, two Yankees assisted Manson in bearing Bernard more than a mile back to a farmhouse where Federal surgeons had improvised a hospital. Wounded men, mostly Unionist, filled the house and its yard. Those assisting Bernard placed him on the grass along with the other casualties. The chaplain of a Maine regiment approached. Remarking that the wounded of both sides would receive the same treatment, he gave Bernard a cup of tea.[36]

Brown also received good care. He recalled his surprise as he sat faint from loss of blood on the cooper shop's back sill, near the Yankees

35 Ibid., 51.

36 Bernard, "The Maryland Campaign," *War Talks*, 30.

William Thomas Morgan. *Courtesy William Turner, Even More Confederate Faces*

drinking cider. One of them brought him a cupful in less than a minute. "He seemed very much interested in my condition, and insisted on going with me, to have my wound attended to," remembered Brown, whom the Northerner led to the hospital.[37]

The enemy allowed private citizens to invite the wounded into their homes. The Marylanders' hospitality ensured that almost all the 12th's wounded received such invitations. "Not only this, but we have been kindly furnished with everything we needed in the way of clothing," Bernard recalled.[38] Brown found himself invited to a doctor's house. He received a carriage ride to visit Bernard and other soldiers from the 12th. The Riflemen's Pvt. William Thomas Morgan wrote, "I could not be more tenderly nursed in my own home."[39] A miller's son and the nephew of Fletcher Archer, Morgan had helped raise a pre-war militia company, the Cockade Cadets, which became part of the 41st Virginia in Mahone's brigade.[40] Morgan had taken two bullets at Crampton's Gap, one breaking a bone in his right leg, the other costing him a finger on his right hand.

The 12th's able-bodied prisoners from Crampton's Gap went directly to Fort Delaware prison and did not fare as well as the wounded. "It was twenty-four hours after we entered the prison before a morsel of food was given," remembered Manson, one of 72 captured officers sharing a casemate in the autumn heat.[41] Each corner of the casemate had a privy. Both sides

---

37 Brown, *Reminiscences of the War*, 34.

38 Bernard Notebook, 81.

39 William T. Morgan to Mother, September 25, 1861, The Lewis Leigh Collection, AHEC.

40 William T. Morgan to Fletcher H. Archer, July, 1861, William T. Morgan Papers, Navarro College Archives, Navarro College, Corsicana, Texas.

41 Joseph R. Manson, Sr., to Joseph R. Manson, Jr., March 2, 1915, Private Collection of William Zielinski.

had a raised platform for sleeping. A small space remained in between for exercise. "This little floor space was soon almost shoe deep in tobacco quids, apple peelings, bones and offal until it became insufferable," Manson recalled.[42] The officers begged the Northerners to clean the place, without success. The Southerners then got permission for their slaves captured with them to do this work. Through these slaves, who had their liberty, the officers could get whatever they wanted from the sutlers. Friends in Baltimore supplied the officers with money.

The regiment's smallest group consisted of approximately 30 soldiers who remained with the colors.[43] At nightfall on September 14, the Yankee VI Corps held Crampton's Gap. Franklin did not push on and seize Kohrersville or attempt to relieve Harpers Ferry but contented himself with posting a skirmish line in Pleasant Valley. The situation of the two Confederate divisions under McLaws remained precarious. Franklin had the angle on McLaws if he tried to escape westward over Elk Ridge through Solomon's Gap. The Federal garrison of Harpers Ferry—still holding out—prevented McLaws from retiring around Elk Ridge's southern end, under the cliffs fronting the Potomac. Marching over a trackless stretch of Elk Ridge between Solomon's Gap and Harpers Ferry would entail abandonment of his trains and artillery. Doubling back eastward between South Mountain and the Potomac through Weverton Pass in search of a Potomac ford seemed suicidal.

McLaws refused to panic. He decided to keep the Yanks in Harpers Ferry bottled up and simultaneously to defend himself against a Unionist thrust southward down Pleasant Valley or westward through Weverton Pass by reinforcing the Confederate line near Brownsville. McLaws entrusted this to Anderson. Luckily for the Southerners, Franklin remained cautious. VI Corps stayed put. McClellan reverted to form. Rather than press his advantage, he acquiesced in his subordinate's inactivity. Before McLaws could reconsider his stance, fortune rewarded his steadfastness. The Federals at Harpers Ferry surrendered. The news reached McLaws at 10 a.m. on September 15. He immediately prepared to withdraw from Pleasant Valley by way of Harpers Ferry. Soon he received orders from Lee, who had decided to unite his scattered forces at Sharpsburg, to proceed there as quickly as

---

42 Ibid.

43 Bernard, "The Maryland Campaign," *War Talks*, 23n.

possible. Lee intended to give battle east of Sharpsburg to Mac's Federals, who outnumbered the Confederates two to one.

The handful of men huddled around the 12th's colors south of Brownsville withdrew with the rest of Anderson's command to a new line that ran from Maryland Heights to Weverton Pass. Anderson consolidated the remnants of Mahone's brigade with Pryor's brigade. Along with Featherston's Mississippi Brigade and Wilcox's Alabama Brigade, Pryor's brigade had joined the Norfolk Division after Second Manassas. The wagon trains of McLaws' command crossed the Potomac on a pontoon bridge. At 2 p.m., when all the trains reached the Virginia side of the river, the rest of his forces withdrew from Maryland. The troops on Maryland Heights led the way. Anderson's men brought up the rear. The 12th did not plod south until dark, crossing the Potomac that night.

At 8 a.m. on September 16, Mahone's brigade arrived at Halltown, four miles southwest of Harpers Ferry. The Virginians slept until 3 p.m., when they trudged north towards Shepherdstown. At 7 p.m., two miles south of Shepherdstown, they stopped for rest. The journey resumed at midnight. Crossing the Potomac back into Maryland at Boteler's Ford, the column headed for Sharpsburg.

Along with the rest of Anderson's division, the 12th neared Sharpsburg at 8 a.m. The trip from Pleasant Valley had thinned the regiment's already sparse ranks. Twenty-three of the brigade's 70 rank and file belonged to the 12th.[44] At least 3 of the brigade's 12 officers belonged to the 12th—Feild, who had caught up with and taken command of the regiment, Jones and Pollard, now a first lieutenant.[45] Pryor's and Mahone's brigades combined had only 300 soldiers.[46]

Anderson's division passed Lee's headquarters on Shepherdstown Road, then paused awaiting orders in a field north of Sharpsburg's main street. The men rested only half an hour. About 10 a.m., a directive came for the division to assist D. H. Hill's division, which manned a sunken road that would soon become known as Bloody Lane.

Brigadier General Roger Atkinson Pryor had formerly edited a Petersburg newspaper. He held the dubious distinction of having declined to fire the first

---

44 Ibid.

45 William W. Chamberlaine, *Memoirs Of The Civil War* (Washington, 1912), 32.

46 Ibid.

shot at Fort Sumter. Now he rode up to his brigade, which still included the remnant of Mahone's brigade. Pryor ordered his command to advance. His troops crossed the fields towards Piper's farm. When they came into view, Yankee artillery let loose. Pryor's soldiers filed across Hagerstown Pike at the double-quick about half a mile south of the Dunker Church. Savaged by the bombardment, they entered Piper's field, stopping at the west side of an apple orchard. After resting a few moments, they formed in a hollow behind the middle of Bloody Lane.

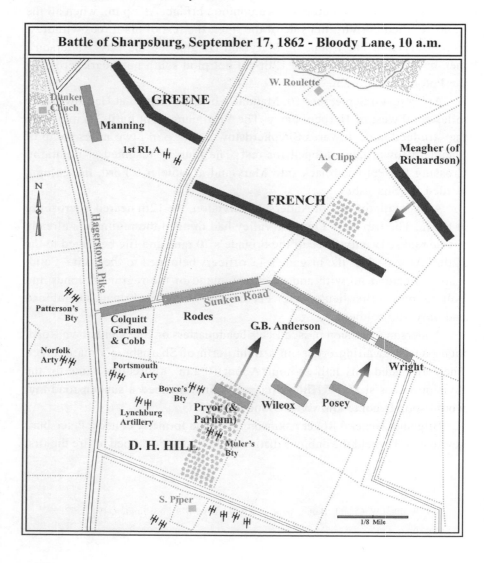

Battle of Sharpsburg, September 17, 1862 - Bloody Lane, 10 a.m.

Anderson suffered a thigh wound and fainted from loss of blood. Command of his division passed to Pryor, its senior brigadier. The division fell apart. In disjointed fashion, Wright's, Featherston's and Pryor's brigades crowded into Bloody Lane. Wright's and Featherston's brigades made piecemeal counterattacks on the Northerners of Richardson's and French's divisions from the line's right and center. The Federals maintained a withering fire of musketry and canister. About noon the Southern line in Bloody Lane collapsed. In the ensuing rout the 12th's soldiers streamed back across Piper's field and down Piper's Lane under fearful fire. They rallied with the rest of their division behind the stone walls bounding Hagerstown Pike. The Unionists charged through the cornfield between Bloody Lane and the Piper orchard, but Secessionist artillery supported by small arms fire from behind the stone walls forced the enemy back. Firing along this line slowly sputtered out. The fighting shifted toward the Confederate right. There the battle culminated when A. P. Hill's division arrived from Harpers Ferry and repulsed a Yankee attack that threatened to cut Lee's line of retreat.

Nine of the twenty-six soldiers the 12th took into action at Sharpsburg became casualties. Eight, including Pollard and Spottswood, suffered wounds. Both survived, but the injuries of two others proved mortal. Still another wounded man fell into enemy hands, joining the regiment's only other loss, an uninjured prisoner of war.[47] But while the 12th took 26 soldiers into combat and lost nine, the regiment left the field with more than 17.

Stragglers were rejoining Lee's army throughout the day, making at least one of the 12th's companies—the Riflemen—bigger going out of the battle than entering. The Riflemen took three soldiers into action, lost one man wounded but gained two stragglers—one of them Shepard.[48] Many of the army's other units had similar experiences. The additional strength gave Lee the confidence not only to remain at Sharpsburg next day but to consider attacking McClellan.[49]

September 18 passed without the battle resuming. Lee found no opportunity to take the offensive. Mac did not renew the previous day's assaults, despite receiving reinforcements. More stragglers caught up with Lee's army, but that

47 Henderson, *12VI*, 106-167; Roll 66, M861, Record Group 109, NA.

48 Bernard, "The Maryland Campaign," *War Talks*, 23n, 43n.

49 D. Scott Hartwig, "Robert E. Lee and the Maryland Campaign," in Gary W. Gallagher, ed., *Lee The Soldier* (Lincoln, Neb., 1996), 351.

Confederate dead in Bloody Lane.
Library of Congress

night he retreated. The 12th crossed the Potomac next morning at Boteler's Ford under Union artillery fire. The armies broke contact after a fight near Shepherdstown between the rear guard of Lee's army and McClellan's van. On September 21, Lee encamped near Smoketown, on Opequon Creek north of Winchester. The 12th soon shifted from the Smoketown camp to another nearer Winchester.

The Maryland campaign had ended. Lee had inflicted two casualties for each he had suffered. Lincoln made the most of Lee's retreat by declaring the battle of September 17 a Federal victory and using it to justify issuing the preliminary Emancipation Proclamation. To make matters worse for the Confederacy, Lee's army was approaching physical collapse. Combat, disease, indiscipline and poor logistics had halved its strength.

The 12th's manpower had declined by far more than half. The regiment now amounted to an understrength platoon.

CHAPTER 8

Fredericksburg

The 12th shuffled into camp north of Winchester hungry, ragged and barefoot. The men remained there a month, resting in glorious autumn weather. McClellan reorganized and reequipped his army. The 12th also reorganized. On October 3, its soldiers elected Feild their lieutenant colonel though he had participated in only two of its fights—Seven Pines and Sharpsburg. Lewellen became the regiment's major.

The troops had enough time to keep themselves clean, but still had no changes of clothing. The lice epidemic intensified. "You could see fellows every night turning their clothes wrong side out and upon asking why they did this they would tell you they were going to Countermarch them to death," wrote Sale.[1] Some men who had made it through the Maryland Campaign broke down and reported themselves sick. The surgeons sent them to hospitals. Primitive by modern medical standards, the hospitals represented an improvement over camp. The attendants kept the hospitals in good order. The food compared well with camp fare.

The number of soldiers with the colors grew. Stragglers returned, as did the sick and lightly wounded from the Peninsula Campaign, and the able prisoners of war from the Maryland Campaign. The Unionists started swapping prisoners from Crampton's Gap during the first week of October.

---

1 John F. Sale to Uncle, February 13, 1863.

The Southern officers from Fort Delaware brought back their slaves "in spite of the many offers they had to remain," recalled Manson.[2]

When the wounded captives recovered enough to travel, they reported to the Federal provost marshal in Frederick to get their paroles. The Northerners shipped these men to Baltimore in filthy boxcars, then confined the prisoners in barracks at Fort McHenry. Enemy officers prohibited rudeness to the captives, who often visited Southern friends in the city. The Confederates had such good times there that the Union authorities shipped them out as soon as possible. As Brown rested in the barracks, he felt thankful for the many kindnesses shown him in captivity. "In my prayers my grateful heart whispered to the recording angel how much I had been blessed," he remembered.[3] From Baltimore steamers carried the captives to Fort Monroe.

Treatment varied aboard ship. Manson received nothing but a few crackers. The captain of Bernard's steamer refused to take money from the prisoners in return for their meals, saying he wished he could do more for them.

From Fort Monroe the enemy transported the prisoners up James River. Their route took them by the Yankee fleet lying at anchor in Hampton Roads, within sight of Norfolk, Craney Island and Malvern Hill.

Exchanges occurred at Aiken's Landing, a few miles below Richmond. The captives included many wounded who had not yet recovered. A long train of ambulances, spring wagons, drays and carts awaited the enemy steamers. A group of the 12th's men disembarked on October 18. They passed along a line of ragged, sallow Federals in Confederate custody. "The sympathy of fellow sufferers caused our men to speak kindly to them, which words they seemed to appreciate," Bernard recalled.[4] The Unionists had lost their liberty at 1861's battle of Belmont, Missouri, under Brig. Gen. Ulysses S. Grant. The 12th's men would become better acquainted with Grant and get used to taking prisoners from him.

The train of ambulances departed with Bernard and his newly-freed comrades expecting a checkup at a Richmond hospital. Then the able would return to the regiment and the wounded would begin 60-day furloughs. Instead, the authorities quarantined all former captives for smallpox. "Many now were the imprecations heaped upon the head of the responsible party,"

2 Joseph R. Manson, Sr., to Joseph R. Manson, Jr., March 2, 1915.

3 Brown, *Reminiscences of the War*, 39.

4 Bernard Notebook, 83.

Bernard remembered.[5] In captivity the exchanged prisoners had rarely gone hungry. In the quarantine encampment, skimpy rations prevailed. The cooks dished out bits of baker's bread and molasses or boiled beef only twice daily. The authorities transferred the former captives to hospitals after a week. There they remained for more than an additional two weeks. Spoiled convalescing in private homes, the wounded from Crampton's Gap did not find the Richmond hospitals the spas they seemed to men who had gone through the Maryland Campaign unscathed.

While the 12th's men made their ways back to Virginia, McClellan remained in Maryland. More than a month after the battle of Sharpsburg, Mac finally put his army in motion. On October 25, the Northerners crossed the Potomac east of the Blue Ridge Mountains, heading toward Warrenton, Culpeper Court House and Gordonsville and seizing the Blue Ridge gaps on their right.

McClellan's advance caught Lee's army reorganizing. The Confederate Congress had recently confirmed Longstreet and Jackson as lieutenant generals and respective commanders of the First and Second Corps. On October 27, Lee sent Davis recommendations for filling vacancies among lesser-ranking general officers. Next day Lee reacted to Mac's advance, dispatching Longstreet's Corps toward Culpeper Court House to block the Federal thrust. Lee left Jackson's corps around Winchester to threaten McClellan's right flank and rear. Longstreet's Corps reached Culpeper Court House during November's first week. Mac moved so slowly that Lee visited Richmond for a few days, leaving Old Pete in command. Lee returned on November 6. That day his recommendations for filling vacancies among the army's lower-ranking general officers became effective—as modified by the War Department, Davis and the Confederate Congress.

On November 7, Unionist cavalry crossed Hedgeman's River on the road to Amissville. Two days later the enemy stopped along Hazel River, six miles south of Hedgeman's and as many miles north of Culpeper Court House. The pause puzzled the Southerners. The reason for it soon became apparent.

On November 5, immediately after the Republicans lost ground in mid-term elections, Lincoln sacked McClellan for having the slows. Lincoln gave command of Mac's army to Burnsîde, now a major general. McClellan got the order relieving him on November 7. Burnside did not take command

5 Ibid., 84.

until November 9, after the army had completed the movement under way at the time of Mac's relief. Burnside wanted to resume the advance, but along another line. He submitted his own plan of invasion to Lincoln, which called for the army to cross the Rappahannock at Fredericksburg, then rush to Richmond before Lee could interpose his army. Lincoln approved.

Unaware of Burnside's designs, Lee continued rearranging his army. The 12th remained in Mahone's brigade of Anderson's division, Longstreet's Corps. The brigade, temporarily commanded by Brig. Gen. Richard B. Garnett, underwent no change. Anderson's division lost two brigades but gained part of one of them back in another brigade, for a net loss of one. Pryor's brigade ceased to exist. Lee stripped Pryor of troops and used the Florida soldiers among them to form a new brigade which became part of Anderson's division. Armistead's Virginia Brigade went to Pickett's Virginia Division.

The Confederate commissary continued failing the front-line soldiers. Inadequate food reached the troops. Inflated prices made it hard for the men to make up for the short rations by purchasing produce from local farmers.

Under Stuart, Lee's cavalry launched a series of probes to gather evidence of enemy intentions. Jeb led the first of these scouts on November 10, reconnoitering toward Jeffersonton, midway between Hazel River and the Rappahannock on the road from Culpeper Court House to Warrenton. At 10 a.m. on November 14, as the regiment stood picket along Hazel River, Stuart arrived there on his way to launch another reconnaissance toward Jeffersonton. To support his cavalry, he asked for the 22nd Georgia of Wright's brigade and the 12th Virginia.

The 12th's men fell in and plodded toward Hazel River. They found that Stuart's cavalry had driven in the enemy pickets. Crossing the river on a log, the Virginians hiked toward Jeffersonton. The Confederate cavalry took thirty prisoners in the village at a cost of four horses. The Southern infantry occupied a conspicuous position on a hill just south of the village, stacking arms and building fires. Citizens came out from the village, welcomed the troops and begged them never to leave again. The Federals had stripped the country of livestock for miles around. The 12th's men noticed the escalation of the war's viciousness. During the previous August, Pope had brought a new note of savagery to the fighting in Virginia, announcing that he would make war on civilians as well as on soldiers, something McClellan had eschewed. Pope had not lasted long enough to put his words into effect, but now Burnside had adopted Pope's policy.

The Secessionist infantry remained in view of enemy scouts until after dark. Then Stuart sent the foot soldiers back to their former positions as quickly as they could march. The cavalry remained at Jeffersonton covering the retreat, but the Northerners left the Confederate horsemen unmolested.

The lack of resistance this reconnaissance met lulled some of the 12th's men into thinking they had finished fighting for the year, but the information gathered supported Lee's growing apprehension that Burnside had decided to approach Richmond via Fredericksburg. Even as the 12th marched and countermarched north of Hazel River, Lee ordered the Richmond, Fredericksburg & Potomac Railroad's destruction between Fredericksburg and Aquia Creek. On November 15, he sent troops to Fredericksburg.

Longstreet's Corps got in motion three days later. Mahone's brigade crossed the Rapidan at Raccoon Ford on the frigid night of November 18. The 12th encamped next day on a windy hillside northwest of Fredericksburg. Orange Plank Road, Mahone's first project as a civil engineer, ran just south of the camp.

Poor logistics beyond Burnside's control prevented him from crossing the Rappahannock before Lee's army could oppose him. The pontoons Burnside requisitioned failed to arrive on time. The Northerners waited for bridging equipment. The Confederates gathered on the low hills overlooking Fredericksburg and prepared to meet Burnside's attack. Every morning, Mahone's brigade marched down from its camps, taking position as the center brigade of Anderson's division, which constituted the extreme left of Lee's line. The 12th occupied a bottom behind Stansbury's Hill, opposite the town of Falmouth on the Rappahannock. Northern and Southern pickets confronted one another across the river. The Confederate sentries had orders not to respond to Federal taunts.

The 61st Virginia Infantry, a newly organized regiment, joined Mahone's brigade. Like most of the brigade, the 61st came from the Tidewater section of Southside Virginia. The unbloodied 61st had twice as many men as any other regiment in the brigade.

The 12th's soldiers spent much of their time drilling and building fortifications. Every week or two, after the troops denuded their surroundings of wood for fires, the regiment shifted its camp. This prevented the soldiers from constructing proper winter quarters. At best, the men dwelt in drafty tents. At worst, they spread their bed rolls in the open. The bitter cold forced them to pair off and bed down together for warmth. A buddy system developed which lasted until hostilities ended. The men called their bedmate their "chum," Todd recalled.[6]

The regiment's ranks continued to fill. The lightly wounded from Second Manassas, such as Todd, returned from their furloughs. The curably ill, like Sale and Whitehorne, returned from hospital. Mahone came back and resumed command of his brigade. The cold weather hindered attention to personal hygiene and drove the soldiers close to one another. The returning men arrived at the lice plague's height. The bugs afflicted the troops so badly that the soldiers would get up at night, take off their shirts, turn them inside out, hold them over campfires and beat the greybacks off with a stick. The insects "would fall in the fire and pop like popcorn," Phillips remembered.[7] Then the men would put their shirts back on still inside out, fasten them at the wrist and return to sleep.

Signal guns warned that the enemy was crossing the Rappahannock before daybreak on December 11. The long roll beat. The regiment formed line. The soldiers expected orders to move out at any moment. They did not build fires on this cold, clear morning. Time passed without the arrival of any directive. The men began shivering. Finally, the order came, "Column forward!"[8] The Virginians started off on the two-mile tramp toward Fredericksburg.

Before the 12th reached its post fronting Stansbury's Hill, Yankee batteries opened fire on the city. Southern sharpshooters there had picked off some of the enemy engineers constructing pontoon bridges. The regiment met civilians streaming out of Fredericksburg. The troops, Sale remembered, found it "truly heartrending to see the poor women and children who had been thus unmercifully turned out of their homes without a place to lay their heads excepting bush huts in the woods or some old out house or other."[9] The sight put the men in a mood to fight.

Shot and shell riddled the houses but did little to keep Confederate marksmen from decimating the enemy bridging details. Federal infantry crossed in pontoons to drive off the Secessionist snipers. Burnside's army needed both December 11 and 12 to bridge and cross the Rappahannock. A disgraceful sack of the city followed.

6 Todd, "Reminiscences,," 73.

7 Phillips, "Sixth Corporal, 12.

8 Todd, "Reminiscences," 74.

9 Sale to Aunt, December 23, 1862.

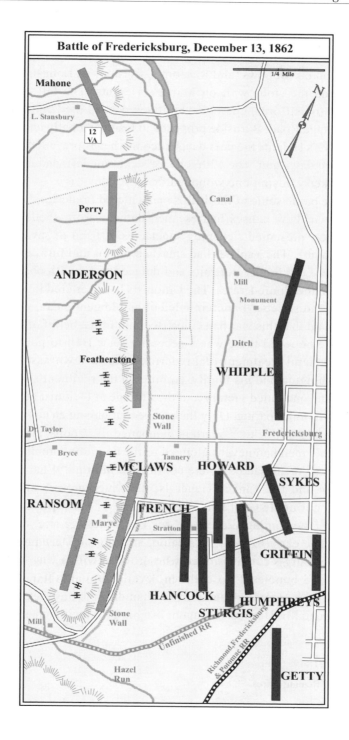

Battle of Fredericksburg, December 13, 1862

1/4 Mile

N

Mahone

L. Stansbury

12
VA

Perry

Canal

ANDERSON

Mill

Monument

Ditch

Featherstone

WHIPPLE

Stone
Wall

Dr Taylor

Fredericksburg

Bryce

Tannery

MCLAWS

HOWARD

SYKES

RANSOM

FRENCH

Marye

Stratton

GRIFFIN

HANCOCK

HUMPHREYS

Stone
Wall

STURGIS

Mill

Unfinished RR

Richmond, Fredericksburg
& Potomac RR

Hazel
Run

GETTY

On December 13, the invaders assaulted Confederate lines more than a mile to the south of Anderson's division. Their attack's right arm made no impression on McLaws' and Ransom's divisions of Longstreet's Corps, placed behind the stone wall on Marye's Heights. The left arm initially pierced Jackson's Corps, but a counterattack pushed the Unionists back to Richmond Stage Road. Burnside proposed to lead personally another assault against Marye's Heights the next day, but cooler heads prevailed. The enemy withdrew two days later. The 12th, on Lee's extreme left, endured shell fire but not musketry, losing one wounded.[10]

After the battle some of the 12th's men entered Fredericksburg and saw a sacked town. Few houses had escaped damage from shells. Some had burned. Others presented sickening spectacles. A band of savages seemed to have run amok. The Yankees had smashed pianos and furniture, punched out the eyes of old family portraits and defaced walls with obscene verses and curses on the Confederates. The Unionists had scattered intimate letters in the yards and streets. "I am reminded of an old gentleman, whom I once knew, who said that this war had converted him into a belief of Hell," Todd recalled. "He believed there was a necessity for a Hell to put such devils in."[11] The Federal treatment of Fredericksburg, a town associated with George Washington and his family, embittered the regiment and the rest of the South. The one-sided victory and the outrage at Unionist atrocities sent Secessionist morale soaring. Only the prospect of having an active campaign instead of going into winter quarters dampened the troops' spirits.

The 12th's men had never belonged to the dwindling numbers of Lee's critics. The regiment had complete confidence in him. "What a difference between him and the Yankee Generals, their men are dissatisfied while ours all hail our noble Genl with cheers whenever his white hair is seen," Sale wrote.[12] The coming year would see Lee's prestige rise, then plunge.

Santa came early to the 12th's camp, arriving on December 22 in the form of Petersburg's commissioner, who drove in with a wagon piled high with boxes and bundles. "No children...ever examined their stockings in the morning with greater glee and frolic than did 'the boys' exhibit as they gathered around Mr. Harrison's wagon, listening for their names to be called

10   *OR*, 21:610.

11   Todd Reminiscences, 78.

12   John F. Sale to Aunt, December 23, 1862.

out," Todd recalled.[13] Each box made someone's heart glad. The wagon carried shoes, shirts, drawers, socks and soap for the Petersburg men, the Norfolk troops and any soldiers of the regiment's three other companies whose relatives in Petersburg remembered them. The extra clothing turned the tide in the struggle against the greybacks. The wagon also brought a heavy load of liquor for the Petersburg men. They kept the alcohol to themselves, guzzling it next day.

December 25 began as Christmas had ordinarily begun in urban Virginia before the war—with crowds of men firing off their guns. The racket caused the detailing of a heavy guard. Several noisemakers found themselves in the guardhouse. Somebody got the better of Mahone. A few days earlier, he had acquired several turkeys. He fattened the fowls in a pen outside his tent. On Christmas morning he stepped out of his doorway to pick one for his dinner but found the birds gone. "Who stole Mahone's turkeys was a favorite 'conundrum' in the Division the balance of the war," Todd remembered. "Our fellows laid it on the Florida Brigade, but I am sure there was enterprise enough in either brigade to perform such an exploit."[14] Suspicion fell so heavily upon the Floridians that the rest of the division nicknamed them "the turkeys."[15] Even the orphans from Norfolk fared better than their brigadier. Their repast consisted of baked beef heart, boiled beef, salt pork, turkey, apples and for dessert some gingerbread. Unfortunately, to wash down this meal they had nothing better than water.

The regiment's soldiers confronted the New Year from a new perspective. They had become unrecognizable to their friends, their families and to some degree to themselves. Almost all the men had on their pants big patches of odd shapes, many colors and various materials, including leather and oil cloth, giving the wearers a ludicrous appearance. The transition from garrison duty to field service burdened the troops with menial tasks previously left to women and slaves. No longer could the men hire cooks or send out their sewing and wash. "I am going to advertise for a husband soon, can wash, sew, cook in fact anything that is required of a really old fashioned wife with some exceptions of course," Sale wrote.[16] The 12th had come under

13 Todd, "Reminiscences," 80.

14 Ibid., 81.

15 Cameron, "Chancellorsville," *War Talks*, 72-73.

16 John F. Sale to Aunt, September 3, 1863.

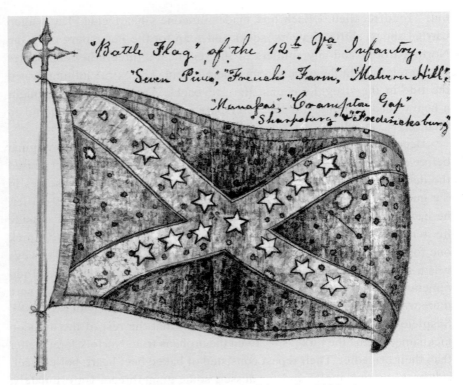

Sergeant John F. Sale's sketch of the 12th's "Old Rag"
John F. Sale Papers, Library of Virginia

enemy fire many times, losing about 300 killed, wounded and captured while becoming hardened to the battlefield's sights, sounds and smells. "I have seen a person's limbs taken off in every possible way without ever feeling the least pity or sorrow for them," Sale commented.[17] The men had exchanged the values of garrison troops for those of combat veterans. Spotless uniforms no longer meant anything to them. Instead, they took pride that more than 150 bullet holes adorned their battle flag, which they called their "old Rag".[18] "You would hardly believe how much attached the fellows feel towards it and it makes them feel proud when going through a town to hear everyone make remarks about how badly she has been used,"

17 John F. Sale to Aunt, November 26, 1862.

18 Sale to Aunt, January 31, 1863.

wrote Sale.[19] A regiment considered a badly torn flag a badge of honor, to cherish as long as a scrap remained. The men thought of their identities differently. Soldiers from different regiments never asked one another's names but called one another by the name of their regiments. "For instance they would call me 12th VA or some of the Woodis Rifles 6th VA and so on," Sale wrote.[20] Each of the regiment's men thought of himself as "12th Virginia."[21]

The regiment presented a far different picture at the end of 1862 than at the previous year's end. The 12th entered 1862 with about 941 soldiers present and absent. As in 1861 the regiment lost one company and gained another. The Meherrin Grays, 123 strong, arrived in April. The Hargrave Blues, 112 in number, departed at May's end. By Seven Pines the 12th had swollen to 1,100 present and absent.[22] Afterward, the flow of men reversed itself. Besides the Meherrin Grays, 306 other men joined the regiment. Four hundred and thirty-two soldiers left the ranks exclusive of the Hargrave Blues who belonged to that company when it exited. The regiment ended 1862 with around 806 men present and absent, a loss of 12 percent.[23] About 300 remained with the colors, far fewer than at the year's beginning.[24]

19 Ibid.

20 Ibid. The Woodis Rifles formed Company C of the 6th Virginia of Mahone's brigade. Wallace, *A Guide to Virginia Military Organizations 1861-1865*, 90.

21 Sale to Aunt, January 31, 1863.

22 Henry Van Leuvenigh Bird to Margaret Randolph, August 29, 1864.

23 Rolls 514-534, M324, Record Group 109, NA; Confederate Rosters, 2:1-56, LV; Henderson, *12VI*, 106-167.

24 William E. Cameron to David A. Weisiger, February 1, 1863, Weisiger Papers, VHS.

CHAPTER 9

Chancellorsville

In the New Year the army's supply lines developed problems. Daily rations dwindled to a quarter pound of bacon and a pound and a quarter of flour or meal. The regiment's soldiers got plenty of bread, but it consisted only of salt, flour and grease. The men went hungry. Morale plummeted. Desertion increased. The picket of Anderson's division, about 250 strong, lost an average of 15 soldiers each night. Only a handful came from the 12th.

Soldiers ventured into the countryside to buy food, ranging far and wide, "like ants, diverging in every direction," recalled Todd, and scouring the country for "anything that could fill their voracious maws."[1] Few farmers wanted to part with their produce for rapidly depreciating Confederate currency.

Company commanders could not issue a pass to go more than a mile from camp. The troops often ran afoul of the division's provost guard. Men who knew someone in this equivalent of modern-day military police might escape punishment. The friendless and the unconnected fared less well.

After the Maryland Campaign's straggling, Lee resolved to improve his army's discipline. This meant roll calls, drills, reviews and evening parades. It also meant examining boards to weed out incompetent regimental officers and swifter, surer and severer punishments for transgressions of the regulations. Mahone excelled as a disciplinarian.

1 Todd, "Reminiscences," 104.

The 12th witnessed the punishment of two men sentenced by a court martial to 39 lashes each. Ordered to protect certain property, they had stolen it instead. A guard detail escorted the culprits to two uprights linked by a cross-bar, stripped the prisoners to their waists and lashed their hands to the cross-bar over their heads. The executioners began administering punishment while the lieutenant in charge counted the lashes.

"It was as distasteful to the detail carrying out the sentence as it was painful to us who had to look at it," remembered Todd.[2] The executioners merely tapped the prisoners with their whips, making a farce out of the proceeding. Mahone, observing this, placed the lieutenant and the executioners under arrest.

"The prisoners have been found guilty of an infamous offense," he said. "It is my duty, however painful, to have the sentence rigidly enforced."[3]

He had another officer carry the sentence out properly.

"If I may judge by the way the prisoners winced, and the appearance of their backs, the new detail did their work effectually," Todd recalled.[4]

The Yankees were stirring again. On January 9, enemy cavalry raided the Orange & Alexandria's crossing of the Rappahannock, far above Fredericksburg. The raid suggested that Burnside might shift his line of advance back towards Gordonsville. By January 19, his army seemed poised to cross the river above Fredericksburg but much closer to the town. Longstreet shifted Anderson's division from Windy Hill to Salem Church, a brick structure on Orange Plank Road. There the division could cover Banks' Ford, about three miles above Fredericksburg.

On January 20, scouts reported the Northerners concentrating for crossings at Banks' Ford and nearby United States Mine Ford, but rain began falling and continued through January 22. The fifth element brought the Unionists to a halt before they reached the river. Their advance became known as the "Mud March." Afterward, internal dissension wracked Burnside's army. Lincoln accepted Burnside's request for relief from command. Burnside and IX Corps went west to the Department of the Ohio. Major General Joseph "Fighting Joe" Hooker succeeded Burnside, then led the army toward winter quarters.

2 Ibid., 85.

3 Ibid.

4 Ibid.

The weather turned cold. Snow began falling on January 27. Eight inches lay on the ground next day. The Confederate troops fought snowball battles. Mahone's Virginians had more experience with snow than the Deep Southerners in the Norfolk Division's other brigades and established themselves as division snowball champions. A battle with Perry's Florida Brigade lasted two hours, but the Virginians finally won. "The way we rolled them around in it was a sight to see," Sale exulted.[5] In a battle with Wright's Georgia Brigade, Mahone's troops "whipped them out easy," remembered Phillips.[6]

One time the Virginians faced both the Florida Brigade and Posey's Mississippi Brigade. The Floridians and Mississippians advanced in battle array, with officers mounted and color bearers carrying pieces of red blanket for banners. They gave Mahone's men time to get ready, then charged. The superior numbers of Deep Southerners overwhelmed the Virginians, who broke after a stubborn fight. The Floridians and Mississippians pursued the Virginians pell-mell through their camp, but Mahone's brigade had kept in reserve the 6th Virginia. Hidden behind the tents at the camp's far end, its men had filled their haversacks with snowballs. The attackers passed the 6th, which emerged from ambush and struck their flank. The fresh troops had a full supply of ammunition. The Floridians and Mississippians had empty hands. They had to stop to make new snowballs. The 6th Virginia pounded them. Mahone's other soldiers rallied on the 6th. With a shout, the entire Virginian line advanced. The Deep Southerners gave way. The Virginians pursued them and captured many of their flags.

Six to eight mail carriers serviced the regiment, keeping the troops in touch with their homes. The mail went through to enemy-occupied and Confederate territory alike. The South's people responded to letters complaining about the lack of food, sacrificing their own comfort to send boxes of provisions to friends and relatives in the army. Petersburg particularly distinguished herself. "I don't think any of our fellows ought ever to forget Petersburg and its kind people," Sale wrote. "Everything that comes from home is divided equally with us no matter what it is."[7]

As February began, high spirits again prevailed. "The morale of the army is superb, the idea of a defeat never occurs to them so great is their

5 Sale to Aunt, January 31, 1863.

6 Phillips, "Sixth Corporal, 13.

7 John F. Sale to Aunt, April 19, 1863.

confidence in their own prowess, and skill of their generals," Edwards wrote.[8] Wounded and captured from the previous year kept returning. On February 1, the 12th had 425 men present, 318 of them present for duty.[9]

The returning men included Bernard. After his exchange and convalescence, he went on detail as a recruiting officer at Cumberland Court House. While there, he remembered, "we lived more like gentlemen of pleasure than ever before or since."[10] When his Crampton's Gap leg wound healed sufficiently to permit service in the field, he at his own request obtained relief from the detail and returned as a private to his original company, the Petersburg Riflemen. "My leaving is my own act unadvised by any person whatsoever and the step I take in returning to my command is only induced by a strong sense of duty which directs me now that I feel myself fit for service, to return where I belong & where ought to be thousands of others not at home or in easy berths," he wrote.[11]

Mahone's brigade broke camp at noon March 15, amid a snowstorm. Rumor had it that Yankee cavalry were heading for United States Mine Ford. The men abandoned their huts and strode into the tempest. Without wagons, they left behind whatever they could not carry on their backs. The Norfolk Blues Artillery and Posey's brigade, all under Mahone's command, accompanied the Virginians. The snow turned to rain and hail. The soldiers tramped along execrable roads. Halting at a fork in Orange Plank Road about ten miles from Fredericksburg, they bivouacked in some woods.

Next day they found the ground covered with snow and ice. Under a clear sky they took the road toward United States Mine Ford, slogging three miles closer to the crossing.

At 4 a.m. on March 17, the officers of Mahone's brigade roused the rank and file from sleep. The soldiers marched down the frozen road to a place overlooking the ford. They waited in line of battle for four or five hours, hoping for a chance to empty a few enemy saddles, but the Federal cavalry did not appear. They had instead crossed the Rappahannock at Kelly's Ford, still farther upriver. "Had they dared to cross at this point, I wager

8 Postscript of February 16, 1863, to Letter, Leroy S. Edwards to Father, February 15, 1863.

9 Cameron to Weisiger, February 1, 1863.

10 Bernard Notebook, 87.

11 George S. Bernard to Father, March 20, 1863.

they would have had a merry time for there was no ground for cavalry and admirable covering for infantry," Edwards crowed.[12] The brigade returned to its bivouac.

The weather made the roads impassable for artillery and wagons, rendering heavy fighting unlikely. The 12th's men built huts for themselves again. The woods resounded with the chop of axes and the fall of trees. The soldiers dug holes in the ground, erected dirt or log walls and stretched tent flies across the top. At one end, they left an entrance which they enclosed with a flap; at the other, they erected a wooden chimney. "Every kind of chimney that was ever thought of is built and every style of shanty, some under the ground and some on top and some half one way half another," Sale wrote.[13] The huts stood scattered about at random. The interiors had little furniture. A single box might serve as lounger, sofa, chair and writing desk. The shanties proved firetraps. "Hardly a night passes over that we do not hear the cry of fire and some poor hellven's house is gone and he has hardly time to get his baggage out of the way," wrote Sale.[14]

For a month the weather remained foul—either rain, snow or hail. The troops rarely had a day of unbroken sunshine. The desolate region near United States Mine Ford yielded little wood except small green pines. The soldiers could barely coax them to burn. Their smoke proved blinding. A few books and fragments of magazines, along with homemade chess sets, enabled some men to pass the time agreeably. Others found the situation unbearable. "It is so dull up here, & so lonesome that I almost die with the blues," Whitehorne wrote.[15]

The troops had extra clothing. They could wash regularly. The greybacks remained for the most part subdued. "But there are men in the Reg[iment] & some in our Company who have enough on them to almost eat them up alive," wrote Manson.[16]

Mahone kept his soldiers from spending too much time in their huts. They took part in drills, roll calls and dress parades, fortified the approaches to the ford and stood picket along the Rappahannock's banks. Initially they

12 Leroy S. Edwards to Brother, March 29, 1863.

13 Sale to Aunt, April 19, 1863.

14 John F. Sale to Aunt, January 21, 1863.

15 James E. Whitehorne to Sister, April 6, 1863.

16 Joseph R. Manson to Wife, April 13, 1863, in Joseph R. Manson Papers, VHS.

found picket duty dull and disagreeable but not dangerous. Yankee infantry had not moved that far up the river. The invaders did not remain absent for long, appearing in gradually increasing numbers. By not taking potshots at the Confederate pickets, they marked themselves as veterans. "Old Sojers hardly ever fire at one another on picket but if a new Regiment goes on opposite you then you may look out," Sale explained. "This is the meanest kind of shooting as you may not expect an enemy near you when whiz comes a minnie."[17]

Rations remained reduced—a quarter pound of bacon and a pound and a half of meal or flour. Boxes of food still arrived from friends and relatives. One came for Sale in mid-March. Manson got something every time Harrison reached the 12th's camp. Greensville's commissioner, on the other hand, failed to satisfy at least one of his county's soldiers. "I dont see why Col S[pratley] cant bring us boxes," groused Whitehorne. "Mr H[arrison] brought Billy Mitchell a bundle of nic nacs. I tell you we did certainly enjoy it . . . ."[18] The boxes had a more lasting effect on morale than on the stomach. The troops grew increasingly dependent on the game abounding in the woods and the fish schooling in the river. "The soldiers catch a great many squirrels, coons & 'Possums—nothing can get away from them," Manson wrote. "They go squirrel hunting without a gun! and get everyone they see."[19] The frequent roll calls to prevent desertion made angling difficult. Men who did not receive boxes from home or share with those who did had to scrounge. The gunners of the Norfolk Blues Artillery ate rats caught at a nearby barn. One artillerist assured Todd that "a fat, corn-fed rat was not bad food to a hungry man."[20]

During April's first week, the winter's 26th and 27th snowfalls kept the ground white. The number of Federals on the Rappahannock's opposite bank increased. Anderson contemplated shifting the camp of Mahone's brigade back from the river.

The weather warmed during the following week. No blossoms appeared on the fruit trees, but the men could walk into the woods and listen to the pheasants drumming on the logs with their wings.

17 Sale to Aunt, April 19, 1863.

18 Whitehorne to Sister, April 14, 1863.

19 Manson to Wife, April 13, 1863.

20 Todd, "Reminiscences," 88.

The Northerners grew active. On April 13, Mahone's brigade prepared to move at daylight. A report had arrived that four enemy divisions were heading for United States Mine Ford. The alarm proved false, but Anderson moved the brigade's camp three miles back towards Fredericksburg.

The roads began to dry. Mahone sent work parties to throw up entrenchments around Chancellorsville, a large brick house at the junction of Orange Plank Road and the road to Ely's Ford. A bridging detail under the Richmond Grays' Capt. James Edward Tyler, a building contractor, hiked over to Germanna Ford, about 10 miles upstream. The detail, which included many of the 12th's carpenters, worked on a military bridge to facilitate the movement of the Confederate horse artillery, then encamped near Culpeper Court House.

During the winter Longstreet's campaign in Southeastern Virginia held the attention of Mahone's soldiers. In late February, Old Pete left Lee's army with Hood's and Pickett's divisions and became engaged in the siege of Suffolk. Mahone's men thought they should have drawn this task. Their brigade had more soldiers from Suffolk's vicinity than any other brigade in the army except Armistead's brigade of Pickett's division, but Mahone's men deferred to the wisdom of their commanders. "We certainly are blessed with Smart, Brave and God fearing Generals and whatever they agree on is always considered best," Sale wrote. "No matter what it is if Genl Lee says do it is all right."[21]

The spring campaign's opening approached. Tension mounted. The price of a substitute rose from $1,800 on March 26 to $3,000 by April 6. "It seems that patriotism is on the wane," commented Manson. "What is to become of us if the fighting is to be done by hirelings altogether?"[22]

The examining boards established the previous autumn hastened to finish weeding out corrupt or incompetent officers, who usually resigned for reasons of health or financial hardship rather than let the boards sack them. Several of the 12th's officers resigned about this time.

The Southern cause's prospects seemed bright. Northern newspapers spoke of Union forces acting only on the defensive until autumn. Lee's army expected to advance upon the enemy, but few soldiers thought the war would end without a fierce struggle.

21 John F. Sale to Uncle, April 26, 1863.

22 Manson to Wife, April 13, 1863.

On April 27, Mahone's brigade kept an extra vigilant watch over the Yankees at United States Mine Ford. Two days later the bridging detail at Germanna Ford came to grips with the invaders.

The detail's 120 men quartered in the old mill building on the south side of the Rapidan—or Rapid Ann, as the soldiers called the river. They had begun building their bridge from the river's north side and they had to row across each day to go to work. After 9 o'clock that morning, word came of a Federal crossing at Ely's Ford, six miles downstream. They gave little credit to the report, but the man Tyler had put in charge of the bridge's construction did not want to risk having the Northerners catch the detail unprepared. He ordered the fifty soldiers then north of the Rapidan to return to the mill building, get their arms and equipment, recross the river and resume work.

This man, Cpl. William Crawford Smith, a former building contractor, had moved from Petersburg to Nashville, Tennessee, before the war. After Virginia seceded he returned to Petersburg to enlist in the Petersburg Old Grays, serving as the regiment's right general guide. The enemy had wounded and captured him at Crampton's Gap.

The first boatload of men to get back to the Rapidan's north bank arrived before 10 a.m. and had worked only a few minutes when an officer of the cavalry's engineer corps confirmed the Federal crossing at Ely's Ford. Tyler, wanting the troops working on the bridge to have warning of the foe's approach, sent ten men from the south bank to picket the road running toward Culpeper Court House from the bridge's northern abutment. The pickets crossed the river and advanced along Culpeper road. On their way to what appeared the best spot for a picket post, they left unguarded a track branching off to the right a short distance from the abutment.

Tyler's remaining sixty men stayed on the Rapidan's south bank. He divided them into three squads. Tyler led one in person, posting it at the ford. Another squad, commanded by Smith, took position to the left of Tyler's, across from the approach to the abutment. The final squad deployed on the far left at the mill building, under a Mississippi officer.

The last boatload of the soldiers at work on the bridge had scarcely reached the top of the river's north bank when an unpleasant surprise greeted them. Enemy infantry from Ruger's brigade of XII Corps had advanced by the unguarded track, slipped in behind the Confederate pickets and attacked.

XII Corps formed the vanguard of Hooker's wing of the Army of the Potomac. Hooker had reinforced VI Corps and stationed it at Fredericksburg facing Lee's right. Fighting Joe was leading the rest of his army around Lee's left flank, intending to drive through the tangled area known as the Wilderness and envelop Lee before the Virginian knew what was happening.

To repel Ruger's Federals, the bridge-builders deployed as skirmishers, but the Northerners overwhelmed and captured them. The pickets on Culpeper road heard the firing behind them and tried reaching the bridge. Finding themselves facing the rear of a line of Unionist skirmishers, the sentries moved unseen upriver through the undergrowth. They discovered a boat and escaped to the Rapidan's south bank.

The three squads already on the south bank engaged the Federal skirmishers lining the north bank. The Secessionists fired until they had nearly run out of ammunition, losing one man killed and another wounded. The squad leaders then had their soldiers retire one at a time. They reassembled beyond the hill in their immediate rear. Looking back as he climbed the hill, Smith saw across the river a long line of battle supported by artillery. Enemy fire pinned down some of his comrades, who surrendered.

Yankee cavalry pursued these Confederate fugitives south of the river. A few fell into enemy hands. Most, taking to the woods, avoided captivity. Keeping the Culpeper road in view, the fugitives retreated until they reached Orange Plank Road about 4 p.m., meeting Secessionist cavalry pickets and reporting the affair at Germanna Ford. The men from the bridging detail decided to halt at the crossroads for the night, or at least until they heard from Mahone. About 80 of the detail had entered captivity, including Tyler and one wounded man from the 12th.

Cavalry pickets brought word of the enemy crossing at Ely's Ford to Mahone that afternoon. Then he received a report that the Northerners threatened a crossing at United States Mine Ford. Soon, news arrived of the enemy column moving east from Germanna Ford. Another courier galloped up reporting a Federal crossing at Fredericksburg.

Mahone issued orders. Couriers dashed back and forth. Within the hour his soldiers had abandoned their winter quarters and put themselves under arms, ready to move on short notice. Wagons filled with baggage crowded the roads to the rear.

"Fall in!" came the order early that evening. The 12th, 500 strong, took its customary position leading Mahone's brigade.[23] The Virginians marched west on Orange Plank Road. At Chancellorsville, they turned right on the road to Ely's Ford. Mahone's brigade deployed in the Bullock farm's field, about half a mile beyond Chancellorsville. Half mile to the left, the division's Mississippi Brigade held the plank road. A mixed detachment from both brigades remained at United States Mine Ford. Two-cannon sections of the Norfolk Blues Artillery supported each of these three forces.

Feild led the 12th. Mahone ordered Feild to picket the road to Ely's Ford. Feild gave this job to the Riflemen. The rest of the brigade bivouacked in line of battle. The Riflemen marched by the flank down the road, passing a schoolhouse designated for the picket post. Near sunset they approached a wooded ridge half a mile beyond. The soldiers in the company's van saw a few figures in blue 100 yards or so ahead. "There they are!" the Riflemen whispered among themselves.[24] Neither side fired. Banks deployed his men as skirmishers in the dense woods on both sides of the road. A steady rain fell. The Riflemen lay on their arms in the damp undergrowth without knowing at what minute the enemy might charge them.

A courier from Mahone reached the bridging detail, bringing an order to reconnoiter toward Germanna Ford. Mahone wanted to ascertain if the Yankees were advancing by that route in force. With two volunteers from the Norfolk Juniors, Smith prepared to reconnoiter. Just before the three started, they saw on a hill half a mile ahead a squad of soldiers. At first Smith thought them Northerners, but they proved the ten men detailed to picket the road from Germanna Ford to Culpeper Court House.

Smith and his two companions pushed through the darkening woods to the Dempsey house, a half mile west of Germanna Ford. A friend of the Dempsey family guided the three by a hog path through a pine thicket to the field at the ford, where a horde of the enemy encamped. After another stop at the Dempsey house, Smith and his two comrades hustled back through the trees to the junction of Culpeper and Orange Plank Roads. Exhausted, they arrived at 1 a.m., reported to Mahone's waiting courier and fell sleep.

Anderson reached Chancellorsville accompanied by his Georgia Brigade. He had orders from Lee to oppose the enemy's advance at Chancellorsville.

---

23 Cameron, "Chancellorsville," *War Talks*, 67.

24 Ibid., 66n.

In a room of the house there Anderson consulted with Col. Carnot Posey, the Mississippi Brigade's commander, and Mahone. Finding the Chancellorsville position unsuitable for defense, they agreed their forces must fall back to the Zoan or Wooden Church, three miles east on Orange Plank Road. Mahone urged Anderson to withdraw under cover of darkness. Anderson decided to retreat in the morning. His other two brigades would join them at the church. The division would oppose the Unionist advance until the rest of Lee's army arrived.

At 2:30 a.m. on April 30, Feild directed the Juniors to relieve the Riflemen on picket. The Juniors completed this operation an hour later. The Riflemen returned to the regiment in the Bullock field. Anderson rose at 4 a.m. Issuing his final orders for the withdrawal of Mahone's command, he mounted up and rode back toward Zoan Church with the Georgia Brigade.

At the junction of the plank and Culpeper Roads, the fugitives from Germanna Ford picked themselves off the damp ground. Retreating toward Chancellorsville, they posted a man every half mile with instructions to retire towards Chancellorsville in six to eight minutes.

At daylight on this foggy, overcast morning, the brigade heard popping caps and a few discharges of rifles from the picket line's direction. Silence followed. Puzzled, Mahone sent forward Cameron, now the brigade's Acting Assistant Adjutant and Inspector General. Cameron rode into the woods beyond the ridge the pickets had occupied. Finding neither the pickets nor the enemy, he returned and reported this to Mahone, who exclaimed impatiently.

Parham sat his horse nearby. Hearing Mahone, Parham dashed off on the same path that Cameron had taken and reached the ground that Cameron had left. A volley issued from some Yankee cavalrymen hidden a few feet away. The bullets missed Parham, but his horse shied. A branch ripped off his hat. He returned shaking his head and cursing the enemy.

Soon one of the Juniors from the company's extreme left returned to camp, explaining what had happened to his comrades. At daybreak a handful of horsemen from the 8th Pennsylvania Cavalry charged down the road from Ely's Ford. The Juniors on picket were standing ten paces apart. The rain had wet their powder. Those not captured had to skedaddle into the thickets. The Keystoners pounded down the road and surrounded the schoolhouse in which the rest of the company was sleeping. The hapless Juniors inside surrendered to a mere eight Federals. Almost the entire company was missing.

At 7 a.m., Mahone approached Feild.

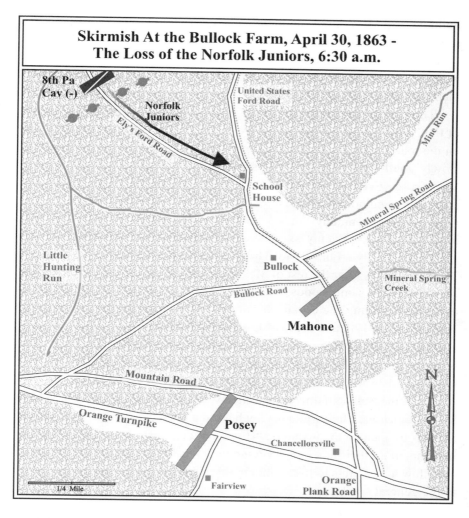

"General Anderson has determined to do now what I advised him to do last night, that is, to fall back to the Wooden Church, about two miles on the road to Fredericksburg," Mahone grumbled. "Had this been done last night under cover of darkness, it could have been done without loss; but now we will have to retreat in the face of a large force of cavalry, and I have determined to leave you here, with your regiment, to cover my retreat."[25]

Mahone explained his plan. Posey would leave one of his regiments on the Plank Road. This would cover his retreat and protect Feild's left. Neither

25 Ibid., 65-74.

Feild nor the Mississippi regiment's commander would retire without first informing the other. Feild would place his men across the road to Ely's Ford. The balance of Mahone's brigade would retreat along this road. Feild would remain for thirty minutes after the rest of the Virginians had passed, then withdraw to Zoan Church.

The 12th plunged into the woods south of the Bullock field. The section of the Norfolk Blues withdrawing from United States Mine Ford appeared on the road running to that ford from Ely's Ford Road. The gunners moved slowly southward near the field's west side. Parham advanced his 41st Virginia to cover the section's retreat. "One of our men dashed up to the guns, the jaded horses then lashed, and was made perhaps some of the best time over rough muddy roads known to the artillerists," wrote Edwards, now a corporal.[26] Enemy skirmishers emerged from the woods after the guns reached Ely's Ford Road. The 41st withdrew.

Ten minutes after the rest of Mahone's brigade had left, a Union general rode out of the same woods. About 100 mounted staffers and bodyguards accompanied him. The cavalcade cantered to the Bullock farm house, 300 yards from the 12th and south of Ely's Ford Road, and turned into the yard. Farther south the bridging detail's remnant emerged from the timber west of the regiment. Seeing the Yankee horsemen north of them, the fugitives hastened eastwardly, reentering the 12th's ranks moments later.

From the Bullock farmyard the enemy general surveyed the 12th through his field glasses. The Virginians lay behind a fence with their guns cocked, anxious to open on the invaders. "How impudent they look as they file into line and sit on their horses, surveying us!" recalled Bernard.[27] Feild would not allow his soldiers to fire, thinking that would bring hordes of the enemy to the general's aid.

A Confederate ambulance appeared, rolling southward on United States Mine Ford Road. "Mister!" a Federal shouted from the trees, "Which way are you going?"[28] The ambulance reversed course, but Unionist skirmishers seized it under the eyes of the 12th's men.

Before 20 minutes had passed, the Northern horsemen in the farmyard retired. Feild sent word to the Mississippi regiment's commander on the

---

26 Leroy S. Edwards to Brother, May 10, 1863.

27 Bernard Notebook, 91.

28 Ibid.

Plank Road that the 12th would fall back in 10 minutes. The courier quickly returned. The Mississippians had already withdrawn. Feild feared the Yanks might flank him on the left. He put his second in command, Jones, in charge of the soldiers in the 12th's left wing, ordering Jones to retreat to the turnpike, form line of battle and await Feild's arrival with the regiment's right wing.

Jones and his men retired. Enemy cavalry burst out of the woods and bore down on Feild's troops. Thirty minutes had not yet expired. Feild doubted his soldiers could cope with the Federal horsemen. He ordered Jones to halt, form line of battle across Ely's Ford Road and await further orders. The cavalrymen rode within 400 yards of Feild's wing, slackened their pace and advanced a skirmish line 150 yards closer. Feild's men brought their muskets down to the aim. The horse soldiers halted and dismounted. Feild gave the order to fire. None of his men's muskets discharged. Their powder had gotten wet. Feild feared his men would lose heart and flee, but none left the line. All began picking the tubes of their guns with pins and re-capping them.

The skirmishers got behind their horses and fired over their backs. The Virginians soon managed a scattering fire, checking the Yanks until the thirty minutes expired. Feild's wing withdrew through the trees to the regiment's left wing. Taking charge of the left wing, Feild ordered Jones to assume command of the right and form another line of battle across the road 200 yards to the rear. Confined to the road by the thick woods, the enemy horsemen took potshots at the Virginians but did not press them. Mahone and his staff awaited the 12th at the plank road. Riding up to Feild, the brigadier extended his hand.

"I am glad to see you, sir," said Mahone. "I thought that you and your whole regiment were captured. I heard the firing and thought it was in your rear."[29]

The 12th hastened to Zoan Church. Now out of the Wilderness, the troops could see the foe following them. "Here we moved on at a lively gate, did not run, but did some fast walking," recalled Phillips, now a second lieutenant.[30] Arriving at Zoan Church at 10 a.m., the men deployed in a pine thicket on the right of Mahone's brigade.

The Confederate line ran along the crests of some hills commanding the roads. Mahone's brigade held the right, on the turnpike. Posey's brigade

---

29 Cameron, "Chancellorsville," *War Talks*, 68.

30 Phillips, "Sixth Corporal," 14.

occupied the center. Wright's brigade held the left on the Plank Road, near Tabernacle Church. The 12th rested. The remainder of the brigade dug rifle pits. Soldiers built a redoubt for artillery on each of the roads.

Two men from the Juniors' right had already made their way back to the 12th. Now half a dozen more appeared. These men had stood sentry away from the road to Ely's Ford. When the enemy overran their company, they skedaddled into the woods. All around them Federals shouted. Sometimes a Yank shot at them. Despairing of escape the Juniors destroyed their letters, rifles and equipment lest they benefit the foe. Finally they struck a path one of the men knew. It led them to the regiment, lowering the morning's loss to thirteen, though all three of the company's officers remained captives.

A sharp skirmish announced the arrival of bluecoats in front of Anderson's division, but the Northerners failed to mount a full-scale attack. Hooker had lost his nerve and would advance no farther. He hunkered down in the Wilderness and hoped Lee would attack him frontally.

The day's remainder passed quietly except for some sharpshooting to the 12th's left. Near noon, a Yank climbed a tree in a farmyard about 100 yards in front of Mahone's brigade. From his perch he wounded two of the men entrenching the guns on the turnpike. It took one of Posey's Mississippians a quarter hour to spot the sniper. Firing at long range, he brought down his prey. Cameron recalled observing through his field glasses "the body falling like that of a wounded squirrel from limb to limb until it struck the ground." Cameron "could almost hear the thud."[31]

Before nightfall, Mahone directed Feild to deploy part of the regiment as skirmishers. Later Mahone ordered the line extended farther right to prevent the Northerners from flanking the position. Feild deployed nearly the entire 12th as skirmishers. The remainder helped dig entrenchments.

"We knew that Hooker's whole army was in our front and that we had only 4,000 men to oppose him, and the balance of Lee's army from 10 to 25 miles away," Feild recalled.[32] Reinforcements came that night, giving Mahone's men a sense of relief. Semmes' Georgia Brigade deployed to the Virginians' right. Wilcox's Alabama Brigade arrived still farther to the right. The isolation of three brigades of Anderson's division, many times outnumbered, ended. Hooker had allowed the initiative to slip away. Lee

31 Cameron, "Chancellorsville," *War Talks*, 51.

32 Ibid., 68.

was gathering his army to attack a force more than twice its size. Part still faced the Federals in Fredericksburg, but most now opposed the Unionists advancing from the west.

Before daybreak on May 1, Feild shifted to the left of his regiment the pickets posted on its right. Semmes' brigade filled the place the skirmishers vacated. At sunrise Feild visited Mahone in his headquarters at the McCarty house, a small building on the turnpike about 100 yards behind the front line. Feild found Mahone washing his face at the well in front of the house. Two hundred yards away, a Confederate general and his staff sat their horses examining the breastworks.

"Who is that officer?" Feild asked.

"Don't you know, sir?" replied Mahone. "Why, that is General Jackson."

Feild looked down the turnpike, filled with Jackson's troops. Returning to the 12th Feild boosted morale by spreading the news of their arrival. During breakfast Mahone's assistant adjutant general rode up, directing Feild to get the 12th under arms and report to the brigadier. Feild moved out with his men in column of fours. Beckoned by Mahone, Feild rode to the turnpike ahead of his regiment. He saw two cannon limbered in the pike with the heads of their horses towards the enemy, which struck him as strange. Mahone's orders surprised Feild even more.

"I wish you to take your regiment with these pieces of artillery down this road," the brigadier said. "You will find a strong picket in the house ahead of you, and on the hill beyond a strong skirmish line. Detach one of your companies to drive in the pickets. Deploy a sufficient number of your companies as skirmishers—if necessary, the whole regiment—and drive in the Yankee skirmishers. I wish you to drive them. Drive them quickly, and until you find the enemy's line of battle. I expect that you and your whole regiment will be captured, but we have a trap set for them, and we will re-capture you."[33] The plan required the 12th to lure the Unionists eastward on the turnpike. Other Confederate forces would move westward on the plank road, then turn north and cut off the Federals. Hooker may have had good reason for hesitating to emerge from the Wilderness.

The advance began at 11 a.m. Mahone's brigade led McLaws' division. The 12th led Mahone's brigade. The remainder of Anderson's division, with Jackson's Corps following, advanced on the left of McLaws' division. Fifteen

33 Ibid., 69.

troopers of the 3rd Virginia Cavalry preceded the 12th and the pair of guns. Where the Southern entrenchments crossed the turnpike, Feild directed the Riflemen to advance ahead of the artillery and drive Federal pickets from near the Alsop house, which occupied one of the ground's many crests. The company's 32 soldiers hastened forward in skirmish order, coming to a small hut on the pike's north side. Behind the hut's broad rock chimney stood an old black woman, gesturing wildly and pointing toward the Alsop house.

"Oh, for God's sake, don't go up there!" she said. "Don't go up there! There are thousands of them up there and they will kill every one of you all."

"Never mind, old lady, we've got a plenty of men just behind us to take care of those Yankees," some of the Riflemen replied as they passed. "Don't be alarmed."[34]

A quarter mile beyond the entrenchments, Banks deployed his first platoon on the turnpike's right and his second on the left. Advancing another quarter mile past several small farmhouses, the Riflemen reached the handful of Confederate cavalry skirmishers. The Southern horsemen confronted dismounted pickets of the 8th Pennsylvania Cavalry behind a brush fence on a crest 300 yards distant.

"Hurry up boys and get a shot at the Yankee cavalry," said the Confederate horsemen's leader.[35] The Riflemen fired. The Keystoners shot back. Banks stood in the road. To his left stood Edwards. On Edwards' left cringed a man white with fear.

"Oh, Captain, Captain, they are shooting down this way," he cried.

"I suppose they are and you will get more yet when you get up in the hill," said Edwards.

"Yes, and they are shooting down this way, too," said Banks.[36]

Feeling sorry for the fellow, Edwards tried to cheer him.

The Riflemen charged up the muddy slope, hindered by the underbrush. Reaching the top they saw the Pennsylvanians among the stunted oaks on another crest 200 yards ahead. A chinquapin patch and some rail and brush fences intervened. Banks' men drove the Keystoners from this position. The Riflemen met the 8th Pennsylvania Cavalry's main body near the Lewis house.

34 Ibid.

35 Todd, "Reminiscences," 93.

36 Edwards to Brother, May 10, 1863.

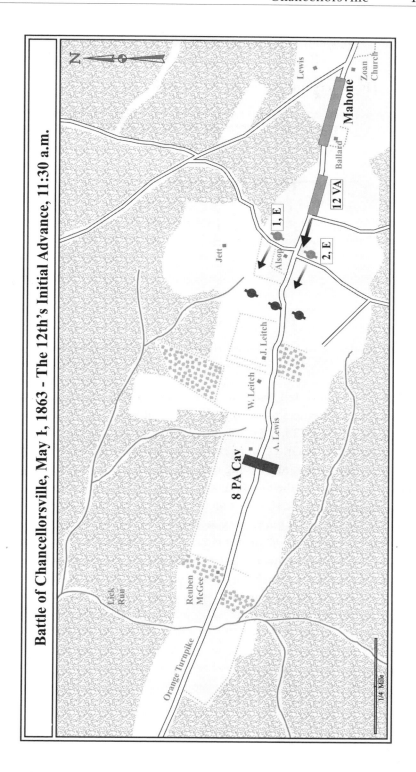

Battle of Chancellorsville, May 1, 1863 – The 12th's Initial Advance, 11:30 a.m.

Lewis

Zoan Church

Mahone

Ballard

12 VA

1, E

2, E

Jett

Alsop

J. Leitch

W. Leitch

A. Lewis

8 PA Cav

Lick Run

Reuben McGee

Orange Turnpike

1/4 Mile

N

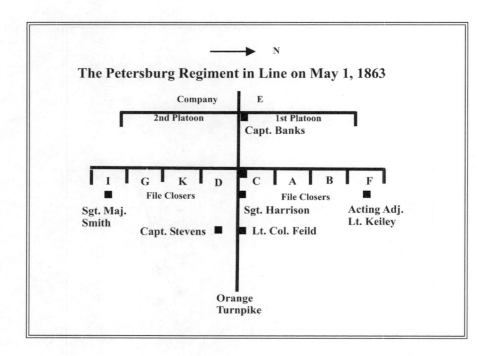

Banks' company fell back to the enemy's former picket line. Banks reported the Northerners too strong for him and asked for reinforcements. Feild deployed the 12th forward on center. The Petersburg City Guard and Petersburg New Grays went right. The Lafayette Guards and Archer Rifles proceeded leftward. Driving his men forward at the double-quick, he extended his line with the Old Grays and Huger Grays on the right and the Richmond Grays and the Herrings on the left. Joining the Riflemen, the line halted and lay down behind the brush fence. The two guns unlimbered and fired over the Virginians' heads for ten minutes, silencing an enemy battery.

Feild's men jumped the brush fence and rushed through the chinquapin. The Pennsylvanian skirmishers withdrew to their regiment on the next crest. The 12th's men came within fifty yards of the brush fence on the chinquapin's other side. They saw some of the Keystoners scattered in the open not fifty yards beyond the fence. Yelling, the Virginians opened fire, which the Pennsylvanians returned. Advancing to the rail and brush fences atop the crest, Feild's troops fired as rapidly as possible, forcing the Keystoners to retire. On the right the Pennsylvanians galloped for their lives out of a wood. The Virginians dropped some of the horsemen.

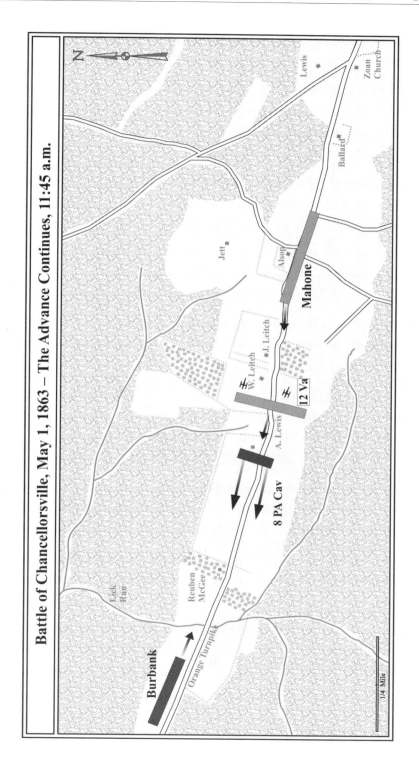

Battle of Chancellorsville, May 1, 1863 – The Advance Continues, 11:45 a.m.

The regiment chased the routed Keystoners from crest to crest for about half a mile. Hurrying over a ridge higher than the rest, the winded Virginians faced a Yankee line of battle 150 yards ahead in the Reuben McGee farm's open field. These Northerners belonged to Burbank's brigade of Sykes' division—Regulars. Spaced five yards apart, the 12th's soldiers confronted a solid column in double ranks the length of their line. The Regulars faced left, double-quicking that way to get on the regiment's right flank. Some of the 12th's soldiers opened fire, wounding several Regulars, causing others to halt and provoking still others to return the fire. The foe dressed line and advanced firing. The Virginians retreated.

Banks fell near the 12th's right with a bullet through his body and another in his leg.[37] The City Guard's Pvt. George Whitfield Ivey tried to get Banks back on his feet.

"Save yourself," said Banks. "I'm badly hurt."[38]

Regulars charged out of the woods skirting the farm. Ivey made for a log hut. With some other Virginians he took cover behind its chimney. They blazed away at the Regulars, who had them surrounded.

"Surrender, you damned rebel!" shouted a big Regular as Ivey prepared to fire for the third time.

The Federal had his finger on the trigger and his bayonet at Ivey's breast.

"Do you intend to shoot a man after he surrenders?" said Ivey, forgetting the musket in his hands.

"You have not surrendered!" came the reply.[39]

A Northern officer stepped up and disarmed Ivey. About 20 of his comrades surrendered with him.

The Virginians reeled backward from crest to crest, turning at every fence to fire on the advancing Regulars. "It was a tight time," Bernard recorded. "Heated and fatigued, we could scarcely get along, and many gave up from sheer exhaustion and were captured."[40]

East of the Leitch houses, the 12th found the rest of its brigade in line of battle, supported by artillery. The line exchanged volleys with the Regulars.

---

37 Banks died of his body wound in September 1871. Cameron, "Chancellorsville," *War Talks*, 52n; Henderson, *12VI*, 108. Phillips visited Banks in Petersburg September 1, 1864. James Eldred Phillips Diary, September 1, 1864, James Eldred Phillips Papers, VHS.

38 Cameron, "Chancellorsville," *War Talks*, 75n.

39 Ibid.

40 Ibid., 70n.

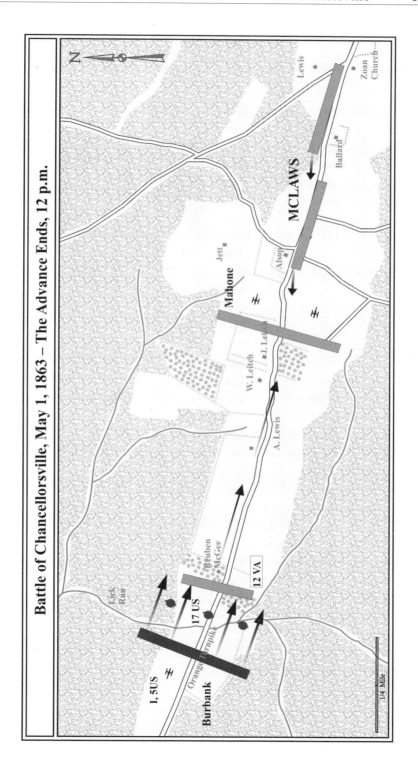

Battle of Chancellorsville, May 1, 1863 – The Advance Ends, 12 p.m.

George Whitfield Ivey. *Ed Miller, "George Whitfield Ivey," findagrave.com, May 25, 2017*

An artillery duel began. The regiment rallied in the rear, mustering about 100 of the 400 it took into action.[41] Mahone's brigade stood firm against an enemy disordered by pursuing the 12th. The Regulars withdrew to the Lewis house, two miles east of Chancellorsville on the turnpike. Mahone let Feild's men rest several hours. Towards evening they rejoined the brigade. Axes resounded to the west as the Federals strengthened their works. That night the regiment's soldiers slept on their arms in line of battle.

Before dawn on May 2, Lee and Jackson conferred and made critical decisions. Stonewall and his corps would march around the enemy army to enfilade its extreme right. Wilcox's brigade would hurry back to Banks' Ford to guard against a Yankee crossing between the Confederates near Chancellorsville and the reinforced division under Maj. Gen. Jubal Anderson Early, dug in around Fredericksburg confronting VI Corps. Lee would face Hooker with only seven brigades, whose troops outnumbered Lee's force around eight to one.

Lee's men sidled left, adjusting for Jackson's departure. At 10 a.m., Mahone's brigade moved by the left flank about a quarter mile to the turnpike's south side. McLaws rode up and asked Feild his name and regiment. Feild identified himself and his unit. McLaws directed him to halt his command and support a battalion of artillery about fifty yards ahead. Feild complied but informed Mahone. The brigadier ordered Feild to move the 12th to the right so that the entire brigade could fit into the position. Mahone did not think that one regiment could adequately support twenty pieces of artillery.

The 12th lay prone on the reverse slope of a hill, fifty yards behind the 1st Richmond Howitzers, unlimbered on the crest. An enemy battery dashed down the turnpike from Chancellorsville to occupy a hill north of the road.

41 Ibid.

The Howitzers opened on the battery, which unlimbered and replied. The Southern artillerists exerted themselves to the utmost. "It did one good, in spite of the great danger we were in, to see how beautifully the men at the pieces worked," recollected Bernard.[42] After 15 minutes the Howitzers silenced the Federal battery. The Southerners cheered. The regiment suffered five casualties from the artillery duel, including First Lt. Nathaniel Macon Martin. He had succeeded Banks in command of the Riflemen. A pellet from a spherical case shot hit Martin in the foot, leaving Second Lt. Anthony M. Keiley in charge of the company. A lawyer in civilian life, Keiley had been serving as the 12th's acting adjutant.

That afternoon the regiment sidled left still farther, deploying on the Plank Road opposite Chancellorsville. Lee established his headquarters behind the 12th. The men could see anxiety on his face and on Mahone's. Their division's left became heavily committed. The center and right remained intermittently engaged.

During a lull Lee told Mahone to feel the enemy "pretty heavily."[43] The 12th stayed in reserve. The brigade's other regiments advanced in skirmish order. The Yankees would not raise their heads above the breastworks to shoot but only held their muskets over with one hand and banged away. The Virginians pushed all the way to the enemy works. A captain of the 6th snatched a Unionist color. The firing reached its crescendo. A body of men double-quicked down the Confederate line from the right. The 12th's soldiers recognized the Florida Brigade. They greeted the Floridians with, "Hello turkey!" The Floridians hallooed in reply, "Hello Mahone!"[44] The Floridians hastened to the division's left and suffered heavy losses.

Before sundown the 12th's men heard artillery far to their front and left. "Thank God!" said Mahone. "There are Jackson's guns."[45]

Lee's gamble paid off. Jackson routed XI Corps on the Federal right. Musketry and artillery fire resounded from that direction until after dark. The 12th's men slept on their arms in line of battle again that night. About midnight a tremendous cannonade began in the regiment's front.

---

42 Bernard Notebook, 95.

43 Cameron, "Chancellorsville," *War Talks*, 72.

44 Ibid.

45 Ibid., 73.

May 3 dawned overcast. The batteries on the 12th's right and in its rear opened. The reply from the Federal artillery must have reminded some soldiers of Frayser's Farm. The "villainous projectiles" howled about their ears "like so many mad demons shrieking out death-knell and doom," Keiley wrote.[46]

The Confederates mounted a concentric assault on the Unionist breastworks around Chancellorsville. With its right on the Plank Road, Mahone's brigade advanced under the Northern batteries' fire. The 12th thrashed through the woods down a gentle slope for a quarter mile. Cheers arose from the converging Secessionist lines. At 10 a.m., the regiment's soldiers saw the enemy wavering. A white flag rose above the foe's works.

The 12th's men rushed through the abatis in front of the fortifications. "When we got inside of the works and saw their strength, we congratulated ourselves that we did not have to charge them," Todd recalled.[47] Within the smoking, blackened fortifications, the soldiers observed the carnage wrought by the Confederate artillery's crossfire. The enemy "were piled on each other in every sort of shape," Phillips remembered. "Some of them was blown to pieces, some heads off from the explosions of caissons and limber chests . . ."[48] Expecting to take many prisoners, the Virginians found only a few. The balance of the Yankees had retreated toward United States Mine Ford.

The regiment formed column and stood in the Plank Road. The men bantered with passing captives. An enemy cannon in the woods to the north fired. Its shell whizzed over the heads of the regiment's soldiers, outraging them. This seemed an act of treachery. Several Southern artillery sections in front of the Chancellor house returned fire, silencing the Federals and satisfying the 12th's men. Ragged and hungry, they eyed the enormous quantities of clothing and food abandoned by Hooker's forces.

"Fall in!" came the order before the Virginians could gather the spoils.

The column, consisting of Mahone's brigade and the four brigades of McLaws' division, all under McLaws, headed toward Fredericksburg on the Plank Road. The Virginians marched in the column's van. As the brigade's right regiment, the 12th led the way. Feild rode at the head of his regiment. Mahone rode ahead of Feild. The troops heard gunfire ahead. Lee rode up to confer with Mahone. The men gave a yell. Trudging back over ground

---

46 Ibid., 63.

47 Todd, "Reminiscences," 97.

48 Phillips, "Sixth Corporal," 15.

they had needed three days to win, they remained in high spirits. "You could scarcely hear anything that was going on," Feild recalled. "Every man was giving his experience during the fight to his neighbor, and evidently thinking that the battle was over and won."[49]

Feild would have reached the same conclusion, but he noticed Mahone's look of deep concern. Lee had informed Mahone that VI Corps had broken through Confederate lines at Fredericksburg and was advancing westward. Early was falling back southeastward along Telegraph Road. Wilcox's brigade was occupying a wooded ridge at Salem Church on the plank road in VI Corps' path. Lee, having defeated the Yankees to his left, now had to halt their onslaught against his right.

A horseman galloping from Fredericksburg pulled up by Mahone.

"General Early says come forward as rapidly as you can," the horseman said. "The enemy are advancing."

Mahone turned in his saddle to Feild, who had spurred his horse forward to hear the message.

"Have your men step out," said Mahone.

Feild reined up until the 12th's van overtook him.

"Step out!" he shouted.

His men became "so quiet you might almost have heard a pin drop," Feild recalled. "Well did they know that this meant another fight and that very quickly."[50]

Near Salem Church Mahone's brigade deployed too hastily to countermarch, filing to the left and forming line behind a ditch bank topped with bushes. In front of the ditch ran a rail fence. A skirt of woods stood in front of the fence. The Virginians had entered this good position the wrong way. Having filed to the left without countermarching, they would have to face rearward to maneuver.[51]

Skirmishing began in less than five minutes. Mahone's brigade confronted Brooks' division of VI Corps. Bullets whizzed through the bushes atop the ditch banks, showering the Southerners with clippings. Mahone ordered

---

49 Cameron, "Chancellorsville," *War Talks*, 73.

50 Ibid., 73-74.

51 A regiment with its right in front had to countermarch and put its left in front to file off to the left and retain the capacity to advance while facing the enemy. Bernard, "Notebook," 97; James Eldred Phillips to William H. Stewart, 190_, James Eldred Phillips Papers, Private Collection of Elise Phillips Atkins, Arlington Heights, Illinois.

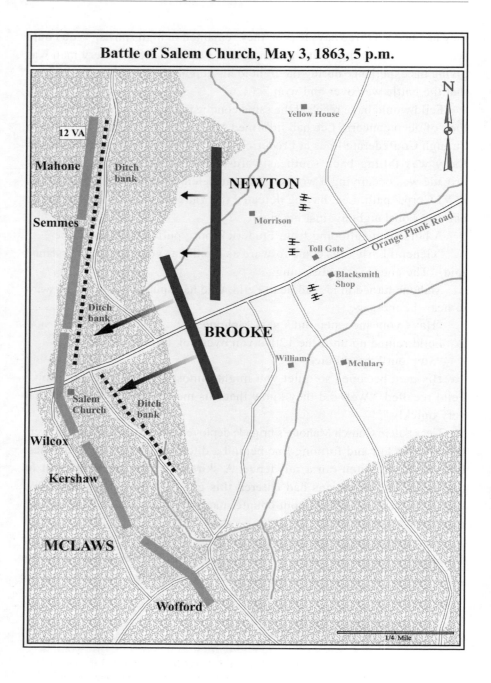

Battle of Salem Church, May 3, 1863, 5 p.m.

his troops farther left to make room for Semmes' brigade. Despite their awkward formation, the Virginians had no difficulty shifting laterally. They now faced Newton's division. The regiment formed the brigade's left. The main Federal attack came to the Virginians' right and met with repulse. The 12th suffered a handful of casualties from stray bullets and shells. The invaders retired half a mile.

On the following day Lee maneuvered to annihilate VI Corps. McLaws and Early positioned their infantry brigades and artillery batteries for a concentric attack. Mahone's brigade shifted still farther left. Early attacked, but McLaws did not. The Confederates failed to destroy the foe. The regiment ended the day in a rifle trench overlooking Banks' Ford. That night the sound of troops crossing came from the bridges at the ford. Shells fired at the bridges by the Southern artillery whizzed over the heads of the 12th's pickets.

On the morning of May 5, the Secessionists near Salem Church found the enemy gone. They hastily buried the dead, laying them in the roadside ditches and covering them with dirt. Rain began falling hard. Early's troops reoccupied their former trenches overlooking Fredericksburg. McLaws' and Anderson's divisions headed for Chancellorsville except for a brigade left to guard Banks' Ford. The soldiers traipsed along the plank road confronted by a grisly sight. The downpour unearthed some of the corpses interred that morning. They floated down the roadside ditches towards Fredericksburg.

The column halted at dark. Mahone ordered Feild to take the 12th and march back to guard against Federal cavalry reportedly in the area. "I told Gen. Mahone that I had done all that human nature could stand—that I had been on the outpost for three nights and was compelled to sleep, and would not be responsible if he sent me on the duty," Feild recalled.[52]

The brigadier responded sympathetically. He directed Feild to move down the road, put the regiment in position to resist an attack, detach a company, send it 200 yards farther down the road and then bed down for the night. Except for the men of the unlucky company on outpost duty, the 12th's soldiers went to sleep on the soggy ground, slumbering soundly until the rising water woke them.

Next day Mahone's brigade rejoined Anderson's division, which advanced to the junction of Ely's Ford Road and United States Mine Ford Road. Lee,

---

52 Cameron, "Chancellorsville," *War Talks*, 74.

suffering from the overconfidence that would lead to disaster in less than two months, had decided to attack Hooker in the fortifications the bluecoats had been building near the Rapidan for the past two days.

The Confederates formed battle lines, then advanced. They could see that the Unionists had built breastworks of oak. "On top of this wood they put on a heavy log with a space between by propping it up to give room to shoot through," Phillips recalled.[53] The men figured that taking these works would cost many lives. "Everybody looked very solemn and had nothing to say but continued to move forwards," Phillips remembered.[54]

Hooker did not get the chance to let Lee snatch defeat from the jaws of victory. The troops, to their surprise and relief, found the Federal fortifications abandoned. From the inside they seemed even stronger. "We could never have taken them by assault," Whitehorne wrote of "the six or eight lines of breastworks not over 75 yard from each other."[55]

The men joked.

"Damn them," a soldier said. "They knew we was coming after them. They had better gotten out when they did or they would have caught hell."[56]

The campaign of Chancellorsville had ended. The 12th had stood in the forefront of battle. The regiment lost five killed, 38 wounded and 55 missing or captured for a total of 98.[57] The wounded included Shepard, whose valor gave rise to the reports that circulated in Southern newspapers after the war of an unnamed "Connecticut school teacher in the 12th Virginia Infantry" deemed "one of the best soldiers we ever saw" and "never known to shirk a fight."[58] Mahone commended the regiment "for its rigid and efficient resistance of the superior force of the enemy while covering the formation of

---

53 Phillips, "Sixth Corporal, 15.

54 Ibid.

55 James E. Whitehorne to Sister, May 11, 1863.

56 Phillips, "Sixth Corporal," 17.

57 Richmond *Whig*, May 12, 1863; Cameron, "Chancellorsville," *War Talks*, 75-76; Henderson, *12VI*, 106-167.

58 The New Orleans *Crescent*, November 20, 1866, p. 2, col. 2, The Daily *Phoenix* (Columbia, S.C.), December 8, 1866, p. 2, col. 3, and the Keowee *Courier* (Pickens, S. C.), December 15, p. 2, col. 3, 1866, quoting The Richmond *Times*, n.d. After convalescing, Shepard became a major in the Commissary Department. Henderson, *12VI*, 155.

our line of battle on the turnpike, Friday, May 1."[59] The soldiers considered the campaign one of their finest feats of arms.

Not everyone shared their opinion. Declaring that Mahone's soldiers "never stood a charge in their lives" and disgusted with the Virginians' rout at Crampton's Gap, Semmes had objected to having his troops fight near Mahone's men.[60]

59 *OR* 25, 1:863.

60 Waters and Edmonds, *A Small but Spartan Band*, 144, citing McLaws to McBride, July 3, 1895. Waters and Edmonds say Semmes *refused* to have his troops fight near Mahone's brigade but Semmes' and Mahone's brigades fought adjacent to one another at Chancellorsville and Salem Church.

CHAPTER 10

Gettysburg

On May 7, the 12th camped anew two miles south of Salem Church. Eight days of marching and fighting had used up the men, who got a hard-earned rest. "My clothes, which were not very sound at the commencement of the engagement, were, in our charges, through woods, bushes and briars, sadly torn in divers pieces," Todd remembered. "I had the various rents fastened up with wooden pegs."[1] Smallpox raged behind Confederate lines. Soldiers previously not inoculated for the disease received vaccinations. Elections took place. Petersburg elected Keiley to Virginia's House of Delegates. Not until December 1 would he resign his commission to serve in the legislature.

One evening at dress parade, Feild censured six soldiers for exhibiting cowardice during the Chancellorsville Campaign. After having their names read out, he ordered them to advance and lay down their arms. He declined to court martial them, preferring to appeal to their "better natures" and such self-respect as remained to them.

"It is within your power to retrieve your reputation by subsequent good conduct," Feild said. "Resume your arms, and by your gallantry in the future efface all recollections of this painful scene."[2]

His address proved effective. "I never heard of any of these fellows behaving badly again," recalled Todd.[3]

1 Todd, "Reminiscences," 98.

2 Ibid., 109.

3 Ibid.

Lee's army again reequipped itself at the expense of a defeated foe. His soldiers found abundant plunder in the enemy works at Chancellorsville. "Our Boys got as many clothes, blankets, small tents, oil cloths, and every thing else they could lug along with them," wrote Sale. "Almost every man in the Brigade has at least two nice flannel shirts and plenty of drawers which they took from their knapsacks besides other articles of clothing."[4] The troops obtained other useful items such as stationery, hard tack, canned goods, muskets, ammunition and artillery. The 12th's men could scarcely believe their good fortune. When they came across 45 premium beeves, slaughtered, dressed and ready to cut up, some feared the Federals had poisoned the meat.

The soldiers made the most of these spoils. The miserable Southern supply system would not permit Lee to subsist his army in northern Virginia much longer. Petersburg and its adjacent counties did their best to supplement the 12th's short rations. Their commissioners visited the army monthly and brought their men "car loads of provisions &c," wrote Whitehorne, who remained unhappy with Greensville's commissioner. "I haven't had enough to eat since the battle," he complained on May 13.[5] Six days had elapsed since his company's last mouthful of meal. The Greensville men resorted to other measures to fill their bellies. Scott sent his slave Nepperson home to Greensville County to bring back something good to eat. Nepperson returned with ham, chicken, biscuits and snaps. "Lucullus sitting in his garden at Rome, or exhibating in his villas at Rusculum and Neapolis, never felt as happy and contented as we, while eating the good things from home," recalled Whitehorne, who tented and messed with Scott.[6]

The soldiers suffered from other privations. "Write me how the children look and don't let them forget me," scribbled Manson, one of the regiment's married men. "I can hardly secure the Baby's features & I know I could never tell that she was my child."[7] He had not visited his home in seven months.

On May 10, Jackson succumbed to the wounds he received helping win at Chancellorsville. "His death produced a deep feeling in the Army but it is the universal conviction that the same God who gave us him can

4 John F. Sale to Aunt, May 10, 1863.

5 James E. Whitehorne to Sister, May 14, 1863.

6 Elmore, *Diary of J. E. Whitehorne*, June 10, 1863, 8.

7 Joseph R. Manson to Wife, May 17, 1863.

also make us others," Sale wrote.[8] The Southerners had suffered more than 13,000 casualties during the campaign, a far higher percentage of those engaged than the 17,000 the Yankees lost. Luckily for the Confederates, prisoner exchanges began soon after the campaign's end.

Four days later Lee traveled to Richmond to confer with Davis and his cabinet. The high command groped for a response to the enemy's progress in Mississippi. Grant, now a major general, had crossed the Mississippi River below Vicksburg. His army was isolating the city. The Secessionist command of Lt. Gen. John C. Pemberton, charged with Vicksburg's defense, would have to abandon the city or endure a siege. Lee thought marching his army into Pennsylvania would force the Federals to withdraw troops from Vicksburg. The conference considered sending soldiers from his army to Mississippi but let Lee have his way, adjourning on May 18. By that time Grant had driven most of Pemberton's army into Vicksburg and was preparing to lay siege to the city.

Lee reorganized his army, transforming its two infantry corps of four divisions each into three corps of three divisions each. Longstreet remained in command of the First Corps. Major General Richard S. Ewell became the Second Corps' commander. Lee put Maj. Gen. Ambrose Powell Hill in charge of the newly constituted Third Corps, which consisted of a division each from both previously established corps as well as a newly organized division. Anderson's division drew the transfer from the First Corps into the Third. The men regretted leaving Longstreet but hoped they would soon take pride in belonging to the Third Corps under their fellow Virginian, Hill.

By June 2, the 12th had shifted to within two miles of Fredericksburg. Good health and good morale prevailed. The troops were enjoying themselves eating, sleeping, telling jokes and smoking their pipes. Rumors of an imminent operation put Mahone's brigade in what Whitehorne called "a state of nervous expectancy."[9] Officers bustled about headquarters conversing in low tones. Couriers came and went. A general hush settled over the camp. At 4 p.m. that day, the long roll beat. The 12th's men struck their tents and prepared to march, learning they would relieve Barksdale's brigade of McLaws' division in Fredericksburg.

8 John F. Sale to Aunt, June 13, 1863.

9 Elmore, *Diary of J. E. Whitehorne*, June 1, 1863, 2.

The 12th's hike began at 7 p.m. The men slogged for two hot, dusty hours and arrived in the desolate city after sunset. The officers of each company detailed a few men for picket duty. The 12th's remaining members quartered in the vacant houses along the main street. "I took a walk over this almost deserted place & examined the many residences torn and riddled with balls & bullets," noted Captain Waddell. "Fredericksburg has indeed suffered terribly."[10] Enemy pickets and a few Yankee camps stood in view on the Rappahannock's other side. Their troops strolled about on the opposite hill.

Next day the Riflemen went on provost guard duty at division headquarters along with a company from the 6th Virginia. The Riflemen disliked this assignment, despite the hospitality of the few remaining citizens of Fredericksburg. "They would share their last crust with a soldier," recalled Todd.[11] The Riflemen preferred the assignment to picketing. They had more liberty when off duty.

The 12th's men joined the rest of the South in anxiety over Vicksburg, besieged by Grant. Word of the repulse of the initial Federal assault on the city cheered the regiment. The news soon became gloomy. "At last accounts Vicksburg was barely holding out, but Johns[t]on had not fallen upon the enemy," Bernard observed. "If we lose Vicksburg, our cause will have received a most damaging blow, equal to, if not greater than any it has yet received."[12]

Lee started shifting his infantry northward, beginning with McLaws' division. The plan called for Hill's Corps to remain at Fredericksburg. The rest of Lee's army would concentrate near Culpeper Court House.

The Federals grew active across the Rappahannock on June 4 but not enough to prevent Lee from dispatching a division of Ewell's Corps to Culpeper Court House.

At 10 a.m. the following day, after the rest of Ewell's Corps had departed for Culpeper Court House, Mahone's brigade got under arms and entered the rifle pits along the river. In full view of the Virginians, the invaders brought their pontoon trains down to the river near Deep Run, below Fredericksburg. Rumors of Lee's departure from Fredericksburg inspired Hooker to order VI Corps to reconnoiter-in-force. At 5 p.m., the enemy's guns near the run began

10 Charles E. Waddell Diary, June 2, 1863.

11 Todd, "Reminiscences," 110.

12 Bernard Diary, June 3, 1863. General Johnston was charged with Vicksburg's relief.

a cannonade. An hour into the bombardment, the company cooks brought hot food to the men on the firing line. The commissary wagon halted 100 yards behind the line. The cooks negotiated the remaining distance on foot.

"Now these Cooks were once brave men," recalled Whitehorne, "but having been detailed as cooks, consequently not accustomed to the whistling of bullets, their courage was nothing to boast of."

The line soldiers teased the cooks.

"They are going to open on us," some wags shouted.

"Boys, look out, there she comes," called others.

The cooks panicked. "They lost all control of themselves and pitched our rations out on the ground and 'got up and got' amid the taunts and jeers of the men," remembered Whitehorne.[13]

Afterward, the barrage abruptly ceased. The 12th's men heard skirmishing. The Northerners had crossed the river again. The prospect of fighting excited the regiment's soldiers. They hoped for a repeat of December's battle. The few civilians still in Fredericksburg reacted phlegmatically. At 8 p.m., the Virginians left the rifle pits and withdrew to the hills above the city, deploying behind the stone wall at the foot of Marye's Heights. The provost guard got under arms and plodded to the rifle pits near Fredericksburg's lower end. Hill expected the Yankees would attempt to throw another pontoon bridge across there, but the rest of the night went quietly. Lee directed Ewell to halt his march toward Culpeper Court House.

June 6 found the Federals entrenched near the riverbank. They showed no inclination to leave the earthworks' shelter, disappointing the Confederates' hopes. VI Corps' reconnaissance had satisfied Hooker that Lee's entire army remained at Fredericksburg. To Lee, the Yankee crossing looked like a feint. He instructed Ewell to resume his march to Culpeper Court House. An enemy battery on Bray's Hill opposite Fredericksburg fired at intervals of fifteen minutes at the heights occupied by Mahone's brigade but failed to draw a reply from the Secessionist artillery. Northern skirmishers approached to within 400 yards of the provost guard's rifle pits, but the night again passed quietly.

On the morning of June 11, news arrived of a fight at Brandy Station two days earlier. Hooker had sent his cavalry in an unsuccessful attempt to break up the concentration of Confederate horsemen east of Culpeper

---

13 Elmore, *Diary of J. E. Whitehorne*, June 6, 1863, 4-5.

Court House. That night the Riflemen traded places with the 6th Virginia's company, then shifted higher up the river.

Vicksburg still had the attention of the 12th's men. "Every day we expect to hear that Johnston with the large force he is said to be collecting for the purpose has fallen upon Grant's rear," Bernard noted on June 12.[14] More news of the northward progress of Lee's army also came. Ewell's Corps was crossing the Blue Ridge into the Shenandoah and heading north, followed by Longstreet's Corps. Few of the regiment's soldiers, still smarting from the Maryland campaign, felt going north could result in any good. "Our men hope that we will be spared a participation in any movement soon to come off by being left here as I am quite sure we will be if the enemy keep any considerable force opposite us," Bernard observed.[15] Many believed their army could not fight as well in Yankee land as on Southern soil.

At 6 p.m. on June 13, the Union batteries on Bray's Hill exchanged a few shots with their Confederate counterparts. Rain put an end to the firing. That night the Southerners in Fredericksburg heard and saw across the river and down by the pontoon bridge what Bernard recorded as "trains moving all night, wagons loading and unloading, hammering as if boxing or unboxing something, and the whole sky illuminated by large fires, one of which seemed to us on post to be about the depot."[16]

Morning revealed that the invaders had retired across the Rappahannock. Finally aware of Lee's move north, Hooker wanted to attack Richmond but received orders from Lincoln to stay between Lee's army and Washington. The last Federals opposite Fredericksburg were hotfooting it up toward Manassas.

At 2 p.m., Mahone's brigade packed up and prepared to follow the rest of Lee's army north. Less than an hour later the Virginians headed westward from Marye's Heights on Orange Plank Road with the remainder of Anderson's division. The regiment had present 31 officers and 403 men.[17]

---

14 Bernard Diary, June 12, 1863.

15 Ibid., June 5, 1863.

16 Ibid., June 14, 1863.

17 George S. Bernard, "The Gettysburg Campaign, The Narrative of a Private Soldier in the Confederate Army, Taken From His Diary and Note Book: An Address Delivered by Geo. S. Bernard Before R. E. Lee Camp No. 1, of Confederate Veterans of Richmond, VA, on the Evening of Friday, November 3, 1893," Petersburg *Enterprise*, March 3–April 7, 1894, Bernard Notebook, 111.

All the 12th's soldiers captured during the Chancellorsville campaign had returned except for a few on sick leave in Petersburg. The prisoners had received even better treatment than those taken the previous year.

The Riflemen remained in the rifle pits in Fredericksburg without receiving orders to join the rest of the 12th on the heights until after it had departed. Leaving the pits one by one and traveling by different streets, the Riflemen reassembled on the heights, catching up with the 12th three miles out of Fredericksburg. Mahone's brigade trekked past Salem Church, then across part of the Chancellorsville battleground. "The weather today is extremely warm, the road dry and dusty and marching very disagreeable," observed Whitehorne. "The men are in fine spirits, joking each other, smoking their pipes and are having lots of fun."[18] The Virginians halted at sunset two miles from Chancellorsville.

On June 15, the troops downed hasty breakfasts and started marching before sunrise, heading across the remainder of the battlefield. The graves remained plainly marked. The stench of decomposing flesh hung in the air. The day grew oppressively hot. The men suffered greatly from fatigue, heat, dust and thirst. Cases of sunstroke appeared. Men began straggling. West of Chancellorsville, the column turned toward Culpeper Court House, crossing the Rapidan at Germanna Ford on a hastily constructed footbridge. The soldiers encamped before sunset in a clover field 10 miles southeast of Culpeper Court House.

Their journey resumed at 7 a.m. They had an easy stroll through Stevensburg. The men closed up and tried to look presentable as they passed the stores and churches along the principal street of Culpeper Court House. The regimental band played "The Bonnie Blue Flag." The column halted at 2 p.m. beyond this town. News of Ewell's victory at Winchester on June 14 arrived.

On June 17, Mahone's troops marched at 10 a.m. with three days' rations in their haversacks, covering the first few miles rapidly. Straggling began early in the scorching heat. A repeat of the Maryland campaign seemed underway. Laggards lined the roadsides, many suffering from heat exhaustion, some from sunstroke. At the brigade's first rest halt, it amounted to a skeleton of what had left camp that morning. Anderson's division forded Hazel River after noon, then encamped in a chestnut grove with a view of

18 Elmore, *Diary of J. E. Whitehorne*, June 14, 1863, 9.

the Blue Ridge. "The men must be drinking in the beauties of the scene if one can judge by their hilarity," Whitehorne noted.[19] The hot weather made sleeping difficult. Their campsite proved impractical. Chestnut wood made poor fuel for cooking fires.

The next day's walk occurred in the same heat, but Anderson and his men took measures that reduced sunstroke and straggling. Anderson called more halts. His soldiers threw away everything unnecessary. Phillips recalled that "the country people flocked around with horses and picked up blankets and threw them on the horses back one by one until the horses grew in size until they looked like elephants."[20] After eight miles the division stopped for three and a half hours. The journey resumed in the afternoon. A thunderstorm overtook the soldiers at Gaines' Cross Roads. Those who had kept their oil cloths that morning did not get very wet.

The troops encamped at sunset in another chestnut grove on a hillside half a mile west of the hamlet of Flint Hill. News arrived that Johnston's relief force had Grant pinned against Vicksburg. The rumor received little credence, as did another that Ewell had invested Harpers Ferry. For some of the 12th's men the slope's pitch alone killed sleep. Rain made it a rough night for others. After the downpour ceased, the weather turned cold. "When I woke up I was almost frozen," Whitehorne recorded.[21]

The tramp of June 19 began soon after sunrise on a cloudy morning. The 12th crossed the Blue Ridge at Chester Gap. The mountain country's luxuriance impressed the soldiers. "How it contrasted with the worn out and devastated country to which we had been so long accustomed!" Bernard remembered.[22] The regiment halted at 1:30 p.m. on a high hill overlooking Front Royal. Resting in bright sunshine, the men watched a thunderstorm below them. After two and a half hours, the hike resumed. Winchester Turnpike took the column through Front Royal, which Bernard found "'sorry' looking."[23] The regimental band played and the soldiers cheered as the village's ladies waved their handkerchiefs.

19   Ibid., June 17, 1863, 12.

20   Phillips, "Sixth Corporal," 18.

21   Elmore, *Diary of J. E. Whitehorne*, June 14, 1863, 9.

22   Bernard, "The Gettysburg Campaign," Bernard Notebook, 110.

23   Ibid.

At sunset the 12th reached Shenandoah River's South Fork. To ford it the troops removed their shoes, socks, pants and drawers. On the opposite bank they began putting back on these items, but word reached them that the Shenandoah's North Fork lay only a short distance ahead. They decided to save themselves the trouble of dressing and undressing again. Falling in with their shoes, socks, pants and drawers in their arms, they headed for the North Fork, passing a white two-story mansion. From this house five or six young ladies ran down to greet the soldiers. The ladies thought for an instant that the men were wearing white pants. A closer look revealed the truth. "The explosion of a shell in their midst would not have produced a more sudden scampering from their place of observation," Bernard recalled.[24]

Night came and rain began shortly before the 12th reached the North Fork. Torrents fell as the regiment crossed. Another brigade had preceded the 12th's men, making the steep northern bank slippery. When the troops tried to climb it, they needed one another's assistance. In the rain and darkness, formations dissolved. Finally reaching firm ground, the soldiers found themselves "in a big Crowd, a perfect mob, no Company, no regiment, no brigade, every man for himself," wrote Whitehorne.[25]

The first sergeants hollered themselves hoarse reassembling their companies. The regiment slogged up the road several hundred yards. There the 12th waited while the rest of its brigade crossed. The rain ceased. The stars began to twinkle. The men remained muddy, soaking wet and very mad, with one exception—the Huger Grays' Pvt. James A. Taylor.[26] The regiment knew him as "Horse Taylor" for his ability to carry "as many coffee pots, frying pans, tin cups, hatchets, blankets, &c. as a horse can pull," observed Whitehorne, who pronounced Taylor's knapsack "the largest in the army."[27] Taylor never got angry. Now in a particularly good humor, he joked and laughed at his comrades in their misery. He sang, jumped up, clapped his feet together and shouted, "Roll on sweet moments, roll on!"[28] Another Gray asked Scott to have Taylor taken out and hanged.

24 Ibid.

25 Elmore, *Diary of J. E. Whitehorne*, June 19, 1863, 15.

26 Henderson, *12VI*, 160.

27 Elmore, *Diary of J. E. Whitehorne*, June 19, 1863, 16.

28 Ibid.

After an hour the column marched again. At 11 p.m. the 12th's soldiers filed off Winchester Turnpike a mile beyond the North Fork, encamping in an old wheat field, "nothing but red clay, old sticks, stuff," Phillips remembered. "When you stooped down you would pull up 8 or 10 lbs. of mud."[29] Phillips used a big rock as a bed. Those who spread their rubber blankets atop pairs of fence rails placed on the earth included Todd and Whitehorne. The men who tried to sleep in the mud did not always succeed. Just as Bernard and his chum had fallen asleep, the water from the soft wet ground soaked through their underlying oil cloth and blanket. Penetrating the thick sleeves of Bernard's woolen shirt and coat and reaching his skin, the water reminded him of the "uncanny condition of things."[30] He and his chum immediately arose. They found it drizzling. Some of the men had made unauthorized fires from the rails of a neighboring fence. The two repaired to one of these blazes and spent the rest of the night alternatively drying and warming one side of their bodies while the other got a fresh wetting.

When the 12th halted, its soldiers had not stacked arms. Each man fixed his bayonet and stuck his musket in the mud up to the muzzle to keep the action clean. The slightest touch would topple a musket. Like many other soldiers trying to move around in the dark, Whitehorne knocked a musket over. It fell and hurt a member of his company. The stricken man jumped up and wanted to fight. Exhausting his vocabulary of invective, he offered 50 dollars to find out who had injured him. The darkness protected Whitehorne. He kept quiet and went to sleep.

Anderson's division received a much-needed respite on June 20. The march did not resume until the afternoon of this cool, pleasant day. Until then, noted Whitehorne, the 12th's men contemplated some examples of Federal occupation, "here a silent chimney, yonder a fine brick house, standing alone, every out house burned, fences gone, everything going to ruin."[31] At 2 p.m., the soldiers got back on Winchester Turnpike, trudging through a severe rain until they turned off on to Berryville Turnpike. Passing through an unsullied area with many attractive residences, the regiment stopped at sunset a mile north of the village of White Post.

29 Phillips, "Sixth Corporal," 19.

30 Bernard, "The Gettysburg Campaign," Bernard Notebook, 110.

31 Elmore, *Diary of J. E. Whitehorne*, June 20, 1863, 17.

Despite the intense heat and pelting rain of the journey north's first week, the troops remained well clad, well shod and very confident. They did not want for food, the absence of which had caused such distress during the Maryland campaign. The countryside's people frequently dispensed ice water and milk to the passing soldiers. The regiment lost only 38 men in a week of marching, "nothing like so great as . . . in the famous campaign of last year," Bernard observed.[32]

In the morning the 12th's 31 officers and 365 men received a day's ration of corn bread.[33] The Virginians resumed their journey at 8:30 a.m. Stone fences lined the macadamized turnpike. The troops found this countryside beautiful. "I think I had rather live in this county than any county I have passed through," recorded Whitehorne.[34] That evening the soldiers pitched camp just shy of the village of Berryville.

They broke camp at 12:30 p.m. on June 22 and traipsed through Berryville. Beyond, the scenery looked as lovely as that of the previous day. "I believe I had rather have one thousand acres of land in this section than the whole of Greensville County," observed Greensville's Whitehorne. "The soil is very fertile Streams clear and pure, woods magnificent and beautiful."[35] After nine miles the soldiers halted at sunset three miles short of Charles Town. Captain Edwin White "Ned" Branch, the Richmond Grays's commander, had become familiar with this village in 1859, when he served in the security detail at John Brown's hanging. Branch ran the blockade into Charles Town that evening.

The 12th moved out again soon after daylight. Before the regiment entered Charles Town, Anderson received a report of the enemy's presence beyond the village. The 12th detached the Riflemen and sent them forward to verify the report, which proved false. As the rest of the regiment walked through the village, the soldiers cheered the ladies who turned out to see them. The men who had attended Brown's hanging pointed out to other members of their companies the jail, the old Court House, the Guard House and the gallows' site.

32 Bernard, "The Gettysburg Campaign," Bernard Notebook, 111.

33 Ibid.

34 Elmore, *Diary of J. E. Whitehorne*, June 21, 1863, 18.

35 Ibid., June 22, 1863, 19.

The 12th stopped at 11 a.m. near the Baltimore & Ohio Railroad, a mile short of Shepherdstown on the Potomac. The troops spent the afternoon scouring the countryside for the luxuries rumored to abound there. Many returned with butter, milk and vegetables. The men heard of Lee's orders to secure enemy property when they entered Yankee land. Despite the strictness of these orders and the inscrutability of Lee's designs, the soldiers remained in high spirits and confident of success. At sunset the regiment went on picket three-quarters of a mile east of its camp, toward Harpers Ferry.

Early on June 24, while the rest of Mahone's brigade and the Norfolk Division passed by, the 12th remained on sentry duty. At 9 a.m. the regiment rejoined its brigade at the Potomac ford below Shepherdstown. With soldiers of the 12th Mississippi of Posey's brigade, the 12th Virginia's men acted as wagon guards for several hours while the trains of Anderson's division crossed. Some of the regiment's soldiers relieved their boredom by building little pens out of sticks and putting into the pens the big black ants that infested the area. "We had lots of fun seeing them fight, sometimes both would get killed," Whitehorne wrote. "It was brutal but we had to have some diversion."[36]

After the trains had crossed, the wagon guards forded the 150-yard-wide river, taking the same road to Sharpsburg as they had the previous autumn, but swinging along at a more leisurely pace. Hiking through Sharpsburg they turned towards Boonsboro, crossed the Sharpsburg battlefield and passed through the village of Keedysville, where a small band of Federal cavalry had captured Wright's son hours earlier. The regiment halted at sundown within a mile of Boonsboro.

In Maryland, unlike Virginia, prosperity prevailed. "Some of our boys went up to the town and bought some molasses the first I have seen since the first year of the war," wrote Whitehorne.[37] The troops saw few displays of Southern sentiment in the villages they passed through that day. "It was amusing to see the long faces of the Union people," Bernard recorded. "They looked as though a funeral procession were passing."[38] The soldiers noticed another difference between Maryland and real Southern soil. "I also saw

36 Ibid., June 24, 1863, 21. This conjures up images of the children in the opening scenes of Sam Peckinpah's 1969 film, *The Wild Bunch*, pitting red ants against scorpions.

37 Elmore, *Diary of J. E. Whitehorne*, 22.

38 Bernard, "The Gettysburg Campaign," Bernard Notebook, 111.

William Evelyn Cameron. *Virginia Historical Society*

samples of Negro equality that I did not like so much," wrote Sale, whose cousin had recently become involved in a fracas with liberated blacks in enemy-occupied Norfolk.[39]

The regiment marched at 6 a.m. on June 25, tromping through the pretty town of Boonsboro with musicians playing "Dixie." Boonsboro gave the Confederates a lukewarm welcome. A few secessionist ladies waved their handkerchiefs at the soldiers. "The inhabitants don't seem to enthuse very much," Whitehorne noted. "They look as if they had rather not see us."[40] National Turnpike took the 12th through what Bernard called "the little Union hole of Benevola."[41] Stopping at a house for water, Cameron saw another side of the village. "Look at Grandma," said the girl who brought him a drink. Back in the hallway waving a sunbonnet, the old woman performed what Cameron remembered as "a very dance of jubilee in the privy of her own dwelling, knowing full well that, did she indulge in public rejoicing, the vengeance of neighbors otherwise affected would be visited upon her after we had passed by."[42]

Beyond Benevola the regiment marched among ripening fields of wheat. At Funkstown ladies displayed the most sympathy toward the Southern cause that the men had yet seen in Maryland. "In this place, I had to submit to having the *buttons* on the sleeve of my jacket cut off by some 4 or 5 young ladies- was sized by them in the street & was not allowed to proceed until I gave up the buttons," recorded Waddell, whose company

39 John F. Sale to Aunt, July 27, 1863.

40 Elmore, *Diary of J. E. Whitehorne*, June 25, 1863, 22.

41 Bernard, "The Gettysburg Campaign," Bernard Notebook, 111.

42 Newsome, Horn and Selby, eds., *Civil War Talks*, 150.

led the brigade through town.[43] The 12th halted at 1 p.m., a mile short of Hagerstown. Mahone's soldiers had a pleasant surprise that evening. The brigade commissary, which had collected several beeves near Berryville, issued a ration of fresh beef.

On June 26, the regiment broke camp at 6 a.m. in rain and mud. Passing through Hagerstown, a pretty city at least as big as Fredericksburg, the soldiers cheered a few female sympathizers. Until now the countryside had resembled the Shenandoah. "Same looking farms, same houses, and almost the same people," Whitehorne recorded.[44] Beyond Hagerstown the landscape looked strange, with an abundance of Morello cherries and what Todd recalled as a contrast between "the great size of their well-built and well-painted barns with the insignificant dwelling houses of the farmers."[45] Maryland differed from Virginia more with every step. The barns grew bigger, the fields and houses smaller. Five muddy miles beyond Hagerstown, the 12th entered what Edwards, now a sergeant, termed "the country of Dutchmen" at the homely village of Middleburg.[46] A few lower class women timidly waved a small Confederate flag. The troops treated skeptically a citizen's characterization of the place as "Copperhead."[47]

The 12th's soldiers did not regret leaving Maryland. They could neither draw upon her resources as upon those of an enemy, nor obtain the support of her citizens as recruits. Lest the Confederates turn passive sympathy into active opposition, they treated the Old Line State's people and their possessions with a consideration not shown in Virginia.

Pennsylvania struck the regiment's men as even more foreign. Mysterious hex signs decorated the barns, which kept growing bigger as the fields and houses shrank still further. Near the houses stood the first Dutch ovens the soldiers had seen. Some mistook the ovens for stills. The farmers seemed paralyzed with fear. Several told Sale that "they thought we were nothing more than a Grand Gang of Cut Throats roaming through the country without

43 Charles E. Waddell Diary, June 25, 1863.

44 Elmore, *Diary of J. E. Whitehorne*, June 25, 1863, 23.

45 Todd, "Reminiscences," 120.

46 Leroy S. Edwards to Father, June 26, 1863. Edwards also referred to the Northern states as "the lands of the Blue Bellies." Ibid.

47 Bernard, "The Gettysburg Campaign," Bernard Notebook, 111.

any commander and committing all manner of depredations."[48] Five miles beyond the Mason-Dixon line, the regiment passed through Greencastle, neither as large nor as pretty as Hagerstown. The troops found everything closed and little evidence of Secessionist sentiment. Few people appeared in the streets. Most who did looked terrified. The soldiers did nothing to justify this fear. The inhabitants would not sell to the Southerners for Confederate money, Federal greenbacks, or even silver, but the men still respected enemy property.

At 1 p.m., the 12th encamped a few miles beyond Greencastle. Lee's restrictions protecting enemy property went by the board. Havoc befell the local farmers. The tired soldiers trampled wheat and built grand fires with fence rails. Pitching their tents in the rain, they seized their beds' makings from hay and straw stacks. They then descended upon the farmers in search of food and found a bonanza of chickens, ducks, pigs, lard, bacon, butter, milk and honey. What the Virginians did not steal, they paid for at low Northern prices and in nearly worthless Confederate money.

Some just wanted to eat. Others wanted to give the Yankees a taste of their own medicine. Several Virginians encountered an officer's manservant slaughtering chickens right and left and asked him why he was killing so many.

"Ah Massa," the slave replied, "the Yanks come to my master house and took every thing he had even to his last nigger and now I am going to get every man in massas company a chicken."[49]

The victim of this vandalism complained to Mahone.

"You are damn lucky if you are not killed yourself," the general replied.[50]

Then Mahone relented, posting a guard who successfully protected the farmer and what remained of his property.

Not all the farms had guards. Returning to their camp that evening with their booty, the Virginians feasted. Dinner tasted all the better for having come from the enemy. The men enjoyed the role of invaders immensely.

On June 27, the 12th broke camp at 6 a.m. The troops passed through the village of Marion and the town of Chambersburg, where people looked glum and scared. War had thinned the population of neither place, unlike

---

48 Sale to Aunt, July 27, 1863.

49 Ibid.

50 Phillips, "Sixth Corporal," 22.

Southern towns. In Chambersburg the 12th encountered a crowd of ladies who had each pinned on her bosom a small "gridiron," as the Virginians called the Yankee flag.[51] The women began calling the Southerners names. The soldiers responded with such profanity that some of the females ran away, but one of the men replied with humor.

"Boys," he said, "those are the kind of breastworks we could charge very easy and take all of the flags."[52]

Outside Chambersburg the column turned from Harrisburg Pike to Baltimore Pike. Lee passed the column on the march, looking "hale and hearty," according to Waddell.[53] Mahone's brigade gave Lee three cheers. At 2 p.m., Anderson's division encamped in a grove of hickory, cedar, pines and white and red oaks near the village of Fayetteville. The soldiers again scoured the countryside for food.

They found the grove delightful. It had abundant and convenient water. The trees provided ample shade. The men received a daily ration of either a half pound of good bacon or a full pound of fresh beef. They supplemented their rations with pickings from the surrounding farms. "To have heard the squealing of pigs, the cackling of chickens, and the quacking of ducks, the luckless victims of the Confederate appetites, one for the instant might have supposed himself on some market square," Bernard recalled.[54] As the soldiers fattened up, their spirits rose.

Not all the 12th's men liked the foraging methods that made for this mirth. "Our soldiers acted very disgracefully in Pennsylvania toward the citizens," Manson recalled. "True, the enemy have done us great damage wherever they have been but we should have taught them better manners."[55] Waddell concurred. "Nothing so demoralizes an army as to be allowed free scope to commit wanton waste and depredations," he noted.[56]

For three nights the grove rang with the Norfolk Division's cheers. Then the period of plenty ended.

51 Sale to Aunt, January 31, 1863; Sale, Diary, June 4, 1864.

52 Phillips, "Sixth Corporal," 22.

53 Charles E. Waddell, Diary, June 27, 1863.

54 Bernard, "The Gettysburg Campaign," Bernard Notebook, 112.

55 Joseph R. Manson to Mother, July 30, 1863, Private Collection of Richard Cheatham.

56 Charles E. Waddell Diary, June 28, 1863.

Lee had led his army north with several objects in mind. He wanted to remove the seat of hostilities from Virginia, subsist his forces in enemy territory and disrupt Federal plans. To draw the Army of the Potomac into a hasty pursuit, fall upon it before it could unite and defeat it in detail constituted his most ambitious goal.

Unfortunately for Lee, his cavalry commander had other ideas. Embarrassed that Yankee horse soldiers had surprised him at Brandy Station, Stuart was trying to restore his reputation with the same sort of ride around the enemy army that had catapulted him to fame the previous year. This movement left Lee in the dark. As his army entered Pennsylvania, he did not know the opposing army's whereabouts. He did not learn that it had crossed the Potomac and was hastening north, or that Maj. Gen. George G. Meade had replaced Hooker as its commander, until the night of June 28-29. Lee learned this not from his cavalry but from one of Longstreet's spies.

Lee ordered his army to concentrate at Cashtown, the center of the road net southwest of Harrisburg. Hill's Corps trudged eastward along the muddy track running from Chambersburg over South Mountain. Heth's division led the way, followed by Pender's division. Mud made for slow going. Anderson's division, at the corps' tail end, left the grove near Fayetteville on July 1.

The 12th broke camp at 4:30 a.m. that day, heading east through town and passing the ruins of the Caledonia Iron Works, which belonged to a prominent Radical Republican Congressman. By mid-morning the troops could hear artillery far ahead. After trudging over South Mountain, they learned that Heth's and Pender's divisions were engaging the enemy near the town of Gettysburg. Soon the 12th met wounded and prisoners headed for the rear.

In Cashtown, eight miles from Gettysburg and six from the fighting, Lee conferred with Anderson. Wondering what had become of Stuart, Lee complained of the lack of intelligence that left him ignorant of whether he faced the whole Federal army or only a detachment. "If it is the whole Federal force, we must fight a battle here," he concluded. "If we do not gain a victory, those defiles and gorges which we passed this morning will shelter us from disaster."[57]

Lee rode forward toward the fighting. Anderson's division shuffled eastward on the wagon-choked road. More and more wounded passed. Five

57 James Longstreet, *From Manassas to Appomattox: Memoirs of the Civil War in America* (Philadelphia, 1896), 357.

miles beyond Cashtown, the Norfolk Division filed off to the right and formed line of battle behind Willoughby's Run. The line crossed the run, halted, closed column and then resumed its advance, stopping at the foot of West McPherson's Ridge at 5:30 p.m. The men saw the battle raging ahead, but no orders came committing them to the fight.

"Man, what in hell are we doing standing here doing nothing?" Phillips said to Branch. "Tomorrow we will catch hell. You see if we don't."[58]

Uniting on the field of battle, Hill and Ewell had crushed two of Meade's seven corps. "There was full time to have thrown our division into action," Cameron recalled. The 10,000 fresh troops in Anderson's division, if committed at the day's close, "would beyond a doubt have swept the already defeated remnants of Meade's advance from the field; and there would have been no battle at Gettysburg."[59]

The Confederates lost heavily in the day's struggle. Lee did not know the whereabouts of the Yankee army's five other corps except that they lurked somewhere to his right. Hill's Corps formed Lee's right. Throwing in the last fresh division of that corps would have rendered Lee's right vulnerable. Anderson's division remained in reserve.[60]

Fighting ceased by 6:30 p.m. Given a discretionary order by Lee to clear the Federals from Cemetery Hill and the other heights south of Gettysburg, Ewell declined to try. Anderson's division occupied West McPherson's Ridge. Most of its men spent the night there, but some scroungers entered Gettysburg, getting into a public hall and pillaging a banquet spread for the return of local troops whose enlistments had expired.

The division's soldiers rose early on July 2. Moving east Mahone's brigade formed line of battle with its right in an open field and its left in McMillan's Woods, a big stand of oak and hickory. The Virginians faced

---

58 Phillips, "Sixth Corporal," 24.

59 Newsome, Horn and Selby, eds., *Civil War Talks*, 152.

60 Mahone held this view. George Morley Vickers, ed., *Under Both Flags: A Panorama of the Great Civil War, As represented in Story, Anecdote, Adventure, and the Romance of Reality, Written by Both Sides; the Men and Women Who Created the Greatest Epoch in our Nation's History* (Philadelphia, 1896), 69. After the battle, a charge was leveled against Anderson in the *Savannah Republican* that Gettysburg would have been a Confederate victory had he arrived earlier on July 1. "Anderson and Pettigrew," Daily Richmond *Enquirer*, July 11, 1863. Mahone and Posey defended Anderson. William Mahone and Carnot Posey to Editor, Semi-Weekly Richmond *Enquirer*, August 7, 1863, p. 2, cols. 2-3.

Ziegler's Grove on Cemetery Ridge, which ran southward from Cemetery Hill.[61] Mahone's headquarters lay behind the Riflemen, on the 12th's right. One hundred yards in front of Mahone's brigade, the gunners of Pegram's battalion served their pieces behind a low rock wall on Seminary Ridge's crest. They were engaging the enemy artillery on Cemetery Ridge. The 12th's soldiers slept unsoundly, cognizant of nearly everything that took place around them. They heard the booming of cannon, the sound of solid shot as it cut through the branches overhead and the cries of men struck by shell fragments. They felt the dirt and grit strike them as cannon balls tore up the earth around them, but still they slept.

Early that afternoon Anderson directed four of his division's five brigades to prepare to advance one after another from right to left across Emmitsburg Road toward Cemetery Ridge.[62] He ordered Mahone's brigade to remain on Seminary Ridge behind and in support of Pegram's artillery and the right of Pender's division.[63] Anderson's orders implemented Lee's plan for an attack on the Northern left. Lee's staffers had informed him that the Unionists had left unoccupied Little Round Top and the southern portion of Cemetery Ridge. Lee wanted Longstreet to march beyond the enemy left, much as Jackson had slipped around the Yankee right at Chancellorsville. Longstreet would get astride Cemetery Ridge and wheel northward, then strike the enemy left flank perpendicularly, as Jackson had struck the Federal right on May 2. Lee placed Anderson's division under Longstreet's orders. It would join the attack as Longstreet's men rolled up the enemy line. Meanwhile, Ewell's Corps would demonstrate against the enemy right.

Lee did not have the intelligence from his army's Cavalry Corps that had facilitated both the formulation and the implementation of the plan for Jackson's flank attack at Chancellorsville. His staffers served him poorly, failing to observe that the Yankee left on Cemetery Ridge did not end near the G. Weikert house, but extended along Emmitsburg Road to Went's Peach Orchard, then swung back to Devils' Den at the foot of the Round Tops.

61 Phillips, "Sixth Corporal," 24-25.

62 Longstreet, in charge of the attack, related that Anderson was to attack with four brigades. Longstreet, *From Manassas to Appomattox*, 369. Anderson's division had five. *OR* 27, 2:322, 343.

63 William Mahone and Carnot Posey to Editor, Richmond Semi-Weekly *Enquirer*, August 7, 1863. See also Elwood W. Christ, "Over a Wide, Hot, . . . Crimson Plain:" *The Struggle For The Bliss Farm At Gettysburg, July 2nd and 3rd, 1863* (Baltimore, 1994) (2nd Ed.), 85-86.

Longstreet and his troops modified Lee's plan twice. They reversed their march order when they discovered that their initial route would not take them around the Federal left unobserved. Afterward they adjusted when they found that the plan did not fit the situation on the Union left. The Northerners held different ground than Lee's staffers had reported. These changes caused substantial delays. Not until late in the afternoon did Longstreet's men attack.

Before the time came for Anderson's advance, a distraction hobbled his division—the Bliss farm, lying in the hollow halfway between Seminary Ridge and Cemetery Ridge and to the 12th's right front. Northern and Southern skirmishers had driven each other back and forth across the farm's fields all day. Shortly before 4 p.m., Anderson decided to seize the farmstead and its massive barn to facilitate his division's advance. This task fell to his Mississippi Brigade, which stood on the right of his Virginians and to the left of his Georgians, Floridians and Alabamians. The Mississippi Brigade's pickets accomplished the mission by 5 p.m. A call reached the 12th—the rightmost of Mahone's regiments—to send a company to support the Mississippians.

Adjutant Cameron approached the Huger Grays.

"Where is Lieutenant Scott?" Cameron shouted.

Scott appeared.

"We are ordered to reinforce the picket line," Cameron said. "Take your company beyond the stone wall, deploy them as skirmishers, advance across the field and when you strike the skirmishers report to the commandant of the picket line."[64]

The Grays advanced by company front at a double-quick. Reaching the stone wall they vaulted it and deployed. At a run they crossed a clover field and jumped a plank fence into the Bliss peach orchard. The storm of shot and shell passed over their heads. They found the Confederate picket line deployed behind another plank fence. "In front of this fence was a wheat field, the wheat being very rank, and as tall as a man's head," remembered Whitehorne.[65] To the Grays' right loomed the Bliss barn. Across the field lurked Federal pickets from Gibbon's and Hays' divisions of II Corps.

About 12 of the Grays entered the barn. Through holes in its sides, with some Mississippians and some soldiers of the 16th Virginia, they sniped

64 Elmore, *Diary of J. E. Whitehorne*, 27-28.

65 Ibid., July 2, 1863, 28.

away at Battery B, 1st Rhode Island Light Artillery, on Cemetery Ridge. This annoyed the Yankees. A battalion of the 12th New Jersey, as well as elements of the 1st Delaware from Hays' division and a company of the 106th Pennsylvania from the Philadelphia or California Brigade of Gibbon's division, advanced to dislodge the Confederate marksmen at about 5:30 p.m. The Jerseymen and Delawareans drove straight across the wheat field toward the barn. The Pennsylvanians double-quicked along a plank fence that ran through the wheat field to the barn's right. They hopped the fence between the wheat field and the Bliss peach orchard. Getting behind the barn, they captured the Grays and other Southerners inside, breaking the Secessionist picket line and flanking the rest of the Grays, who withdrew in good order. The Unionists also retired, carrying off their prisoners.

The retreating Grays reached the plank fence between the orchard and the clover field. "About face!" they heard. The command came to reoccupy the position near the Bliss barn. A shrapnel burst about twenty paces to Whitehorne's right. He felt a sharp blow on each leg and thought dirt kicked up by the shell had struck him.

The Federal Capture of Bliss' Barn—and Many Huger Grays
Gettysburg National Military Park

"You are hit," said Scott, who stood by Whitehorne's side.[66] A shell fragment had taken off nearly half his right calf. A ball had passed between the bones of his left calf without fracturing them. Scott advised Whitehorne to go to the rear. He limped back by the way he had come but could not find the field hospital of Mahone's brigade. The Federal barrage had forced it to relocate to a safer place. A black cook guided him to the field hospital of Wilcox's Alabama Brigade.

The time for the four brigades from Anderson's division to advance arrived after 6:20 p.m.[67] The three right brigades charged as planned. Wilcox's brigade attacked first, followed by Lang's Florida Brigade, then Wright's Georgia Brigade. The advance of Anderson's division broke down with Posey's Mississippi Brigade, which had spent itself in the skirmishing on the Bliss farm. To the Mississippians' left, Mahone's Virginians remained on McPherson's Ridge in support of Pegram's guns and Pender's right.[68]

Against stiffening resistance Wilcox's and Lang's brigades gained the upper reaches of Plum Run and Wright's Georgians almost summited Cemetery Ridge. Desperate counterattacks by Federals of II Corps halted them. Enemy pressure built upon Wilcox, Lang and Wright to retreat. Ammunition ran low. Wright and Wilcox sent couriers to Anderson demanding support. The couriers found him and his staffers reclining in a ravine behind the Mississippi Brigade instead of overseeing the division's advance. Anderson dispatched his aide-de-camp, Capt. Samuel D. Shannon, with orders for Posey's brigade to send forward its right—the 19th and 48th Mississippi—on the left of Wright's Georgians, and for Mahone to shift to the right and advance on the left of the two Mississippi regiments.[69]

The 19th and 48th Mississippi charged toward Emmitsburg Road on the left of Wright's Georgians. Meanwhile, Shannon reached Mahone with

---

66 Ibid.

67 *OR* 27, 2:618.

68 See notes 62 and 63, above.

69 Shannon told Wilcox the order from Anderson to Mahone was "to advance." Douglas Southall Freeman, *R. E. Lee: A Biography*, 4 vols. (New York, 1934), 3:555. That the order included a sidle to the right is apparent from the brigade's subsequent movements—otherwise the shift to the right would have resulted from another order from Anderson to Mahone. Phillips, "Sixth Corporal," 24; Stewart, *A Pair of Blankets*, 97-98; Bernard, "The Gettysburg Campaign," Bernard Notebook, 112-113; Newsome, Horn and Selby, eds., *Civil War Talks*, 133, 155-156. Posey confirmed that Mahone was ordered to the right. *OR* 27, 2:634.

Anderson's order to shift to the right and advance. Mahone reacted to this change of plan with disbelief.[70]

"No," he said, "I have orders from General Anderson himself to remain here."[71]

Shannon moved on before Mahone recovered from his astonishment and complied with Anderson's order.[72]

Brigadier General Carnot Posey brought up first the 16th and then the 12th Mississippi to support the 19th and 48th Mississippi on his right, leaving only a skirmish line on his left. The Unionists in front of Posey's left threatened that flank of his brigade, and Posey sent a courier to Mahone asking for a regiment to support the Mississippians' left. The courier arrived after Mahone received the order from Anderson to shift to the right and advance, which precluded literally complying with Posey's request though the shift provided the support sought.[73] The attack of Posey's right sputtered. Only a few men from the 19th and 48th Mississippi reached Emmitsburg Road. None neared Cemetery Ridge except for a handful from the 48th Mississippi on the Georgia Brigade's immediate left.[74]

Mahone's brigade left its skirmishers in place. About dark, the Virginians sidled around 200 yards to the right behind the worm fence on the crest of Seminary Ridge until the brigade's right stood behind the left of Posey's skirmishers. This put the Virginians on the left of the body of Posey's brigade and unmasked the left of Mahone's brigade from behind the right of Thomas' brigade of Pender's division. Mahone's men silently advanced about 400 yards through the Bliss wheat field to the plank fence that separated it from the Bliss orchard. The Virginians faced the Brian farm on Cemetery Ridge, between Ziegler's Grove and the Copse of Trees. Had they gone forward, they would have found themselves near Wright's left, but by this

---

70 As the late Dr. John T. Hendron of Steger, Illinois used to say, "Order plus counterorder equals disorder."

71 Freeman, *R. E. Lee*, 3:555.

72 Shannon did not remain long enough to see Mahone move and mistakenly told Wilcox that Mahone did not move. Ibid.; Phillips, "Sixth Corporal, 24; Stewart, *A Pair of Blankets*, 97-98; Bernard, "The Gettysburg Campaign," Bernard Notebook, 112-113; Newsome, Horn and Selby, eds., *Civil War Talks*, 133, 155-156; *OR* 27, 2:234.

73 Ibid.; Janet B. Hewett, et al., eds., *Supplement to the Official Records of the Union and Confederate Armies* (100 Vols.) (Wilmington, N.C., 1994-2001), 5:405-407.

74 Donald C. Pfanz, *Gettysburg: The Second Day* (Chapel Hill, 1987), 386-387.

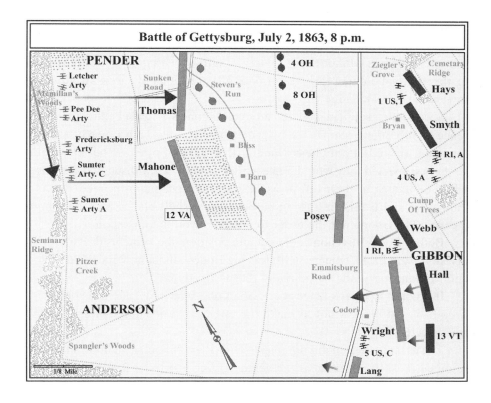

time the Northerners were repulsing the rest of Anderson's division as well as Longstreet's men.[75]

Too late to assist the rest of their division, the Virginians remained in their advanced position, where they might participate in another assault—this one beginning far to their left. East of Cemetery Hill Ewell converted the demonstration of his corps into an attack. On Ewell's far left as twilight gathered, Johnson's division seized a toehold on Culp's Hill. On Johnson's right at nightfall, Early's division broke into the enemy trenches on East Cemetery Hill. Rodes' division maneuvered to attack

75 Ibid.; Phillips, "Sixth Corporal, 24; Stewart, *A Pair of Blankets*, 97-98; Bernard, "The Gettysburg Campaign," Bernard Notebook, 112-113; Newsome, Horn and Selby, eds., *Civil War Talks*, 133, 155-156. Bernard thought this move occurred "about dark." Ibid., 133; Bernard, "The Gettysburg Campaign," Bernard Notebook, 112. Cameron believed it happened around about three o'clock in the morning. Ibid., 155. Phillips thought the move took place about 10 p.m. Phillips, "Sixth Corporal," 24. Stewart recalled that the move occurred at "night." Stewart, *A Pair of Blankets*, 98.

West Cemetery Hill on the right of Early's division. Pender's division of Hill's Corps prepared to advance on the right of Rodes' division, toward Cemetery Ridge. Mahone's brigade, the only fresh body of Confederates to the right of Pender's division, stood where it could join an advance toward Cemetery Ridge.

Secessionist soldiers gathered around Mahone's brigade behind the plank fence on the Bliss farm. On the brigade's far right, the 12th's men could still see some arrive but only heard the muffled tread of others. The regiment's soldiers suspected they would make a night assault. They discussed fastening white bandages to their left arms in case their suspicion proved true. To their right and front, the fuse of an occasional shell blazed an arc through the sky. The troops felt the order to advance would come soon.

Before Rodes' division could get into position, the Federals drove Early's division from East Cemetery Hill, leaving Rodes' division, Pender's division and Mahone's brigade without any reason to advance.

In front of the plank fence at 10 p.m., Longstreet and Anderson conferred.

"It would be best not to make the attempt," Longstreet said. "Let the troops return."[76]

The assault column did not disperse for several hours. Mahone's brigade rejoined its skirmishers near the center of Lee's army at 2:30 a.m.

Brief artillery exchanges punctuated the morning of July 3. The 12th's men lay behind breastworks they had erected. The Herrings relieved the Huger Grays on picket duty and skirmished around the Bliss farm. The struggle swayed back and forth until about 11 a.m., when Yankees from Hays' division burned the Bliss barn.

Lee marshaled his forces for a blow at the Union center on Cemetery Ridge. With Hill ailing, Lee put the reluctant Longstreet in charge of the attack. The four brigades of Heth's division from Hill's Corps and two brigades from Pickett's division of Longstreet's Corps formed the assault column's front line, with Heth's men on the left and Pickett's on the right. The column's second line consisted of two brigades from Pender's division of Hill's Corps behind Heth's men and Pickett's third brigade behind his other two. Anderson's division formed the third line. Wilcox's and Lang's brigades would follow behind the right of Pickett's division. The rest of the Norfolk Division—from right to left, Wright's, Posey's and Mahone's

76   Newsome, Horn and Selby, eds., *Civil War Talks*, 156.

brigades—would support Heth's and Pender's troops in the column's center.[77] Mahone's brigade would advance along the same axis as Davis' brigade of Heth's division, marching one brigade in from the first line's extreme left.[78] Thomas' and McGowan's brigades of Pender's division would advance in the third line on the left of Mahone's brigade. Still farther left stood 1,800 soldiers of Rodes' division prepared to join the attack. Part of McLaws' division would move forward in the third line to the right of Anderson's division.[79]

At 1 p.m., the Southern artillery unleashed its preliminary barrage. Yankee batteries replied. Deadly missiles of all sorts, sizes and shapes filled the air around the 12th, howling, shrieking, whistling, moaning. Some immense projectiles rhythmically rushed like railroad trains. Every instant ordnance struck the ground in front of the regiment or whistled over its ranks. Shell fragments "rained through the limbs of the trees almost as regularly as the pattering of hail storms," Cameron remembered.[80]

One hundred yards in front of the 12th, on the eastern crest of Seminary Ridge, shot and shell struck continuously among the Confederate batteries. Caissons and limber chests exploded, dismembering men and horses. "It was piteous to see the poor animals walking about with terrible wounds, and to hear their groans," recalled Todd.[81] In the hollow between the ridge's crests, the 12th's body began taking casualties. Falling limbs injured some soldiers, Federal metal others. Twenty yards behind the regiment, Davis'

---

77 An article in *Gettysburg Magazine* argues that Mahone's brigade was omitted from Pickett's Charge for Mahone's insubordination on July 2 when, as we have seen above, there was no insubordination—just confusion from Anderson's contradictory orders—and the evidence cited in the article contradicts the article's argument. Bradley M. Gottfried, "Mahone's Brigade: Insubordination or Miscommunication," *Gettysburg Magazine*, No. 18, July 1998, 75-76.
Another article in the same issue of *Gettysburg Magazine* refutes the aforesaid article and shows that Mahone's brigade was indeed among the troops intended to support the first wave of Pickett's Charge. Richard Rollins, "The Second Wave of Pickett's Charge," *Gettysburg Magazine*, No. 18, July 1998, 104-105. See also Bernard, "The Gettysburg Campaign," Bernard Notebook, 112-113; Newsome, Horn and Selby, eds., *Civil War Talks*, 133-134; Jeffrey D. Wert, *Gettysburg: Day Three* (New York, 2003), 238-239; Vickers, ed., *Under Both Flags*, 70.

78 Newsome, Horn and Selby, eds., *Civil War Talks*, 157.

79 Rollins, "The Second Wave of Pickett's Charge," 105-110. Added to the 12,500 in the first wave, the troops in the second would have brought the total nearer the 30,000 Longstreet thought necessary for success. Ibid., 109.

80 Newsome, Horn and Selby, eds., *Civil War Talks*, 157.

81 Todd, "Reminiscences," 133.

brigade occupied higher and more exposed ground. A shell struck among a group of this brigade's men. Exploding at their feet, it blew them into the air, recalled Cameron, "in such a mass of blood that some one cried out that a flag had been carried away."[82]

Mahone's soldiers had never endured such an intense bombardment. They did not stand firm. Some burrowed with their bayonets. Others hid behind trees that would not have stopped a bullet, much less a cannonball. The antics of the Archer Rifles' Pvt. John Heffron amused his comrades. A shell would explode on his right. The former lumber mill laborer would spring up "as if possessed with a demon of unrest," and dash to the left. Another shell would strike on his left. He would leap frantically in some other direction. "And so . . . he passed from trench to tree from pillar to post, and was actually consoled, no doubt, with the idea that he was dodging death," Cameron remembered.[83]

Feild observed that the barrage had shaken his men. Jumping up, he drew his sword and walked up and down the 12th's line.

"Steady!" he shouted.[84]

His coolness reassured the troops. Then he issued an order that always improved morale. He called for the ambulance men to carry off the wounded. The sight of the stretcher-bearers at work under fire completed the restoration of order.

The Riflemen's Pvt. Robert Randolph Henry, Todd's former chum, was carrying orders to the division on detached duty as a courier for Anderson. Henry rode into a maelstrom of shot and shell so fierce that nothing could remain in it long and live. His horse did not survive. Henry flattened himself on the ground behind a tree, with his head close to the trunk, which shells had almost severed. Fearing the tree would fall and crush him, he rose, fled to a different section of the division, delivered the orders and returned to Anderson unscathed.[85]

The bombardment slackened at 3 p.m. Cheers came from behind the regiment's right. The men of Davis' brigade stepped over the Virginians and

82   Newsome, Horn and Selby, eds., *Civil War Talks*, 157.

83   Ibid.

84   Todd, "Reminiscences," 131.

85   "Maj. Robert Randolph Henry," Clinch Valley *News* (Jeffersonville, VA), March 24, 1916, p. 3, cols. 1-2. We do not know what orders Henry was carrying.

marched across the crest of Seminary Ridge. Minutes passed. The enemy artillery's thunder reached a crescendo. Volleys of musketry resounded. Soon broken groups of the assault column scuttled back over the crest.

"Fall in, men!" the non-coms of Mahone's brigade cried.[86]

A moment's hesitation followed. The order had come too late. Coordinating four divisions and parts of two others had proven impossible. Only two divisions and portions of two others had gotten into action. The attack had failed. The men knew that beyond the crest lay an open field more than three quarters of a mile wide. In their minds' eyes they could see their brigade and division raked by artillery fire as they crossed the field, then decimated by musketry and hand-to-hand fighting as they assaulted the enemy breastworks on Cemetery Ridge.

Chappell, now a first lieutenant and in command of the Archer Rifles, ended this hesitation. Leaping up, he threw off his blanket roll. In seconds all but three of the regiment's officers and men stepped across their earthworks and formed line of battle. The brigade's other regiments came up on the 12th's left and dressed on their colors.

Most of the regiment's soldiers remained silent.

"Make up your minds to go until a bullet stops you, and we will take the works," said a private in the Lafayette Guards.[87]

Mahone advanced from his post behind the 12th's right.

"Attention!" he shouted. "Forward!"[88]

In perfect order the line began crossing the 100 yards to the wall at the crest. Before the brigade reached the wall, a rider appeared heading toward the brigade across an open field to the right. He waved excitedly, spurring a gray horse covered with foam.

Longstreet had the responsibility of ordering forward Mahone's, Posey's and Wright's brigades in support of the assault, but he had waited too long as his lack of faith in the attack became a self-fulfilling prophecy.[89] The three brigades could no longer help and Longstreet directed Anderson to halt them. They would only add to the casualty list. The rider—one of Anderson's couriers—handed Mahone an order stopping his brigade. "The order for me to go in after Pickett's assault had failed was countermanded," Mahone

---

86   Todd, "Reminiscences," 132.

87   Newsome, Horn and Selby, eds., *Civil War Talks*, 159.

88   Bernard, "The Gettysburg Campaign," Bernard Notebook, 113.

89   Rollins, "The Second Wave of Pickett's Charge," 113; *OR* 27, 2:360, 615.

recollected.[90] "I must confess that I was greatly relieved," Todd recalled.[91] Posey's and Wright's brigades also halted. Longstreet had the responsibility for ordering Wilcox's and Lang's brigades forward, waited until they could no longer do any good but, conflicted, ordered them forward anyway.[92]

The Virginians retraced their steps. Lee rode among the assault column's fragments, rallying fugitives in case of a Yankee counterattack. Despite the numerical superiority of the Federals, Meade declined to take the offensive. The day's remainder passed in skirmishing.[93]

On the morning of July 4, the regiment numbered 222 muskets and 22 officers.[94] Except for sharpshooting and minor artillery duels, the day passed quietly. A drenching rain began that afternoon. The 12th's men dined on three-day old cornbread. At dark they withdrew as quietly as possible, leaving fires along the lines burning brightly. The Confederates abandoned most of their seriously wounded and headed southwest, toward Fairfield. "We feel mortified at our failure, but rather pleased at the idea of once more going toward Dixie," remembered Bernard.[95] The war's bloodiest, most intense

90 Vickers, ed., *Under Both Flags*, 70.

91 Todd, "Reminiscences," 132.

92 Rollins, "The Second Wave of Pickett's Charge," 112-113.

93 Mathematical modeling based on Lanchester equations developed during the First World War to determine the numbers necessary for successful assaults shows that with the commitment of one to three more infantry brigades to the nine brigades in the initial force, Pickett's Charge would probably have taken the Union position and altered the battle's outcome, but the Confederates would likely have been unable to exploit such a success without the commitment of still more troops. Michael J. Armstrong and Steven E. Soderbergh, "Refighting Pickett's Charge: mathematical modeling of the Civil War battlefield," *Social Science Quarterly* 96, No. 4 (May 14, 2015), 1153-1168. The authors do not include Wilcox's and Lang's brigades in the initial force. Ibid., 161. Commitment of Anderson's entire division with the initial force would have supplied five additional brigades and around 5,000 more men, making the attack force fourteen brigades and from 15,000 to 18,000 men. Ibid., 161, 164. These numbers would practically have guaranteed a lodgment at the Angle and refuted Longstreet's assertion that "thirty thousand men was the minimum of force necessary for the work." Ibid., 164; Longstreet, *From Manassas to Appomattox*, 386. Rollins has identified another five brigades and one regiment scheduled for the second wave of Pickett's Charge from Pender's and Rodes' divisions, as well as at least another brigade from McLaws' division, all of which would have brought the attack column still nearer the 30,000 Longstreet thought necessary. Rollins, "The Second Wave of Pickett's Charge," 105-107. Inclusion of these troops would have made Pickett's Charge even more irresistible.

94 Bernard, "The Gettysburg Campaign," Bernard Notebook, 114.

95 Ibid.

battle had ended. The 12th's casualty figures conveyed the battle's ferocity. Though uncommitted, the regiment lost 41 soldiers, almost as many as at Seven Pines or Malvern Hill: 2 killed, 28 wounded and 11 missing. The wounds of two proved mortal. Ten other wounded fell into Yankee hands. The enemy captured 10 of the missing soldiers, all skirmishers. The 11th deserted.[96]

The 12th marched on Hagerstown Road all night in the rain. The passage of the army's wagon trains and artillery churned this road into a quagmire. The troops slogged along in inky darkness through mud and water up to their knees. Trying to keep together, they called out the names of their companies, but stragglers abounded. "Often I was only guided by Col. Feild's white horse, and I have an impression that more than once I took hold of his tail," Cameron recalled.[97]

The regiment tramped through Fairfield toward South Mountain. At daybreak July 5, those remaining with the colors found themselves climbing the mountain again, but toward a different pass than on the way to Gettysburg. Halfway up, they halted. The regimental cooks caught up with them. The famished soldiers wolfed down their rations. After an hour or two, the men plodded over Monterey Pass. The cooks distributed rations again near Frog Creek, at the mountain's foot. Mahone's brigade stood picket on a commanding point a mile east of Magnolia Springs. Morale remained low despite a rumored Confederate victory over Grant at Vicksburg. At sunset the Virginians pitched their tents, made comfortable beds of straw and looked forward to a sound sleep. At nightfall marching orders arrived. The men disliked giving up the prospect of a good night's rest, but the idea of heading homeward mollified them. They trudged along behind a long line of guns and wagons, making scant progress. The troops halted before daylight, bivouacking in the ugly village of Waterloo.

Mahone's brigade rested for most of July 6. Many soldiers wrote home and informed their families of their safety. They did not understand the movements of the enemy or of their own forces. They did not know their destination. Some believed they would return to Virginia. Others thought they would remain in Yankee land. At 5:30 p.m., they left Waterloo. A long, slow hike beside a wagon train began. The troops shuffled through

96 Henderson, *12VI*, 106-167; Rolls 514-534, M324, Record Group 109, NA.

97 Newsome, Horn and Selby, eds., *Civil War Talks*, 160.

the respectable looking village of Waynesboro into Maryland, then through Leitersburg. Near a stone bridge beyond the town, the 12th's soldiers saw other men leaving the road and running to a house 100 yards up the creek. Curiosity made some follow. Before they reached the house, they smelled whiskey and met troops returning to the road with liquor in tin cups, canteens and horse buckets. Behind the house stood a large still. Around it surged a crowd eager for alcohol. A tall soldier stood on the still's rim, straddling it. With his long arms he reached down and with a tin ladled whiskey into canteens and other receptacles held up to him. The men who visited the still left in high spirits, but down the road stood a guard who relieved each soldier of his canteen and drained it of liquor. Those in the rear observed that the guard stopped only those who remained on the turnpike. They retained their precious fluid by leaving the road and passing through adjacent fields.

At 7 a.m. on July 7, badly in need of rest, the 12th stopped two miles northeast of Hagerstown. A rumor spread that the army had retired merely to obtain more artillery ammunition and that it would make a stand at Hagerstown. Only the rumor's latter part proved true. The regiment stood in line of battle on Salisbury Ridge July 10. Meade again refused to attack. The retreat resumed that afternoon. The 12th headed for Hagerstown. The men slumped through the town "feeling rather crest-fallen," recalled Bernard. "We had not accomplished so much as we had anticipated when we marched so proudly through the same place less than two weeks before."[98] The column took the turnpike to Williamsport, but three miles beyond Hagerstown turned onto a road to the left. The Virginians walked a short distance down this road before bivouacking. It looked as if Mahone's brigade would soon recross the Potomac.

At 8 a.m. on July 11, the Virginians departed their encampment. Leaving the road, they struggled southeastwardly through woods and across fields. The men sensed they were not heading for the Potomac. After a mile and a half, they formed line of battle and halted. Soon they built breastworks, "five minutes of which work caused the fences near us to disappear like frost before the sun," recalled Bernard.[99] When the fence rails gave out, the troops used shocks of wheat. Only a little skirmishing disturbed their peace the rest of the day.

98 Bernard, "The Gettysburg Campaign," Bernard Notebook, 115.

99 Ibid.

The 12th's men had not headed for the Potomac because the recent rains had swollen the river. Lee's army could not cross until the river subsided, or the Confederate engineers constructed a pontoon bridge. That meant digging in and offering battle to the victorious, more numerous and better supplied Yankees. The Southerners occupied a line that stretched about six miles northward from Downsville on the Potomac to around a mile and a half south of Hagerstown, covering the only road from Hagerstown southwestward to Williamsport. Hill's Corps held the Confederate line's center.

Quiet prevailed on July 12 until evening, when picket firing grew brisk. The Juniors drove back the enemy's skirmishers. The Riflemen, in the reserve line of skirmishers for Mahone's brigade, could hear the drums in the enemy's camp, so close had the Yanks approached.

Hunger grew uncontrollable the following day. A flock of sheep grazed in a field of grass between the line of battle and the skirmishers. Mahone watched his soldiers' mouths water. He did not share Lee's squeamishness about plundering private property or offending Marylanders.

"Boys, if you want a lamb, help yourself," said Mahone.[100] The famished Southsiders slaughtered the unlucky animals in less than twenty minutes. Hanging the carcasses on fence rails, the men divided the meat among themselves. At first, they had no condiments, but a search of the countryside disclosed a supply of fish salt at a deserted house.

The retreat resumed at dark. The 12th's men felt disappointed that the Unionists had not attacked, as did Lee. Meade's caution disappointed Lincoln as well. The President would never forgive the Pennsylvanian for his failure to destroy the defeated Southern army during its retreat from Gettysburg.

Mahone's troops soon reached the public highway, which they found "ankle-deep with mud and water of about the consistency of batter," recalled Bernard.[101] The tired soldiers slogged for hours in the drizzly darkness.

On the morning of July 14, the regiment approached Falling Waters. The North Carolinians of Pettigrew's brigade occupied the roadside with their shirts off, killing lice. At 11 a.m., the 12th Virginia halted for a rest on a hill about a mile and a half from Falling Waters. Many men descended to a stream at the hill's bottom to wash their aching feet. The regiment resumed its march, leaving these men behind.

---

100 Phillips, "Sixth Corporal, 29.

101 Bernard, "The Gettysburg Campaign," Bernard Notebook, 116.

Shortly, a rattle of musketry startled the stragglers. Minnies struck the branches over their heads. Enemy cavalrymen were charging into the middle of Pettigrew's brigade. Several Tarheels "came rushing down the hill pell mell," recalled Todd, one of the stragglers.[102] The North Carolinians, when asked what had happened, replied in the usual manner of the panic stricken that the Northerners were cutting them to pieces. The Tarheels quickly rallied and overwhelmed the Yankee horsemen. The 12th's stragglers hastened up the hill to find their regiment gone. Gathering up their arms and baggage, they hurried to catch up with the colors.

At 1 p.m., under enemy artillery fire and beneath the eyes of Lee, Mahone's brigade crossed the Potomac on a pontoon bridge that the army's engineers had completed that day. The Virginians cheered Lee, who raised his hat in reply. "How rejoiced we were at the idea of being once more on Confederate soil!" remembered Bernard.[103] The army's rear guard finished crossing before evening, then cut the bridge loose. Many stragglers fell into the hands of the enemy, whose policy toward prisoners had changed since Chancellorsville. Secessionists captured now would have to wait until late 1864—if not until months after the war's end—before they left Federal prison camps.

Mahone's men marched through Martinsburg on July 15, receiving a sullen reception. The gloomy town had many Union sympathizers. After passing through Winchester, the regiment's soldiers reached Bunker Hill, a wooded ridge resembling a fortification. The army stopped amid fields of blackberries. "As soon as the men threw off their trappings they swooped down on the field like a flock of blackbirds," Todd recalled.[104] That day the troops finally credited the reports of Vicksburg's fall. "How unfortunate this catastrophy is," recorded Waddell.[105] News of Port Hudson's fall came two days later.

Lee had expected to advance into Loudoun County, east of the Blue Ridge, but the swollen Shenandoah blocked his army's path. Waiting for the water to ebb, he sent out foragers, had wheat threshed and milled and fed his army with Virginia bread and Pennsylvania beef. Before a week ended,

102 Todd, "Reminiscences," 139.

103 Bernard, "The Gettysburg Campaign," Bernard Notebook, 115.

104 Todd, "Reminiscences," 140.

105 Charles E. Waddell Diary, July 15, 1863.

the Union army crossed the Potomac east of the Blue Ridge. Enemy cavalry seized the passes into Loudoun County. Lee feared the invaders would bottle him up in the Valley while their main body moved on Richmond. He ordered Longstreet to take his corps and occupy Manassas and Chester Gaps before the enemy reached them. By this time the Shenandoah had fallen enough for the engineers to throw a pontoon bridge over its torrent. Longstreet's Corps crossed the river, securing the gaps on July 21. Ewell's Corps shifted to Madison Court House. The enemy followed McClellan's path of the previous autumn and advanced to Warrenton.

Hill's Corps followed Longstreet's Corps. On the same day as Longstreet's men seized Manassas and Chester Gaps, the 12th plodded through Winchester, Front Royal and Flint Hill. On July 25, after following Longstreet through Chester Gap, the regiment encamped in a pleasant orchard about a mile north of Culpeper Court House. The 12th's troops found Virginia prices as high as when the army had left for Yankee land. "I bought some articles the other day for which I paid $4 that in ordinary times could have been purchased for 20 cents exactly," Sale lamented.[106]

Their leaders encountered controversy. Southern newspapers printed criticisms of the handling of Anderson's division and Mahone's brigade at Gettysburg. Anderson and Mahone fired off replies. The Virginians' failure to support the charge of Wilcox's, Lang's and Wright's brigades on July 2 caused bitter feelings within the Norfolk Division and led to gibes about giving Mahone's men wooden weapons and transferring their muskets to soldiers who would fight.[107]

The regiment's men assessed the campaign. The assault on Cemetery Ridge evoked unprecedented criticism of Lee. "This charge was one of the

106 John F. Sale to Aunt, August 10, 1863.

107 Waters and Edmonds, *A Small but Spartan Band*, 144. Much of the derision stemmed from the mistaken assumption of Wilcox and Wright that because their brigades and Lang's had peremptory orders to advance, so did Posey's and Mahone's brigades. Freeman, *R. E. Lee*, 3:555-556; Christ, *The Struggle for the Bliss Farm*, 40; Edwin B. Coddington, *The Gettysburg Campaign: A Study in Command* (Morningside, OH, 1979), 421, 759. Mahone and Posey denied they had peremptory orders to advance. William Mahone and Carnot Posey to Editor, Richmond Semi-Weekly *Enquirer*, August 7, 1863. Neither Wilcox nor Wright knew that Mahone's brigade *did* move, though Wright ought to have known part of Posey's brigade advanced beside Wright's brigade. Phillips, "Sixth Corporal," 24; Stewart, *A Pair Of Blankets*, 97-98; Bernard, "The Gettysburg Campaign," Bernard Notebook, 112-113; Newsome, Horn and Selby, eds., *Civil War Talks*, 133, 155-156; *OR* 27, 2:634.

most uncalled for acts that was committed," commented Phillips.[108] Many decided that the army ought to do the rest of its fighting on its own soil, but dismissing this view as "all fudge," Sale wrote, "No men ever did better than ours did at Gettysburg but the Yankees were too many for us besides with a much superior position to any they have ever held against us."[109]

108 Phillips, "Sixth Corporal," 26.

109 John F. Sale to Aunt, August 16, 1863.

CHAPTER 11

Second Brandy Station

A belief had developed among some of the 12th's men that singing "A Soldier's Life Is Always Gay" would precipitate a battle next day. Late on July 31, some soldiers gathered to sing. One proposed singing "A Soldier's Life Is Always Gay."

"Do not sing that song," another objected. "If you do, tomorrow we will have a fight. This has been our experience."[1]

The others ignored him and sang the song:

> *The rich have cares we little know of,*
> *All that glitters is not gold,*
> *Merit's seldom made a show of,*
> *And true worth is rarely told.*[2]

August 1 opened quietly. About noon Bolling arrived at headquarters with the same horse and wagon that had brought him to Second Manassas. Feild and Cameron prevailed upon Bolling to stay and share their meager dinner of sheep's hamlet washed down with what Cameron called "a wretched apology for coffee."[3] Afterward, Bolling departed. Surgeon Claiborne arrived and challenged Cameron to a game of chess. They sat at

---

1 Bernard Papers, SHC.

2 Miller and Lanier, eds., *Poetry and eloquence of Blue and Gray*, 348-349.

3 William E. Cameron Diary, August 1, 1863, "An Affair with Cavalry," William E. Cameron Papers, UVA.

a table beneath the trees, out of the bright sunshine, arranging the pieces on a board carved with a penknife by a private in the Richmond Grays. A group of idle officers gathered to kibitz. The game ended in stalemate prolonged by Claiborne's reluctance to accept a draw. "So in peaceful and contemplative mood we continued to pore over the position, never dreaming that any foe more dangerous than our knights or bishops were within miles of us," remembered Cameron.[4]

A cannon boomed. A shell whistled by and burst above the tents a few yards away. "It was as if a flash of lightning had come from a cloudless sky," Cameron recalled.[5] The game ended. Drums beat the long roll. Men buckled on their equipment as they hurried into line. Grooms saddled the horses of the field and staff. The regiment stood ready to move. Rumor had it the Yankees had crossed the Rappahannock and driven in the Confederate cavalry pickets. A staff officer from Anderson galloped up. Fighting Dick himself reined in his horse soon afterward. Mahone, remembered Cameron, "appeared on the scene as promptly as though summoned by Aladdin's lamp."[6] The brigadier directed Feild to advance into the thick woods facing the 12th's camp on the north. This would cover the rest of the brigade's assembly.

The regiment's soldiers plunged into the timber. Skirmishers deployed from the color company at the double-quick. Cameron sat on his horse overseeing the line's deployment. The Old Grays' Capt. Robert R. Bowden approached Cameron. Bowden had disgraced himself by dereliction of duty in previous campaigns. He had just returned to the 12th that day after recovering from a Chancellorsville wound and subsequent infections. He carried a brand-new saber of the English pattern, "a very handsome weapon, with burnished steel scabbard, & vastly superior to the pattern with which our officers were furnished," Cameron recalled.[7] Weak from hospitalization, Bowden asked Cameron to carry the sword. Cameron took it, fastened it to his saddle and laughed.

"You almost certainly will get into action today," he said.[8]

4 Ibid.

5 Ibid.

6 Ibid.

7 Ibid.

8 Ibid.

The 12th struggled forward through the underbrush. Before the troops had gone 300 yards into the trees, they came under fire from enemy skirmishers—cavalrymen of Buford's division, which the Florida Brigade had halted.[9] The regiment kept advancing. Soon the men emerged from the woods into the broad plain that stretched almost unbroken to the Rapidan, more than five miles distant.

The 12th's right rested on the Orange & Alexandria, which ran northeastwardly from Culpeper Court House to Brandy Station in the plain's middle. Across the tracks, abreast of the regiment, advanced the 12th Mississippi thrown out as skirmishers for the rest of Posey's brigade.[10] Confederate cavalry, Hampton's and Jones' brigades, hovered in solid columns on the 12th Virginia's left. The horsemen's firearms and sabers glittered in the sunlight. A line of Yankee skirmishers faced the regiment's soldiers, mounted to their left and dismounted dead ahead. Behind the skirmishers blue coated squadrons on the next of the countryside's gentle ridges awaited "their opportunity to swoop down upon our thin line," Cameron remembered.[11] The rest of the Virginians remained behind the 12th's left, standing in line of battle at order arms with colors flying near the woods through which the 12th had passed. "It gave us a very comfortable feeling to know they were there," recalled Cameron.[12]

The regiment's soldiers opened fire. The Northern skirmishers replied with carbines. Pressed by the Southern infantrymen, the enemy cavalrymen grudgingly gave ground. Federal bullets kicked up the dust near the Virginians. A Unionist cannon on the 12th's right fired upon the regiment's soldiers until the retreating blue skirmishers neared the cannoneers. Then the artillerists limbered up and galloped back to the next crest.

A couple hundred yards into the plain, the regiment met stiffer resistance. The men of both sides took cover behind anything that would protect them. The firing grew brisk. The 12th resumed its advance but became overextended. Cameron went to the left to lead that wing of the regiment. Feild remained with and directed the right. Cameron passed behind the Old Grays, finding

9 *OR* 27, 2:609.

10 "Army Correspondence, The Fight in Culpeper," Richmond Daily *Dispatch*, August 6, 1863.

11 Cameron, "An Affair with Cavalry."

12 Ibid.

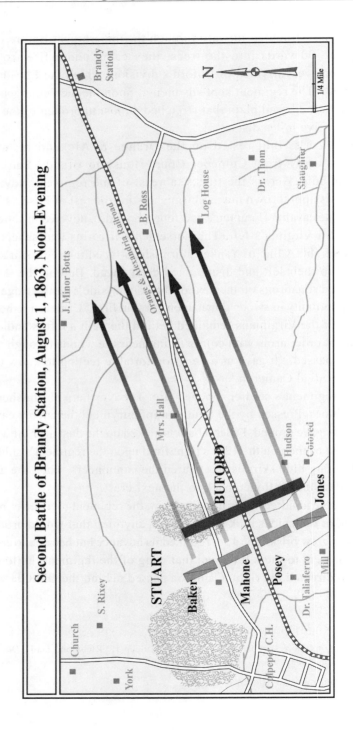

Second Battle of Brandy Station, August 1, 1863, Noon-Evening

a junior lieutenant in command. Calling for Bowden, Cameron learned he had fallen out before the Federal skirmishers fired their first shot.

The Union horse soldiers withdrew slowly, rallying at each successive crest. About a mile beyond where the 12th emerged from the forest, the Federals made an obstinate stand in an orchard of young trees. Near the orchard the regiment suffered its first casualties.

Heffron was behaving more coolly under fire than at Gettysburg. Leaping to the foremost rank, he loaded and fired as if on a rabbit hunt.

"Why, Jack," Cameron said, "The boys told me you were afraid to fight."

Heffron grinned sheepishly.

"I used to be, Adjutant, but see me chase 'em now."[13]

The 12th dislodged the enemy from the orchard, then advanced into a depression. The Hall house, halfway to Brandy Station, stood on the opposite crest. The Unionists held the regiment's soldiers there briefly. Cameron thought he detected signs of an attempt to outflank the 12th on its left. He called on a private in one of the nearest companies to bear a message to Feild. The private objected to the trip of nearly half a mile across the open field in point blank range of Yankee sharpshooters. Before Cameron could insist, the Archer Rifles' Sgt. Samuel Seay volunteered to go. Seay threw his leg over the fence to the right of his company to start on his mission. A ball struck him in the heel, inflicting a disabling wound. Showing no anxiety about the injury and making no outcry at the pain, he overwhelmed with oaths the private who had refused to go. Then a bullet plugged the private's left leg.

"Served you right, damn you," cried Seay. "Pity you weren't killed."[14]

The regiment took the Hall house crest. The soldiers continued northeastwardly with their right still on the railroad. Several times the Federal horsemen threatened to charge the thin Virginia line. Each time the 12th's men formed little squares and frightened off the enemy troopers.

Near the Botts farm the firing intensified. A Yankee bullet passed through the right side of the red-faced Branch's chest. He threw his hands up and fell to the ground. Phillips went to Branch's assistance. Keiley approached them.

"Well, Anthony, I am a goner at last," said Branch.

"Oh, Ned, I hope it is not so bad as you expect," Keiley replied.

"Oh, yes, it is."[15]

13 Ibid.

14 Ibid.

15 Phillips, "Sixth Corporal," 32.

Anthony M. Keiley. *Virginia Historical Society*

Branch soon spit out his chaw of tobacco. The color fled from his face. He died before the stretcher-bearers could carry him to Dr. Claiborne.

The Rifles included a pacifist of sorts. Private Benjamin H. Hays, an apprentice carpenter, considered it sinful to kill even an enemy in battle. On many fields he had refrained from firing his musket. Second Brandy Station was proving no exception. At the Botts farm Chappell observed Hays' reluctance to use his weapon. An accomplished swearer, Chappell ordered Hays to fire and added emphasis with numerous oaths. The profanity produced results.

"Lieutenant," Hays replied, "if you will stop cursing, I will begin firing."[16]

Evening approached. Another charge brought the 12th's soldiers within sight of Brandy Station. "General Stuart dashed up, superbly mounted as usual, and be-sashed & be-plumed like another Murat," remembered Cameron.[17] Two pieces of horse artillery accompanying Stuart unlimbered among the 12th's men.

The guns opened on the Northerners, who tried to deploy from the grove at the town. The combined fire of cannon and muskets drove them to cover before they could form a squadron. They attempted to place a battery in the opening in front of Brandy Station. The 12th's sharpshooters forced the gunners away before they could bring their pieces to bear. Fire from the regiment's extreme right, which occupied a bluff on the railroad, particularly galled the invaders.

The Virginians kept pressing forward. On horseback among the Riflemen, Stuart hummed an air and called out encouragement to the 12th's soldiers as they drove back the enemy. He impressed the troops favorably by speaking to them kindly and encouragingly. Knowing how far they had pushed and

---

16 Bernard Papers, SHC.

17 Cameron, "An Affair with Cavalry." Cameron alludes to Joachim Murat, Marshal of France, King of Naples, a leader of Napoleon Bonaparte's cavalry.

observing their fatigue in the heat, he would say, "Rest a little, boys, and then pour it to them."[18]

Near sunset the regiment reached a branch just west of the town. "Let's go across, boys," said Stuart.[19]

The 12th entered a cornfield on the branch's other side. The Yankees gave up the fight. Cheering wildly, the regiment's soldiers swept into Brandy Station. The Southern cavalry advanced and took over the pursuit. Stuart asked the 12th's men what unit they belonged to. They told him that they belonged to the Petersburg Regiment of Mahone's brigade.

"Present my compliments to the General, and say that he should be proud to command such superb soldiers," said Stuart, bowing low in his saddle.[20]

Night soon fell. The 12th's men retired to the woods where their advance had begun. On the way Cameron found Bowden sitting dejectedly by the roadside. Cameron offered Bowden his sword back, but Bowden declined it, saying he had resolved to resign because his bad heart could not stand the excitement of battle. Cameron was too elated by Stuart's praise for the regiment to let this encounter depress him. He hastened to pass Stuart's compliment on to Mahone.

"Wait until you see Stuart's report," Mahone said coolly.[21]

Long afterward, Cameron read that report expecting fulgent praise for the regiment. The Federals had trounced the Confederate horse soldiers and pushed them back to the outskirts of Culpeper Court House. Once the 12th appeared on the scene, Stuart's forces had not fired a shot except for his horse artillery. Despite this, Cameron recalled, "not one word was said by the Southern Rupert of the troops who had saved him from utter discomfiture that evening."[22] The regiment lost one killed and seven wounded. One of the wounded would die of his injuries.[23] Command of the Richmond Grays passed to First Lt. Robert Mayo, Jr. Bowden resigned 11 days after the fight, leaving the Old Grays under Pollard, now a first lieutenant.

---

18 Charles E. Waddell Diary, August 2, 1863.

19 Cameron, "An Affair with Cavalry."

20 Ibid.

21 Ibid.

22 Ibid. For Stuart's report, see *OR* 27, 2:725.

23 Ibid., 2:336; Henderson, *12VI*, 128.

There is no such thing as a minor skirmish for a participant. Any fight can amount to the war's biggest battle for a soldier involved. A fatal wound ends his existence. A lesser injury might cripple him for life.[24]

There is no such thing as a small loss. The 12th had suffered many more killed or mortally wounded in other actions, but Branch's death evoked unparalleled mourning.

The regiment's officers called an unprecedented meeting on August 5 to give expression to the 12th's grief. Waddell commanded the regiment at the time and chaired the assembly. Cameron served as secretary.

Captain Ned's comrades lauded his patience, courage, endurance, cheerful acceptance of hardship, self-denial, fortitude and gallantry. "Irreparable," they considered his loss, "in the dress-room, around the camp-fires, in the family gatherings of the regiment." They despaired of seeing another with "his cheerful disposition, his efforts to please, his friendliness, his social accomplishments."[25]

The bluecoats had killed the best-loved man in the regiment.

24 Colonel David Baldwin, III, United States Army, provided this insight.

25 "Tribute of Respect," Richmond Daily *Dispatch*, August 18, 1863, p. 2, col. 2.

CHAPTER 12

Meade Versus Lee

Enemy movements prompted Lee to withdraw from the Rappahannock to the Rapidan. The 12th left Culpeper Court House on August 3 and arrived at Orange Court House next day. The retreat exposed Culpeper County again to the invaders' ravages. "Fences all gone, fields uncultivated, stock & negroes driven away and in fact houses without inhabitants all serve to impress on the mind more fully the malignity of our enemies," Sale railed.[1] The men saw refugees carrying such necessities as they could, keeping the army between themselves and the Federals.

A quiet spell followed. The regiment camped on a hill in the beautiful country along the Rapidan. The soldiers could see the plains of Culpeper County beyond the river. To the west loomed the Blue Ridge. Rain fell almost every other evening. The thunderstorms provided grand spectacles. The clouds formed in the mountains and approached until the tempest broke over the camp. Sometimes the wind carried away tents and the warm rain soaked the inhabitants and their belongings.

Company and regimental officers caught up with paperwork. The 12th's record-keeping reached its high-water mark. Mahone kept up his brigade's discipline and drill. Just as in Norfolk, his Virginians had a battalion drill every morning and a brigade drill every evening, each two hours long. Inspections, reviews and picket duty also kept the men on their toes. "We

1 Sale to Aunt, August 10, 1863.

have the name of the best disciplined &
drilled Brigade in this Army but I tell
you we earn the name if hard drilling
ever earns anything," recalled Sale.[2]

Mahone posted a guard around
the camp. Nobody could get out
except to fetch water from a spring.
Sometimes the Virginians felt as if
they did not even have time to wash,
but they managed to participate in
the army's ongoing religious revival.
Ministers from Petersburg traveled to
Orange Court House and preached,
including Reverend Platt. Despite
short rations and long drills, the
soldiers read religious tracts and
sang from hymn books. Around 200
converted. Several prayer meetings
took place nightly.

The troops also found time for amusement, playing a game called "Hot
Jackets." Each participant had a hickory switch. As best he could, he laid
it on his opponent. "The sound of the cuts resound[s] through the camp,"
remembered Sale.[3]

Mahone lived in luxury. Visiting him, his wife boarded in a comfortable
farmhouse. Todd, now a sergeant on detached duty as acting ordnance officer
of Mahone's brigade, had grown up with Mrs. Mahone in the village of
Smithfield in Isle of Wight County. She often invited him to dinner with
the general. Todd frequently partook of Mahone's excellent cigars. The
general's courier scoured the country and kept Mahone supplied with butter,
eggs and other delicacies. The general had brought from Norfolk a slave

2 John F. Sale to Aunt, September 3, 1863.

3 Ibid.

named Tam and trained him as a cook.[4] Sale called Mahone "Old Porte" or "Porte" because he seemed to live as luxuriously as the Sultan of Turkey.[5]

As in May the Northerners were making progress in the west. Now they were maneuvering Bragg's army out of Chattanooga. As in May Lee favored taking the offensive in Virginia, but this time Davis overruled Lee. Longstreet received orders to transport two divisions of his corps to Georgia. Elements of his third division would go to Richmond and Charleston. Preparations for the move commenced on September 6. Longstreet's Corps departed two days later. Because of lax security in Richmond, the enemy knew the destination of these troops before they left.

Lee reviewed his remaining forces. The review of Hill's Corps occurred on September 11 in a beautiful valley with gently swelling hills on either side. Officers' wives and ladies from the surrounding country graced the scene. Wearing full uniform and mounted on his dappled gray, Traveller, Lee occupied a rise in front of the center of the line formed by the corps. His staff surrounded him. As his veterans passed in review, his face lit up with admiration. The three divisions resumed their positions. Lee, followed by his staff, rode at a gallop along the line of between 10,000 and 15,000 men. "The old hero looked the embodiment of grace and martial bearing," recalled Todd. "Coming to a wide ditch 'Traveller' cleared it with a bound, while the general held his seat as if he were a part of the horse."[6]

The long hours of drilling paid off for Mahone's brigade in this review. In marching and soldierly bearing, the Virginians surpassed any other brigade in the corps and lived up to their reputation as General Lee's Regulars, but something else made them unique—a bayonet on each man's musket. Mahone would not grant a furlough to any man lacking the certificate of his captain that the applicant had a bayonet. Soldiers hardly ever used the bayonet in combat. Veterans in other units threw them away to lighten their loads on long marches. Mahone's brigade had not yet fought hand-

4 Todd, "Reminiscences," 144.

5 John F. Sale Diary, May 25, 1864, John F. Sale Papers; ibid., June 29, 1864. He also referred to Mahone as "Billy" (Ibid., September 25, 1864) and as "Billy Mahone" (Ibid., October 3, 1864). None of the 12th's soldiers referred to Mahone as "Little Billy," though Wise's circle referred to Mahone that way. John Sergeant Wise, *The End of an Era* (Cambridge, MA, 1899), 320-321.

6 Todd, "Reminiscences," 148.

to-hand, but one day the men would thank God that Porte insisted they retain these weapons.

A few skirmishes occurred along the Rapidan, causing the 12th to shift camp several miles east to Rapidan Station, but a major clash of arms did not seem imminent. The revival resumed in Lee's army. The ministers who preached to the 12th included Edwards' father. The regiment had recovered from the Gettysburg campaign. All the men had clothes and shoes and lacked only hats. The ranks refilled until the 12th's aggregate strength totaled about 500. "Nearly all the Hospital 'Rats' have returned to duty," one of Whitehorne's cousins in the Huger Grays wrote to the sergeant, who was convalescing at home in Pleasant Shade.[7] He had not fallen into enemy hands at Gettysburg because a hospital steward had found room for him in a spring wagon.

Cold weather arrived by September 27. Word came of the Confederate victory at Chickamauga, where Longstreet's Corps played a key role. "The news from the Western army causes us to be profoundly grateful to the God of battles," wrote Edwards.[8] The regiment shifted camp again, this time a mile northwest to Clark's Mountain. The revival proceeded despite the presence of only a single chaplain in the brigade. Reverend Peterson had resigned late in 1862. His position remained vacant. Weisiger, who had rejoined the regiment, created a fuss by declining to fill the post. "There is still much religious interest manifested in the Brigade," wrote Edwards to his father, a candidate for the position.[9]

Bragg's army besieged the defeated Federals in Chattanooga. The Northerners drew upon their other armies to assemble a relief force. Two infantry corps traveled to Tennessee from Meade's army. Lee sought to capitalize on their departure by launching his army on what Edwards called a "great flank."[10] Two of Meade's remaining infantry corps held positions just north of the Rapidan. His other three encamped farther north, by Culpeper Court House. Lee intended to turn the Unionist right, drive Meade's army into the confluence of the Rappahannock and the Rapidan and destroy it in that trap.

7 n.a. to Whitehorne, September 16, 1863, Whitehorne Papers, LV.

8 Leroy S. Edwards to Father, September 27, 1863.

9 Leroy S. Edwards to Father, October 4, 1863.

10 Leroy S. Edwards to Father, October 11, 1863.

The 12th broke camp at Clark's Mountain on October 8 and slogged westward through Orange Court House in what Phillips termed "a fine slow rain."[11] The muddy, shivering troops encamped at Liberty Mills on the Rapidan. "We are very bad off for shoes, nearly half of the Regiment is barefoot," noted Waddell.[12] The regiment moved out at daybreak October 9, crossed the Rapidan and hobbled northward, halting within two miles of Madison Court House, near the Blue Ridge's foot. The journey resumed at 7 a.m. next day. A ramble through woods and fields by every imaginable byway took the 12th's men northeastward beyond Robinson River. "No engineer could give you an idea of the sinuosities of our route." wrote Edwards.[13] They encamped on Hazel River's south bank at 7 p.m.

On October 11, they forded the river and trekked along its north bank for several miles in clear weather. "The forest is robed in all the glory of colors that October can paint," Edwards wrote.[14] The troops emerged from the woods before noon, re-crossing the river and heading for Culpeper Court House on the road from there to Front Royal. A report of Yankees in line of battle ahead halted the column at 1 p.m. but proved false. Three hours later the regiment bivouacked five miles northwest of Culpeper Court House. "We all feel that on the morrow another collision with our ancient foe must take place," Edwards wrote.[15] The Confederate trap appeared ready to spring on the invaders. Despite hard marching and short rations, the troops displayed high spirits and felt optimistic about the outcome of Lee's maneuver.

But the "great flank" failed. Meade did not allow Lee to envelop him but was retreating up the Orange & Alexandria toward safety. The Federals burned the railroad bridge over the Rappahannock, leaving their stragglers to cross the river as best they could. Lee kept trying to head off the enemy. Ewell's Corps engaged in a narrow flanking movement on the right. Hill's Corps made a wider swing on the left. The 12th's soldiers broke camp at 10 a.m. on October 12. By twilight they had trudged cross country to Amissville. Next day they crossed the Rappahannock at Waterloo Bridge, halting that afternoon in an oak grove within two miles of Warrenton. Their

11 Phillips, "Sixth Corporal," 33.

12 Charles E. Waddell Diary, October 8, 1863.

13 Leroy S. Edwards to Father, October 11, 1863.

14 Ibid.

15 Ibid.

sutler overtook them with a wagonload of gingerbread, quickly selling out in return for Confederate money or liens on the men's pay. The tired troops also feasted on white oak acorns. "Ate them like chestnuts, roasted them, boiled them, burnt them & boiled them to make coffee," Phillips recalled. "They made splendid coffee and was a splendid appetizer, provided you could get the eatables."[16]

On the morning of October 14, the men began a jaunt taking them through Warrenton and the villages of New Baltimore and Buckland Mills. As they strolled through Greenwich, another hamlet, the enemy's deserted campfires still burned. Hill's column moved faster and faster. The 12th's soldiers spotted Bristoe Station on the Orange & Alexandria and heard firing which soon became heavy. An enemy corps was crossing Broad Run. Hill was trying to strike this corps. In his haste he failed to detect the Federal II Corps approaching along the Orange & Alexandria's embankment beyond his right.

Cooke's and Kirkland's North Carolina brigades of Heth's division led Hill's attack. The division's other two brigades and the guns of McIntosh's battalion supported the North Carolinians. II Corps took position behind the railroad's cuts and fills, opening fire on the right of Cooke's and Kirkland's brigades. The Tarheels wheeled and charged the railroad embankment. The Northerners blasted the North Carolinians. Many of the surviving Tarheels surrendered. The rest fled. The Unionists counterattacked, seizing five cannon of McIntosh's battalion and threatening to overwhelm the supporting brigades of Heth's division, Walker's brigade on the left and Davis' brigade on the right.

Anderson's division advanced to prevent this. As the lead brigade's lead regiment, the 12th deployed first, in a field on the right of Davis' brigade. The Herrings went forward as skirmishers. The other companies formed line of battle. The rest of Mahone's brigade took post on the 12th's right, but the Yankees did not press their counterstroke farther. Hill did not renew his attack. His men came under heavy cannon fire. A battery between one half and three quarters of a mile distant shelled the regiment. "Nothing but a horizontal position would save us," Edwards wrote.[17]

16 Phillips, "Sixth Corporal, 33.

17 Leroy S. Edwards to Father, October 15, 1863.

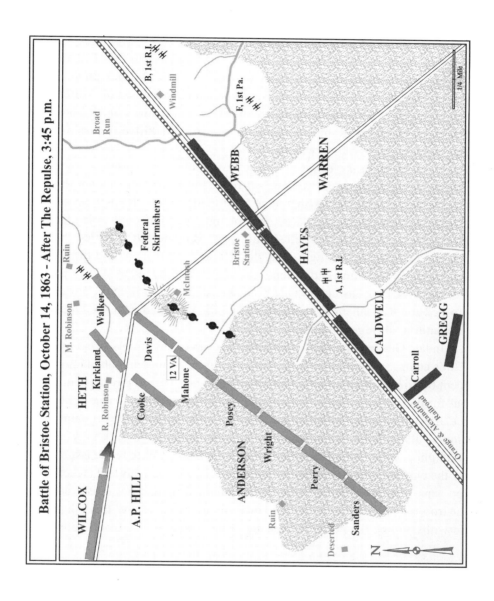

Battle of Bristoe Station, October 14, 1863 – After The Repulse, 3:45 p.m.

Heth's division lost heavily. Anderson's division suffered fewer than a score of casualties. The 12th lost one man wounded, but his injury proved fatal.[18] The repulse evoked angry criticism of Hill. "Had we continued to march the day before instead of halting in the Grove, we could have been bosses of the situation," Phillips concluded.[19]

That night a light rain fell. By morning the invaders had vanished, retiring to their old entrenchments around Centreville. Lee did not pursue. The Bristoe Station campaign ended. The regiment remained on the battlefield, camping near the railroad amid wire grass, broom straw, stunted pines and other scrubby trees. Rabbits abounded. The soldiers killed droves of them and had all the food they wanted.

Lee's army broke camp at 1 a.m. on October 18, withdrawing down the Orange & Alexandria. Mahone's brigade hiked in clear weather through Greenwich, reaching Rappahannock Station at sunset. "It came up a small shower of rain in drops as large as your thumb and as cold as ice, almost make one have a chill," recalled Phillips.[20] Mahone felt gratified that his brigade had not lost a single straggler. He halted his men, had them close up and dress their line and ordered the regimental bands to strike up "The Bonnie Blue Flag" as his brigade bivouacked. Next morning the Virginians crossed the Rappahannock on pontoons and encamped near the Orange & Alexandria's bridge abutments.

In late October and early November, a series of cold fronts swept over the 12th's camp. Some soldiers had first class winter clothes and blankets sent to them by friends or relatives. Other men could only afford government issue, but for once the government provided abundant clothing, partially because the army lay at the Orange & Alexandria's railhead. The government issue clothes also proved of good quality. The troops received dark gray jackets and light gray pants and caps. Those who disdained Confederate issue could try the clothing abandoned by the Federals—light blue pants and jackets, and red caps with blue bands. Only shoes remained scarce, but those reaching the troops excelled in quality. "The majority of the shoes are 'English make,' notwithstanding the perfect Blockade of the 'old Ape,'" crowed Sale.[21]

---

18 Henderson, *12VI*, 106-167.

19 Phillips, "Sixth Corporal," 34.

20 Ibid.

21 John F. Sale to Aunt, November 1, 1863.

On November 5, Lee and Letcher reviewed the army's Cavalry Corps on the broad plain between Culpeper Court House and Brandy Station. Hundreds of Lee's infantrymen and artillerymen attended. The governor and the general, surrounded by staff officers and subordinates, conducted the review from a knoll. Confronting them stood a line of cavalry extending for more than a mile. Regiment by regiment, the horsemen moved by the right flank in column of fours, then wheeled into line of battle. Each regiment took its position, one behind the other, at intervals of 100 yards. In this formation the cavalry advanced at a walk toward Letcher and Lee, who saluted each regiment and took salutes in return as the horsemen came opposite the knoll. "Nearby was a mounted cavalry band, which discoursed as each regiment passed in review beautiful music, the soft and liquid notes of which floated dreamily away in the balmy atmosphere, delighting all who heard it," remembered Bernard.[22] The formation then turned, coming within 200 yards of the reviewing stand. At a command the lead regiment dashed forward in line of battle with drawn sabers brandished overhead and glittering in the sun. Howling the Rebel yell, the troopers passed the reviewing officers at a gallop. One regiment after another repeated this maneuver until the entire command had galloped by.

The Bristoe Station campaign belatedly inflicted another loss on the regiment. During November's first week, a court martial found the Archer Rifles' Pvt. Joseph H. Adams guilty of cowardice at Bristoe. A "small poor scrawny" printer from Petersburg and a "natural born coward," Adams "could not fight even if he wanted to," recalled Phillips.[23] Adams had already been court-martialed in April. Convicted of going absent without leave, he had been sentenced to 30 days in the regimental guardhouse, the first 10 on bread and water. His sentence also required him to walk around the regimental camp wrapped in two blankets every alternate two hours for fifteen days, wearing a sign that said, "absent to get blankets."[24] This time the tribunal sentenced Adams to death by firing squad.

Adams got a reprieve courtesy of Meade and his army. The Confederates could not defend Kelly's Ford, four miles down the Rappahannock from the Orange & Alexandria's former bridge. The high ground east of the

22 Bernard Papers, SHC.

23 Phillips, "Sixth Corporal," 36.

24 Henderson, *12VI*, 106-167.

Rappahannock commanded the western bank. A strong Federal force could cross at any time. The Secessionist defenders could only delay the Northerners long enough for reinforcements to gather behind the ford. To counter a Yankee thrust across the river at Kelly's Ford, Lee retained a bridgehead on the Rappahannock's east bank at the old railroad crossing. The bridgehead would allow him to threaten the Northern rear just as a Unionist crossing at Kelly's Ford would menace the rear of his army.

The Federals had originally dug the bridgehead earthworks, consisting of two redoubts and a line of rifle pits. The Secessionists turned them to face the foe and worked hard strengthening them. The bridgehead accessed the Rappahannock's southern bank by a pontoon bridge about 800 yards above the railroad crossing. The camps of Lee's army extended for several miles opposite the bridgehead. Hill's Corps encamped above the bridgehead, Ewell's Corps below.

On November 7, Hays' Louisiana Brigade of Early's division held the works in the bridgehead. That afternoon a strong force of Yankee infantry from III Corps pushed across Kelly's Ford. Another powerful Union contingent approached the bridgehead, which Early reinforced with Hoke's North Carolina Brigade. The 12th's soldiers struck their tents, packed their baggage and eased down to a hill above the railroad abutments. At sunset Mahone's brigade formed line of battle on the slope, shivering in the frosty air. They heard heavy firing across the river a few hundred yards to their right, at the bridge's site. Detached from the rest of the brigade, the 12th's soldiers at dark deployed as pickets among the tall weeds in the bottomland near the river. Further chilled by the dampness, the men saw the Northerners charging the bridgehead's earthworks "by the flashes of their rifles, looking like fire flies," remembered Bernard.[25] The invaders—VI Corps—captured Hays' and Hoke's brigades. Early confirmed the bridgehead's loss, then ordered the pontoon bridge cut loose. The 12th remained near the river bank less than an hour before returning to high ground. The regiment, minus one man who fell into enemy hands, stood picket there until 4 a.m.[26] Then the 12th retired toward Culpeper Court House. With the bridgehead gone and the enemy III Corps across the river at Kelly's Ford, Lee saw no alternative to withdrawal.

25 Bernard Papers, SHC.

26 Henderson, *12VI*, 106-167.

The 12th rejoined the army two miles short of the court house. Lee had formed line of battle there at right angles to the Orange & Alexandria. Mahone's brigade, on the right of Hill's Corps, threw up earthworks just left of the tracks. The Yankees appeared at 3 p.m. and threatened Hill's left. Mahone's Virginians remained facing the enemy until dark. Then the Southerners built fires along their line and the retreat resumed. The regiment plodded through Culpeper Court House along the railroad. The cold made the march miserable. "Walking was fatiguing, and resting was freezing," Edwards wrote.[27] At daybreak the men crossed the Rapidan on pontoons, halting before noon on the bleak north slope of a hill at Bell's farm, several miles from the river and a mile nearer Orange Court House than their September camp. They began building new quarters.

Quiet prevailed November 9, a windy day of rain and snow. The line of the Rapidan discouraged the Federals from further operations. The arrival of Harrison's wagons initially cheered the Petersburg men, but news from home about the activities of speculators aroused one of the 12th's soldiers to fury. Adopting the pen name "Alpha," he wrote to the Petersburg Daily *Register*'s editor demanding that profiteering cease.[28]

The men improved their new accommodations. Their morale remained high and their confidence in Lee almost unshaken though Meade had now defeated Lee three times in a row: at Gettysburg, at Bristoe Station and at Rappahannock Bridge. Defeating Lee in Northern territory or Northern Virginia would not meet the Lincoln administration's burden of persuading the Northern electorate to give Abe another term in office in the coming presidential election. If Meade did not capture Richmond, or an equivalent success did not come elsewhere, Lincoln could expect to lose the election. The Union would likely elect a Democratic administration that might well abandon the war.

Mahone sent for Tyler. Porte had horses ready. The two officers mounted and began riding.

"You will come along this way where I have had the fences pulled at each place," said Mahone.

"What do you want me to do?" asked Tyler.

"Dammit I want you to shoot a man tomorrow," replied Mahone.[29]

27 Leroy S. Edwards to Father, November 10, 1863.

28 Petersburg Daily *Register*, November 20, 1863.

29 Phillips, "Sixth Corporal," 36.

Adams had accompanied the regiment under guard on the retreat and into its new encampment. "Sitting around so many campfires he had become smoked equal to a piece of bacon," recalled Phillips. "He had become changed in color so one could scarcely recognize him."[30] On the morning of November 10, Adams may have thought that he would have his sentence commuted or that he would receive another reprieve. Two men from the 16th Virginia sentenced to death for desertion had already had their execution postponed that day.[31] "The poor fellow seemed little concerned as he passed me a few moments ago under guard," Edwards wrote.[32] Most condemned men in the Confederate army were not executed. Family members, friends and politicians interceded on the offenders' behalf. Davis often commuted the sentences, annoying his army commanders and hurting discipline.

The brigade gathered down by a creek that afternoon. The Virginians formed three sides of a square, facing inwards. The fourth side remained open. The condemned man's open grave and the stake which would hold him for the fatal bullets occupied the middle of that side. Adams stood nearby waiting. Perhaps even yet he hoped that an order for his reprieve would arrive, but his luck had run out. "There was no one to intercede for him and get him off," recalled Phillips, who thought Adams looked more smoked than ever.[33] His last walk began. He and his entourage started on the formation's left and marched slowly along the ranks of soldiers.

First came the 12th's band, playing a funeral dirge. Tyler followed with the firing squad. Next marched four men bearing an empty coffin. Behind the coffin came Adams. A chaplain walked at his side. Adams displayed "abject fear and wretchedness," Bernard remembered. "His very gait, shambling as he moved unsteadily along, was that of a man thoroughly undone by fright."[34]

When the procession reached its destination, Tyler blindfolded Adams and tied his hands behind him to the stake. Adams composed himself. Expressing himself ready to die, he asked Tyler not to give the command to fire but to blow his little whistle instead. Tyler gave preliminary orders to the firing squad, then blew his whistle. The first volley failed to kill Adams—a sad

---

30 Ibid.

31 "Shot," Staunton *Spectator* (Staunton, Virginia), December 1, 1863, p. 2, col. 2.

32 Edwards to Father, November 10, 1863.

33 Phillips, "Sixth Corporal," 37.

34 Bernard Papers, SHC.

commentary on the regiment's marksmanship. He only lurched forward. The stake held him upright. A second volley dispatched him. On the way back to camp, the brigade marched past his corpse. "I did not witness the execution and am glad of it," noted Waddell, a member of the court martial that had sentenced Adams to death.[35] Waddell's company was working on breastworks.

By November's last week, the soldiers figured they had gone into winter quarters. Little fighting took place except for an occasional Federal probe and the skirmishing that accompanied Confederate efforts to harvest the corn behind the enemy pickets north of the Rapidan. The 12th's pursuits included not only checkers, chess and reading but cards, dancing, improvised backgammon and music. A log hall served as chapel and music hall. "Some of the concerts were very creditable," Todd recollected. "The best received performances were the negro minstrel concerts."[36] Serenading parties became fashionable. Serenaders customarily received invitations to partake of "creature comforts."[37]

Amid this bustle some lads plumbed the depths of sloth. Bernard, whose messmates had topped the chimney of their tent with a flour barrel for better draft, remembered, "Rarely did any member of the mess do anything for the benefit of the mess unless it was his turn to do it." One day as they lay in their tent, they learned that their chimney was on fire. Instead of rushing to the door to knock down the burning barrel, they wasted time arguing about whose turn it was to act. They knew they should dig a small ditch around their tent, pitched on a hillside, but Bernard recalled "we reasoned that we might probably move our camp before the next rain, in which event the labor constructing a ditch might be saved." One night as they slept on the tent's floor, a downpour began. The rain ran down the slope, into the tent and into their bed, "from which we quickly bounced up, almost in the plight of drowned rats."[38] They dug the ditch next day.

Other soldiers had their minds on a more spiritual plane. "Nothing so quickens our spiritual life as the constant sense of our approaching dissolution in our mind," wrote Manson as he prepared for the possibility of death.[39]

35   Charles E. Waddell Diary, November 10, 1863.

36   Todd, "Reminiscences," 159.

37   Ibid.

38   Bernard Papers, SHC.

39   Joseph R. Manson to Sister, November 13, 1863, Joseph R. Manson Letters, Private Collection of William T. Zielinski.

Owens, an active Mason, helped organize a Masonic Lodge for Mahone's brigade—the Kadmiel Military Lodge. The Masons met in the log building. Their members included Manson.

The consensus that campaigning had ended for the year proved mistaken. Grant relieved the Federal army besieged in Chattanooga. The Yankees then compelled Longstreet's command to abandon its siege of Burnside's Corps in Knoxville. Meade received intelligence that his army outnumbered Lee's by two to one. The Unionist had his bluecoats prepare rations for eight days. On November 26, his army crossed the Rapidan, threatening to turn the Confederate right and get between Lee's army and Richmond. Next day the regiment broke camp and headed eastward on Orange Plank Road. Beyond Verdiersville the 12th's men turned toward Locust Grove, on the Wilderness' fringe. Anderson's division was marching to the assistance of the Second Corps, which Early led because of Ewell's illness. As the farther east of Lee's corps, Early's Corps had contacted the invaders first and was battling them. The Norfolk Division, crossing Mine Run, formed line of battle near Locust Grove. At 10 p.m., on orders from Early, Anderson's troops retired to a stronger position behind the run and bivouacked.

On November 28, a cold rain fell all day. Lee withdrew Ewell's Corps and Anderson's division to the still stronger line extending from Hume's Old Shop to Zoar Church. The Norfolk Division took position between Orange Turnpike and the plank road, on the left of Heth's division. The 12th deployed in support of some artillery.

That night the rain stopped, the wind rose and the temperature plummeted. The detailed men and the staff found some respite from the weather. Todd sheltered his ordnance train in a pine thicket. Doctor Samuel T. Dickinson, who had succeeded Doctor Baker as the 12th's assistant surgeon in April upon Baker's promotion to surgeon of another regiment, fixed his quarters in the hollow behind the ridge the regiment defended. Assisted by his mulatto slave, Dickinson built out of boulders there a formidable structure capable of accommodating his slave, his horse and himself. It amused Lee as he rode by in the morning. Stopping to inquire who had built the fort, he complimented Dickinson on his engineering.

The frontline soldiers' plight had nothing amusing about it. "The keen north wind had a clear sweep over our poor fellows as they lay in line along their elevated position behind hastily constructed breastworks," Todd recalled.[40]

40 Todd, "Reminiscences," 161.

The Federals pushed their lines closer to Anderson's division on November 29. A battle seemed imminent, but no attack came. The 12th's men improved their breastworks in the bitter cold. Next morning the Northerners shelled the artillery supported by the regiment. Projectiles fell among the 12th's men but hit none of them. A Union battle line emerged from the trees in the regiment's front, threw out skirmishers and started to advance but then retired without assaying the Southern position, disappointing the Virginians. "We could have given them such a flogging as would sink Chancellorsville into insignificance," wrote Edwards.[41] A close look at the Confederate line convinced Maj. Gen. Gouverneur Kemble Warren, the Federal II Corps' commander, that his troops could not take the Southern position. This scuttled Meade's plan, formulated upon Warren's previous assurance that he could turn the Secessionist right.

December 1 also passed without a Union attack. That evening the Juniors stood picket. A few advanced and took cover behind trees, playing a rough game with their Northern counterparts until dark. A sentry would fire and hit the tree that shielded his opposite number. The latter would sing out, "That's a good shot, now give me a show."[42] Lee decided to assume the initiative because of a report from the Cavalry Corps' Maj. Gen. Wade Hampton that the Confederates could turn the Union left. That night Lee attempted "an undertaking of the Jackson stamp," Edwards wrote.[43] Anderson's and Wilcox's divisions prepared to attack the Yankee left at daybreak. The Norfolk Division would open the ball.

The 12th's soldiers left their breastworks early December 2, taking Catharpin Road and obscure by-ways toward the unguarded enemy flank. They were forming line of battle when a messenger overtook them. The Northerners had retreated. "Old Meade Crawfished out," commented Sale.[44] Anderson's division pursued the Federals for about eight miles, but not even cavalry could overtake the Yanks. Lee's army made, wrote Edwards, "a most harassing march" back toward Orange Court House.[45]

---

41 Postscript of December 3, 1863, to Letter, Leroy S. Edwards to Father, November 29, 1863.

42 John F. Sale to Aunt, December 23, 1863.

43 Postscript of December 3, 1863, to Letter, Edwards to Father, November 29, 1863.

44 Sale to Aunt, December 23, 1863.

45 Postscript of December 3, 1863, to Letter, Edwards to Father, November 29, 1863.

Next morning the regiment reoccupied its quarters on Bell's farm. "I am fatigued, but the sight of my *chimney* puts life in me," recorded Waddell.[46] Some regretted that the enemy had not attacked. Meade had done so little, wrote Sale, "it put me in mind of the Mother Goose story about the 10,000 men who marched up the hill and then marched down again."[47] Others rejoiced just to have survived. "Thank God the battle is over and twice victorious are we in that we bring back into our old winter quarters in Orange, our entire force, no man in the Brigade during the campaign having received a scratch," Edwards declared.[48]

Reports arrived that the Unionists were going into winter quarters. The Virginians opened letters that awaited them in camp. They hoped Harrison, Spratley and the other commissioners would soon bring boxes of delicacies from home and Harrison arrived after sunset. Some soldiers calculated when their turns would come for a 15-day furlough. Of every 100 infantrymen, one at a time could go. This increased to two men out of every 100 after December 15.

Thieves plundered the flour in the brigade commissary. A teenage slave carrying a musket loaded with hard peas was posted to protect the remaining rations. A private from the 16th Virginia approached the commissary too closely. The sentry shot the white man in the face, then brought the musket down on his head, killing him. Hearing of this, some of the brigade's men wanted to lynch the lad. Mahone's intervention saved him.[49]

Virginia prepared to inaugurate her new governor, "Extra Billy" Smith, who had served in Mahone's brigade at French's Farm. Weisiger filled the 12th's vacant chaplain's position with Rev. Samuel V. Hoyle on the recommendation of Edwards' father.

An epidemic began of itch, a contagious eruption caused by a mite that burrows in the skin. The first symptoms consisted of "a few suspicious looking pustules" on the hands, Todd recalled. "The disease, with the 'Scotchfiddle' accompaniment, rapidly developed and was soon in full bloom."[50] Incubation took about two weeks. The affliction spread through the entire regiment because the troops slept in pairs for warmth. Some cured themselves with

---

46 Charles E. Waddell Diary, December 3, 1863.

47 John F. Sale to Aunt, December 13, 1863.

48 Postscript of December 3, 1863, to Letter, Edwards to Father, November 29, 1863.

49 Benjamin H. Trask, *16th Virginia Infantry* (Lynchburg, VA, 1986), 20.

50 Todd, "Reminiscences," 162 a.

folk remedies. Phillips dug up some "poke stink root" and boiled it in a cooking kettle to make a wash. At bed time his messmates stripped and he spread this potion on them. "No more camp itch after that," he remembered. "When first applied it would tickle you all over and would bring out great welts as if you had been whipped with a cowhide."[51] Others did not rid themselves of the itch until spring, when the surgeons issued chloroform ointment. "But it was verily 'old scratch' while it lasted," recalled Todd.[52]

The troops suffered from other afflictions as well. "*Snowing* & wood as scarce as *whiskey*," recorded Waddell.[53] The surrounding countryside lay destitute. "Our prospects are very hard for a Christmas," Sale wrote on December 23. "We can procure nothing scarcely here and what we can the most enormous prices are charged for them."[54] But 10 wagons were rolling up from Petersburg. They arrived on a very cold Christmas Eve. Almost every soldier with relatives in Petersburg received a bundle. The townspeople forwarded parcels smuggled through enemy lines from Norfolk. Through Mrs. Waddell, Sale received a package containing boots, a suit of clothes, a hat, underclothes, socks, soap and thread, among other items. "Everything suited to a fraction fitting as if they were made for me, as well as could-have been done had I been where they were made," he commented.[55] The boxes for the Petersburg troops far outdid the bundles for the other men and contained "anything you might name not forgetting a liberal supply of Liquor," wrote Sale.[56] The Petersburg soldiers did not wait for Christmas but promptly got drunk.

Compared with the previous year, 1863 represented light duty for the 12th. The troops fought less but only a trickle of men entered the regiment while a relative flood departed. The regiment had begun the year with about 806 soldiers. A mere 37 men joined. At least 147 left permanently.[57] The latter included Brown and York Archer, medically discharged because of their 1862 wounds. The 12th shrank by 14 percent to around 696 soldiers present and absent. Fewer than two-thirds of these lads remained with the colors.

51 Phillips, "Sixth Corporal," 37.

52 Todd, "Reminiscences," 162 a.

53 Charles E. Waddell Diary, December 23, 1863.

54 Sale to Aunt, December 23, 1863.

55 Sale to Uncle, December 28, 1863.

56 Ibid.

57 Rolls 514-534, M324, Record Group 109, NA; Confederate Rosters, 2:1-56, LV; Henderson, *12VI*, 106-167.

CHAPTER 13

The Wilderness

Lee's army had exhausted the available rations near Orange Court House. He had to disperse his forces to subsist them. Anderson's division withdrew to the southern part of Orange County. Preparations to move the camp of Mahone's brigade began on January 2. One hundred men from the 12th walked about 10 miles down the Orange & Alexandria to Madison Run Station, halfway between Orange Court House and Gordonsville. Three-quarters of a mile from the station, the detail reached a bluff. The soldiers began clearing out an oak grove. They endured an unusually cold night, then continued clearing throughout the following day and January 4 as well. On that day the rest of the 12th's men struck their tents at 9 a.m. These soldiers and the brigade's remainder shuffled through a snow squall toward their new camp, arriving at dark. They spent the rest of the week building quarters. The usual ramshackle village arose. By Saturday the troops had finished their huts, moved into them and made them comfortable. The various activities of winter quarters resumed. Detachments from the regiment crushed stone to pave the road between Madison Run Station and Orange Court House.

Mahone grew increasingly active. "He directed his attention towards increasing the efficiency and strength of his brigade," recalled Todd. "He made strenuous efforts to get back the absentees, detailed men, and skulkers."[1] Porte consolidated the regimental bands into a Brigade Drum and Fife Corps

1 Todd, "Reminiscences," 168.

of twenty drummers and five fifers, which played reveille and tattoo for the brigade and practiced an hour a day in front of his headquarters. The consolidation freed many regimental musicians for other duties. Mahone also provided his men with shoes. His colonels detailed to brigade headquarters any shoemakers in their regiments. Porte sent to Richmond for the tools necessary to manufacture footwear. Swapping green hides for leather, he bartered with the residents of Orange and the neighboring counties. Soon he had a shoe factory operating.[2]

The two soldiers of the 16th Virginia reprieved on the day of Adams' death came up again for execution on January 10.[3] No reprieve or commutation came for them this time. "The execution took place on a bitter winter afternoon when the leaden skies were unrelieved by a ray of sunshine, while the sad winds moaned through the trees as if Nature seemed attuned to the melancholy work at hand," remembered Todd.[4] One of the condemned men met his fate well, kneeling unassisted at his stake and pulling the cap over his eyes while the firing squad's captain blindfolded and bound the other. The onlooking soldiers brooded. "Thinking for instance that man was once somebody's darling and how much care, attention, & cost it requires to raise a child to manhood," Phillips recalled.[5] The Virginians marched past the lifeless bodies. "All seemed sad for a moment, but the hearts of soldiers are so hardened, that before reaching the camp the merry laugh and joke could be heard as if nothing had happened," recorded the Petersburg Riflemen's Pvt. John R. Turner, a former clerk at a dry goods store wounded at Second Manassas.[6]

Postmaster General John Reagan, a Texan, had organized a mail service considered one of the Confederacy's few successes. But nothing short of a letter a day could satisfy homesick young men. As of the double execution, Edwards had not yet received New Year's greetings from his family. Thawing his frozen ink, he wrote of Reagan, "He is a slow coach,

2 For the art of making shoes out of hides, see "Important to Planters," *The Carolina Spartan* (Spartanburg, SC), October 27, 1864, p. 1, col. 3. The author, "Lieut. H. W. Fields, 12th Virginia Infantry," was First Lt. Hubbard W. Feild of the Huger Grays, who retired with "chronic congestion of the brain" August 19, 1864. Henderson, *12VI*, 124.

3 "Shot for Cowardice," Richmond Daily *Dispatch*, January 15, 1864, p. 1, col. 59.

4 Todd, "Reminiscences," 176.

5 Phillips, "Sixth Corporal," 40.

6 John R. Turner Diary, Bernard Papers, SHC.

that Texas friend of mine."[7] The soldiers from enemy-occupied territory had a bigger problem with mail. As of January 23, Sale had not received a letter from his family in Norfolk since December 21, when he received one written November 26. He would not receive another until April 17. Major General Benjamin F. Butler commanded the Yankees occupying Norfolk. He wanted to destroy the morale of its hostile citizens and their relatives in Confederate uniform and gave high priority to discouraging and intercepting their correspondence. Mail carriers knew they could sell their letters to the invaders. Some embraced this opportunity rather than risk smuggling the missives through enemy lines.

The troops also suffered from want of food. The Confederate Commissary Department had failed them again. The local farmers did not want to part with their produce for nearly worthless scrip. The soldiers often did without meat, sometimes without any dinner.

During February's first week, Mahone's brigade reenlisted with few exceptions for the war's duration. This amounted to an empty gesture. Those who did not reenlist would be conscripted back into their units anyway. But the near unanimity in reenlisting signified the Virginians' determination to continue fighting.[8]

The 12th reached the zenith of its literary powers that week. On February 2, the Riflemen's Pvt. Charles Miller Walsh commenced teaching "a class to write" in a day school established under the auspices of the Young Men's Christian Association to instruct pupils free of charge in the elementary branches of an English education—spelling, reading, writing, grammar and arithmetic.[9] Walsh ran a literacy class rather than a seminar in creative writing, but it fitted that one of the Riflemen should give such a course. More letters, diaries and memoirs would survive from this company than from all the regiment's other companies put together. Nineteen of the 40 soldiers of the 12th who had attended college or graduate school, 25 of the 50 who took commissions in other units and only 3 of the 57 illiterates belonged to the Riflemen. The company represented the flower of Petersburg.

Thieves continued ravaging the brigade commissary. Weisiger, the brigade's senior colonel, on February 10 issued a directive on the absent

---

7 Leroy S. Edwards to Father, January 10, 1864.

8 "Re-Enlistment," Daily Richmond *Dispatch*, February 9, 1864, p. 1, col. 5.

9 Charles M. Walsh Diary, February 2, 1864, AHEC.

Mahone's behalf, to search the camp of each of the brigade's regiments for missing bacon, flour and leather. Weisiger claimed that nobody suspected the troops.[10]

Warm weather arrived February 20, bringing a resumption of inspections, drill and dress parades. On February 22, the soldiers drew sugar and coffee besides their other rations. The amounts of the delicacies struck some as a bad joke. "This sugar & coffee when called out sounded very loud but when we saw it the amount was so small it was not worth speaking about, 30 or 40 grains & about an ounce of brown sugar," recalled Phillips.[11] Private John Kayton of Phillips' company, wounded at Chancellorsville, became enraged, threw down his ration, put his foot on it and ground it into the dirt. Cooler heads attempted to salvage the delicacies.

On February 27, Mahone established a Brigade Pioneer Corps, consisting of expert axemen and practical workmen. They would serve as combat engineers.

Two days later the Federals launched the Dahlgren Raid. The 12th's men heard cannon fire from the direction of Charlottesville at 1 p.m. Custer's brigade of Federal horsemen was feinting to draw Lee's attention westward and clear the way to Richmond for raiders with orders to kill or capture Davis and his cabinet. The long roll beat for three hours. Then the 12th's men bundled up and tramped to Madison Run Station. At 5 p.m., they boarded the Orange & Alexandria for Rivanna Bridge on the Virginia Central, two miles east of Charlottesville. The soldiers arrived at 9 p.m., in a hard rain. The men had no tents and scrambled to find dry places to sleep.

The soldiers remained guarding the bridge in rain and cold on the following day. Some fashioned leaky shelters out of corn stalks. "Red mud all over the place," Phillips observed.[12] "Nearly ankle deep," recorded his fellow Richmond Gray, Sgt. Oscar Oglesby Mull, a native of Maryland.[13] A train derailed, killing one bystander and breaking the legs of another. Snow fell that night.

Custer's brigade withdrew. Mahone's Virginians boarded the cars at 1:20 p.m. on March 2, returning to Madison Run Station at dark. Awakened at

10 Trask, *16th Virginia Infantry*, 20.

11 Phillips, "Sixth Corporal," 39.

12 Phillips Diary, March 1, 1864.

13 Oscar O. Mull Diary, February 29, 1864, in Oscar O. Mull Papers, VHS.

1 a.m. next day and herded onto the cars again, the 12th's soldiers reached Gordonsville at sunrise. An hour later the Petersburg Old Grays, Huger Grays, Herrings and Archer Rifles went on picket. The rest of the regiment remained in reserve. By this time, the Dahlgren Raid had fizzled out.[14] Porte's men took the cars for Richmond at 5 p.m., but only got as far as Louisa Court House before they reversed course and returned to Madison Run Station, traipsing into their camp at 1 a.m. Stoking up the fires in their frigid huts, they huddled together for warmth.

Within a few days a new battle flag arrived at the 12th's camp, replacing the regiment's old rag and reminding the troops that fighting would soon resume.[15] The men figured the coming campaign would be the war's hardest and wrote home asking for little notebooks to keep diaries. Bible study groups proliferated. Bernard and Edwards belonged to the same study group. On Sundays the men filled the 275 seats of the brigade's rustic church. The faint-hearted began looking for soft spots in the rear or opportunities to desert.

Lee combed the rear areas for the able-bodied fellows he thought abounded there. "Alpha" wrote, "The 'bomb proofs' in Petersburg and Richmond are disgorging the hale, hearty, fat and sleek clerks from their several departments under the operation of the recent conscript law and our ranks are visibly augmented by this cogent recruiting agent."[16] Lee took such draconian measures that soldiers who did not qualify as able-bodied declined going on detail. Whitehorne had sufficiently recovered from his Gettysburg wounds to return to light duty with the 12th, but he declined to go on detail to Lynchburg, fearing hospitalization or getting ordered back to the regiment as fit for duty as soon as he came up before one of Lee's Boards of Examiners. "Detailed men have to be examined monthly, & their Capt. notified how they are, & as soon as they are fit for duty, they are

---

14 The Confederates did not forget this attempt to assassinate the Davis administration. Before the war's end, to eliminate the Lincoln administration, they launched an operation that the Dahlgren Raid may have inspired. The Secessionist operation had more success than the Dahlgren Raid. Though it would not annihilate the administration, it killed Lincoln. See generally William A. Tidwell, James O. Hall and David Winfred Gaddy, *Come Retribution: The Confederate Secret Service and the Assassination of Lincoln* (New York, 1997), 245-251; William A. Tidwell, *April '65* (Kent, OH, 1995), 156; Edward Steers, Jr., *Blood on the Moon* (Lexington, KY, 2001), 4, 45-46.

15 Bernard, *War Talks*, 184.

16 "Camp 12th Va. Reg't, A. N. V., March 24th, 1864," Petersburg Daily *Register*, March 28, 1864, p. 1, col.2.

sent to their commands," explained Whitehorne.[17] The return of detailed men and convalescents and the assignment of conscripts increased the regiment's strength.

The 12th drew picket duty on the Rapidan March 21. The men departed camp at 7 a.m. that warm, cloudy morning. The Brigade Drum and Fife Corps accompanied them as far as Orange Court House. The regiment arrived at the site of the Orange & Alexandria's bridge over the Rapidan at 11 a.m. The Petersburg New Grays, Lafayette Guards, Riflemen, Richmond Grays and Norfolk Juniors drew outpost duty. The remaining companies went into reserve, quartering in the filthy rooms of some abandoned houses and stores. That night the weather turned cold. The soldiers on outpost duty doubled up in their tents. The men in the buildings resolved to brave the dangers of fire and "the Confederates"—lice.[18] These soldiers ignited blazes in such stoves and gratings as they found and shared blankets, oilcloths and overcoats.

Two days afterward, just as the 12th returned to camp from picket duty, Mahone rejoined his brigade after an absence of several weeks during the session of Virginia's General Assembly. Sixteen of every 100 men had been getting furloughs before Lee's recent suspension of them because of interrupted rail service in the Carolinas. Now they resumed, but went to only one of every 100. Provisions remained scarce. The regiment's officers went on one ration a day.

On April Fool's Day the troops again drew token amounts of sugar and coffee besides the other available rations. A week later came a day of fasting and prayer—the eighth day since January 19 that at least some of the 12th's soldiers had gone without dinner. By this time many suffered from malnutrition. Some experienced nyctalopia. They could not see in the dark and feared to take a step without someone guiding them. Malingerers complained of this affliction to get out of night picket duty. Their company commanders devised a method of determining the truth of such complaints. Two strong, sharp-eyed soldiers seized the complainant by the arms and tried to run him into all the stumps in camp. If the complainant cleared every stump and did not bark his shins once, his officers considered him miraculously cured and put him on picket.

17 James E. Whitehorne to Sister, March 23, 1864.

18 Bernard Diary, March 24, 1864.

John E. Laughton, Jr. *Virginia Historical Society*

Around this time a blockade runner entered Wilmington, North Carolina, one of the few Confederate seaports remaining open. The ship's cargo of globe sights, Enfield rifles and English-made ammunition profoundly influenced the course of the coming campaign. When the sights, rifles and ammunition reached Orange Court House, Lee's chief of ordnance rewarded the care that Mahone's men had shown in maintaining their arms. He allowed Porte to have the men still carrying Springfield rifles exchange them for the superior Enfields. Mahone's brigade thus finally achieved homogeneity of arms, conferring on the brigade a signal advantage. Its ordnance officer had to supply only a single type of ammunition. "I am quite sure there was not another brigade in the army that had such uniformity of arms," recalled Todd, the brigade's acting ordnance officer.[19]

The sights and ammunition made possible one of the war's most important changes in the structure of Lee's army. Lee was finally organizing sharpshooter battalions, authorized by the Confederate Congress two years earlier. The sharpshooter's battalion in Mahone's brigade was created on April 12. Porte ordered each of his five regimental commanders to form a company consisting of two commissioned officers, two sergeants, two corporals, thirty privates and two ambulance corps members. He specified experienced, capable officers possessed of their men's confidence. In the rank and file, he wanted veterans of established reputation for faithfulness and reliability in action, capable of enduring the extra hardships anticipated, and good marksmen. The five companies numbered eleven officers and one hundred and eighty men. The officers included Feild, commanding the

19 Todd, "Reminiscences," 169.

battalion. The Lafayette Guards' Second Lt. John E. Laughton, Jr., originally a Richmond Gray, served as the battalion's adjutant and commanded its Company C, composed of soldiers from the 12th. Regulations called for treating the battalion as a separate regiment of the brigade, except that its soldiers drew rations and pay from their parent companies.

Like the rest of Mahone's brigade, the sharpshooters carried long-range, small bore Enfield rifles, but the marksmen used a long, English-made cartridge, never any ammunition of Confederate manufacture. The battalion also possessed two globe-sighted rifles for sniping. Every day the sharpshooters engaged in target practice at ranges of from 50 to 1,000 yards. At first they used chains to mark off the distances, but soon they became so proficient at estimating the range that they stopped using the chains. Soldiers who did not measure up returned to their companies. Others replaced them.[20]

Lee ordered his army to prepare to march on April 5, but the 12th's soldiers did not send their baggage home until April's last week. Officers' wives also went home then. The Riflemen's Pvt. James Edward Nash—one of the few to fight at Sharpsburg, captured at Chancellorsville and wounded at Second Brandy Station—solicited from Petersburg's people contributions for the relief of sick and wounded men from the city on behalf of the brigade's Young Men's Christian Association.[21]

Morale ran high in the regiment, the army and the South. "I believe I am engaged in a righteous cause and if God wills that I should live, am willing to put up with the dangers and hardships of my life a much longer time to secure our independence," wrote Sale.[22] Lee's army had recovered from the terrible winter and stood in better condition than ever, but it faced its most formidable foe yet. Lincoln had put his most successful general—Grant—in charge of all the Federal armies. Grant had come east and stationed himself with Meade's army, intending to give Lee and his army the same treatment given the western Confederate forces at Fort Donelson, Vicksburg and Chattanooga.

---

20 John E. Laughton, "The Sharpshooters of Mahone's Brigade: A Paper Read by Captain John E. Laughton, Jr., Before Pickett Camp, Confederate Veterans, Richmond, VA." *SHSP* (1894), 32:98-101.

21 Bernard, "The Maryland Campaign of 1862," 23n; Henderson, *12VI*, 144.

22 John F. Sale to Aunt, April 22, 1864.

By April 30, a rainy day, everyone knew that the spring campaign could open any minute. Suspense built. Word came that the price of gold had risen to $184 per ounce on the New York Stock Exchange.

On the clear night of a stormy May 3, the Virginians received orders to march at 7 a.m. the next day. They formed column along Orange Plank Road at 7:30 a.m. Three hours later Mahone's brigade left Madison Run Station at the head of Anderson's division. The brigade numbered 1,600 muskets.[23] The Virginians plodded toward the Wilderness, resting often. Rumor had it that the Yankees had crossed the Rapidan at Germanna Ford. Grant was trying to turn Lee's right and get between Lee's army and Richmond, forcing the Southerners to attack at a disadvantage. At 5:30 p.m., the regiment's soldiers halted at their old camp at Bell's farm.

May 5 dawned clear and warm. Mahone's brigade broke camp at 2 p.m. The pace remained slow. Word came that fighting had begun near the Wilderness. So far, Grant's attempt to turn Lee's right had not succeeded. Waiting on the roadside for rations held up the Virginians for two hours. They shambled into Verdiersville at 9 p.m. and bedded down.

The troops fell in at 2 a.m. on May 6. Rubbing the sleep from their eyes, they picked up what little baggage they were carrying and resumed their hike. The rest of the night they "met nothing but wounded men, some walking, some hobbling on a gun used for crutches, some in ambulances aiming to get back," Phillips recalled.[24] First light showed that the regiment had finally entered the Wilderness. "This place does not belie its name for it consists of miles upon miles of uncultivated swampy land," wrote Sale.[25] Volleys of musketry ahead confirmed that the soldiers would soon participate in a great battle. They reached the field at 8 a.m., during a lull in the fighting.

Lee had intended to ruin Grant's debut in the east by engaging him in the Wilderness. The Virginian hoped the terrain would neutralize the enemy's numerical advantage. But the need to disperse his forces to subsist them prevented Anderson's division and Longstreet's Corps from joining the fray on its first day. Grant's troops were doing most of the attacking, driving into Ewell's Corps on Orange Turnpike and, farther south, into Hill's Corps on Orange Plank Road. Longstreet's Corps, originally ordered to approach the

23 Todd, "Reminiscences," 181.

24 Phillips, "Sixth Corporal," 42.

25 John F. Sale to Aunt, July 9, 1864.

Unionists on Catharpin Road around the Federal left, shifted northward to Orange Plank Road because of the enemy pressure along that line. Anderson's division reached the battlefield just after Longstreet's soldiers prevented Federals under Maj. Gen. Winfield Scott Hancock from overrunning the heavily outnumbered troops of Heth's and Wilcox's divisions. Now the Southerners were seeking to regain the initiative.

Longstreet took charge of Confederate operations along the plank road. Mahone's brigade and the rest of the Norfolk Division came under Longstreet's command. The Virginians filed to the right off the plank road. The 12th led the way as, remembered Phillips, "the sun rose up appearing in the center of the wood and was as red as a ball of fire."[26] The Virginians passed the site of a Confederate field infirmary. Phillips recalled that "arms and legs had been amputated and thrown in a pile like cord wood." He turned to Second Lt. Patrick Henry Kelley of his company, a former wheelwright, and remarked, "Pat, if this don't demoralize our men, nothing on earth will do it."[27]

About a third of a mile into the woods, the brigade's other four regiments joined the 12th, forming line of battle at a right angle to the road, facing east.[28] From left to right stood the 6th, 16th, 61st, 41st and 12th Virginia. The sharpshooters deployed 150 yards in front of the battle line. Mahone's brigade rested. Portions of Field's and Kershaw's divisions 200 yards farther east held the enemy at bay.[29]

Major General Martin L. Smith, Lee's Chief Engineer, found an unfinished railroad cut beyond the brigade's right. The cut led into the left rear of the invaders pushing westward on the plank road. When word of the cut reached Brig. Gen. William Tatum Wofford, he suggested using it for an attack on the Northerners. Longstreet ordered Lt. Col. Gilbert Moxley Sorrel, his chief of staff, to lead Wofford's brigade of Kershaw's division

26 Phillips, "Sixth Corporal," 42.

27 Ibid.

28 Ibid.; Turner, "The Battle of the Wilderness, *War Talks*, 96, 98; William Mahone to Edward B. Robins, May 9, 1879, Military Historical Society of Massachusetts Collection, Mugar Library, Boston University, Boston, Massachusetts.

29 Letter, n.a., May 6, 1864, quoted in Petersburg *Express*, May 12, 1864, reprinted in Richmond *Whig*, May 14, 1864; John W. H. Porter, *A Record of Events in Norfolk County, Virginia, from April 19th, 1861, to May 10th, 1862, With a History of the Soldiers and Sailors of Norfolk County, Norfolk City and Portsmouth Who Served in the Confederate States Army or Navy* (Portsmouth, VA, 1899), 198.

and G. T. Anderson's brigade of Field's division into the cut.[30] As soon as they deployed and Longstreet's other men unmasked Mahone's brigade, Old Pete wanted Wofford's and G. T. Anderson's brigades to strike northward while Mahone's brigade pushed east.[31]

Sorrel required until 10:30 a.m. to get Wofford's and G. T. Anderson's brigades into the cut. Mahone meanwhile explained the plan of attack to his officers, instructing them to swing round to the north and in doing so to dress to the left.[32] His regiments would conform their movements to those of their left guides.[33] By 11 a.m., the men of Longstreet's Corps in front of Mahone's brigade had withdrawn.[34] Sorrel rode to a position ahead of the 12th's right wing and gave the order to advance. The Rebel yell resounded through the woods. Sorrel grasped his hat in one hand and the reins of his horse with the other.

"Follow me, Virginians!" he shouted. "Let me lead you!"[35]

The sharpshooters struggled forward over marshy ground and through tangled underbrush. Soon their left reached an opening of 70 by 40 yards. The marksmen saw Yankees on the opening's other side moving by column of fours to the Confederate right at the double-quick. The sharpshooters opened fire. The enemy shot back, wounding Feild and others. The rest of the brigade came up behind the marksmen. Only slightly wounded, Feild ordered the sharpshooters to charge. Hearing the order, the other Virginians charged with them.

---

30 Turner, "The Battle of the Wilderness," *War Talks*, 96, 98; Mahone to Robins, May 9, 1879.

31 Richmond *Whig*, May 14, 1864; Porter, *A Record of Events in Norfolk County*, 198; Laughton, "The Sharpshooters of Mahone's Brigade," *SHSP*, 32:101; John Michael Priest, *Victory Without Triumph: The Wilderness, May 6th & 7th, 1864* (Shippensburg, PA, 1996), 78, 89-90; Robert E. L. Krick, "Like a Duck on a June Bug: James Longstreet's Flank Attack, May 6, 1864," in Gary W. Gallagher, ed., *The Wilderness Campaign* (Chapel Hill, 1997), 244, 260n Longstreet in his report, written on the basis of hearsay long after the battle, mistakenly located Mahone's brigade between Wofford's and Anderson's brigades. *OR* 36, pt. 1, 1055.

32 Turner, "The Battle of the Wilderness," *War Talks*, 98.

33 Bernard, Appendix, *War Talks*, 312.

34 Richmond *Whig*, May 14, 1864; Porter, *A Record of Events in Norfolk County*, 198.

35 Turner, "The Battle of the Wilderness," *War Talks*, 96.

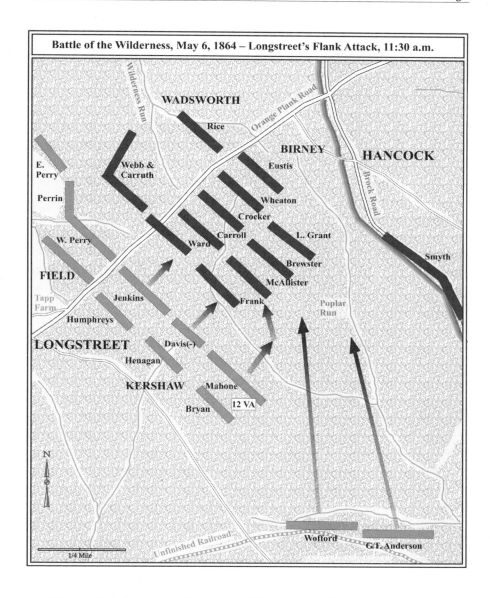

Battle of the Wilderness, May 6, 1864 – Longstreet's Flank Attack, 11:30 a.m.

Mahone's brigade overlapped the Union left, which extended just south of the plank road.[36] The 12th struggled through the clinging vines in line of battle and reached the bottom of a slope that rose less than 150 yards ahead

36 G. Moxley Sorrel, *Recollections of a Confederate Staff Officer* (New York, 1905), 241; Longstreet, *From Manassas to Appomattox*, 561-562; *OR* 36, pt. 1, 1055.

to a crest with marshy flats to its right and left. Through the thick foliage and undergrowth, the 12th's men glimpsed blue uniforms and a Yankee flag among the scrubby oaks atop the crest.

"Come on Virginians!" cried Sorrel, cantering ahead of the regiment's right.[37]

The regiment loosed a volley. Its soldiers howled the Rebel yell, surprising the Northerners in Frank's brigade, Barlow's division. These Federals skedaddled. The 12th's men ran up the slope, loading and firing, yelling and cheering. The Yanks sprinted eastward. "They fled pell-mell before us, leaving their light camp equipage scattered in every direction, making scarcely any resistance," Turner recalled.[38]

Pivoting on the 6th Virginia, Mahone's brigade wheeled left to face north and enfilade the Unionists.[39] The Virginians surged around the exposed left flank of McAllister's brigade, Mott's division, smashing that formation despite its efforts to change front to meet their onslaught. Mahone's men drove toward the plank road, enfilading and routed one hapless bluecoat brigade after another. Confederate troops north of the Virginians—Jenkins' brigade of Field's division and part of Davis' brigade of Heth's division—also pitched into the foe. Musketry and abandoned Federal campfires set the woods ablaze. The smoke permitted the 12th's men to catch only glimpses of the fleeing enemy, but the Virginians killed and wounded many of the Northerners. The Old Grays' Pvt. Leonidas H. Dean, a member of the ambulance corps, distinguished himself, dragging many wounded Yankees out of the burning woods, but he could not rescue them all. Some perished in the flames.

One blaze caused the rightmost eight companies of the 12th to break off from the rest of the brigade. The other two companies—the Herrings and the New Grays—remained on the right of the 41st Virginia, the next regiment in line.[40] The eight companies with the 12th's colors pursued the Federals to the plank road, firing at them all the way. The invaders rallied on Wadsworth's division of V Corps. The Virginians pressed forward under heavy fire. Members of Mahone's brigade again began to fall. Porte was

---

37 Bernard Diary, May 7, 1864.

38 Turner, "The Battle of the Wilderness," *War Talks*, 88.

39 Bernard, Appendix, *War Talks*, 312; Phillips, "Sixth Corporal," 43 ; Porter, *A Record of Events in Norfolk County*, 197-198.

40 Bernard, Appendix, *War Talks*, 312; Turner, "The Battle of the Wilderness," *War Talks*, 104n.

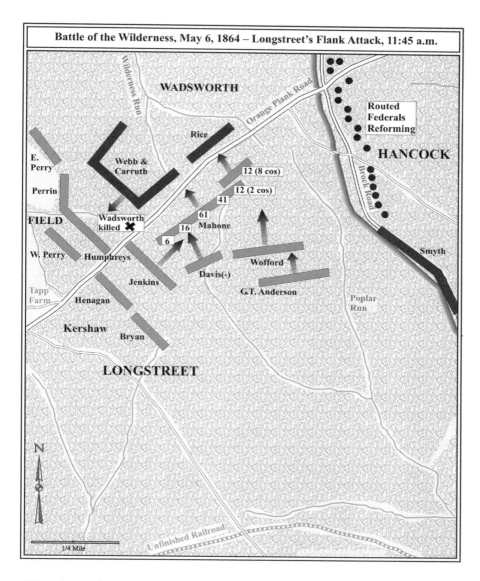

Battle of the Wilderness, May 6, 1864 – Longstreet's Flank Attack, 11:45 a.m.

riding immediately behind the Riflemen. "Steady in the 12th!" he said.[41] The Northerners bunched up in front of the 6th Virginia on the brigade's left. Mahone headed in that direction to get his former regiment moving again. In front of the 6th, Maj. Gen. James S. Wadsworth fell with a bullet through his brain.

41 Ibid., 105.

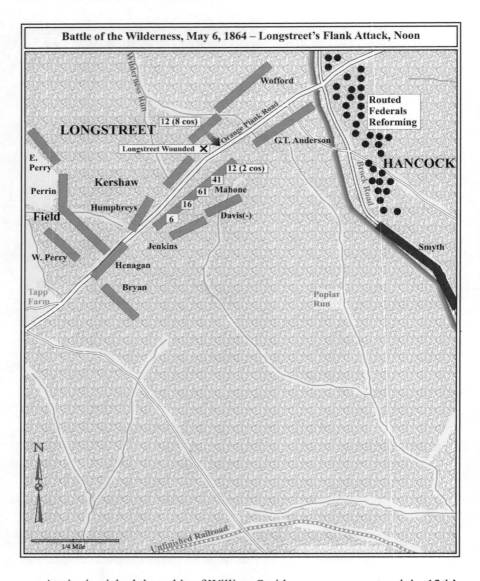

Battle of the Wilderness, May 6, 1864 – Longstreet's Flank Attack, Noon

A minnie nicked the ankle of William Smith, now a sergeant and the 12th's color bearer. Ensign Benjamin Harrison May took the battle flag. "A splendid fellow he was, as brave as a lion and as gentle as a woman," remembered Bernard.[42] May had just obtained his medical degree in Philadelphia when the war began, but he enlisted as a private in the Petersburg City Guard and

42 Ibid., 91.

served with his four brothers. After Second Manassas killed brother John, mortally wounded brother George and crippled brother James, Mahone detailed Ben as assistant surgeon of the 12th to keep him out of harm's way. But as the 1864 campaign's opening approached, Ben begged Porte for permission to carry the regiment's colors. Mahone assented. Ben became the 12th's ensign on April 17.

Now May floundered knee deep through a swamp toward the plank road. Sorrel spotted him. "He was doing all that man could do with his colors, but seemed to be somewhat embarrassed by the bushes, and I thought perhaps I might help him to get them forward, mounted as I was," Sorrel remembered.[43] He rode up and asked for the colors, which May refused to yield.

"We will follow you," May told Sorrel.[44]

Enemy resistance broke. At the plank road the 12th gave a volley to the Federals. They tried to rally again on the opposite side around Carruth's brigade of Stevenson's IX Corps division.[45] The Virginians ran over the 4th United States Infantry.[46] Sorrel dashed westward on the plank road toward Longstreet, who was pounding through the woods north of the road leading forward part of Jenkins' brigade, under a grand corps flag of a new design.[47] May could not see that the other regiments of Mahone's brigade were slowing as they approached the road. He led the eight companies with the 12th's flag beyond the road in pursuit of the Northerners. "One of them had a stand of colors which we kept shooting at," recalled Phillips. "We cut the tassel off but the flag & bearer escaped."[48] Weisiger thought his troops would have captured the flag if supported by the rest of the brigade. "The balls fell around me like hail," he wrote.[49]

The Riflemen's Pvt. James A. Farley, formerly an apprentice baker, was serving in the sharpshooter battalion. Despite wounds in the face and shoulder, he charged across the plank road to the regiment's most advanced position. The eight companies with the 12th's banner halted 50 yards beyond

43 Ibid., 90.

44 Ibid., 88.

45 "The Battle of the Wilderness," Richmond Daily *Dispatch*, May 19, 1864, p. 1, col. 5.

46 Ibid.

47 Turner, "The Battle of the Wilderness," *War Talks*, 98.

48 Phillips, "Sixth Corporal," 43.

49 David A. Weisiger to Wife, May 7, 1864.

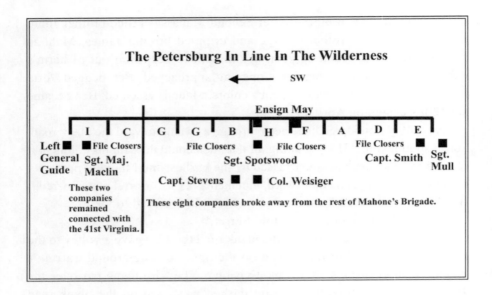

the road in a ravine about six feet deep. They exchanged fire with the enemy. Many more of the regiment's soldiers caught bullets. Weisiger ordered his troops to fall back. They reformed, turned around and climbed the gentle slope to the road. The eight companies with the 12th's colors neared the road. Longstreet rode within 100 yards of their right. A scattering fire began, then a sharp volley from men 40 or 50 yards ahead of the 8 companies. "The enemy are in our rear, and we are in a bad box," thought the troops with the 12th's flag, immediately falling on their faces, then realizing that Southern soldiers had unleashed the volley.

"You are firing into your friends!" the men with Weisiger shouted. "Show your colors!"[50]

Most of the bullets had flown around the flags, the best targets. The regiment's three soldiers struck by the volley included two of the color guard.[51] Instead of diving for cover, May made himself even more conspicuous. "Ben May stood upon a stump, with his lithe, graceful form, a smile upon his face, waving our battle-flag until it was recognized," recalled the Riflemen's

---

50 Turner, "The Battle of the Wilderness," *War Talks*, 92.

51 Bernard Diary, May 7, 1864; Leroy Summerfield Edwards to George S. Bernard, March 25, 1891, Bernard Papers, SHC. Part of this letter appears in Turner, "The Battle of the Wilderness," *War Talks*, 93-94.

Sgt. William Watson Tayleure.[52] Captain Hugh Ritchie Smith, brother of William Smith and Cameron's replacement as regimental adjutant (Cameron, promoted to captain, was serving as Mahone's AAG), waved a handkerchief atop the point of his sword. The musketry quickly stopped. The companies with the 12th's colors recognized the troops firing on them as men of their own brigade. The minnies had come from the 41st Virginia.[53]

"Boys, we are *so sorry!*" its soldiers cried. "We are *so sorry!!* We did not know you were our friends."[54]

All three of the 12th's soldiers struck by the 41st's fire perished. Two of the Old Grays, Color Cpl. John Mingea, who had returned from Tennessee with his friend William Smith to fight for Virginia, and Cpl. William A. Jelks, died instantly. The New Grays' First Sgt. Benjamin B. White, a former clerk and another member of the color guard, took a bullet "on the side of the head and a portion of his brain ran out," recalled Phillips. "We left him on the ground going around & around on his elbow not knowing what he was doing."[55] The 41st wounded Longstreet seriously in the shoulder and Brig. Gen. Micah Jenkins mortally in the head as they rode past with their new corps flag. "Our loss of these was more deeply regretted than of those who were shot by the enemy," Sale observed.[56]

The 12th's men rested on the road's north side. The First Corps soldiers who had charged out of the railroad cut continued the advance. The Northerners withdrew to their breastworks on Brock Road. Late that afternoon, those breastworks caught fire. The Southerners charged through the smoke and seized them, but could not hold them and the attack stalled.

The regiment withdrew across the road onto the ground it had covered in its swoop on the Union left. The men halted, lay down and snatched what sleep they could behind the sharpshooters, who stood picket. "The

52 Ibid., 94n.

53 Todd and Phillips said this unequivocally and Todd was positioned to know as a member of Mahone's staff. Todd, "Reminiscences," 191. Phillips, "Sixth Corporal," 43. Bernard said, "They were fired into by the 41st, and I hear also a part of the 61st regiment...." Turner, "The Battle of the Wilderness," *War Talks*, 93. Nobody claimed the two companies of the 12th with the 41st fired the shots.

54 Ibid., 92.

55 Phillips, "Sixth Corporal," 43.

56 Sale Diary, May 6, 1864.

woods were on fire, and the cries of the wounded made the night hideous," remembered Feild.[57]

The 12th lost five killed and forty-seven wounded.[58] The injuries of seven proved mortal.[59] The regiment's wounded shared Dr. Claiborne's infirmary with Wadsworth until his removal to the field hospital of Kershaw's brigade, where he expired.[60] Longstreet later said Mahone's brigade behaved "very well," the 12th "most gallantly."[61] Weisiger wrote that the regiment had "covered itself with glory."[62]

Roused at 7 a.m., the Virginians found the Yankees had remained to face them. "Many thought Grant would recross the river last night, and it was remarked this morning by a member of Gen. Hill's staff that anybody else but Grant would have done so," recalled Bernard.[63] Hooker had retreated the previous spring after a less severe drubbing. Sunrise revealed another horror. "I could see the forms of men on the ground in all directions & took for granted they were troops sleeping and did not know any better until daybreak the next morning," Phillips recalled. "They were dead men we had killed on the 6th."[64] Nothing but heavy skirmishing developed that day. The troops took advantage of this. "I washed my face for the first time in 3 days," recorded Mull, the regiment's acting right general guide.[65] The shoeless White staggered into the 12th's bivouac. Phillips carried him to an ambulance corps man, who brought White to the regiment's infirmary. There White died.

After breakfast Anderson's division retired 400 yards, going into reserve with Heth's division. Some of the 12th's soldiers dug trenches and lay in them for the rest of the day. Others buried the dead. "Those who did not have blankets, we would cut off a piece of their blouse and cover their faces over

---

57 Laughton, "The Sharpshooters of Mahone's Brigade," *SHSP*, 32:101-102.

58 Weisiger to Wife, May 7, 1864.

59 Henderson, *12VI*, 106-167.

60 Turner, "The Battle of the Wilderness," *War Talks*, 97.

61 Bernard Diary, May 7, 1864.

62 Weisiger to Wife, May 7, 1864.

63 Bernard Diary, May 7, 1864.

64 Phillips, "Sixth Corporal," 44.

65 Mull Diary, May 7, 1864.

to keep the dirt off of them," recalled Phillips.[66] Some of the regiment's men visited the troops in front of them, Bryan's Georgia Brigade of Kershaw's division. The Georgians kept at their sides several loaded muskets taken from the enemy and wanted to stay on the front line potting away at the foe rather than take their turn resting in the rear. "The fun is as good as at a camp meeting," said one of them.[67]

Southern ordnance officers scoured the battlefield for equipment abandoned by the Federals in their flight from the flank attack. Todd collected several wagonloads of splendid muskets. Unionist wounded continued coming in to the 12th's position on litters. Sale reviled these troops as mercenaries, but pitied them in their misery, giving them water or coffee. "I felt most sorry for a youth who was shot through the lungs," Sale noted. "I could but think of his mother and friends who would look for his return but would never see him again as he died after much suffering."[68]

Lee reorganized his army. Anderson took over Longstreet's Corps. Mahone became commander of Anderson's division. Weisiger succeeded to the command of Mahone's brigade. Feild took charge of the 12th.

The sun set. Weisiger's brigade trudged to the front. Lee was preparing to send Anderson's Corps southeast to Spotsylvania Court House to prevent the bluecoats from turning the Secessionist right. The Virginians relieved Bryan's brigade after "a worrying time of halting and stumbling around," Mull recalled.[69] They did not lie down to rest until 2 a.m.

66 Phillis, "Sixth Corporal," 45.

67 Bernard Diary, May 7, 1864.

68 Sale Diary, May 6, 1864.

69 Mull Diary, May 7, 1864.

CHAPTER 14

Spotsylvania

Roused at 6.30 a.m. on the clear, warm and quiet morning of May 8, the 12th's men hobbled a mile to their right to erect breastworks running at a right angle to the previous line of Lee's army. Hill and his staff rode past the regiment at 1 p.m. An hour later came the announcement that with Hill too ill to command, Early had taken charge of Hill's Corps. Mahone's division departed for Spotsylvania Court House at 3.15 p.m., hiking southeastward through the woods by the right flank.

Weisiger's brigade as usual led the way. Its sharpshooters formed the vanguard. The Virginians followed the line of Confederate earthworks, then a lane. After two miles the 12th replaced the marksmen in the lead. The Riflemen deployed in front of the regiment on both sides of the road. The sharpshooters retired behind the Riflemen but remained ahead of the rest of the 12th. The column followed the zigzagging lane into more open country. Coming out of the Wilderness seemed "about the same as coming out of a dark house or room into the open air where the sun is shining," recalled Phillips.[1] The troops passed Early and his staff sitting on their horses.

The Riflemen advanced three-quarters of a mile to another country lane diverging to the east. Continuing southeastward, they met a line of Confederate cavalry pickets along a rail fence to their left at 5 p.m. A quarter mile ahead, atop a plateau affording views to the east and southeast,

---

1 Phillips, "Sixth Corporal, 45.

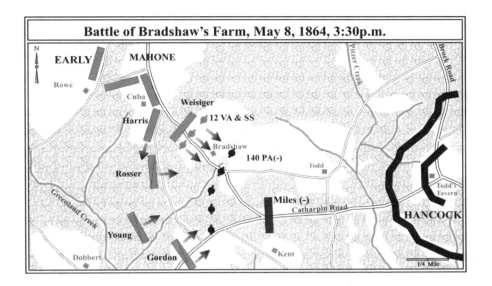

Battle of Bradshaw's Farm, May 8, 1864, 3:30p.m.

stood a lone horseman. He "looked like a statue," Phillips remembered.[2] The regiment halted at the fork. The Riflemen proceeded as far as the horseman—Mahone, mounted on a stump-tailed steel gray taken from Yankee cavalry earlier that day.

Early rode up to Mahone and told him to reconnoiter toward Todd's Tavern, which stood about a mile and a half east on Brock Road—the Federal army's route to Spotsylvania Court House.

"Drive in cavalry and halt before infantry pickets," said Early.[3] Encountering cavalry would mean that Mahone's men threatened the right flank of the Federal foot soldiers marching toward Spotsylvania Court House, while meeting infantry would signify that not all the Unionist infantry had passed Todd's Tavern yet. Early added that Lee did not want a general engagement. Feild approached Mahone, who pointed toward a handful of soldiers 800 or 900 yards eastward, on the Bradshaw farm.

"Take your men down there and see who those people are," said Porte, passing on Early's instructions.[4]

The Riflemen returned to the regiment, then traipsed eastward along the other lane with their right in the open and their left in dense timber.

2 Ibid., 46.

3 Edwards to Bernard, March 25, 1891.

4 Phillips, "Sixth Corporal," 46.

Advancing half a mile into desolate country with a few rude houses, they struggled over a wooded hill. With the sharpshooters behind them, the Riflemen entered a field.

A line of soldiers stood in front of a cluster of small pines on another rise around 350 yards ahead. The Riflemen and sharpshooters advanced down the slope to determine who the soldiers were. The 12th's balance deployed as pickets. The rest of the brigade formed line of battle behind a fence near the top of the forested hill. The division's other four brigades deployed two on each side of Weisiger's brigade. Fitzhugh Lee's division of cavalry held the ground on the infantry's right. No exchange of fire took place with the troops on the rise, who struck some of the Riflemen as possibly Northerners.

The Confederate skirmishers passed a branch, then edged off to the right of the track they had been following and started up a crest. By the time the Riflemen reached the worm fence at the top, their line had contracted to 75 yards. In front of them stood the Bradshaw barn and beyond, the Bradshaw house and outbuildings. Having advanced about 100 yards, the Riflemen now could see that the line of soldiers standing in front of the pines consisted of 20 or 30 unarmed Yankee infantrymen picking up their knapsacks and putting them on in a leisurely fashion. The Riflemen thought these Unionists stragglers.

About 50 yards beyond the branch, the Riflemen passed to the barn's right. The Northerners in sight and many hidden by the pines unleashed a hail of bullets. These Yanks belonged to the 140th Pennsylvania of Miles' brigade in Barlow's division of II Corps. The Riflemen dashed for the house, flinging themselves to the earth in the surrounding hollow. Hugging the ground behind the hollow's rim, they could not see the Pennsylvanians or return the fire. They lay there for several minutes under the Keystoner musketry. Three members of the company got under the shelter of some dependencies on the left, giving the Pennsylvanians a brisk peppering. The sharpshooters supported the Riflemen. The rest of the regiment advanced to provide still further support.

The Keystoner musketry slackened. Five Riflemen dashed forward to a bridge over another branch to the southeast: Edwards, Bernard, Walsh, Pvt. Ello K. Daniel—a South Carolinian who had previously served in the 13th Virginia Cavalry—and Pvt. Frank M. Robbins. They hastened up another hill. At the top stood a fence, about 70 yards from the Pennsylvanians in front and an equal distance from the Bradshaw house. All but Bernard made it over the fence. Then the Keystoner fire intensified again as the 184th Pennsylvania of Miles' brigade came to the support of the 140th. The five Virginians hit the dirt. "It was the hottest sort of a hornet's nest, & it seemed that a thousand riflemen had determined to make mince meat of our unhappy little party," Edwards recalled.[5]

Someone shouted from the Bradshaw house for the five to retreat. The fence Edwards had mounted with ease while advancing, he remembered, while withdrawing "seemed to have grown into a regular ten rail fence & the top rails were being by the enemy's bullets converted into kindling wood."[6] He and his comrades threw off some of the top rails to facilitate their retreat. They asked the soldiers at the Bradshaw house for covering fire. The troops at the house complied. The 12th's remainder fired with them.

The men at the fence fled down the hill. Pennsylvanian skirmishers rushed after them and gave them a galling fire as they retreated to the branch and its bridge. At the branch the five's paths diverged. Edwards and Daniel took cover in the branch's gully. Bernard, Walsh and Robbins continued up the slope toward the Bradshaw house and its outbuildings. The sharpshooters and the Riflemen's main body retired from the house toward the rest of the 12th. Walsh and Robbins caught up with the other skirmishers and headed back toward the brigade's battle line.

Bernard lagged the others withdrawing from the fence. Minnies whistled past him. Bullets struck the ground around him. Exhausted from the previous three days, loaded down with his musket and other equipment, he could manage only a slow trot. Finally, he passed through a set of draw bars in the fence around the house and outbuildings. He staggered out of the enclosure and tottered northwestward toward the barn.

Edwards watched from the branch, just below the bridge. "Your gait was tantalizing," he later informed Bernard, "if you had been a young lover looking for violets for his sweetheart on some quiet hillside your speed would have been greater."[7] Bernard reached the barnyard, putting the Bradshaw barn between himself and the Pennsylvanians, then slowed to a walk and followed the other skirmishers back up the slope.

5 Edwards to Bernard, March 25, 1891.

6 Ibid.

7 Ibid.

Crouching in the gully, Edwards and Daniel thought they saw soldiers of the 16th Virginia and followed the branch toward them. A Keystoner flanking party got into the branch below the two and cut them off. Edwards and Daniel fell into enemy hands.

A Union battle line from the balance of Miles' brigade advanced across the plateau on the heels of the Confederate skirmishers. Weisiger's brigade knelt in the woods behind the fence near the hilltop. The Riflemen and the sharpshooters took their places in the line of battle. The Virginians fired and broke the Yankee formation. The Federals recoiled and did not renew the attack. The whole engagement lasted an hour and a half. After nightfall the Northerners retreated, leaving their dead and wounded on the field. The 12th had lost three killed, eighteen wounded and two missing—Edwards and Daniel.[8] The Virginians who survived the action unscathed lay down and slept in line of battle.

The Confederate thrust toward Todd's Tavern had significant repercussions. During the struggle between the Secessionists and II Corps, V Corps had been unsuccessfully charging Anderson's Corps at Laurel Hill, two miles northwest of Spotsylvania Court House. The Confederate advance toward Todd's Tavern had appeared to Meade an attempt to turn his right. This discouraged Meade from sending reinforcements from II Corps to V Corps that might have permitted V Corps to batter its way through to Spotsylvania Court House and get between Lee's army and Richmond.[9]

The officers of Weisiger's brigade roused their men at midnight. The troops staggered two miles, bivouacking on Shady Grove Church Road at 1.30 a.m. Their officers woke them again early. No bread rations had arrived, just a little meat. The Virginians plodded toward the Confederate right. The march on that clear, hot morning fatigued them. They reached Spotsylvania Court House at 1 p.m., formed line of battle and erected breastworks. Long after dark, their bread ration arrived. The troops began to eat supper. At midnight, before they could finish, orders came to march to the Confederate left. Grumbling, the men smothered their fires and trudged off into the darkness. They fell in behind Heth's division, reaching the high ground overlooking Block House Bridge on Po River at 3 a.m. The Norfolk Division halted there and bivouacked. Detached from Weisiger's brigade, the

---

8 Bernard Diary, May 9, 1864.

9 Gordon C. Rhea, *The Battles for Spotsylvania Court House and the Road to Yellow Tavern, May 7–12, 1864* (Baton Rouge, 1997), 81.

12th went to sleep in line of battle. Heth's division kept shuffling southward along the Po's left bank.[10] This unit would cross the Po farther downstream, near Long's Mill, then turn north to smite II Corps, which had cut the road from Shady Grove Church to Spotsylvania Court House.

The sun rose on another hot day May 10. The regiment's men not on picket took advantage of their position near the river. Some bathed their blistered feet. Others, like Phillips, fished in a millpond. Noon approached. Skirmishers of II Corps probed for a crossing of the Po, threatening a two-gun section of McIntosh's battalion. The 12th advanced to support the artillery. "We grabed up the line of fish & put them in haversacks and in 15 min. we was in a fight," recalled Phillips.[11] The regiment's soldiers charged up a hill alongside Wright's Georgia Brigade, coming out on a road and driving off enemy skirmishers of Barlow's division. The woods caught fire. Wounded Yankees burned. The 12th suffered no casualties.

In high spirits the men rested. "Grant seems the most obstinate of men but he cannot confront us much longer," Bernard recorded. "I hear Gen. Lee says he has been attempting the most hazardous thing he ever heard of—i.e. any attempt to outflank a victorious army."[12]

At 5 p.m., the 12th crossed the Po at the double-quick with the rest of Mahone's division. II Corps was withdrawing from its position across Shady Grove Church Road. Heth's division pressed the Federals. The Norfolk Division took position on the right of Heth's division. The regiment's soldiers formed line of battle, still attached to Wright's brigade. They faced a Federal battery expecting to charge the guns, but the order to advance did not come. II Corps lost a gun for the first time ever, to Heth's division. Mahone's troops lay in line of battle that night.

The 12th withdrew to the woods on the morning of May 11. The soldiers erected breastworks. That afternoon, the invaders shelled the timber. Skirmishing began in the regiment's front, leading the men to think the Northerners were advancing, but the Union skirmishers retreated. At 3 p.m., rain began to fall. Reunited with the rest of Weisiger's brigade, the men pitched their pup tents, which sheltered the troops from a downpour that lasted through

10 Bernard Diary, May 10, 1864; Sale Diary, May 10, 1864; Nathaniel H. Harris to William Mahone, August 2, 1866, William Mahone Papers, LV.

11 Phillips, "Sixth Corporal," 47.

12 Bernard Diary, May 10, 1864.

the night. Rumor had it "that Grant had laid down his pontoons at Falmouth & had crossed some cavalry & his wounded stragglers," noted Bernard.[13] Similar reports reached Lee. The Yanks were retreating, he concluded. He ordered the guns withdrawn that night from a salient known as the Mule Shoe, in his line's center, east of where the 12th and the rest of Mahone's division camped. But Lee had erred. II Corps was massing for an assault on the Mule Shoe's tip.

Pursuant to Lee's error about Grant's intentions, the 12th's officers shook the rank and file awake at 3 a.m. on the morning of May 12 and told the men to prepare to march in pursuit of the Unionists. The troops waited in the rain. Dawn came at 5 a.m. Heavy discharges of artillery and musketry broke out to their right, where Lee had discovered his error and ordered the artillery back into the Mule Shoe. But the guns arrived just as 20,000 Federals swarmed over the Mule Shoe's fortifications. The artillery only swelled the captures of the Unionists, who also took prisoner most of Johnson's division of Ewell's Corps.

About two miles west of the Mule Shoe, Jim Phillips had outpost duty with his brother, Sgt. Robert L. Phillips, another member of the Richmond Grays. They could see the Grays and Juniors, consolidated at the time, putting on their equipment and beckoning to the soldiers on outpost. Illness afflicted Bob Phillips. Jim begged him to stay in camp.

"I would rather die than to have anyone say I shirked duty," Bob replied.[14]

The brothers rejoined their company, learning that the rest of the division had already double-quicked toward the Mule Shoe. Weisiger's brigade then followed. The 12th's men marched as fast as the mud permitted until they arrived 200 yards behind the Mule Shoe's eastern face. Then Lee rode up to the column, which halted. Early, Mahone, Weisiger and their staffs joined Lee for a conference. They formed a knot of more than 20 horsemen in full view of the Union batteries of IX Corps, which opened fire. A shell struck among the horsemen, disabling the mounts of two couriers and ending the conference. The column resumed tramping eastward. Not needed for the fight in the Mule Shoe, the Virginia Brigade slogged through the rain and mud to the Confederate line's right, on the road from Spotsylvania Court House to Fredericksburg.

---

13 Ibid., May 14, 1864.

14 Phillips, "Sixth Corporal," 49.

The Virginians remained there while fighting raged to their left. At 10.30 a.m., the men trekked back westward to where the shell had broken up the conference. Lee rode up to the column again, this time accompanied by a single staffer. Again, the column halted. Lee passed a stand of pines. IX Corps' gunners again opened on him. Shells of two batteries firing from the column's front and right burst in front of the pines. One missile exploded near the 12th, but injured nobody.

The column proceeded again, still westward. The soldiers trudged through the pines under the enemy artillery's crossfire. Beyond the pines, the brigade wheeled to its right and deployed behind a hill. Minutes later, the order came to return to the pines. The men took another severe shelling and dodged. Feild ordered the dodging stopped. The shelling slackened, then resumed its previous intensity. A shell passed near Feild, who dodged. "Stop that dodging," his men shouted.[15]

Weisiger's brigade filed outside the Confederate breastworks near Heth's Salient, which extended to the edge of a plateau at the base of the Mule Shoe's eastern side. The Virginians formed line of battle facing northward at right angles to the fortifications. Marching and countermarching put the 12th on the brigade's left. The regiment's left rested against the breastworks. Its line extended eastward down the plateau's steep slope to level ground.[16] The Virginians stood about 100 yards behind Lane's North Carolina brigade of Cadmus Wilcox' division. The Virginians overlapped the Tarheels' left. This rested in an oak wood southeast of Heth's Salient.[17] Mahone, in charge of this force, remained near an ice house at the southern edge of the woods— too far back to command effectively.[18] Ahead of the Virginians and North Carolinians, Unionists of IX Corps held the breastworks of Heth's Salient. They had seized the fortifications' eastern face from the snout of Heth's Salient northward after the initial success of II Corps at the Mule Shoe's tip. Lane's and Weisiger's brigades had orders to advance along the line of breastworks and clear them of Federals.[19]

15 Ibid., 47.

16 Ibid., 51; "Records of Service," Captain E. H. Flournoy, December 27, 1915, Files of H. E. Howard, Inc., in Cavanaugh, *6th Virginia Infantry*, 45-46. Bernard Diary, May 14, 1864.

17 Ibid.; James H. Lane, "History of Lane's North Carolina Brigade: Battle of Spotsylvania Court-House—Report of General Lane," *SHSP* (1881), 9:148.

18 Richmond *Whig*, May 19, 1864.

19 Cadmus M. Wilcox, Report of Operations, Lee Headquarters Papers, VHS.

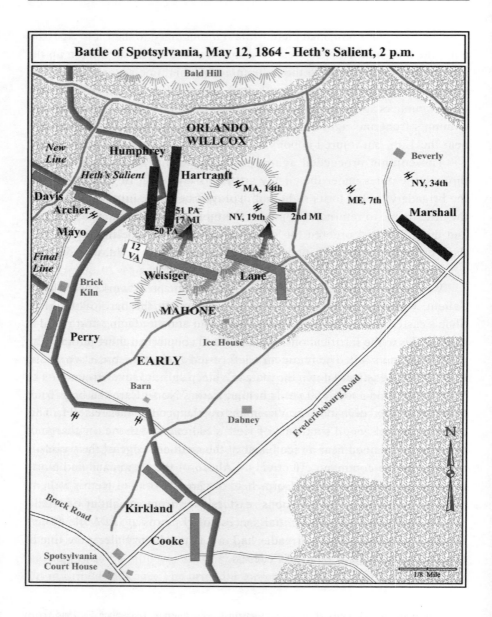

Battle of Spotsylvania, May 12, 1864 - Heth's Salient, 2 p.m.

At 1 p.m., the Tarheels advanced northeastwardly with their left in the oak wood and their right across a brook. The Virginians struggled to follow through the dripping forest. The North Carolinians emerged from the trees. Fifty yards ahead stood the 19th New York Battery, part of a row of Unionist guns, and two regiments of Humphrey's brigade of Orlando Willcox's IX Corps division. The Tarheels charged. Brigadier General James H. Lane dispatched

Benjamin Harrison May. *Virginia Historical Society*

a courier to Weisiger proposing that Weisiger's brigade move up on the North Carolinians' right. Together they would swing back to their own lines, enfilading the row of enemy batteries and enveloping the Northern infantry.

But the Virginians had already become engaged. They had kept stalking northeastwardly along Heth's Salient, coming under heavy shelling from Federal guns. The 12th arrived within about 200 yards of a Yankee battery. The regiment's men saw a line of battle lying down a few paces ahead of them.[20] Thinking it Lane's brigade, they halted. Soon they recognized as blue the rain-sodden coats of the soldiers in the line ahead. Weisiger's troops loosed an enfilading volley into the left flank of the Unionist infantry—the balance of Humphrey's brigade and behind it Hartranft's brigades of Orlando Willcox's division. Some of the bullets flew on into the backs of the North Carolinians charging the New York battery. The Virginians charged into the left of the Federals ahead of them.

A savage melee erupted in front of the 12th's center and left. Ben May held the regiment's flag in one hand. With his other he blazed away with his revolver. A Federal plugged him from less than 10 feet away. The colors fell to the Richmond Grays' Cpl. William Carrington Mayo. A graduate of Yale fluent in a dozen languages, this engineer had returned from France on a blockade runner in early 1863 and immediately enlisted, refusing an officer's commissioner. Mayo's hold on the banner lasted just seconds. A Yankee drilled him in the chest. The New Grays' Pvt. Allen Washington Magee seized the flag.

Dean grabbed a musket and captured a beautiful stand of colors from the 51st Pennsylvania Infantry along with eight Keystoners.[21] Bob Phillips

20 Bernard Diary, May 14, 1864; Stewart, *A Pair of Blankets*, 130.

21 *OR* 36, 3:802; Statement of Napoleon Bonaparte Simmons, Notes of St. George Tucker Coalter Bryan.

perished in the melee. In the regiment's right front, the invaders scattered like sheep. "Just as we got to the edge of the woods where the enemy were I caught a glimpse of hundreds of them skiddadling through the pines," observed Bernard.[22] Weisiger's brigade took flags and 400 prisoners, most of them seized by the 12th and the 41st Virginia—the unit immediately to the 12th's right.[23] Weisiger's brigade sent the Unionists to the rear unguarded. Every Virginian who could shoulder a musket had to remain with the colors to cope with the enemy in front.[24]

Farther east Lane's brigade repeatedly charged the Federal artillery and its screen of enemy infantry. Yankee canister and minie balls hit the Tarheels from the front. Stray rounds from Weisiger's men struck the North Carolinians from the rear. Lane's brigade took a guidon from the New York battery, but the rest of the artillery blasted the Tarheels, who recoiled into the oak wood. There bands of Lane's troops and groups of Northerners captured and recaptured one another.

Still in the rain and still under enemy fire, the Virginians searched for friends and relatives among the dead and wounded. Casualties continued mounting. Jim Phillips took the watch and ring from his brother's corpse, then stood with his back to the enemy talking to Cpl. Israel F. Disoway of the Riflemen, a dentist known as Dr. Disoway. Phillips felt a bullet pass his ear. The minnie, he remembered, "cut a tremendous gash" in the right side of Disoway's neck. Blood spurted out. Disoway slapped his hand over the wound and ran to the rear.

"My goodness he will die," Phillips said to himself.[25]

The remnant of the 12th's color guard stood near a dogwood. A shell burst among these soldiers while Phillips was talking to Doncey Dunlop, recently returned to the ranks from a detail as wagon master with the regimental quartermaster. Two of the color guard died instantly. Magee, wounded in the left forearm, dropped the flag. Phillips ran around the dogwood and picked up the colors. Nearby William Smith, the lone member of the color guard still on his feet, had recovered from his wound of six days earlier. Phillips

22 Bernard Diary, May 14, 1864.

23 Ibid. The 41st's First Lt. Charles E. Denoon claimed 300 of the prisoners and 3 flags for his regiment. Richard T. Couture, ed., *Charlie's Letters: The Correspondence Of Charles E. DeNoon* (Collingswood, N. J., 1982), 96.

24 Stewart, *A Pair of Blankets*, 130.

25 Phillips, "Sixth Corporal," 48; Henderson, *12VI*, 121.

gave the flag to Smith, who got through the fight unscathed despite the hail of lead that the colors drew in his direction.

Weisiger's brigade retired. In the rear, mutual recriminations began with Lane's troops. The Tarheels and Virginians quarreled over who had captured a color of the 17th Michigan of Hartranft's brigade and some of the prisoners.[26] Having gone off in two different directions to fight out of sight of one another, each brigade complained of lack of support from the other.

The Virginians reformed near Spotsylvania Court House. With Cooke's North Carolina brigade of Heth's division, Weisiger's men ventured out of the breastworks near the close of day, reconnoitering on the Spotsylvania Court House—Fredericksburg Road.

Feild stepped off to the roadside, examining the enemy earthworks through his field glasses. A shot struck him on the hip, knocking him unconscious. Jones took command of the 12th. Cooke's and Weisiger's brigades advanced on opposite sides of the road, driving Federal skirmishers out of two lines of breastworks. Just before nightfall, the Tarheels and Virginians halted in front of a third line of works held by a Union battle line. Fighting ceased at dark. Weisiger's brigade withdrew through the downpour to the Confederate line's extreme right. Exhausted, the troops pitched their tents and went to sleep.

The regiment had captured its first enemy flag and helped end the threat of Burnside's Corps to the Mule Shoe, but at heavy cost. The foe had killed 12 and wounded 42 more, 9 mortally. Another wounded soldier fell into enemy hands and three unwounded men also became prisoners.[27] The regiment had experienced its bloodiest day since Second Manassas, where the men had at least given a hasty burial to their dead. This time the troops left the corpses of their comrades on the field.

Despite the capture of flags and prisoners, dissatisfaction with Weisiger's performance prevailed in the 12th. "Our Colonel, commanding Brigade, is a 'poor stick' and can handle a set of men with as much celerity, and tact,

---

26 Stewart, *A Pair of Blankets*, 130; Couture, ed., *Charlie's Letters*, 96; Reports—Spotsylvania battle—flag capture controversy—Lane's versus Mahone's brigades (May 1864), James H. Lane Papers, Auburn University Special Collections & Archives Department, Auburn University, Auburn, Alabama; J. S. Harris, *Historical Sketches of the Seventh Regiment North Carolina Troops, 1861-'65* (Mooresville, NC, 1893), 47-48; Phillips, "Sixth Corporal," 48; Bernard Diary, May 14, 1864; Sale Diary, May 12, 1864.

27 Ibid.; Henderson, *12VI*, 106-167; Semi-Weekly Richmond *Enquirer*, May 17, 1864, p. 3, col. 4.

as a cow a broomstick," Sale noted without specifying exactly what the brigadier had done wrong.[28] The men thought they would have accomplished more if Mahone had led them though Porte had never led a more successful movement. Nonetheless, they called for him to resume command of his old brigade.

May succumbed to his wound four days later. Before he died, he sent a message to Sorrel about their encounter in the Wilderness: "Tell Colonel Sorrel I could not part with the colors, but we followed him."[29]

28 Sale Diary, May 25, 1864.

29 Turner, "The Battle of the Wilderness," *War Talks*, 106.

CHAPTER 15

To the Cockade City

W eisiger's brigade departed Spotsylvania Court House late on the night of May 21, as Grant tried again to get around Lee's right. The 12th had lost another soldier, wounded by a Unionist sharpshooter six days earlier.[1] The dead remained unburied—an unprecedented situation. Phillips thought it disgraceful and inhuman "to march away & leave their dear bodies lying on the ground with nothing to protect them and to shelter them from the many wild animals which we have in this lonesome wilderness. . . ."[2] One day he would take the matter into his own hands.

The Yankees left the Confederates in possession of the battlefield. As in the Wilderness, abandoned equipment littered the ground. Southern ordnance officers like Todd made a haul, recovering 122,000 pounds of lead in the form of bullets. The Secessionists would recast this lead in Richmond and fire it back at the Northerners before the campaign's close.

More than two weeks in the enemy's presence had worn out men and equipment. "Barefoot to day, and each step feels as if treading on nails," Sale noted on May 22.[3] The troops crossed North Anna River at dark, bivouacking near Hewlett's Station on the Virginia Central at 10 p.m., exhausted.

---

1 Henderson, *12VI*, 119.

2 Phillips, "Sixth Corporal," 52-53.

3 Sale Diary, May 22, 1864.

About 4 p.m. next day, Federal gunners zeroed in on the regiment's camp. "Shell literally rained," Sale observed.[4] The 12th's soldiers hurried off with the rest of Mahone's division toward Jericho Mills. There Cadmus Wilcox's division was trying to drive V Corps back across the North Anna. The regiment arrived too late to participate in the unsuccessful Confederate attack. It went into line of battle in front of some rapidly firing guns.

Early May 24, Weisiger's brigade shifted two miles southeastwardly to a new position near Anderson's Depot on the Virginia Central, three miles northwest of Hanover Junction. The exhausted Virginians stacked arms and slept until after sunrise, then reformed line of battle and entrenched. The Donaldsonville Louisiana Artillery unlimbered along the 12th's line. The position seemed impregnable, though the Union artillery enfiladed it from across the North Anna. "The boys are only afraid the Yanks will not charge them," Sale wrote.[5] The enemy did not charge them, but attacked to their right.

Ledlie's brigade of Crittenden's IX Corps division had crossed the river at Quarles' Mill at 1 p.m., advancing through the woods toward the right of Mahone's division. This rested on Ox Ford. Bates' brigade of Crawford's V Corps division went forward on the right of Ledlie's brigade. The Northerners inched ahead through the trees, with the 12th Massachusetts from Bates' brigade facing the Virginia Brigade's sharpshooter battalion.[6] Right of the Virginians the Alabama Brigade and farther right the Mississippi Brigade fronted Ledlie's brigade. The artillery fire on the 12th Virginia's right became incessant. The skirmishing in that direction intensified throughout the afternoon. As 6 p.m. approached, thunderclouds loomed. The sharpshooter battalion of Weisiger's brigade double-quicked toward the right, deploying facing north in front of the adjacent Alabama Brigade, opposite the right of Ledlie's skirmish line—the 35th Massachusetts' Companies A, E and F.[7] The Confederate marksmen advanced Indian style, from tree to tree, firing as they

4 Ibid., May 23, 1864.

5 Ibid., May 24, 1864.

6 Benjamin F. Cook, *History of the Twelfth Massachusetts Infantry (Webster Regiment)* (Boston, 1882), 133; Col. James L. Bates replaced Col. Richard Coulter in command of his brigade after his wounding May 18, 1864. Gordon C. Rhea, *To the North Anna River: Grant and Lee, May 13-25, 1864* (Baton Rouge, 2000), 380.

7 A Committee of the Regimental Association, *History of the Thirty-Fifth Regiment Massachusetts Volunteers, 1862-1865* (Boston, 1884), 238-240.

went. Ledlie's skirmishers withdrew. The Virginian sharpshooters piled up the rails of an old fence for protection. The Alabama Brigade's marksmen took post on the Virginians' right. Ledlie's skirmishers returned and attacked, supported farther to their left by the rest of their brigade in line of battle.

The Confederate sharpshooters fought in three-man teams, firing by file, with one rifle always kept loaded. The marksmen fired so steadily and accurately that they repulsed the charge of Ledlie's brigade with loss. The bluecoats charged a second time, then a third. Some fell within 30 feet of Weisiger's sharpshooters. But the Secessionists pushed the enemy back. The Virginian and Alabamian marksmen held off the right of Ledlie's brigade for two hours while the rest of Ledlie's brigade dashed itself to pieces against Harris' Mississippi Brigade closer to the North Anna.[8]

The storm broke, soaking the battlefield. Ledlie's troops retreated to the river. Weisiger's sharpshooters returned to their brigade's picket line. The marksman company from the 12th had lost two men. Enemy fire killed the Lafayette Guards' Pvt. Benjamin George, recently returned from a detail as a teamster. The Herrings' Pvt. Thomas Weaver also perished.[9]

Grant had walked into a trap. Mahone's division formed part of the western leg of an inverted V with its apex at Ox Ford's bluffs on the North Anna. While VI Corps, Crawford's division of V Corps and Crittenden's division of IX Corps threatened the western leg of the V, II Corps crossed the river south of Ox Ford and probed the V's eastern leg. This gave Lee the opportunity to leave part of his army to hold the western leg of the V and concentrate the rest against II Corps. Reinforcing II Corps from the Federal western wing would require troops to cross the river twice. Illness and a lack of capable corps commanders prevented Lee from springing the trap. Longstreet faced a long convalescence from his disabling Wilderness wound, Anderson lacked experience, Ewell had not recovered from his collapse at Spotsylvania, Hill had returned to command of his corps but had since performed poorly and Stuart lay dead, mortally wounded defending Richmond against Federal cavalry on May 11. That night Grant grasped his predicament and ordered his men to halt and entrench.

The pickets continued firing rapidly on the clear, warm morning of May 25. Yankee skirmishers were back reconnoitering the Confederate main

8 Laughton, "The Sharpshooters of Mahone's Brigade," 102-103.

9 Bernard Diary, May 24, 1864.

line of resistance. The sharpshooters of Weisiger's brigade drove in the opposing pickets. The marksmen advanced 600 yards to the river, passing over the dead and badly wounded left during the night by the retreating Federals.[10] The 12th's sharpshooter company suffered three casualties. The enemy killed the City Guard's Pvt. Bradley Payne, a Northerner by birth who had become a good soldier after his conscription. The foe wounded the New Grays' Pvt. Joseph C. Robinson along with Tyler, the company commander.[11] Leadership of the company passed to Laughton. Relieved before noon by the 41st Virginia, Weisiger's marksmen returned from the river, burying more Union dead than their battalion had men.

Seventy-five yards separated the pickets. They kept up a spirited exchange of fire amid the showers that fell throughout the next day. The regiment got a special treat in the evening. A rumor about increased rations proved true. The men each drew a pound of chewing tobacco and small amounts of coffee, sugar and molasses. They also got half a pound of pork instead of a quarter pound of bacon. For the first time, they received chewing tobacco, plugs about a foot long and three inches wide. Immensely pleased, the soldiers engaged in what they called "a big eat."[12] As they chowed down, Grant was abandoning his North Anna lines and shifting southeastwardly in another attempt to turn Lee's right. This time the Federals headed for the Virginia Central and the Richmond & Fredericksburg railroads.

Since the successful Federal dawn attack of May 12, the Southerners had risen at 3 a.m. every day. At sunrise on the cloudy morning of May 27, the pickets reported that the Northerners had left their front and were retreating across the North Anna. The division's sharpshooters pursued, capturing a few stragglers who stated that "Grant cannot induce them to charge our works, as they have gotten enough of it," Sale recorded.[13] Soldiers from the rest of the brigade searched the abandoned Union trenches for equipment. So far during the campaign the men had provided themselves with Uncle Sam's tents and oilcloths. Today the haul consisted of blankets and frying pans.

Mahone's division headed southward at noon. The 12th followed a wagon train and some artillery. Continual starting and stopping exhausted the

10 Laughton, "The Sharpshooters of Mahone's Brigade," *SHSP*, 32:103.

11 Sale Diary, May 25, 1864.

12 Ibid., May 26, 1864.

13 Ibid., May 27, 1864.

Weighing out rations
Frank Leslie's Illustrated History of the Civil War

men. They crossed South Anna River and some of its tributaries in thickly forested country. Birds filled the trees. The woods resounded with their songs. "They are as gay as can be and they are the only happy creatures in sight," Sale observed. Too tired to converse, the troops only grunted "the most absurd wishes" about their officers, the wagons and the guns ahead, noted Sale.[14] The regiment bivouacked at 10:30 p.m. In the cool night air, a man began singing:

> *Jesus, Lover of my soul,*
> *Let me to Thy bosom fly,*
> *When the nearer waters roll,*
> *While the tempests still are high.*[15]

Others joined in. In minutes, the entire camp had taken up the hymn.

14 Ibid.

15 Ibid.

Next day some of the first reinforcements to reach Lee's army during the campaign met Mahone's soldiers about five miles northwest of Atlee's Station on the Virginia Central—Breckinridge's division from the Shenandoah, where the division had helped defeat a Federal thrust at New Market on May 15, and Finegan's Florida Brigade from its home state. The arrival of these units caused little cheer. Together with intelligence from Union prisoners, it convinced the Virginians that another battle would soon begin.

Finegan's brigade, three big regiments strong, became part of Mahone's division. The brigade consisted "mostly of very young, half grown men, and not very healthy & strong looking," Phillips remembered. They appeared "a pitiful sorrowful looking crowd" and did not seem to know why they had come to Virginia.[16] Compensating for the dwindling numbers of "the turkeys" in Perry's Florida Brigade, Lee consolidated the two Florida brigades under Brig. Gen. Joseph Finegan, who impressed the 12th's soldiers favorably.

The regiment took up the march again after noon, passing through Atlee's Station. At sunset, the troops bivouacked in woods a mile and a half to the station's southeast. For the first time since leaving camp on May 4, they got an unbroken night's sleep.

By May 30, the 12th's soldiers had erected eleven lines of breastworks since the campaign's beginning. They regretted not firing a shot from behind any of them. Hill's corps was digging in while, farther east and south of Totopotomoy Creek, Grant sought to outflank Lee with V Corps. Lee tried to strike V Corps near Bethesda Church with Ewell's Corps—now under Early—supported by Anderson's Corps. The Northerners retreated into their entrenchments, then repulsed Early's troops.

Grant continued sidling left on June 1. Lee, concerned about the impending arrival of Unionist reinforcements, conformed to Grant's movements. The Federals disappeared from in front of Hill's Corps and Breckinridge's division. Confederate pickets advanced but soon found the enemy.

The Unionists again disappeared from the division's front on the sultry morning of June 2. This time the Northerners really had departed— southeastward, as usual. At 11 a.m., the 12th's soldiers headed toward the Confederate right by way of Mechanicsville. At dark they stopped on the old Gaines' Mill battleground near a battery which had unlimbered on a site exposed to counterbattery fire. Rain began as the men excavated earthworks

16 Phillips, "Sixth Corporal," 54.

to protect the battery, uncovering skeletons of soldiers killed almost two years earlier. Nobody knew whether the bones belonged to friend or foe.

The Yankees attacked in the rain at daybreak on June 3. Mahone's division stood in reserve about a quarter mile behind Colquitt's Georgia Brigade of Hoke's division, which had reinforced Lee's army from Petersburg. "I was awaked by the shrill scream of a shell passing immediately over me," wrote Bird, who had recovered from his Malvern Hill wound and a bout with typhoid and returned to the ranks.[17] The battle raged for three hours. Cannonballs and minie balls constantly whizzed over Mahone's men in their breastworks. "A round shot covered up 8 of us," wrote Bird, "to the amusement of everyone except we buried ones." The troops greeted solid shot with cries of, "Catch it out!" When a shell came, they yelled, "Let it bounce before you catch it!"[18]

Skirmishing and occasional artillery fire continued until dark. A crash of musketry several hundred yards to the regiment's right startled the troops. The sound "would have drowned the roar of Niagara," wrote Bird.[19] Breckinridge's division and Finegan's brigade were driving the Federals from rifle pits they had seized that morning. "For 45 minutes the earth quivered like a person in mortal agony," Bird wrote.[20] The firing gradually ceased. A Confederate cheer told of another victory. The remainder of Mahone's division, still in reserve, shifted half a mile rightward through woods, pelted by Union shells. Weisiger's brigade relieved Wharton's brigade of Breckenridge's division in the front line near McGee's farm on Turkey Hill, close to the Chickahominy. The Virginians deployed on the Floridians' right and to the left of Cadmus Wilcox's division.

Another rainy day followed. The invaders did not renew their assaults. Yankee sharpshooters annoyed the 12th's men, whose earthworks lay in an open field less than 300 yards from the Federal trenches. Fifty yards separated the skirmishers of both sides. "We are frequently greeted with the sound of Minnies, in fact we cannot show our heads above the lines for fear of being shot," Sale observed. "This is beginning to be somewhat like

---

17 Henry Van Leuvenigh Bird to Margaret Randolph, June 3, 1864.

18 Ibid., Postscript of June 4, 1864.

19 Ibid.

20 Ibid.

Vicksburg."[21] The Purcell Artillery of Pegram's battalion unlimbered along the regiment's line, opening on the Unionist skirmishers toward evening but failing to drive them back. On the 12th's front, a shell cut down a gridiron. The Northerners declined to raise the banner again.

Unionist sharpshooters remained active on June 5, a cloudy day, wounding one of the Lafayette Guards mortally and two of the regiment's other soldiers less severely.[22] That evening fatigue parties from the 12th and the other regiments of Weisiger's brigade filled in the rifle pits in front of Finegan's brigade. The rest of the 12th's soldiers went on picket. A few panicky fellows set off a fusillade.

The fatigue parties labored until daybreak among the Yankee corpses. The pickets withdrew at 8:30 on this clear, warm morning to within 50 yards of the works because of a rumored two-hour armistice for the burial of the dead. The rumor proved untrue. Firing resumed. Northern sharpshooters wounded three of the 12th's men, one mortally.[23] By midday the Unionists became so quiet that Mahone began to think they had disappeared again. He decided to find out if an enemy battle line held the works opposite his troops. In the afternoon the 12th sent a man from each company to report to the 41st Virginia's Capt. James Smith. They would form part of his 100-man reconnaissance patrol from the Virginia and Mississippi Brigades.

Phillips, commanding the Richmond Grays, asked his sergeant whose turn had come for hazardous duty. The sergeant called out the name of Pvt. Samuel S. Clarke, a watchmaker who had returned to the ranks in January after a stint as an attendant and then a ward master in a Richmond hospital. Partially blind, Clarke begged Phillips to excuse him. Phillips yielded, asking his sergeant whose turn came next.

"E. K. Gunn," the sergeant replied, and Phillips thought, "no better ever lived."

Private Eugene Kinkaid "Blocker" Gunn, one of the men who had stepped more than once into the 12th Virginia, had worked as a clerk in civilian life. He had enlisted in the Grays in 1861. Discharged the following year to accept a lieutenant's commission in the Otey Artillery, he rejoined the Grays in 1864.

21 Sale Diary, June 4, 1864.

22 Bernard Diary, June 6, 1864; Henderson, *12VI*, 106-167.

23 Sale Diary, June 6, 1864; Henderson, *12VI*, 106-167.

"Damn it," Gunn said. "I have to be called on all the time to do duty for another."

"Blocker," said Phillips, "this is a very important task to perform and it requires sure enough men and you are in my judgment the man to fill the place."[24] Gunn reported to Smith as ordered.

The reconnaissance patrol rushed forward, driving Federal skirmishers, who belonged to Miles' brigade of Barlow's division, from their rifle pits.[25] Killing and capturing many of the enemy, the Southerners dashed to within 40 yards of the Union breastworks. A volley in their faces told them the foe still occupied the works in force. They started back toward their own lines, except for Chappell. He charged closer, emptied his pistol at the Northerners and cussed them, then joined the retreat.

The enemy flung a flanking column beyond the retiring Southerners' right, threatening them with capture. The division's sharpshooters came to their rescue, shooting and capturing an officer from the 2nd New York Heavy Artillery of Miles' brigade within 100 yards of the Secessionist rifle pits. Three of the 12th's men fell into enemy hands: Pvt. David Fitzhugh May, the last of the five May brothers still with the colors, and Sgt. Patrick Raferty, a clerk born in County Galway, Ireland, both of the City Guard; and luckless Blocker Gunn.[26] Chappell returned to Confederate lines unscathed.

The reconnaissance patrol included Dean. Afterward, he again impressed his superiors favorably. A wounded Yankee private lay between the lines begging his friends to retrieve him. Dean shouted to Chappell, the officer of the guard then, for permission to fetch in the wounded Federal. Chappell refused permission, telling Dean the enemy would shoot him. The wounded bluecoat overheard this conversation. He begged his friends not to fire. Dean dropped his musket, shucked his equipment and slipped out between the lines. The Unionist was suffering so much that he begged Dean to shoot him. Dean brought in the wounded Northerner, who gave his watch and knapsack to Dean in gratitude.

That evening the rumored armistice for burial of the dead prevailed from 8 p.m. to 10 p.m. The Yanks violated the truce—not all of them who

24 Phillips, "Sixth Corporal," 56.

25 Sale Diary, June 6, 1864.

26 Phillips, "Sixth Corporal," 56; Phillips Diary, June 6, 1864; Henderson, *12VI*, 106-167; Bernard Diary, June 7, 1864; *Richmond Whig*, June 11, 1864.

ventured between the lines returned to their positions by 10 p.m. The 12th's soldiers, still on picket, joined the other skirmishers of both sides in nearly nightlong firing.

The Virginia Brigade's sharpshooters relieved the regiment at daybreak. The 12th's men spent the day sleeping. Breckinridge's division departed for Charlottesville to reinforce the Confederates in the Shenandoah, defeated at Piedmont two days earlier. Weisiger's sharpshooters brought their Federal counterparts under control, but another foe was getting out of hand. "Soldier's friends are more plentiful now than I have seen them for over a year," Sale noted. "There is but one way to get rid of them and that is a frequent use of boiling water and thumbnails."[27] The evening's truce for the burial of the dead went more smoothly. The Secessionist pickets traded tobacco to their Northern counterparts for coffee.

By June 8, the videttes of both sides had reached a tacit agreement not to fire on one another. This emboldened the Unionists to become, Sale observed, "very saucy."[28] Though warned off, Yankee skirmishers advanced so close to the Confederate sentinels that the Southern officers ordered them to fire. A few shots made the Federals keep their distance. That evening a stray ball wounded the Herrings' Second Lt. Erastus Ferguson, shot less than a month earlier at Heth's Salient.[29] The 12th's men spent the night keeping watch and improving Purcell Artillery's position. One-third went on duty at a time.

Whitehorne, after a month of guarding the brigade's wagon train, returned to the ranks. "I have never yet, nor do I ever expect, to volunteer for any dangerous service," he recalled.[30] Now he had endured the disrespect of his immediate superior long enough and explained, "I am not going to Bootlick or humiliate myself to any officer in order to keep an easy place. . . ."[31] The superior "said I was a fool not to keep a soft place when I had one," remembered Whitehorne.[32]

27 Sale Diary, June 7, 1864. By "soldier's friends," Sale meant lice.

28 Ibid., June 8, 1864.

29 Ibid.

30 Elmore, *Diary of J. E. Whitehorne*, 6.

31 James E. Whitehorne to Sister, June 9, 1864.

32 Elmore, *Diary of J. E. Whitehorne*, 49.

Fletcher Archer. *Virginia Historical Society*

Having risen by 3 a.m. on June 9, nearly all the 12th's men went back to sleep at daylight. The sleepers sprawled, Sale recorded, "in every conceivable position in the trenches."[33] Northern bullets continued taking their toll, wounding one of the Old Grays and striking Weisiger but only bruised him.[34]

The incessant strain of the campaign, which had exceeded in length and bloodshed any previous campaign of the war, had left its mark on the men. Nearly all wore haggard expressions and longed for peace. The soldiers took advantage of the relative lull in the action. "I washed and changed my clothes for the first time since the 1st of May—part of the 'honor & glory' of soldiering," Bird wrote. "Does that accord with your preconceived notions of a soldier's life?"[35]

A battery of Confederate mortars emplaced during the night opened fire next morning. The Yanks remained very active. Federal sharpshooters to the regiment's left wounded three men. The enemy took another lad prisoner.[36] Startling news came—a report that Butler's Army of the James had seized Petersburg the previous day. These Unionists had menaced Petersburg from the Bermuda Hundred peninsula at the confluence of the James and the Appomattox for more than a month. "The Petersburg boys all had very long faces," noted Sale.[37] The daily newspapers' arrival brought clarification and relief. The Northerners had failed to take the city. The Confederate units that fought off the bluecoats included the Petersburg Artillery and the 3rd Battalion, Virginia State Reserves. Fletcher Archer, now a lieutenant colonel,

33 Sale Diary, June 9, 1864.

34 Bernard Diary, June 10, 1864; Henderson, *12VI*, 106-167.

35 Henry Van Leuvenigh Bird to Stanley Beckwith, June 10, 1864.

36 Phillips Diary, June 10, 1864; Henderson, *12VI*, 106-167.

37 Sale Diary, June 10, 1864.

commanded the latter. Keiley served as a private in Archer's battalion and fell into enemy hands.

Butler's swipe at Petersburg alerted the Southern high command to the city's vulnerability, and orders increased its garrison. The loss of Petersburg would cut one of Richmond's two lines of communication with the Deep South—the Richmond & Petersburg. Cutting the other—the Richmond & Danville Railroad—would isolate Virginia.

On June 11, incoming ordnance from the Federals slackened. Yankee prisoners complained of the brisk fire maintained by the Confederate pickets. A stray minnie struck the Richmond Grays' Pvt. Joseph Weller in the left shoulder as he lay in his tent, "bullet going in square from the left side which was a mortal wound," recalled Phillips, who had served his apprenticeship with Weller's father.[38] Weller did not expire until October 27.

The sentries of both sides resumed firing at daybreak on June 12. The regiment lost two wounded.[39] The Richmond Grays went on picket that clear, warm evening. Lee sent Early's Corps to oppose the Union advance up the Valley.

Grant had been contemplating the wreckage of his plan for the Virginia campaign. His forces had failed to destroy Lee's army, failed to drive it into the Richmond defenses and failed to reach a position that would permit them to cross James River directly to Bermuda Hundred. Butler had failed to invest Richmond from the south, failed to cut permanently any of the rail lines leading into the Confederate capital from that direction and failed to keep open the way from Bermuda Hundred to Richmond's southern approaches. Major General Franz Sigel had failed to sever the Virginia Central though his successor, Maj. Gen. David Hunter, was renewing the effort. Major General Philip Henry Sheridan, Grant's cavalry commander, dispatched June 7 to link up with Hunter or cut the Virginia Central, was failing in both missions. All this had cost the Yankees more than 60,000 casualties.

But Grant had a knack of using his failures as stepping stones to success. This capacity did not fail him now. He still intended to capture Richmond by severing its supply lines. But now his troops would cross the James below the Appomattox's mouth, ensnaring the Confederate capital in a wider envelopment. Petersburg would constitute the first Union objective Southside.

---

38 Phillips, "Sixth Corporal," 55; Sale Diary, June 10, 1864; Phillips Diary, June 11, 1864.

39 Ibid., June 12, 1864; Henderson, *12VI*, 106-167.

Seizing the city would cut the Richmond & Petersburg's connections with the Deep South. Proceeding to sever the Richmond & Danville might well compel the Secessionists to abandon Richmond.

Late on the night of June 12, most of Grant's Northerners pulled out of their Cold Harbor lines and headed for Wilcox's Landing and Windmill Point on the James. The horse soldiers of Wilson's division and the infantry of V Corps created a diversion, pushing out on Charles City and Darbytown roads and shoving the Southern cavalrymen of Gary's brigade back toward Richmond. The movements of Wilson's division and V Corps had their intended effect. Lee posted his forces to deal with two possibilities—that Grant's entire command was advancing through Riddell's Shop on the Confederate capital, or that he was preparing to cross the James from the vicinity of Malvern Hill to Bermuda Hundred.

Next morning before 8 a.m., scouts and skirmishers from Mahone's division advanced a mile and returned having found no Yankees except a few stragglers. A report came that the Federals were crossing the Chickahominy and heading for the James. Weisiger's brigade advanced to reconnoiter at 9 a.m. but made no contact. News had just arrived of the nominations of Lincoln and Andrew Johnson by the Baltimore Convention. Hugh Smith informed Bernard that the regiment had suffered 159 casualties since the campaign's beginning, mostly in the Wilderness and at Spotsylvania.[40] Ten days near the Unionists at Cold Harbor had accounted for 4 men taken prisoner and 14 others wounded, 3 mortally.

The 12th's soldiers started off on one of the corduroy roads laid by McClellan for his "change of base" in 1862. The Virginians were leaving Cold Harbor for good. The regiment had gotten its first taste of full-fledged trench warfare in the Cold Harbor lines. This kind of warfare had other peculiarities besides the use of mortars, the dominance of sharpshooters and the proliferation of lice. An institution called the "grapevine telegraph" developed. "When anything not of much importance is to be sent it is

---

40 The sources cited up to this point in chapters 13-15 indicate this number, which does not include the bruise suffered by Weisiger and exceeds by 13 the 146 casualties for the same period in Alfred C. Young, III, *Lee's Army* (Baton Rouge, La., 2013) 304. After the 12th had suffered six more casualties, its adjutant told Bernard that the regiment had lost 149 in battles and skirmishes during the campaign—23 killed in battle, 17 died of wounds, 97 wounded and 12 missing. Bernard Diary, July 18, 1864. Lee's order not to include among casualties the slightly wounded who were not incapacitated and returned quickly to the ranks may account for the differences. *OR* 25, 2:798.

passed from one man to another until it reaches its destination," Sale noted. "Something or other is passing during the whole day. . . ."[41]

Mahone's men had also experienced their first encounter with a new foe. The division's pickets captured a black soldier and brought him to the rear. Seeing an African American in arms incensed some Secessionists. "The poor creature was almost frightened to death as he looked around on the scowling faces of the curious crowd," Todd recalled. "He was ashy pale." A rear echelon officer from another division and a few men took charge of the prisoner, leading him into the woods, where they shot him. "It was a cruel murder and worthy only of a man who skulked in the rear," Todd declared.[42]

"Our route lay through the country across swamps and ever way except a good one," Sale observed. "How on earth any man did to find his way through this place I can't see."[43] The men crossed the Chickahominy and White Oak Swamp as well. They followed the familiar Charles City Road southeastward. At noon they heard musketry in the direction of the Frayser's Farm battlefield. A sharp action was going on at Riddell's Shop between Cadmus Wilcox's division and the Yankees. The 12th's soldiers turned off Charles City Road to proceed by a country lane to Darbytown Road. They came within enemy rifle range. The Lafayette Guards' Cpl. William Parker Faison took a minnie in the right leg.[44]

Heavy skirmishing continued all afternoon. Wilcox's division forced back the Federals. Mahone's division formed line of battle about two miles from Malvern Hill. Porte's men entrenched. At sunset Weisiger's brigade abandoned its earthworks, advanced a quarter of a mile and after much delay fortified again. Part of the 12th went on picket at midnight.

The men woke up next morning to find themselves in the battered but blossoming Frayser yard, within 150 feet of the Frayser house, which had served as a Union hospital during the battle of June 30, 1862. Bones covered the ground. At 6:30 p.m., Weisiger's brigade withdrew 400 yards to a wooded hill covered with bones. "Friends and foe are alike scattered around," noted Sale.[45] The sky had clouded. The weather was turning cool.

41   Sale Diary, June 12, 1864.

42   Todd, "Reminiscences," 216-217.

43   Sale Diary, June 13, 1864.

44   Bernard Diary, June 14, 1864; Henderson, *12VI*, 123.

45   Sale, Diary, June 14, 1864.

A light rain began to fall. But the order to pitch their tents among the trees lifted the troops' spirits. For only the second time since leaving their camp near Madison Run Station, the 12th's soldiers enjoyed the luxury of unrolling their blankets and going properly to bed. Before retiring, they prepared to march at nine the next morning. That night Meade's army started crossing the James. Returning from the Cold Harbor lines by ship, XVIII Corps of Butler's army landed at Bermuda Hundred.

By dawn on June 15, the rain had stopped. Fair weather returned. About to fall in, Weisiger's brigade had its marching orders countermanded. The Virginians remained among the bones on the wooded hill until late afternoon, then returned to the Frayser yard. Disorganization, misunderstandings, caution and the increased Cockade City garrison prevented the Unionists from attacking Petersburg before evening. XVIII Corps seized more than a mile of the Secessionist fortifications east of the city, but II Corps arrived too late to attack. Beauregard, the Confederate commander in Petersburg, abandoned his lines opposite Bermuda Hundred, concentrating nearly all his men against the Federals Southside.

At 10 a.m. on June 16, Mahone's division withdrew four miles to Fussell's Mill on Darbytown Road. Many soldiers took advantage of their inactivity to wash clothes in Bailey's Creek. The Unionists continued their efforts to take Petersburg. The previous day's tramping and fighting had fatigued the Federals in front of the city. XVIII Corps shortened its lines. II Corps failed to launch a dawn assault as planned. Meade arrived, taking charge of the Unionists in front of Petersburg but developing tunnel vision, focusing on the two Secessionist divisions in front of him and failing to consider flanking them out of the town. Butler's men occupied the empty Confederate trenches opposite Bermuda Hundred. Grant hesitated to interpose his forces between Lee and Petersburg. Lee shifted Anderson's Corps across the James to cope with this threat. The sun was setting when the Northerners menacing Petersburg launched their second assault. They took little ground. Confederate counterattacks kept them awake all night.

Meade kept hammering away. A dawn attack by the newly arrived bluecoats of IX Corps cracked the second Confederate position east of Petersburg on June 17. The terrain prevented the Yankees from exploiting their success. V Corps arrived but still Meade did not attempt to outflank the city's defenders. Anderson's Corps recaptured the Confederate lines opposite Bermuda Hundred, denying the Federals their tardily perceived opportunity to bar Lee's path into Petersburg. The fighting in front of the city continued until long after dark. A Confederate counterattack drove the Unionists from most of their gains. Beauregard's men withdrew to a line several hundred yards nearer Petersburg. At Fussell's Mill that night, the 12th prepared to march at 8 a.m.

The terrible tramp of June 18 began five hours earlier than expected. The regiment's soldiers arrived at Chaffin's Bluff at 9 a.m., rested briefly, then crossed the James on a pontoon bridge. They reached the Richmond & Petersburg Turnpike by noon. "Here on every side could be seen traces of the sharp fighting between Butler's and Beauregard's forces, such as breastworks, rifle pits, rail road track torn up, cross ties burned, &c. &c.," remembered Whitehorne.[46] In the fearful heat, the 12th's men were spitting cotton. Artillery horses broke down, causing delays in the infantry column. The troops straggled "mightily," noted Phillips, a straggler himself because of gravel getting into his shoes through holes in their sides and cutting his feet.[47] After sitting down on the stoop of a sawmill on Swift Creek to take off his shoes and empty them of gravel, he needed half an hour to catch up with his company though he hiked as hard as he could, reaching his men near Petersburg. He had often wondered why men straggled, and now he knew.

Beauregard's withdrawal of the previous evening had its desired effect. The Yankees took hours to reconnoiter the new Confederate lines, then launched a disjointed series of ineffectual assaults. Weisiger's brigade halted on the Appomattox's north bank at the foot of Dunn's Hill. The Virginians waited for orders designating the position they would take once they crossed Pocahontas Bridge. Ahead loomed the roofs and steeples of Petersburg. The troops heard firing in the distance.

46 Elmore, *Diary of J. E. Whitehorne*, 50.

47 Phillips Diary, June 18, 1864.

CHAPTER 16

Jerusalem Plank Road

The arduous trek of June 18 and the thrill of their reception by friends and loved ones left the 12th's soldiers in poor condition next day to meet a Yankee attack. "I am perfectly broken down have been asleep all day, have just waked up (3 p.m.)," Whitehorne remembered.[1] But the invaders launched no further assaults, contenting themselves with a little shelling. Few men undertook anything more ambitious than running the blockade into town. "A number of persons came out to see the 12th," Phillips recalled. "Eatibles was being brought out all day."[2]

With no Yankees in front of Weisiger's brigade, quiet prevailed until June 21. Then the foot soldiers of Meade's II and VI corps skirmished with Confederate cavalry and Cadmus Wilcox's infantry division screening the Weldon Railroad southwest of the 12th. Nonetheless, 50 men from Weisiger's brigade got passes to go into Petersburg at 6 that evening, provided they returned before 8 a.m. on June 22 or immediately in case of a Federal attack.

The movements of II and VI corps began Grant's second offensive at Petersburg. He intended to envelop the city with infantry from the Appomattox below the city to the Appomattox above, severing the Weldon and South Side railroads. His cavalry would cut Richmond's remaining rail link with the Deep South—the Richmond & Danville.

---

1 James E. Whitehorne to Sister, June 19, 1864.

2 Phillips Diary, June 19, 1864.

On June 22, the Unionist horsemen of Wilson's and Kautz's divisions wrecked Reams Station on the Weldon Railroad 12 miles south of Petersburg, then pounded westward. II Corps advanced to a position opposite the city's fortifications for a mile west of Jerusalem Plank Road. Constructed from 1862 until early 1864, these fortifications—called the Dimmock Line after Capt. Charles H. Dimmock, the engineer who had overseen their construction—ringed Petersburg for about 10 miles from the Appomattox above the city to the Appomattox below, and contained emplacements for 55 batteries connected by earthworks for infantry. A couple miles south of II Corps, VI Corps again advanced through wood and swamp toward the Weldon Railroad near Globe Tavern.

Mahone's headquarters occupied a tent behind the Dimmock Line's Battery 29, just west of Jerusalem Plank Road. Battery 29 would become known as Fort Mahone, or Fort Damnation. It stood across from what would become the Federal earthwork known as Fort Sedgwick, or Fort Hell. Lee and Hill rode to Porte's headquarters and surveyed the situation. The Northerners opposite were erecting breastworks facing the Dimmock Line. Lee directed Hill to drive them back. Hill seemed content, as on the previous day, to employ Cadmus Wilcox's division to defend the railroad farther south. Mahone, because of his activities with the Norfolk & Petersburg, knew the ground around the Cockade City like the back of his hand. He volunteered to attack.

Porte sent scouts up the deep ravine near the Branch house, a mile and a half west of Jerusalem Plank Road. From the Branch house the ravine took the scouts to the Johnson farm, more than a mile south. They located the left flank of the forward line of II Corps in the woods a short distance east of the ravine but failed to detect the left of a second line of II Corps' troops about a mile southeast.[3]

Mahone selected the Virginia, Georgia and Alabama Brigades of his division for a flank attack. About 1 p.m., the Virginians dropped their baggage, pulling out of the works between Battery 33 and Battery 36. "Everyone instantly commenced surmising where was our probable destination," noted

---

3 Major General Gouverneur K. Warren's Sketch of Federal Position at Globe Tavern Evening of August 18, 1864; OR 42, 1:433, 2:276; Map of Battle of Jerusalem Plank Road, June 22, 1864, John Willian Papers, Private Collection of John Horn. The rear line of II Corps angled away from the front line and the Confederate works, standing closer to them on Jerusalem Plank Road than farther left. Ibid.; OR 40, 1:352, 354, 366, 382, 404, 416. Willian was then a major on the staff of Mott's division. Ibid., 412.

Sale.[4] Porte did not want to arouse Federal suspicions. His soldiers withdrew from the Dimmock Line one by one. The men remaining in the Confederate fortifications increased the intervals between themselves, filling the places of those who had left.

The regiment marched at 2 p.m. Mahone led his three brigades through the ravine into the left rear of II Corps' first line unobserved by the Federals, forming his line of battle in the Johnson farm's field. His sharpshooters skirmished with the Union pickets of Barlow's division, the westernmost division of II Corps. This division's front line formed a carpenter's angle, with two brigades in a return running southwardly for a couple hundred yards from another of the division's brigades in the corps' first line, which ran east-west at this point. Miles' brigade of Barlow's division remained in the corps' second line, about a mile southeast of the first and running at an angle of sixty-five degrees to it. II Corps' other two divisions of four brigades each had two brigades up and two brigades back. The front line of the division next to Barlow's—Mott's—also occupied an east-west line while its second line stood from a half to three quarters of a mile to the southeast. The front line of the easternmost division, Gibbon's, held a line running southwestwardly from Battery B, 1st New Jersey Light Artillery, which had unlimbered on the site of the future Fort Sedgwick. In the middle of Gibbon's division's front line stood the 12th Battery, New York Light Artillery, dug in between two of the division's brigades. About 900 yards southeast of this line ran another with the division's remaining two brigades.

Porte aligned his forces on a north-south line perpendicular to their own works. His men confronted the western face of the return of Barlow's division. The First Maryland Artillery prepared to advance on the far left, facing open country. To the artillery's right, Porte posted Sanders' Alabama Brigade, and farther right, the Georgia Brigade. Both brigades confronted woods and Federal skirmishers. Weisiger's brigade stood in reserve behind the Georgia Brigade.

Mahone wanted Cadmus Wilcox's division to position itself on the immediate right of his own three brigades. In the attack Wilcox's division would conform its movements to those of Porte's brigades. As Mahone's brigades struck the first Federal line's left, Wilcox's division would strike deep into its rear and prevent the Unionists from escaping. Mahone attempted

4 Sale Diary, June 22, 1864.

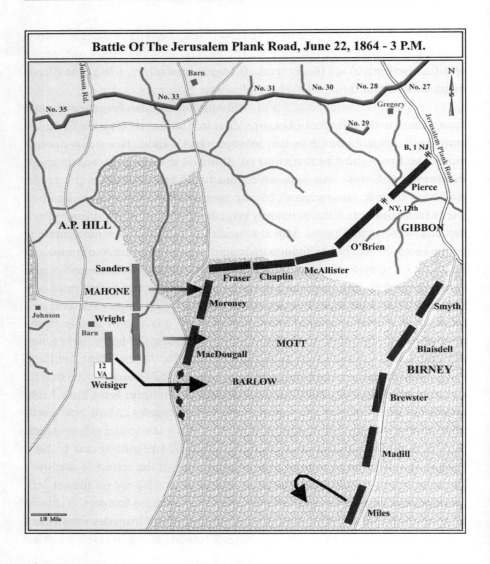

Battle Of The Jerusalem Plank Road, June 22, 1864 - 3 P.M.

to convey his plan to Wilcox through Hill. Captain Victor Jean Baptiste Girardey, a French born, Louisiana educated Georgian on Porte's staff, communicated the plan to Hill near the Davis house, on the Weldon Railroad around a mile southwest of the second Federal line. Hoping to prevent any misunderstanding, Girardey proceeded to Wilcox, who had already interposed his division between VI Corps and the Weldon Railroad east of the Aiken house, a couple miles southeast of the Davis house. Girardey explained the plan to Wilcox.

"Captain, I don't know what I was sent here to do," said Wilcox. "General Hill promised to overtake me and give me further instructions."[5]

When the corps commander issued his orders, they revealed that he had indeed misunderstood Mahone. Hill's orders called for Wilcox to strike straight north, parallel to Jerusalem Plank Road, instead of joining Mahone nearer the Johnson farm. Wilcox played it safe and elected to follow Hill's orders rather than the design conveyed by Girardey and dispatched two brigades due north. Wilcox's other two brigades remained facing VI Corps between the Aiken house and the Jerusalem Plank Road. The absence of Wilcox's division from Porte's right made his attack riskier. The second line of II Corps could outflank Mahone's troops flanking II Corps' first line.

Around 3 p.m., the First Maryland Artillery rolled forward, unlimbered in the open field near the Federal breastworks and opened fire. The batteries along the Dimmock Line also let fly. Under cover of this barrage, the Alabama and Georgia brigades hopped a worm fence and plunged into the woods. They howled the Rebel yell's "Ki-yi" and pushed the Unionist skirmishers back on the main bodies of their brigades in the return.[6] Weisiger's brigade had gone only a few steps forward when, with withering volleys, the Federal line in the return stopped cold the Alabamians and Georgians. Miles' brigade was advancing from II Corps' second line when Mahone's soldiers advanced. The increased volume of fire alarmed Brig. Gen. Francis Channing Barlow, who ordered Miles' brigade to double-quick back to the second line of Unionist works.

Porte deployed Weisiger's brigade on the Georgia Brigade's right. The Virginians double-quicked into position by the right flank. Union fire wounded one of the New Grays. Then Weisiger's men outflanked the Yankee flank guard. "We faced by the left flank & moved down on the enemy and drove them pell mell out of their temporary breastworks made of wood," Phillips recalled.[7] The two Federal brigades in the return skedaddled. The Alabamians and Georgians then rolled up the brigade from Barlow's division

---

5 "A Reply to a Communication Published by Gen. C. M. Wilcox in the *New Orleans Times*, of January 1st, 1872," 17, William Mahone Papers, Folder 2, Library of Virginia; see also "Military Operations Around Petersburg, the Mine, etc." by Cadmus M. Wilcox, written for the *New Orleans Times* in response to Mahone's article in the *Historical Magazine*, Folder 2, LV.

6 Gilbert Adams Hays, *Under the Red Patch; Story of the Sixty-Third Regiment, Pennsylvania Volunteers, 1861-1864* (Pittsburgh, 1908), 257.

7 Phillips, "Sixth Corporal," 58.

in the first line while the Virginians swung through the woods between the two Unionist lines and gobbled up prisoners sprinting for the rear. Barlow's division "melted away like ice in the sun," recorded Whitehorne.[8] Next, the Confederates flanked the first line of Mott's division, which fled without much resistance except from the 1st Massachusetts Heavy Artillery on the division's far right. They rolled up Mott's division "like a sheet of paper," Whitehorne noted.[9] Fugitives from the first Federal line disordered the second, too far back in the thick timber to provide much support or flank the flanking Secessionists.

One of the Secessionist batteries in the Dimmock Line brought the Southerners under fire and disordered them. Mahone turned to one of his couriers, Pvt. James Hamilton Blakemore, a native of Tennessee on detached duty from the Riflemen. Blakemore galloped to the Dimmock Line and delivered the order for firing to cease.

Mahone's troops regrouped and struck the left of Gibbon's division as Wilcox's two northbound brigades encountered Unionist videttes in the swamps and chaparral between the Vaughn farm and Jerusalem Plank Road. When Porte's men were nearing the 12th New York Battery, the skirmishing between Wilcox's men and the Unionists became audible to the south. Mahone directed Blakemore to guide himself by the sound and find Wilcox with the following message: "I am driving the enemy back upon his main works. If you will promptly bear down with your command in the direction of my firing we can sweep everything before us."[10]

On his way, Blakemore spotted Northerners advancing toward Mahone's right. There Maj. Thomas Sumter Mills, Porte's Assistant Adjutant General and an "herculean seven footer," known as "the kid glove major," was also carrying a message to Wilcox. Mills and some Georgians escorting him fell into the hands of the 26th Michigan of Miles' brigade.[11] Blakemore found Wilcox about a mile and a half southeast of the Johnson farm, near Jerusalem Plank Road. Wilcox ordered his two brigades still facing VI Corps to leave skirmish lines behind and follow the rest of his division

8 Elmore, *Diary of J. E. Whitehorne*, 51.

9 Ibid.

10 "A Reply to a Communication Published by Gen. C. M. Wilcox in the *New Orleans Times*, of January 1st, 1872," 19.

11 *OR* 40, 2:308; "Capture of Confederate Officers," Washington D.C. *Evening Star*, June 25, 1864, p. 2, col. 1; "Thomas Sumter Mills," May 7, 2017, www.findagrave.com.

to Mahone's assistance. "Progress was very slow," recalled Blakemore. "Something seemed to act as a hitch every few paces."[12]

The Norfolk Division's skirmish line pitched in with a frontal push against Gibbon's division. The Virginians, Georgians and Alabamians rolled up the left brigade of Gibbon's front line, the Philadelphia or California Brigade. The Southerners scrambled over the earthworks of the 12th Battery, New York Light Artillery in the middle of Gibbon's front line, striking from the rear the bluecoats of Pierce's brigade to the east. Entire Union regiments surrendered and the Confederate advance broke down under the weight of prisoners.[13] The 20th Massachusetts and the 36th Wisconsin turned to face westward and ended the rout.

Porte's men had seized four 3-inch rifles from the 12th New York Battery, at least eight stands of colors and more than 2,000 stand of small arms.[14] The 12th Virginia formed the extreme right of Mahone's formation but did not become hotly engaged, taking neither flags, nor cannons, nor many prisoners.

A hasty counterattack by part of Pierce's disorganized brigade and two regiments from the Corcoran or Irish Legion of Gibbon's second line failed. The Secessionists braced for a better organized Yankee counterstroke. The ambulance corps men tended the dead and wounded. Confederate artillerists limbered up the captured guns and brought them within Southern lines. Porte's infantrymen turned the captured breastworks to face the foe. Each man provided himself with several captured muskets. Mahone summoned Harris' Mississippi Brigade and a section of artillery. Receiving Mahone's order around 4 p.m., the Mississippians arrived within an hour.

The Federals struck again at dusk, employing another regiment of the Corcoran Legion and the 8th New York Heavy Artillery, as well as elements

12 "A Reply to a Communication Published by Gen. C. M. Wilcox in the *New Orleans Times*, of January 1st, 1872," 20.

13 John D. Smith, *The History of the Nineteenth Regiment of Maine Volunteer Infantry, 1862-1865* (Minneapolis, 1909), 210; St. Clair A. Mulholland, *The Story of the 116th Regiment, Pennsylvania Volunteers in the War of the Rebellion, the Record of a Gallant Command* (Philadelphia, 1903), 275; H. L. Patten to "Dear Col.," July 10, 1864, Association of Officers of the 20th Massachusetts Volunteer Infantry, "Reports, Letters & Papers Appertaining to 20th Mass. Vol. Inf." (Boston, MA: Boston Public Library, 1868), 234-235.

14 "The War News," Daily Richmond *Examiner*, June 25, 1864, p. 2, col. 1; Edwin C. Bearss, with Bryce A. Suderow, *The Petersburg Campaign: The Eastern Front Battles, June-August, 1864* (El Dorado Hills, CA, 2012), 168-169.

of Smyth's brigade, all from Gibbon's second line. The attack fell primarily upon the Mississippi Brigade. The Northerners drove in the Confederate pickets, hotly pursuing them through the dense undergrowth back to the breastworks. The Southern battle line held its fire. The Yankees came within 10 or 15 feet. Then the Secessionists blazed away with all the muskets at their disposal. Southern cannon flung shells over the infantry's heads into the oncoming Federal ranks. The Unionists recoiled. The roar of musketry died down, but the shells had set the woods on fire. Soldiers of both sides hustled to drag the wounded away from the flames.

Around that time, Wilcox's vanguard filed into the Johnson field.[15] "It did not require any large degree of military experience to see at once that the movement was not what was expected, and that the time for this command to prove of practical use upon that occasion had passed," remembered Blakemore.[16]

At 10 o'clock that night Mahone's troops began returning to their lines. The men carried with them the last spoils of their victory—the small arms captured. "Every man was required to carry off as many muskets as he was able to tote," recalled Phillips.[17] He bore away four on his shoulders.

Southern pickets remained in the captured fortifications. "These pickets were stationed some twenty or thirty yards apart, and could not plainly be seen on account of darkness, though the moon gave some light," remembered Whitehorne.[18] Just before daylight, Scott directed Whitehorne to go along the vidette line and instruct one soldier at a time to leave his post and quietly return to the regiment. After relieving all but the last picket, Whitehorne saw a man standing behind a pine bush and walked toward him. Before Whitehorne had taken many steps, he heard a low whistle to his right and rear.

"You were walking right up to that Yankee," said the last vidette. "I have been watching him all night."[19]

The two hastened back to Confederate lines.

---

15 Cadmus M. Wilcox, Report of Operations.

16 "A Reply to a Communication Published by Gen. C. M. Wilcox in the New Orleans Times, of January 1st, 1872," 20.

17 Phillips, "Sixth Corporal," 58.

18 Elmore, *Diary of J. E. Whitehorne*, 52.

19 Ibid.

Porte's troops stood in high spirits. His three brigades had routed seven Union brigades and withstood the counterattack of a eighth, inflicting on II Corps 650 killed and wounded and 1,742 captured.[20] The 12th had suffered two wounded and three captured.[21] The often critical Sale wrote that of all the affairs his regiment had participated in thus far during the campaign, this one "far outshown all the others in good management and success."[22] Sale did not know of Hill's failure to coordinate the efforts of his division commanders.

The results did not please everyone. Illness had prevented Pvt. Alva Benjamin Spencer of the 3rd Georgia's Company C, the Dawson Grays in Wright's Brigade, from participating, but he wrote to his sweetheart: "Our brigade was in advance & did the greater part of the fighting. They were *supported* by other troops of our division but they are entitled to *all* the honor. The Virginia papers however, give all the praise to Mahone's brigade (Va.)."[23] Spencer had been wounded at South Mills on April 19, 1862.

The 12th's men slept till 10 o'clock next morning. A few lucky soldiers drew passes to spend the day in town, including Waddell. "He looked worn, weary and dusty," noted his wife.[24] She provided him with a bath and some clean clothes—luxury for the captain, who had not taken off his coat for a month. He had removed his shoes only twice during that time. Mrs. Waddell gave him breakfast, which he wolfed down.

The Juniors and Richmond Grays relieved part of the 6th Virginia on picket. The rest of the 12th tramped off down Halifax Road with the remainder of Mahone's division. That afternoon Porte's forces encountered troops from VI Corps demolishing the Weldon Railroad near Globe Tavern, six miles south of Petersburg.

Knowledge of the previous day's II Corps debacle rendered Maj. Gen. Horatio Wright, commander of VI Corps, justifiably cautious. He was keeping his left firmly anchored to Second Swamp, which ran eastward just

---

20 Noah Andre Trudeau, *The Last Citadel: Petersburg, Virginia, June 1864-April 1865* (El Dorado Hills, CA, 2014), 75.

21 Bernard Diary, June 24, 1864; Henderson, *12VI*, 106-167.

22 John F. Sale to Aunt, July 9, 1864.

23 Clyde G. Wiggins, III, ed., *My Dear Friend: The Civil War Letters of Alva Benjamin Spencer, 3rd Georgia Regiment, Company C* (Macon, GA, 2007), 128.

24 Mrs. Charles E. Waddell Diary, June 23, 1864.

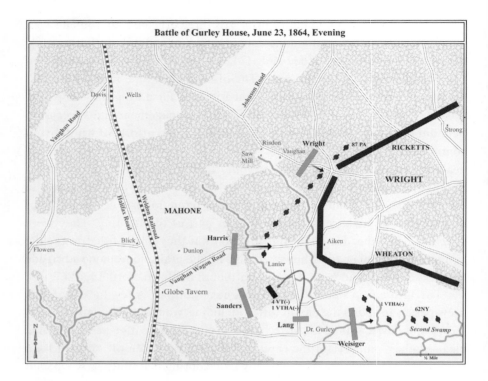

Battle of Gurley House, June 23, 1864, Evening

south of Globe Tavern and appeared to protect that flank against the kind of maneuver that had undone II Corps. His main line ran north and south about a mile east of the railroad. Wright's skirmishers advanced to the rails just north of Second Swamp. The pickets formed a salient with a battalion of sharpshooters from the 3rd Vermont of the Vermont Brigade in Getty's division and some troopers from the 18th Pennsylvania Cavalry tearing up the track at the salient's nose.

Mahone drove southward along the railroad. With his Mississippi Brigade he pushed the salient's nose eastward, back on supports from the 4th Vermont and 1st Vermont Heavy Artillery in a hollow west of the Lanier house. Porte's Georgia Brigade shoved the salient's northern shoulder eastward, separating those supports from Truex's brigade of Ricketts' division on their right and seizing a wood that had given the men in the hollow a retreat route northward. With his division's Alabama Brigade, Mahone jammed in the salient's southern shoulder. His Virginia Brigade stalked eastward through the open ground around Dr. Gurley's house, pushing back pickets of the 62nd New York and from the 1st Vermont heavies. This cut off the retreat route from the hollow southward and uncovered a blind road running through the trees east of the hollow.

On the Gurley farm, Lieutenant Laughton of the 12th's sharpshooter company encountered Sergeant Peter Donnelly of Company C of the 1st Vermont heavies. "I supposed him to be a scout sent out to make a reconnaissance, and as that was my business also, I ordered him to halt," Laughton recalled. "He defiantly refused the second time and he turned to leave when I fired and he fell." Laughton approached Donnelly, who could no longer speak but made signs for water. Laughton gave Donnelly water but he soon died. "I deeply regretted that I had no time to bury him," Laughton remembered.[25]

Around sunset Girardey, now Mahone's Acting Assistant Adjutant General, guided the Florida Brigade northward from Dr. Gurley's house along the blind road. Scattering more enemy skirmishers, the Floridians occupied an open field providing the last escape route for the Vermonters in the hollow west of the Lanier house. Led through the timber by their commander, Col. David Lang, the Floridians attacked the surrounded Vermont men from behind. After a brief firefight, the Floridians took about 400 prisoners, mostly from the 4th Vermont Infantry and the 1st Vermont heavies.[26]

As night approached, Porte probed the main line of VI Corps for weak spots but failed to find one. VI Corps retreated to the Williams house on Jerusalem Plank Road. Mahone's soldiers had worn themselves out. Hill ordered them back to Petersburg. The regiment reached its position near Battery 35 shortly before midnight, not having lost anyone.[27]

Despite their fatigue, the troops in Mahone's division prepared to march early on June 24, a very hot, humid day. Lee intended to use them to exploit a counterattack against the Union right, along the Appomattox, by Field's and Hoke's divisions. The assault failed. The division stood down from the morning's level of alertness. Harrison rode out with what Sale termed "little extras."[28] Grant finally realized the extent of June 22nd's disaster and

25 David Faris Cross, *A Melancholy Affair at the Weldon Railroad: The Vermont Brigade, June 23, 2864* (Shippensburg, PA, 2003), 35; "Local and State Items," *The Rutland Weekly Herald*, October 12, 1865, p. 3, cols. 3-4. The newspaper quotes a letter from Laughton to Donnelly's sister. Id.

26 Bernard Diary, June 24, 1864. Cross, *A Melancholy Affair at the Weldon Railroad*, 72, 74.

27 Ibid., 254 n.4.

28 Sale Diary, June 24, 1864.

halted his infantry's attempt to envelop Petersburg. In the fighting of June 22 and 23, the Southerners inflicted about 3,030 casualties at a cost of around 714.[29] Mahone's division had almost singlehandedly thwarted the Yankees.

Grant knew that worse would come when his cavalry raiders tried to return to Federal lines. He had led the raiders to expect that Union infantry would invest Petersburg south of the Appomattox and that Sheridan's cavalrymen would tie up their Confederate counterparts north of the James. Either eventuality would have precluded Secessionist interception. But the failure of Grant's foot soldiers to attain their objectives and Sheridan's June 24 defeat at Samaria Church left the tired horse soldiers in Wilson's and Kautz's divisions vulnerable.

The raiders and their pursuers staggered back toward Petersburg in intense heat. After Samaria Church Lee dispatched his ranking cavalryman, Maj. Gen. Wade Hampton, to destroy Wilson's and Kautz's divisions. Hampton arrived at Stony Creek Station on the Weldon Railroad at noon on June 28. He contacted the returning Northern horsemen half an hour later, asking Lee to send infantry to hold the Reams Station railroad crossing, 12 miles south of Petersburg. Lee dispatched Mahone with Finegan's and Sanders' brigades. The rest of the Norfolk Division rested near Battery 35.

On the morning of June 29, Porte's two brigades of infantry united with the Secessionist cavalry. The combined force routed the returning Yankee raiders. Fifteen cannon and 1,000 prisoners fell into Southern hands in the first battle of Reams Station. The Confederates departed Reams for Petersburg just before the arrival of VI Corps, which Meade had dispatched to the assistance of Wilson's and Kautz's divisions earlier in the day. Back at Battery 35 that evening the Juniors, Huger Grays and Richmond Grays went on picket, relieving part of the 6th Virginia.

Next morning the rest of the 12th plodded down the Weldon Railroad. Weisiger's brigade deployed at Globe Tavern, tasked with protecting the wagons carrying the spoils of the previous day's victory. The Virginians returned to the breastworks that night. News greeted them that they must go back down the railroad at two o'clock next morning. The three companies of the 12th on picket duty, relieved at 10 p.m., got the same unpleasant order.

The men marched before first light on July 1 along with the rest of Mahone's division, Cadmus Wilcox's division and Kershaw's division. Some

29 Trudeau, *The Last Citadel*, 77.

artillery and cavalry accompanied the infantry. This force headed for Reams Station to smite VI Corps, reported entrenching there. But the regiment halted two miles short of Reams when the cavalry discovered that VI Corps had departed. The Southern infantry trudged back to Petersburg in the heat, dust and humidity. Many men fell by the wayside exhausted, including soldiers never known to have given out before. Porte's knowledge of the ground around Petersburg, which had enabled him to surprise the Yankees and inflict disproportionately high casualties on them June 22 and 23, had made his division Lee's fire brigade. "[Mahone] is fast gaining a reputation for his skilful tactics, in fact is getting most too popular for me as we have to do the marching & fighting to gain his name," Sale observed.[30] Sick and spent, Sale needed to hitch a ride in an ambulance to get back to Petersburg.

Grant reportedly boasted that he would have his 4th of July dinner in Richmond. But his forces launched no attack on his reputed "lucky day," the anniversary of the surrender of Vicksburg.[31] Petersburg's citizens had flinched under the fire of his artillery for weeks and feared he would employ even bigger guns. The bombardment of Petersburg got under the skin of the Confederate soldiers, like the sack of Fredericksburg. The shelling jeopardized the lives of innocent women, children and old men. The troops had "long since ceased to expect anything but barbarity from a people we once thought much better and who were the models of Philanthropy and great aiders of all plans for the improvement of the condition of their fellow creatures," Sale noted.[32] The soldiers hoped a just God would frown on such wickedness.

Some areas had many damaged houses. Many people piled cotton bales or sandbags against the sides of their homes for protection. Others dug holes for refuge. Still others abandoned their houses, dispersing throughout the countryside to wherever they could obtain shelter. No one remained where most of the shells fell. Where they burst only occasionally, ladies walked about seemingly unaware of any danger. "The Yanks cannot make excuse that the shells are those thrown at our troops as they never come near our line of battle but pass way over it," observed Sale.[33]

30 Sale Diary, June 29, 1864.

31 Bernard Diary, July 2, 1864.

32 Sale Diary, July 2, 1864.

33 Ibid., July 3, 1864.

The Wilson-Kautz Raid interrupted mail service. As of the Fourth, Whitehorne had not received a letter fewer than 3 weeks old from his home fewer than 40 miles south of Petersburg. But the material situation of the Confederate soldiers around the city improved. Regular pay also resumed.

The regiment was drawing picket duty at least once a week. Some found it the most disagreeable portion of a soldier's life except battle. Only those who had stood near the enemy, sometimes not more than 75 yards away, could understand a sentinel's loneliness. "Then it is that one's thoughts run to wild confusion, now you wonder what the Yankee opposite you is doing or thinking, is he trying to creep on you?" Sale noted. "Or is he like yourself thinking of his enemy's intentions?"[34] Sometimes the bored pickets would catch a dog, tie a canteen to the animal's tail and shoo the canine toward Union lines. At night, the sentries would occasionally try to draw enemy fire by yelling, hurling burning brands into the air and waving blazing lightwood tied to well sweeps.

One evening the 12th's pickets engaged in a heavy exchange of small arms fire. The exhausted captain commanding nodded off to sleep. Soon a few discharges of Northern muskets awakened him. Seeing a swarm of lightning bugs, he shouted orders: "Look at the Yanks, boys! Pour it into them! They have a crossfire on us!"[35] Peals of laughter informed him of his error.

Had the generals left it up to the rank and file, few bullets would have flown along the breastworks held by Mahone's division. Bird might take his rifle to the front to try to transfer his blues to some Northern family, but ordinarily the pickets of both sides made informal truces. Gathering between the lines, they swapped rumors, jibes, newspapers, coffee and tobacco. Sometimes they sat down for a game of cards. Whenever the sentries' separate peace became too obvious, their officers ordered them to fire continuously at one another.

Occasionally, to keep the Southerners awake all night, the invaders bombarded them with mortars. More often it grew very quiet. Except for the occasional discharge of a musket or cannon, the 12th's soldiers would have thought no Yankees remained near. On July 10, the Confederates thought the Federals had indeed left pursuant to Early's threat to Washington. Secessionist batteries loosed three rounds. Southern infantrymen mounted

---

34 Ibid., July 7, 1864.

35 Ibid., July 13, 1864.

Henry Van Leuvenigh "Birdie" Bird.
Virginia Historical Society

the breastworks, cheering as if about to charge. The Unionists quickly disabused the Secessionists of the notion that they had departed.

The lull in the fighting left the 12th's men with a lot of time on their hands. Officers resumed keeping records. Soldiers who had not written home since the campaign's beginning caught up on their correspondence.

Others read books. Men from the areas raided by Wilson's and Kautz's divisions searched for runaway slaves among the blacks recaptured at Reams Station. A few lucky soldiers went on furlough. Almost everyone spent time socializing with friends or relatives in other units or Petersburg. On July 13, Phillips called on former comrades in the Purcell Artillery. Men from the old Petersburg Battalion visited former comrades in Pegram's Battery, previously Branch's Field Artillery, still earlier Company K, 16th Virginia, but originally Lee's Life Guard in the 12th. On June 17, during Grant's opening assaults on Petersburg, Pegram's Battery had unlimbered on a crest east of the city. The battery's position had since come to form an angle in the Confederate earthworks known as Pegram's Salient.

One and two-day passes abounded. Some men on leave attended services held by Reverend Platt in the basement of St. Paul's Episcopal Church. The congregation consisted almost entirely of soldiers and included Lee. Platt did not pass the collection plate. "He thought the poor fellows had but little money to spare from their own great need," recorded Mrs. Waddell.[36] She attended at least one such service with her husband.

Before mid-month rumors flew about Early's raid into Yankee land. Unionist accounts represented him as "raising quite a rumpus," and described Early as "everything hideous," recorded Sale. Southern soldiers scoffed, having seen the devastation the invaders wreaked in Confederate territory. "But did he treat their people with one 5th the cruelty with which our citizens are treated they well might call him monster," Sale noted.[37]

On July 27, Heth's division pulled out of the trenches to the regiment's right and crossed the James to help oppose Hancock, who was threatening Richmond from Deep Bottom with a mixed force of infantry and cavalry. Grant hoped that Hancock would at least draw enough Southerners from Petersburg that Burnside's troops might spring a surprise on the remaining Confederates and capture the city.

The Federal general-in-chief had come to a standstill in front of Petersburg. Major General William Tecumseh Sherman was reaching a stalemate outside Atlanta. Early still threatened Washington. Other Confederates were invading Missouri and menacing New Orleans. The prices of gold and foodstuffs in Yankee land were rising. The Northern peace party's ranks were swelling. The Confederacy's future looked bright.

Soon it would appear brighter.

36 Mrs. Charles E. Waddell Diary, July 3, 1864.

37 Sale Diary, July 11, 1864.

CHAPTER 17

The Crater

"**On** the night of 29th of July, Gen'l Lee had reason to anticipate that the enemy designed somewhere an assault the next morning," remembered Mahone.[1] Just after midnight orders reached him to have his men under arms from daybreak until after sunrise. The soldiers entered the trenches at 3 a.m. Rumor had it that they could expect a Federal attack beginning with an explosion.[2] By daybreak the picket firing had already grown rapid. But no explosion had taken place.

"Let's go back to sleep," said one of the 12th's men. "They are not going to do anything."[3]

He spoke too soon. "Just as the sun was showing his first light everything was convulsed with a heavy jar and a noise as if a park of artillery had been opened," noted Sale, whom illness confined to camp. "Immediately after this a dreadful chorus of artillery commenced."[4] At 4:44 a.m., a giant column of dust, smoke and debris rose with the dawn for a background. The 12th's soldiers manned the breastworks near Battery 33. They knew that something extraordinary had happened two miles to the northeast. A rumor came from the direction of the huge cloud, already dissipating. The

---

1 William Mahone, *The Crater* (Petersburg, n.d.), 3.

2 Phillips to Stewart, 190_.

3 Ibid.

4 Sale Diary, July 30, 1864.

Northerners had exploded a mine, blowing a hole in the Confederate line. They were pouring into the earthworks around the gap.

Shortly after 6 a.m., Col. Charles S. Venable of Lee's staff galloped past the regiment toward Mahone's headquarters in the Branch house. Venable carried a message for Porte to send two brigades to support Bushrod Johnson's division. The Virginians of Weisiger's brigade and the Georgians of Wright's brigade drew the assignment, dropping back one by one from their places in the breastworks. In the cornfield behind the works, out of the enemy's sight, the two brigades formed column. They marched with the Virginians in the lead. Mahone accompanied the column, riding at its head with Venable.

Weisiger's brigade advanced left in front.[5] The sharpshooter battalion went in place of the 6th Virginia's right wing and led the column.[6] The 6th's right wing had relieved the marksmen the previous night. The order to march came before the sharpshooters took their usual places on the picket line.

The path of the two brigades took them along a series of military roads near the ravine of Lieutenants Run, still out of the foe's sight. But shot and shell from the enemy guns fell everywhere. John Crow, now a corporal, tramped along near his chum and fellow member of the Riflemen, Pvt. David Meade Bernard, Jr., the younger half-brother of George Bernard. Meade was arguing about a girl with Maj. William Norborne Starke, Assistant Adjutant General of Hill's staff. A nearly spent solid shot rolled toward Crow. He began to put out his foot to stop the cannonball.

"Get out of the way!" Starke or Bernard yelled. "It will break your leg!"[7]

Porte left the column before it reached the Ragland farm's peach orchard, southwest of where Jerusalem Plank Road intersected New Road. He headed for a conference with Beauregard and Maj. Gen. Bushrod Johnson. The latter two explained the situation. The Yankees had exploded a mine under Pegram's Salient, annihilating part of Elliott's South Carolina Brigade of Bushrod Johnson's division and destroying Pegram's Battery.[8] The explosion obliterated a section of the main trench, leaving a pit 135 feet long, 97 feet

---

5 Elmore, *Diary of J. E. Whitehorne*, 53.

6 Phillips to Stewart, 190_.

7 Bernard, "Appendix," *War Talks*, 151.

8 At least 5 of the 23 gunners killed by the blast had once served in the 12th. Ibid., 326; Henderson, *12VI*, 106-167.

wide and 30 feet deep—the Crater. The Federals had charged into the Crater, taking the main trench on both sides as well as the retrenched cavalier—a trench across the base of Pegram's Salient. Beauregard had originally intended for Mahone to turn his troops over to Johnson for the counterattack. Now Beauregard suggested that Mahone lead the counterattack. Porte agreed.

At the Ragland house Mahone's men halted, dropping their knapsacks, blanket rolls and other baggage. This, remembered George Bernard, "to the veteran plainly bespoke serious work, and that in the near future."[9] Weisiger's brigade, under heavy fire, was already taking casualties. A shell struck a young Scottish sergeant of the 41st Virginia and tore off his leg. He reeled and fell, exclaiming, "Oh! my poor mother! What will she do!"[10]

The troops departed the Ragland house, advancing along the edge of the hills skirting Lieutenants Run. About 100 yards east of the bridge over the run, they entered New Road. Trudging back west to within a few paces of the bridge, the 12th's men filed northward up the east side of the run's ravine to Hannon's ice pond. A military footpath led them eastward along the pond's length to its head. Union projectiles threw up geysers a few feet away. Another ravine took the column to a covered way crossing Jerusalem Plank Road near Blandford Cemetery.

At the plank road the troops halted, countermarching by battalions in the covered way, each on its own ground.[11] This reoriented the brigade's components. Each would now lead with its military right instead of its left but would also have its rear ranks in front.[12] The battalions' order within the brigade stayed unchanged. The 12th remained on the brigade's left, the 6th's customary place. The 6th's left wing and the sharpshooters still occupied the 12th's customary place on the brigade's right.

Mahone rejoined the column, dismounting on the roadside. He paused with some officers and watched his old brigade pass. Going ahead up the covered way, he reconnoitered shortly after 8:15 a.m. The Yanks occupied

9 Bernard, "The Battle of the Crater," *War Talks*, 151.

10 Ibid., 151n.

11 Statement of James Eldred Phillips, No. 64, October 1, 1903, in William H. Stewart, Crater Legion Reminiscences, ACWM.

12 Henry Van Leuvenigh Bird to George S. Bernard, June 30, 1880, Bird Family Papers. Part of this letter appears in Bernard, "The Battle of the Crater," *War Talks*, 221. Had the brigade's battalions not countermarched, the men would have had to line up with their backs to the enemy to maneuver, as at Salem Church. Phillips to Stewart, 190.

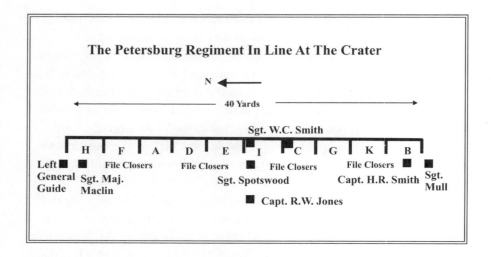

The Petersburg Regiment In Line At The Crater

the Crater in force. They also held the trenches for 200 yards to its north and 150 yards to its south. Porte counted so many flags around the Crater's lip that he dispatched courier Robert Henry down the covered way and past his former comrades in the 12th with an order to bring up Sanders' Alabama Brigade. Mahone then showed Girardey where to place Weisiger's and Wright's brigades for the attack. Girardey led the two brigades northeastward along the covered way that crossed the plank road. The column's head reached an angle where the covered way entered a gully that ran southeastward toward the captured earthworks. The angle, on high ground, exposed the men to Yankee view. Girardey wanted to conceal the column's strength and make the troops harder to hit. He ordered them to run through the angle into the gully one at a time. Passing the angle, they could see the works north of the Crater filled with thousands of the enemy. The sight of as many as 21 gridirons there made some soldiers despair of surviving the coming fight.[13]

The gully led to a bend in a swale running down from the south, then turning eastward. The Virginians stalked southward up the swale. Porte stood at a mortar battery in a little arbor a few yards south of the gully's mouth. Weisiger went by at the Virginians' head.

"Form your brigade for the attack and inform me when you are ready," said Mahone.[14]

13 Bernard, "The Battle of the Crater," *War Talks*, 186.

14 Ibid., 217.

"On the left by file into line!" came the order.[15]

Weisiger's men began forming line of battle.

"Give them the bayonet," said Porte to passing soldiers.[16]

The 12th's flag went by Mahone. The color guard asked him what he wanted done about the bluecoats swarming around the Crater and the banners waving above them. He "remarked emphatically that he wanted all the colors but no prisoners," recalled Bird, a color guard corporal.[17]

Near the general stood a member of Elliott's brigade.

"Show them no quarter, boys, they raised the black flag on us and showed us none," urged the South Carolinian.[18] He declared the Virginians would face mostly black troops.

"General, no prisoners today, but the black flag," one of the 12th's men said.[19]

At. home on leave in Petersburg when the mine exploded, Dean had rushed back to the 12th despite the entreaties of his mother and sisters to remain. Wearing a white calico shirt with red stripes from the knapsack of the Yank he rescued at Cold Harbor, he had reached the regiment before it began its trek to the Crater.

"Do you want any prisoners?" Dean asked Mahone.[20]

The Virginians filed up the increasingly shallow swale. The 12th's men glanced left, looking up the hill where Pegram's Salient stood. A little line of breastworks skirted the hill's base, appearing as if men had scratched them out with their bayonets that morning. Reinforced by the 61st North Carolina, a fragment of Elliott's brigade had held the Federals along this line from the retrenched cavalier's loss until the Virginians' arrival.

Weisiger's brigade halted with its line of battle formed. From left to right stood the 12th, 41st, 61st and 16th Virginia, the 6th Virginia's left wing and finally the sharpshooter battalion.[21] The 12th's left lay 80 feet

---

15 Ibid., 190.

16 Ibid., 153n.

17 Bird to Bernard, June 30, 1880.

18 Bernard, "The Battle of the Crater," *War Talks*, 190.

19 Bernard, "Appendix," *War Talks*, 315.

20 Statement of Napoleon Bonaparte Simmons. Simmons did not record Mahone's reply to Dean.

21 Bernard, "The Battle of the Crater," *War Talks*, 153, 186.

Richard Beale Davis. *Virginia Historical Society*

south of Mahone, who remained at the mortar battery under the arbor. From there the 12th's line extended for the first 40 of the 200 yards that the brigade's front stretched to the right. The Virginians advanced twenty yards up the slope. Their line curved, with both flanks more advanced than the center, conforming to the hill's shape. Weisiger's men lay flat on their faces to conceal themselves from the Federals in the captured works on the hilltop.

The view ahead proved as sobering as the view from the angle. Whitehorne, in the Huger Grays next to the 12th's left, counted 14 flags flying from the captured works. "The thought passed through my mind that, if each flag represented a regiment, and our five depleted regiments had to oppose that force, we had indeed serious work," he recalled.[22] Another member of his company felt even more alarmed—Horse Taylor, whom Whitehorne considered "the greatest and one of the very few cowards in the army."[23] Taylor had yet to participate in a fight. Today his comrades hustled him to within 200 yards of the Yanks before he sensed their presence. Looking up at the hordes of Unionists around the Crater, he grew terrified. That his comrades might shoot him if he skedaddled frightened him more.

In the regiment's center Meade Bernard raised his head, hastily counting 21 enemy battle flags. Getting back to his place in line, he felt his "earthly career was approaching its close."[24] The 12th's company of sharpshooters had an even less pleasant view of the captured works.[25] "The battle-flags seemed almost as thick as cornstalks in a row, and the whole face of the earth, including the ditch which our men formerly occupied, fairly teemed

22 Ibid., 180.

23 Elmore, *Diary of J. E. Whitehorne*, June 19, 1863, 16.

24 Bernard, "The Battle of the Crater," *War Talks*, 190.

25 Ibid., 185.

with the enemy," remembered Pvt. Richard Beale Davis, a former student at Randolph-Macon College detailed to the marksmen from the Riflemen.[26] Farley, recovered from his Wilderness wounds, stood next to Davis and pointed to the nearest stand of Northern colors.

"Dick," said Farley to Davis, "when we start, go for that flag."[27]

In the Old Grays on the regiment's extreme right, Dean too pointed to a Unionist banner.

"I mean to take those colors," he said to Pvt. Thomas Valentine, a fellow Old Gray.[28] Valentine, a substitute, in turn indicated a flag that he intended to capture.

Others prepared for battle differently. George Bernard found on his right Pvt. Robert Emmett Butts, a fellow member of the Riflemen and Petersburg's bar. Butts' proper position lay on Bernard's left. Bernard believed a man's proper place in battle the safest for him.

"Emmett, suppose we change places?" Bernard said. "I am in yours and you are in mine."

"Certainly," Butts replied, with a pleasant smile.[29]

A courier rode up to Jones, the 12th's commander. Awakened by the mine's explosion while at home on leave in Petersburg, Jones had placed the ladies of his family in the cellar and then dashed to the battlefield. The courier summoned Jones to a briefing of regimental commanders. Jones went immediately, walking in front of the battle line. He arrived just as Mahone ordered Wright's brigade to hasten into line on the right of Weisiger's brigade. Mahone then turned to the regimental commanders of both brigades.

Porte explained that only the Virginia and Georgia brigades stood between the enemy and Petersburg. They had to drive back the foe and reestablish the Confederate line immediately.

"If we don't carry it by the first attack we will renew the attack as long as there is a man of us left or until the works are ours," he said. "Much depends upon prompt, vigorous, simultaneous movements."[30]

26 Ibid., 187.

27 Ibid.

28 Statement of Napoleon Bonaparte Simmons.

29 Bernard, "The Battle of the Crater," *War Talks*, 155.

30 Ibid., 154.

Richard Watson Jones. *Virginia Historical Society*

From the brigade's right, Weisiger sent his aide-de-camp, Capt. Drury A. Hinton, to tell Mahone the Virginia Brigade stood ready to advance. Hinton walked down the line ordering officers to have their men hold their fire until they reached the Northerners. As soon as Hinton had passed the 12th, Jones returned from the briefing and stepped in front of the regiment.

"Fix bayonets!" he said.

Those who still had bayonets struggled to comply. Soldiers with unusual foresight gave an extra turn to the screw that held the bayonet shank on their musket barrels.

Jones told his men that they must charge and recapture the works.

"They are only one hundred yards distant," he said. "The enemy can fire but one volley before the works are reached."

At the command "forward," they must rise and advance at a double-quick with a yell, not stopping to fire until they reached the works.

"Every man is expected to do his duty," he said.[31]

The Archer Rifles' First Sgt. Thomas Emmet Richardson stepped in front of the regiment and removed his hat. Tall, strong and athletic, he had worked as an iron moulder before the war.

"Boys, if you ever wanted to do anything for the old Cockade City, now is the time," he said. "Follow me."[32]

As Richardson finished, Hinton delivered Weisiger's message to Mahone.

"Tell Colonel Weisiger to wait for an order from me or Captain Girardey," replied Porte.[33]

31 Ibid.

32 Earl J. Hess, *Into the Crater: The Mine Attack at Petersburg* (Columbia, SC, 2010), 149.

33 Bernard, "The Battle of the Crater," *War Talks*, 224.

Bullets from the Crater cut up the ground around the 12th. Every minute or two, someone cried out for the ambulance corps to remove another wounded soldier. The men knew the situation had become critical. The time had come to do something. The troops were rapidly growing demoralized. They must either advance or retreat. But Wright's brigade had not yet positioned itself to attack. Georgians were still passing behind the Virginians.

Southern cannon were pasting the captured earthworks. Some Virginians looked up to assess the bombardment's effects. They saw Federals jumping out of the trenches as if preparing to charge. The men on the right of Mahone's line disobeyed orders, opening fire. Some invaders dove back into the works. Others started forming line of battle while bullets spun one of their officers around until he fell. Hinton was returning to Weisiger on the right of the brigade's line. Girardey joined the two a moment later. A magnificently attired Union officer emerged from the earthworks carrying a gridiron.

"Captain, had I not better go in now?" said Weisiger to Girardey.

"No, General Mahone desires to annex Wright's brigade on to you and send you in together," Girardey said.[34]

Dashing back down the brigade's line, Girardey stopped halfway between Mahone and the 12th's left.

"General, they are coming!" he shouted to Mahone.

Porte turned from giving instructions to the Georgians. He saw the Northerners massing.

"Tell Weisiger to forward," Mahone replied.[35]

Pulling out his sword, Girardey dashed to his right. Behind the Riflemen, just before reaching the regiment's colors, he turned left and leaped over the line of prone soldiers.

"Charge! Follow me!" he shouted, waving his sword.[36]

It was 8:45 a.m.

The Riflemen and the men of the adjacent companies sprang to their feet. At a trail arms they double-quicked up the hill. They gave a yell that grew tremendous as the troops right and left took it up, jumped up and joined the charge.

34 Ibid., 179n.

35 Ibid., 214.

36 Ibid., 190. Technically in command, the line officer Weisiger wanted credit for the charge led by the staff officer Girardey. Ibid., 217, 222.

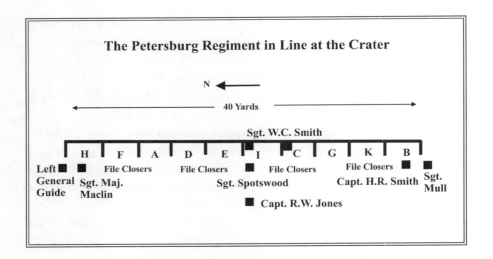

The Petersburg Regiment in Line at the Crater

On the sharpshooter battalion's right, near Weisiger, soldiers of the regiment's marksman company heard a shout to their left. Looking that way, they saw the Yankees preparing to charge. One of the 12th's sharpshooters leapt up and fired.

"Forward!" he yelled.[37]

The rest of the marksmen jumped to their feet.

"Charge, boys!" they cried.[38]

Away the Virginians went, over the field with fixed bayonets.

"Don't fire!" shouted Weisiger.[39]

His soldiers charged with about a regiment and a half from Wright's brigade, fragments of Elliott's South Carolina Brigade and elements of some North Carolina regiments from Ransom's and Clingman's brigades. The troops who had fired at the Yanks massing outside the Crater had not had time to reload.

"The entire line rose up as one man," recalled Crow. "It was like a dress parade."[40] The parade did not last long. Officers screamed for the line to change course obliquely to the right, toward the Crater. Unionist musketry took its toll. A bullet in his left leg disabled Whitehorne before he advanced

37 Ibid., 222.

38 Ibid., 187.

39 Ibid., 222.

40 Bernard, "Appendix," *War Talks*, 315.

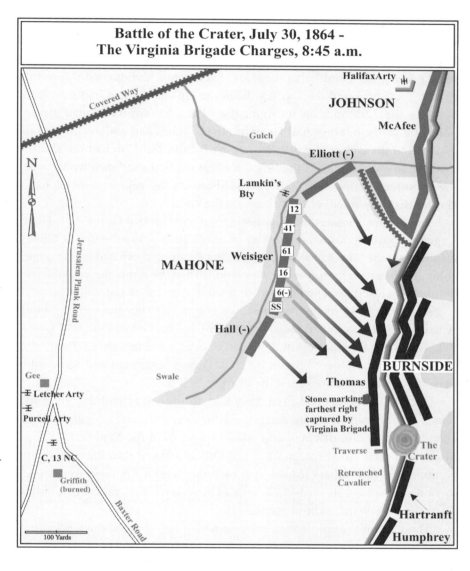

**Battle of the Crater, July 30, 1864 –
The Virginia Brigade Charges, 8:45 a.m.**

twenty paces. The first of the 12th's sharpshooter company hit included the City Guard's Pvt. Benjamin F. Eckles, who had enlisted while a student. He went down with a ball through his left ankle. Some men disobeyed orders and returned fire. Crow had charged halfway up the hill when a black soldier rested his rifle on the shoulder of a Federal officer. The African-American shot at Crow. The ball whistled near his head. Crow and two others shot back. The black fell.

The men on the right were charging obliquely in that direction faster than the rest of the brigade. The line quickly stretched more than 100 feet beyond its original length. The soldiers moved at different speeds. They no longer advanced shoulder to shoulder. Their ranks had opened. More than twenty feet separated the swiftest from the slowest. A gap had developed between the 12th and, on its right, the 41st. The Virginians had already gone 100 yards, but they had 100 more to go. Jones had underestimated the distance to the captured works by one-half. Still, the 12th had the shortest distance to cross of any of the brigade's regiments. Jones' men would reach the captured earthworks first. The soldiers on the regiment's left had a shorter distance to cover than those on the right.

The Federals unleashed a withering volley. The Old Grays' Pvt. Henry Eugene Chase, a former carpenter in the 12th's sharpshooter company, recalled that the "fire had a staggering effect," cutting down and laying out his comrades like "a windrow in a wheatfield." Then, he remembered, "the men untouched closed, touched elbows and went ahead with redoubled pace."[41]

Amid the body of the regiment, Valentine fell shot through the body. A ball mortally wounded Dean in front of his messmate, the Old Grays' Pvt. Napoleon Bonaparte Simmons, an apprentice shoemaker. "I was shot by a negro," said Dean.[42] Simmons took Dean's testament and some other personal effects, then rejoined the charge.

Once the Federals had fired, they had no time to reload. Howling like fiends and brandishing cold steel, the 12th's ragged veterans panicked the enemy, a collection of black and white troops from the Yankee IX Corps. Some Unionists stood frozen in terror. Others slinked into the ditches and bombproofs. Still others leaped over the main trench's parapet to run back to Yankee lines. At 30 yards the regiment blasted the Federals with a volley. Then the Virginians went in for the kill.

About 25 of the soldiers on the regiment's left reached the works first, piling into the hapless Unionists among the ditches and traverses stretching 10 or 15 yards from the main trench on its Secessionist side. Some of the 12th's men, like Crow, descended into the ditches to seize prisoners. Others, like Pvt. Putnam Stith, Jr., another member of the Riflemen, leaped up on the traverses. From there they fired down on the black Federals. "I

41 Statement of Henry E. Chase, No. 44, August 17, 1903, in Stewart, Crater Legion Reminiscences.

42 Statement of Napoleon Bonaparte Simmons.

saw men slam their bayonets in the enemy and fire their guns off in them there," remembered Phillips, to the Riflemen's right. "I also saw them knock the enemy on the heads with the but of their guns & others cut them with swoards."[43]

At the Virginia Brigade's extreme right, the sharpshooter battalion neared the ditches and traverses last. A murderous volley exploded from the Crater on their right and from Northerners in front of the marksmen. Laughton charged to within 30 feet of the retrenched cavalier. An enemy bullet broke his right arm, then burrowed into one of his lungs. Sergeant Marcellus W. Harrison, detached from the Riflemen, took a minnie in the face at three feet, dying instantly. A ball grazed Weisiger's stomach. Turning over command of the brigade to the 6th's Rogers, Weisiger hobbled off the field with Hinton's assistance.[44] The sharpshooters had already lost more than half of their men when they came to grips with the Federals. One ditch "was literally filled with them, crouching in every conceivable attitude, with their palms raised, crying for quarter," Davis recalled.[45] He reached the flag that Farley had pointed out. A bullet pierced Davis' right arm just above the elbow. Despite this, he stripped the banner from its staff and jumped with the flag into the ditch.

Some Confederates went berserk, yielding to what Sale termed a "Devil's Joy."[46] Many had relatives or friends in Petersburg. The defenders feared the African-Americans charging out of the Crater would have these people at their mercy if the city fell to their assault. "The knowledge of dishonor to the loved ones behind us if we failed and victory before us if we succeeded carried everything before it resistlessly," remembered Bird.[47] The Secessionists disarmed white prisoners, sending them to the rear unescorted. Few captured blacks received quarter. The Confederates butchered many on the spot.[48]

43 Phillips to Stewart, 190_.

44 Bernard, "The Battle of the Crater," *War Talks*, 219. Hinton said that Weisiger was not wounded until after 11 a.m., but Hinton was generally not a reliable witness. Ibid., 223.

45 Ibid., 187.

46 John F. Sale to Aunt, August 24, 1864.

47 Henry Van Leuvenigh Bird to Margaret Randolph, August 5, 1864.

48 Dorsey N. Binion to Sister, August 10, 1864, Michael F. Musick Collection, AHEC. Binion belonged to the 48th Georgia, which charged with the Virginia Brigade.

Surviving blacks tried to cross the field toward captivity. Southerners firing from the recaptured works tried to shoot them in the back.[49]

Some of the 12th's men made their way up the ditches to the main trench unhindered. Meade Bernard fired his musket into the massed Federals, then followed a winding traverse, "meeting several unarmed, terrified negroes, some wounded and some not, all begging for mercy and trying to get to our rear."[50] Members of the regiment paused to take these Yankees prisoner.

Other men from the 12th got pinned down in the ditches. Seventy-five yards north of the Crater, George Bernard fired his musket into the fleeing Unionists, then jumped into a ditch. At its other end stood a black soldier pointing his gun at Bernard and grinning. Bernard had an empty rifle. He could not shoot the fellow. Nor could Bernard employ the bayonet. He had lost his in the Wilderness. The ditch's narrowness prevented him from clubbing his musket. Nor could he safely turn his back on the man. In front of Bernard yawned a recess in the ditch's wall big enough to hold a horse. Dashing into the recess, Bernard reloaded his musket as quickly as possible.

Those who had bayonets thanked heaven they had not thrown them away. The Richmond Grays' Pvt. Thomas Walsh, a small but strong soldier known for his proficiency in bayonet drill, had a fierce hand-to-hand contest with a Yankee officer. Walsh employed his rifle and bayonet against the Unionist's saber. They parried vigorously with one another. Walsh lunged and drove his bayonet through the officer's body. The Federal fell still slashing at Walsh.

The 12th's men also employed the butts of their muskets, which weighed about 10 pounds, making fearsome clubs. Three black Federals charged the Herrings' Sgt. James L. Welton, a Portsmouth man who had left school to join the army. Welton's gun misfired. "Emmet Richardson rushed up behind them at the opportune time, killed one with the butt of his gun, which the force of the blow broke off, and then with the barrel, he dispatched the other two," Welton recalled. Richardson brained several more blacks the same way.[51]

The most savage fighting occurred in the main trench. Meade Bernard entered it behind a youth from Elliott's brigade. White and black Federals

---

49 Bernard, "Appendix," *War Talks*, 315-316.

50 Ibid., 190-191.

51 Statement of James L. Welton, No. 20, July 14, 1903, in Stewart, Crater Legion Reminiscences. "The Battle of the Crater," an 1869 painting by John Elder, depicts the charge of the 12th Virginia Infantry at the Crater. Kevin M. Levin, *Remembering the Battle of the Crater: War as Murder* (Lexington, KY, 2012), 40, 137.

filled the trench, some running, some fighting. Meade saw to his left the
kid from Elliott's brigade. A big black soldier stood over the youth trying to
bayonet him. The kid held the bayonet, resisting with all his might. Meade
lunged with his own bayonet at the African-American's side but "struck
plumb on his hip bone." The black dropped his musket, seizing Meade's
weapon. A Northern lieutenant stuck a pistol in Meade's face, demanding
Meade's surrender. Meade, seeing his comrades pouring into the trench,
thought it safer to fight on. He kept trying to get control of his musket.
The lieutenant pulled the trigger. His pistol misfired. "As quick as thought
he again cocked it, and putting it to my face, pulled trigger and it fired,"
Meade recalled. But Meade's arm had knocked it out of position. Its bullet
missed him.[52] The Richmond Grays' Pvt. Jacob Bransford "Jake" Old, a
former tinsmith wounded at King's School house, bayoneted the lieutenant.
The youth from Elliott's brigade picked up a big pistol. With its butt he
struck on the forehead the black struggling with Meade, felling the African-
American. Meade stepped back into the traverse to reload. He nearly shot
one of Beauregard's staff officers by mistake.

More ferocious fighting took place by the regiment's sharpshooters.
Neither side gave any quarter. The Richmond Grays' Pvt. Isadore "Lovey"
Lovesteen, who had returned to the ranks that spring after a Malvern Hill
wound followed by light duty in the Medical Purveyor's Department as a
liquor clerk, fell into the Crater during the melee, emerging unscathed. Davis
stuffed under his jacket the enemy flag he had seized. Then disaster struck.
The 16th Virginia's New Jersey-born Capt. William Wallace Broadbent led
the sharpshooter battalion that day. He cried out, "Come on, boys, they
have captured Rogers!" Davis and his fellow sharpshooters dashed with
Broadbent to the right. A hand-to-hand struggle raged. Chase lost sight of
Broadbent and took a bayonet in the chest. The Old Grays' Pvt. Samuel E.
Brown, a coach painter, saved Chase's life by shooting the bayonet's owner.

Broadbent fired his pistol several times into the crowd. He and his troops
recaptured Rogers. Then came a rush of men from the parapet's other side
into the trench. Fifteen Federal bayonets fatally pierced Broadbent. Davis,
looking right, saw the Unionists on the Crater's rim manhandling a Napoleon
into position to rake the trench. Twenty yards to his left, an immense traverse
blocked his view. Few of his comrades remained in sight. He decided to

52 Bernard, "Appendix," *War Talks*, 190-191.

risk the run over the traverse into the trench beyond, thinking Confederates occupied it. He had gone just a few steps when he heard someone say, "Bayonet that man!" Terrified, he sprang out of the works, running back to the ravine the brigade had deployed from. There he collapsed, exhausted.[53]

The Southerners got the upper hand in the main trench. "No furlough wounds given there and no quarter either—prayers for mercy and the groans of the wounded were alike hushed in death," remembered Bird.[54] The Secessionists turned to massacring black soldiers in the trench. Fifty yards left of the sharpshooters, African-Americans fled terror-stricken. Confederates beat and shot these men. One black ran down the trench towards a group of Secessionists. A Southerner in hot pursuit drew a bead on the soldier. The Confederate fired at the African-American though the bullet might well have struck one of the many nearby Secessionists. A minute later, near the outer end of one of the ditches, a black non-commissioned officer stood begging for his life. One Southern soldier struck him with a steel ramrod. Another aimed a musket at him. The man with the musket fired. The African-American clapped his hand to his hip, begging for mercy. The soldier with the ramrod kept whipping him. The man with the musket reloaded it, placed its muzzle against the African-American's stomach and fired again. The black soldier fell dead. George Bernard and others witnessing the incident from their positions in the trench a few feet away expressed their horror.

"That is too bad!" exclaimed Bernard and others witnessing the incident from their positions in the trench a few feet away. "It is shocking!"[55]

Ten minutes after the Confederates entered the trench, its floor lay strewn with the corpses of United States Colored Troops. In places one could not walk through the trench without stepping on them.[56] Mopping up consisted of giving the *coup de grace* to wounded African-Americans. "The only sound which now broke the stillness was some poor wounded wretches beging for water and quieted by a bayonet thrust which said unmistakably "'[Drink your blood—you won't be thirsty anymore],'" Bird recalled.[57] After briefly

53 Ibid., 187-188.

54 Bird to Randolph, August 5, 1864.

55 Bernard, "The Battle of the Crater," *War Talks*, 159.

56 Ibid.

57 Bird to Randolph, August 5, 1864. Bird used French in the letter: "Bois ton sang—tu n'aurais plus de soif." This paraphrased an English knight's remark to a French opponent

pausing, the Secessionists attended to the hundreds of prisoners who were making their way to the rear. "The order was given to kill them all and rapid fire told plainly how well and willingly it was obeyed," remembered Bird.[58]

Finally, Porte sickened of the slaughter and ordered it stopped.[59] Four hundred and six Federal prisoners reached the safety of the Confederate prisoner pens immediately after the Virginia Brigade's charge. Though almost half the Unionists facing the Virginians consisted of African-Americans, the prisoners included only twenty blacks.[60]

The 12th's new battle flag had flown untouched before that morning. Now five balls had pierced its bunting. Three more had struck its staff. Within a minute of when Smith planted the staff on the works, a ball from the Northerners knocked it down. Smith stuck it back on the works. The enemy shot the flag down again. Yet again it went up. Yet again it went down—this time with a shattered staff. Smith bound its pieces together by lashing them to a ramrod. Once more the banner went up. Union minnies riddled its bunting.

Mahone posted the Georgians still in the swale to deal with any reverse suffered by the Southerners in the works, then dashed up the hill into the main trench. Entering it among the 12th's soldiers, he worked his way toward the right, passing the Riflemen. Butts and Meade Bernard stood side by side on the step standing about nine inches above the trench floor. They aimed at the Federals fleeing from the Crater back to their own lines. Butts warned Porte not to expose himself, then turned and fired over the parapet. A Yankee fell.

"I got him!" cried Butts.[61]

Then a ball in the forehead killed Butts instantly. He fell to the trench floor at Mahone's feet.

Porte conferred with Rogers in the retrenched cavalier.

---

in a 14th century fight during the Hundred Years War: "Bois ton sang . . . le soif te passera . . . " Christophe-Paulin de la Poix, Chevalier de Freminville, *Le Combat des Trente, Poeme du XIV.e Siecle, Transcrit sur le Manuscript Original, Conserve a la Bibliotheque du ROI, et Accompagne de Notes Historiques* (Brest, 1819), 52.

58   Bird to Randolph, August 5, 1864.

59   Ibid.

60   "By Telegraph," Richmond Daily *Dispatch*, August 1, 1864, p. 1, col. 7.

61   Bernard, "The Battle of the Crater," *War Talks*, 192.

Fewer than 10 minutes had passed since the Confederates reached the works. They had cleared the Unionists out of the main trench north of the Crater and all but 50 yards of the retrenched cavalier to the south. A traverse in the retrenched cavalier marked the limit of the ground recaptured. The Northerners beyond had only held by barricading the trench with corpses.

Mahone made defensive dispositions, posting his surviving sharpshooters, he later wrote, "to make death the penalty to those of the enemy who were attempting to escape and get back to their own lines."[62] Then he dashed back to the swale, readying the Georgians to charge. Weisiger, slowly making his way off the field, found Porte at the arbor.

"Weisiger, you and Joe Johnston are always getting yourselves shot," Mahone quipped.

"Yes, General Mahone, and if you would go where General Johnston and I go, you would get shot, too," Weisiger replied.[63]

At Jerusalem Plank Road, Weisiger passed Beauregard and Col. Samuel Paul of his staff.

"You all have covered yourselves with glory," remarked Paul.[64]

Some of the Virginia Brigade's wounded experienced the benefits of fighting near home. Shot in the shoulder after the main trench was secured, Stith met Davis on the way to the rear. The two staggered together up the ravine near Hannon's ice pond to the ambulances. Dr. Thomas J. Vance, the 12th's former assistant surgeon, probed their wounds, gave each man a drink of whiskey, then dispatched them in an ambulance to Dr. Claiborne at McIlwaine's Grove. Reaching Sycamore Street, near the home of Davis' father, Davis asked a boy to tell his father of his slight wound and destination. Half an hour after Davis' arrival at McIlwaine's Grove, his father met him carrying a bottle of homemade wine in each hand. When Davis looked under his jacket for the enemy flag he had taken, it was gone.

The remainder of Wright's brigade charged the Crater from the ravine at 10 a.m. with the 17th South Carolina. The Virginians fired at the Federals as rapidly as possible to keep their heads down. Nearly every Southsider standing at the parapet used his own musket and one or more of the hundreds

---

62 Ibid., 215.

63 George S. Bernard, "Great Battle of the Crater: The Work of Mahone and Weisiger at the Fight," *SHSP* (1900), 28:205.

64 Bernard, "The Battle of the Crater," *War Talks*, 192.

of abandoned Yankee weapons lying along the trench. The Georgians veered off to the left in the face of ferocious fire from the Crater. The invaders were using the 12-pounder Napoleon from Pegram's Battery that Davis had seen them mounting as well as another that had escaped his attention.

The Virginians fired steadily at Unionists attempting to run the gauntlet from the Crater across the field to their own lines. The Northerners constantly crawling in and out of the Crater also afforded targets. Soldiers from the rear echelons dashed into the front line to get off a few rounds at the bluecoats. Todd, still acting ordnance officer of Weisiger's brigade, fired at the enemy from beside the body of his friend, Butts.

Wright's brigade tried again to carry the Crater and to its south the retrenched cavalier at 11 a.m. Again the Virginians provided covering fire. The lead from the Crater still proved too hot for the Georgians, who again recoiled.

Broiling under the fierce sun, the 12th's tired, thirsty soldiers potted away at the enemy. Confederate mortars lobbed shells into the Crater. Southern infantrymen tossed captured muskets into the pit bayonet-first. Before 1 p.m., the Alabamians of Sanders' brigade replaced the Georgians in the ravine. Weisiger's troops yet again provided covering fire. The Alabama Brigade stormed the retrenched cavalier south of the Crater. The Federals in the pit hoisted a white flag. The Alabama Brigade hurled itself over the Crater's rim, into the pit and compelled the Yankees there to surrender after a vicious hand-to-hand struggle. Unionist prisoners poured out of the Crater, making their way to the Secessionist rear under a barrage from their own batteries. Some became victims of friendly fire.

Quiet prevailed for rest of the day. The 12th's men attended to their wounded. "I was removed from the battle field by one of my own Company who was wounded in the arm and leg, with the assistance of four negro prisoners who carried the stretcher," Laughton recalled.[65] The regiment's soldiers threw corpses out of the works to get more room. "We draged them out with gun slings around their necks & four of our men would lift them," recalled Phillips. "Others was rolled over the works towards the enemy &c. and we got rid of them for a while."[66]

65 Statement of John E. Laughton, No. 55, September 19, 1903, in Stewart, Crater Legion Reminiscences.

66 Phillips to Stewart, 190.

Smith examined the regiment's colors. Seventy-five bullets had passed through the flag. Nine had struck the staff.

Weisiger's brigade had lost at least 283 killed, wounded and missing.[67] Casualties in the 12th numbered 23 killed or mortally wounded and 23 wounded of 10 officers and 140 men engaged.[68] The casualties included 5 killed and 8 wounded in the regiment's complement of 15 sharpshooters.[69] "The Battle of The Crater was the crowning glory of our brigade," recalled Todd.[70] The Virginians had helped kill 504 Federals, wound 1,881 others and take 1,413 prisoners, 19 flags and 1,916 stand of small arms.[71] They assisted in recapturing four cannon. Mahone received a promotion to major general. Girardey got one of the Confederate army's biggest promotions ever—from captain to brigadier general. The Virginians established themselves as members of their army's elite.

Weisiger's brigade ordinarily elicited comments about its appearance, not its fighting prowess. It set the standard for the good order of its camp and wagon train.[72] Its soldiers had initially referred to themselves as "a Saratoga trunk regiment" or the "Kid Glove Boys." But no troops employed bayonets more effectively. Spit and polish enhanced proficiency in close combat because of Mahone's insistence that his soldiers not throw away

---

67 Weisiger to Henry B. Perry, April 26, 1896. Bernard gave 270 as the total. Bernard Diary, August 6, 1864.

68 "Battle of the Crater: Roster of the Members of the 12th Virginia Infantry, Mahone's Brigade, who were Engaged," *SHSP* (1903), 31:271-274; "Paroles of the Army of Northern Virginia, R. E. Lee, Gen., C.S.A., Surrendered at Appomattox, C. H., Va., April 9, 1865," *SHSP* (1886), 15:350; Anne Banister Pryor, "A Child's Recollections of War," *Confederate Veteran* (hereinafter *CV*) (1931), 39:55; Henderson, *12VI*, 106-167; Statement of Robert George Thompson, Notes of St. George Tucker Coalter Bryan; Mamie Yeary, comp., *Reminiscences of the Boys in Gray, 1861-1865* (Dallas, 1912), 634; Todd, "Reminiscences," 245-246; James E. Whitehorne Diary, April 3, 1865, James E. Whitehorne Papers, SHC; "List of names at the Crater Petersburg," James Eldred Phillips Papers, VHS; Rolls 514-534, M324, Record Group 109, NA; Bernard, "The Battle of the Crater," *War Talks*, 192; Bernard, "Appendix," *War Talks*, 316, 324-325.

69 Bernard Diary, August 2, 1864.

70 Todd, "Reminiscences," 237.

71 Bernard Diary, August 8, 1864; John F. Schmutz, *The Battle of the Crater: A Complete History* (Jefferson, NC, 2009), 335. Estimates of Confederate losses range from 400 killed, 700 wounded and 40 missing or captured for a total of 1,140, to as high as a total of 1,612. Hess, *Into the Crater*, 200.

72 Douglas Southhall Freeman, ed., *Lee's Dispatches* (Baton Rouge, 1957), 369.

their bayonets. They whipped the invaders as badly as anyone could have wished in the desperate hand-to-hand fighting at the Crater.

The soldiers of Weisiger's brigade would remember this battle above all others. Asked to render his self-conception in pictorial form, a Confederate fighting man would have drawn himself standing between home and an armed slave urged on by a Yankee abolitionist. At the Crater the 12th and the rest of its brigade lived this scenario, achieving the ideal victory for soldiers who referred to the overall conflict as "the John Brown War."[73]

Yet the United States Colored Troops had made a positive impression upon almost all the Virginia Brigade's soldiers. Bird detested the African-American bluecoats and felt that they had gotten what was coming to them, writing about the Crater fight in general, "The negroes' charging cry of 'no quarter' was met with the eternal cry of 'amen.'"[74] But he proceeded to write about the United States Colored Troops, "They fought like bulldogs and they died like soldiers."[75] Before the war's end, members of the 12th would pay the ultimate compliment to the black infantrymen some of them had massacred at the Crater.

73 Phillips, "Sixth Corporal," 32.

74 Bird to Randolph, August 5, 1864.

75 Ibid.

CHAPTER 18

Globe Tavern and
Second Reams Station

At nightfall the 12th shifted rightward with the rest of its brigade, halting among the corpses in the retrenched cavalier behind the Crater. The bodies probably included Farley's, never identified. Simmons and another man crawled out and rolled Dean's body into a blanket. With one of them pushing and the other pulling, they slid the corpse into the Confederate works.

Passes spared some men spending the evening in this terrible place. Late that night a few went into Petersburg, telling relatives and friends about the fight. The City Guard's Cpl. James Blair Banister visited what remained of his family in their home at Franklin and Jefferson Streets. There the morning's bombardment had broken windows and felled trees. His brother Thomas had obtained a medical discharge from the 12th the previous year. Their father, William C. Banister, had died fighting under Fletcher Archer in the city's defense on June 9. Blair's younger brother Norborne, 15, was dying of illness contracted during the same action. Blair's blood-spattered clothes shocked his family.

Back at the Crater, the regiment's soldiers slid down the slope to remove their dead and succor the wounded. Two men from each company oversaw burying squads of captured black soldiers. They worked through the night putting many bodies into a mass grave less than 100 feet behind the Crater and shoveling a thin layer of dirt over the corpses. But they could not bury all the bodies in a single night's work.

In the fearful heat the uninterred corpses quickly decomposed. The stench grew terrible. Few soldiers enjoyed their breakfasts of hard-tack and fried pickle-pork next morning. The Yanks opened negotiations for the burial of the dead between the lines. By evening the invaders had obtained permission to bring water to their wounded. The interment of the corpses between the lines occurred on the morning of August 1. The Unionists assigned the job of burying these bodies to such able-bodied African-Americans as remained in Meade's army. These soldiers interred several hundred more corpses in a common grave.

Relieved that night, Weisiger's brigade returned to its position between Batteries 33 and 34 near Walnut Hill. Mahone sent for Smith and presented him with the staff of one of the gridirons the brigade had captured at the Crater. Smith cut down the staff, then transferred to it the 12th's bullet-torn old rag.

The 12th's men resumed the routine established during the lull before the battle. They visited the wounded as well—of both sides and of both colors. The regiment's soldiers recognized some of the blacks who had fought against them. Todd went to the hospital to visit a wounded African-American, an acquaintance's butler in prewar Norfolk.[1]

On August 6, the Confederates sprang their own mine in front of Wise's brigade, just south of the Crater. Fortunately for the Southerners, they did not charge. Their tunnel had not reached the Yankee trenches. The mine exploded harmlessly between the lines.

Three days later about 3 p.m., the 12th's soldiers saw distant smoke, then heard the attenuated noise of another terrific explosion. A Confederate spy had slipped a time-bomb into an ammunition barge at City Point, nearly killing Grant.

On the morning of August 14, the dull rumble from Deep Bottom announced Grant's fourth offensive of the Petersburg campaign. Wright's brigade, led by Girardey, and Sanders' brigade departed for Deep Bottom that afternoon. Weisiger's brigade returned to the breastworks that night.

At 2 p.m. on August 16, the Virginians fell in without striking their "raghouses," as the men called their tents.[2] "This order caused many to have a heavy feeling in that portion of the body known as 'The Haversack,'"

1 Todd, "Reminiscences," 240.

2 Sale Diary, August 15, 1864.

recorded Sale.[3] Two hours earlier Northerners under Hancock had stormed Confederate earthworks at Fussell's Mill held by Girardey's troops. Hancock's men killed Girardey and threatened Richmond. Weisiger's soldiers relieved Harris' Mississippi Brigade on the division's left, near Battery 30. The Virginians strung themselves out in one rank, taking over the positions of both Sanders' and Harris' brigades. The Mississippi Brigade departed for Fussell's Mill that evening.

At 2 o'clock on the rainy morning of August 18, Confederate batteries bombarded the Federals massing on the left of Grant's lines. The 12th went on picket that day. The regiment's soldiers swapped Indian bread—as the Unionists called cornbread—for coffee with Yankee sentries. Reports arrived of a Federal cavalry raid on the Weldon Railroad where the Vaughn and Halifax roads joined. The rest of Weisiger's brigade relieved the 12th at dark. The nightly artillery firing from 2 a.m. to 4 a.m. prevented the men from sleeping.

The Herrings and the sharpshooters drew picket duty in the next morning's rain. The troops learned that the previous day's commotion had involved more than cavalry. V Corps of Meade's army had reached the tracks near Globe Tavern and advanced up the rails almost to the W. P. Davis house, about a mile and a half south of the Dimmock Line. The Unionists tore up the railroad all along their route. Setting the ties ablaze, they heated the rails red hot and twisted them into Maltese crosses, the emblem of V Corps. Davis' and Walker's brigades of Heth's division attacked, driving the Northerners back three quarters of a mile. But the Yanks proved too many for the Confederates, who retreated to the Davis place.[4]

Before noon Weisiger's brigade prepared to march. The Virginians supposed they would leave camp soon to renew the fight for the Weldon Railroad. Instead, they returned to their quarters to await orders and worry about friends and relatives affected by the Federal advance. About 1 p.m., the troops fell in and headed up the ravine behind the breastworks—the same ravine that had taken them to victory against II Corps on June 22. Today their destination lay down the Weldon Railroad. Five brigades—Davis' and Walker's of Heth's division, Colquitt's and Clingman's of Hoke's division and Weisiger's of Mahone's division—were venturing out to drive away the Yankees.

3 Ibid., August 16, 1864.

4 Horn, *The Battles for the Weldon Railroad, August 1864*, 172.

These troops moved pursuant to a suggestion Mahone had made the previous day. It had gone up the chain of command and met with Beauregard's approval. He had charge of the Petersburg front during Lee's absence north of the James. Mahone proposed to send a force through the gap in the Union lines he knew must exist between V Corps and the rest of Meade's army. This force, while another proceeded down the Weldon Railroad and clutched the invaders' front, would strike the exposed right of V Corps. The intended result would resemble Mahone's June 22 rout of II Corps. Beauregard directed the two brigades from Heth's division to advance down the railroad and clench the front of the Federals while Mahone smote V Corps' right with his old brigade and the two brigades of Hoke's division.[5]

Colquitt's brigade led the way past Porte's headquarters and up the ravine that had led to victory on June 22. Clingman's brigade followed, then Weisiger's brigade. Each moved by the left flank. The 6th Virginia marched at the head of Weisiger's brigade, the 12th at its rear. Weisiger had quickly recovered from his Crater wound and led his brigade.

Mahone's soldiers reached the open field in front of the Johnson house. Forming line of battle, they crossed the field to the woods at its southeast corner. So far, the column had taken Porte's route of June 22, but now it plunged southwestward into the brush in a downpour. The men struggled through the tangled creepers. The Virginians consoled themselves by picking and eating the ripe whortleberries abounding, reminding men in the 12th and 41st of the whortleberries lining their route to Seven Pines.

Soldiers from Hoke's division at the column's head pierced the picket line formed by the old Iron Brigade, and the pickets retreated to either side of the penetration. Weisiger's brigade passed the enemy sentinels' abandoned dinners, smoking by little cooking fires. Mahone adjudged his force in the Yankee position's right rear. He formed line of battle facing west, with Colquitt's brigade on the left and Clingman's on the right. Weisiger's brigade stood in column of regiments behind the left of Colquitt's brigade, with the 12th in the column's van. Porte summoned his brigadiers to a meeting, giving them their instructions, then sending his command forward. Unionist shells began bursting about the Virginians as they double-quicked westward.

Clingman's brigade enveloped the right of the Federal advanced line running through the woods on the southern edge of Johnson cornfield. At the

5 Ibid., 148-150.

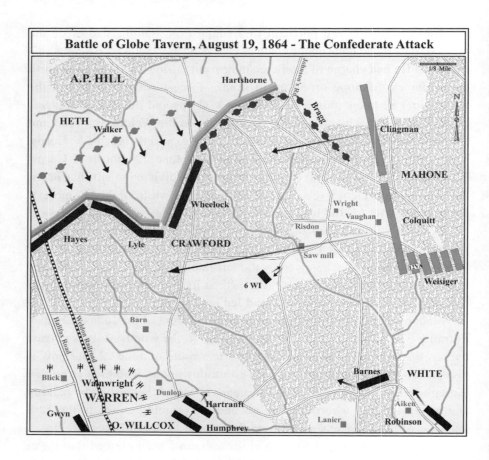

Battle of Globe Tavern, August 19, 1864 - The Confederate Attack

sound of the firing, Davis' and Walker's brigades drove down the Weldon Railroad against the front of this line. The larger part of Colquitt's brigade swept through the trees behind the line. The Georgians captured Northerners trying to escape back to the Globe Tavern clearing and the main Yankee line.[6]

The Unionists had a complicated defense plan. Warren, now commanding V Corps, intended for his infantry, moving by the flank, to evacuate the advanced line if attacked. His artillery, posted in the Globe Tavern clearing, would then blast any attacking Confederates. The plan went awry and contributed to the success of the Secessionist attack. The left of Colquitt's brigade, about 200 men, emerged into the clearing from the woods. The Federal artillery commander thought the V Corps infantrymen were evacuating the

6 Ibid., 150-154.

advanced line as planned. He opened fire on the breastworks he thought the Confederates now held. But few of the unfortunate Yankee foot soldiers had budged. Fired upon from front, flank and rear, they surrendered in droves.[7]

Clingman's brigade rolled up the Union front line all the way to the Weldon Railroad. Near the tracks, the Georgians on the right of Colquitt's brigade captured a brigadier general. Four Federal brigades practically ceased to exist. A fifth lost half its strength. Colquitt's and Clingman's brigades broke down under the weight of their prisoners. Chaos prevailed in the 500-yard-wide belt of woods between the Globe Tavern clearing and the Davis farm. Squads from both sides captured and recaptured one another.[8]

Mahone ordered Weisiger's brigade, still in reserve, southwestward toward the opposing batteries. The 12th advanced to a small branch running southward about half a mile northeast of Globe Tavern. Sunset approached on this rainy, dismal evening. The regiment's soldiers shifted southwardly along the branch. They had slightly rising ground in front of them and a small body of second growth pines 100 yards to their rear. They saw, no more than 150 yards to their right front, the backs of soldiers in line of battle facing north. Some of the 12th's men favored attacking the rear of this battle line. Richardson leaped to the branch's west side, starting up the bank.[9]

"Come on boys!" he said. "They are Yankees! Let's charge 'em."[10] Other members of the regiment hesitated. The soldiers in front of them seemed too quiet for Unionists, given that they must have known of the presence of Weisiger's brigade in their rear. The 12th did not charge. The Virginians faced the back of Hartranft's brigade of Orlando Willcox's division of IX Corps. Willcox's division had already reinforced Warren at Globe Tavern when the Confederates attacked. Hartranft's brigade had just finished pushing the left of Colquitt's brigade out of the Globe Tavern clearing and back into the woods. These Federals had no idea that Confederates menaced their rear. Weisiger, seeing Unionists to his right, halted at the branch, fearful of leading his men into a trap. Porte had led him to expect Federal reinforcements to come from the direction of Jerusalem Plank Road, Weisiger's left.

7 Ibid., 155-157.

8 Ibid., 157-160.

9 Ibid., 163-164.

10 Bernard Papers, SHC.

Mahone, seeing Globe Tavern in the distance, rearranged his forces. The time had come for the *coup de grace*. He looked for men from Clingman's brigade in an open field near the Risdon saw mill, finding only Brig. Gen. Thomas Lanier Clingman being carried from the field on a stretcher with a wound that would cost him a leg. Mahone rode on to Brig. Gen. Alfred H. Colquitt, visible on the opening's fringe. Colquitt had only the approximately 150 Georgians Hartranft's brigade and the Yankee guns had driven from the Globe Tavern clearing.

Porte sent the men from Colquitt's brigade southward down the branch occupied by Weisiger's brigade. The Georgians filed past the 12th and took position on the left of Weisiger's brigade.[11] Less than 10 minutes since the regiment arrived in the branch, the 12th and the right of the 41st faced about and advanced to the pines' edge east of the branch, on the Georgians' left. Weisiger disposed these men facing east to ward off the anticipated Unionist counterattacks. Orders from Warren took Hartranft's brigade westward and away from the Virginia Brigade's unprotected rear.

Mahone believed that with a few more brigades he could capture all the Federals on the Weldon Railroad. He dispatched two staff officers and a courier to contact Hill at Maj. Gen. Henry Heth's headquarters far to the right, near the Davis house. The two staff officers left a few moments apart. The second followed the customary short distance behind the first. They passed through the woods swept by Colquitt's and Clingman's brigades and teeming with stragglers and fugitives of both sides rushing this way and that, capturing, escaping and recapturing one another. Within minutes, a squad of Northerners snatched the Southern staffer in the lead. The second staffer rallied a band of Confederates and freed his comrade. Unionists captured this group in turn and led it through the rear of Weisiger's brigade toward Yankee lines. Mahone put himself at the head of a body of his men and rushed the bluecoats, capturing them and freeing their prisoners.

The courier, Robert Henry, took a cart path that ran farther east than the route taken by the staff officers. Henry got lost in the dense thicket, almost impossible to penetrate on horseback, and came to the clearing around the Lanier house. No more than 150 yards away he saw two limbered batteries of Federal artillery followed by infantry and a train of ambulances—the

---

11 Ibid. Bernard mistakenly thought these men belonged to Clingman's brigade.

head of White's division of IX Corps, floundering westward through the mud from Jerusalem Plank Road to rescue V Corps.

To avoid capture, Henry turned back. At a sharp bend in the path fewer than 100 yards from where he had left Porte, Henry met two Union horsemen. Pulling an inoperative pistol captured at the Crater, he took them captive and when he reached Mahone, presented his prisoners to the general. One of the Northerners, Col. William R. Hartshorne, had commanded a Yankee brigade destroyed by Clingman.[12]

Privates George William May of the City Guard, a native of Lunenburg County captured at Chancellorsville and afterward detailed to the Commissary Department in the Florida Brigade, and Alexander M. Miles of the Old Grays, a former member of the provost guard, were enjoying leave in Petersburg that day. Learning that the regiment was going out to fight, they grabbed their Enfields and hotfooted it out of town together to join the 12th. Rushing into the woods that had stymied Mahone's staffers, May and Miles saw Federals advancing towards them. Thinking that retreat would lead to death while standing and fighting would result in captivity, the two Virginians ducked behind some trees and conferred. They resolved on bluffing the bluecoats.

When the Unionists arrived within hearing, May stepped forward and demanded their surrender, telling the Yanks that he had a regiment behind him while another was bearing down on their flank. Some of the Unionists threw down their arms immediately, but the officer leading them hesitated. Hidden in the underbrush, Miles made enough noise to suggest many Confederates advancing. The threat of overpowering numbers silenced the officer. The whole party lay down its arms and marched in double file to where May stood. May placed himself at the column's head. Miles emerged from the timber and posted himself at the column's rear. The two Virginians led within Confederate lines a captain, a lieutenant and 25 privates whose chagrin knew no bounds when they discovered the deception.[13]

Unable to contact Hill, Porte knew he would have to rely on his own resources to finish off Warren's force. Before Mahone could react, White's

---

12 "Maj. Robert Randolph Henry," *Clinch Valley News* (Jeffersonville, VA), March 24, 1916.

13 "From the *Petersburg Express* of Wednesday, From the Front," *The Daily Confederate* (Raleigh, NC), August 26, 1864, p. 2, col. 3; *The Chattanooga Rebel* (Griffin, GA), September 3, 1864, p. 1, col. 3. Both versions mistakenly name George Henry May instead of George William May, both of whom belonged to the City Guard, but George Henry May had died on May 22, 1863. Henderson, *12VI*, 140.

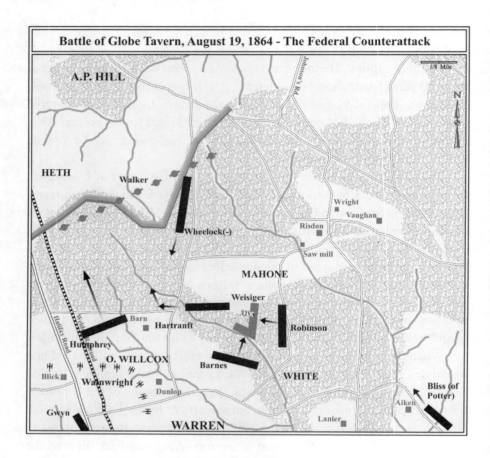

Battle of Globe Tavern, August 19, 1864 - The Federal Counterattack

division struck from the east and began the fight—isolated from the rest of the struggle around Globe Tavern—known to its participants as "the No Name Battle."[14] The 14th New York Heavy Artillery of Robinson's brigade appeared in the pines about 150 yards east of the 12th and opened fire. The 12th's soldiers hit the ground and shot back. Through the gloom they could see nothing but the flash of the foe's rifles and occasionally a man's figure. The 12th soon started taking bullets not only from its front, but from its right flank and rear. The minnies from the right and rear—the south and southwest—came from Barnes' brigade of White's division, which was struggling with the 6th, 16th, 61st and the left of the 41st on the Globe Tavern clearing's eastern fringe. About 75 yards separated the backs of the

14 William H. Stewart and Whitman V. White. "The No Name Battle," *Blue and Gray* (January 1895), vol. 5, no. 1, 29-35.

William Crawford Smith.
U. S. Army Historical Education Center

men in the 12th, at the top of the J formed by the brigade, from the backs of the troops in the 41st's left, at the J's lower lip. Despite the unnerving Federal crossfire, the Southerners remained full of fight, repeatedly charging the bluecoats through the dense underbrush. Most of the 12th's soldiers lost their bayonets in these charges.

Casualties mounted fast. George Bernard heard groans several feet to his left. A fellow member of the Riflemen, Pvt. Richard Avery Machen, lay badly wounded. A former building contractor, Machen had returned to the regiment from a detail as ward master of Petersburg's Virginia Hospital. Bernard tried to cheer Machen, telling him the battle would soon end and then the ambulance corps would take him from the field.

Jones, the 12th's commander that day, received a slight wound. Tom Walsh was standing between Weisiger and William Smith, pointing to a sword leaning against a tree and inquiring about the blade's ownership when a bullet hit him in the face, killing him instantly. For at least 12 feet on each side of the regiment's banner, every man of the color guard fell killed or wounded except Smith and Bird.

Ammunition ran low for the Virginians. They lay down, determined to wait until the enemy closed with them, then use the butts of their muskets on the bluecoats. "We had all made up our minds not to be captured as we knew well enough that Mahone men neither asked nor gave quarter," Bird wrote.[15] White's division did not charge but poured in a devastating fire from 80 yards away. The IX Corps men seemed to surround Weisiger's Virginians and Georgians. The 12th's men stripped their colors from the staff and hid them in a haversack to save them from capture.

Standing behind the 12th, Weisiger gave his horse to Hugh Smith and sent him to tell Mahone that the Unionists threatened to surround Weisiger's force. On the way, Smith met Henry bearing an order from Porte for Weisiger to withdraw and reform.

The Federal firing slowed. Weisiger took advantage of this to implement Mahone's order. On the left the 12th had to withdraw only a few paces. The Virginians and Georgians reformed their lines and began hastening northward out of the Unionist vise. "It was 'no time to swap jack knives,'" wrote Bird.[16] The Virginians and Georgians left 60 prisoners and about

15 Henry Van Leuvenigh Bird to Margaret Randolph, August 20, 1864.

16 Ibid.

200 stand of arms in enemy hands. They also abandoned their dead and badly wounded. The Northerners pursued and firing briefly returned to its former pitch. Hartranft's brigade began retracing its steps eastwardly, threatening the Southerners' retreat. Weisiger displayed a flag of truce to inform the attendants left with the badly wounded to surrender. The flag of truce delayed the Unionist pursuit and the Secessionists broke contact with the foe. Contrary to Bird's fears, the captured Mahone men received every courtesy from the white IX Corps men, who did not undertake to avenge their black comrades massacred by Porte's troops at the Crater.

Night fell. Mahone's men returned to the Johnson farm, then slouched back to the Confederate works. The Virginians had not run the Federals off the Weldon Railroad but had helped Colquitt's and Clingman's brigades get away with their prisoners. Weisiger's men reoccupied their position at Walnut Hill. The Georgians who had fought alongside the Virginians plodded back to Petersburg to rejoin Colquitt's brigade. Bernard described his regiment and its brigade as "pretty well fagged out after the evening's expedition."[17] Morale remained high. "What our Div. can't do—can't be done," wrote Bird.[18] Later he added, "I feel much better satisfied when our Division is engaged because I know that it is in good hands and will go farther and do more than any other division."[19]

Ninety-four officers and men of the approximately 600 the brigade took into action belonged to the regiment. The 12th had 6 killed, 29 wounded and four captured among the brigade's 187 casualties. Those whose wounds did not prove mortal included former ambulance corps man Joe Maclin, now the regiment's sergeant major. Seven of his wounded comrades fell into enemy hands. One of them died there—Machen. The uninjured prisoners included two ambulance corps men left to tend the wounded.[20] The 12th suffered a higher percentage of casualties than it had at the Crater, more than 41 percent as opposed to just under 31 percent, a remarkable percentage.[21] But

17 Bernard Papers, SHC.

18 Bird to Randolph, August 20, 1864.

19 Henry Van Leuvenigh Bird to Margaret Randolph, September 8, 1864.

20 Henderson, *12VI*, 106-167; Petersburg Daily *Register,* August 22, 1864, p. 2, cols. 2-3; Bernard Diary, August 20, 1864. Miles and May, who fought independently of the 12th, are not included among the ninety-four.

21 Fox, *Regimental Losses*, 556-558. See Table 3.

Hill's Corps had struck the Yankees a terrible blow. At a cost of about 600 casualties, the Confederates had inflicted more than 3,000, including around 2,700 prisoners.[22] Globe Tavern represented a brilliant feat of Confederate arms of the sort that Southerners were coming to associate with Mahone. But largely because of the IX Corps troops, the Weldon Railroad remained in Federal hands and the fight therefore amounted to a Union victory—albeit a Pyrrhic victory because Grant could not afford to lose five men for every Secessionist put out of action.

That night Beauregard prepared to attack Warren's force the following day, the third in a row. Heavy cannonading resounded along the lines held by Hill's Corps. Bernard noted that the day's exertions had left him and his comrades "too sleepy to get up to see what was 'to pay' although the battery not 50 yds from our tent was lumbering away pretty freely."[23] Lee wanted to strike a concentrated blow along the Weldon Railroad on August 20. But Beauregard and Hill failed to scrounge up satisfactory forces. Beauregard postponed the attack until August 21.

Cavalry scouts reconnoitered the enemy left. Among them rode Roger Pryor, serving as a private. He shinnied up a tree, then returned to headquarters to report the Federal left unanchored and vulnerable. At 3 p.m., orders reached the 12th to have cartridge boxes filled and one day's rations cooked by 7 p.m. The regiment's soldiers interpreted this to mean a night march through Dinwiddie County to get behind Warren. But at 6:30 p.m., new instructions arrived. The men would form at the breastworks with muskets and equipment at 7 p.m. "What does this mean?" Bernard recorded. "Perhaps we are to open on the enemy."[24] The 12th's soldiers fell in at the appointed hour, underwent an inspection, then filed down the breastworks to their left. "This move pleased us much, surmising that we were not to take part in the move against the enemy on the Weldon RR," noted Bernard.[25] Moving so quietly that they drew no Yankee shells, the Virginians relieved Finegan's Florida Brigade. The 12th's men found themselves surrounded by troops not usually encountered in the trenches. To free enough veterans to drive the Northerners from the Weldon Railroad, Lee scraped the barrel's

22 Horn, *The Battles for the Weldon Railroad, August 1864*, 172.

23 Bernard Diary, August 20, 1864.

24 Ibid.

25 Ibid.

bottom. The regiment's new neighbors included the Petersburg Militia, the City Battalion, train guards, clerks, cooks, musicians and every straggler the provost guards could gather.

At 1 a.m., the Floridians trudged out of the breastworks with the rest of Mahone's division except the Virginia Brigade. Hill was going to attack the Union left based on Pryor's reconnaissance. Hill's force included elements of several other divisions. The Confederate batteries opened before daybreak that foggy morning. By 9 a.m., the sun had finally burned away the mist. The 12th's men heard cannon fire and musketry rise to battle pitch, last for two hours and by 1 p.m., almost cease. The regiment awaited news of what had happened. It did not arrive until late in the afternoon. Hill had directed an attack on the Yankee left that might have succeeded the previous day. But the lull in the fighting allowed Warren to withdraw several hundred yards and fortify another line. Hill and Mahone found the old line abandoned, then discovered the new one. They tried to modify their attack plan without further reconnaissance. Their soldiers met with a stiff repulse. A South Carolina brigade suffered the envelopment and near annihilation the Virginians had narrowly escaped on August 19. Lee finally abandoned to the Federals the Weldon Railroad, which he had declared indefensible on June 19.[26]

During the morning of August 24, a rumor circulated that the brigade was going to escort one of the wagon trains that had just started hauling supplies around the break in the Weldon Railroad. The wagons went from Stony Creek to Petersburg via Dinwiddie Court House to get around the Federals in their fortifications at Globe Tavern. About 1 p.m. came the "everlasting" order: "Prepare to move and leave your baggage!" Sale recorded, "Generally thinking every one can form some idea or at least imagines he can—of where we are going when such orders come but this time they fooled all the knowing ones."[27] The Virginians left the breastworks at 4 p.m. with the division's Alabama Brigade. They trekked westward, reaching Boydton Plank Road near Battery 41. About four and a half miles from Petersburg, they turned left from the plank road onto Duncan Road. This narrow country lane led them through a thickly wooded swamp. A battalion of artillery accompanied the column. On the roadside rested stragglers from

26 Freeman, ed., *Lee's Dispatches*, 252.

27 Sale Diary, August 24, 1864.

other infantry brigades ahead. "From the troops along our expedition is not that of guarding a wagon train," Bernard observed.[28]

Grant wanted to wreck the Weldon Railroad as far as Hicksford, 40 miles south of Petersburg. He intended to begin by destroying the tracks down to Rowanty Creek, about 15 miles below the city. This task fell to Miles' division of II Corps and Gregg's cavalry division. On August 23, Hampton and the cavalry corps of Lee's army probed these two divisions near Reams Station, five miles north of the railroad's Rowanty Creek crossing. Hampton saw the Yankees' weakness and isolation. He rushed a message to Petersburg suggesting that Lee send infantry to smash the bluecoats. The assignment went to Hill, who left the Confederate trenches with eight infantry brigades, including Weisiger's brigade and the Alabama Brigade, both under Heth. The 12th's men bivouacked at 11 that night 200 yards from the dam of Armstrong's Mill Pond. There Duncan Road crossed Hatcher's Run, a tributary of Rowanty Creek. As Hill and Hampton planned the next day's battle, the soldiers bedded down with orders to march at four next morning.

The appointed hour came and went. Hill was ailing and his column did not move. The sun rose. His men remained in camp. Soon the infantry got in motion—slow motion. The Virginians and Alabamians trudged along at the column's rear, halting and resting frequently. They crossed Hatchers Run near the mill dam, then plodded down Duncan Road until they came to Dabney Road, where they bore left. Tramping onward to Vaughan Road, they turned right. They slogged along until they veered left onto Monk's Neck Road, crossing Rowanty Creek on Monk's Neck Bridge. Monk's Neck Road acquired the name of Depot Road as it continued eastward to Reams Station. Two or three miles from the previous night's camp, the Virginians and Alabamians lay down in the woods. At 1 p.m., they moved on and formed line of battle a mile and a half from the railroad. By 3 p.m., they had hiked to within a mile of the tracks. Then they waited.

Hampton's first plan had called for the cavalry to strike from the south while the infantry pushed in from the west at 9 o'clock in the morning. The plan fell apart when Cadmus Wilcox, whose division led the infantry column, encountered a small force of Federal cavalry east of Monk's Neck Bridge. Wilcox deployed his men in line of battle. The head of the Confederate infantry column did not arrive near Reams Station until noon.

28 Bernard Diary, August 24, 1864.

Hampton had then made a second plan, which called for his cavalry to lure the Federals south while the Secessionist infantry struck from the west. This plan also failed. Gibbon's division of II Corps had reinforced the Union detachment at Reams Station the previous day. Hancock himself had arrived to take command. He did not fall for the Confederate horsemen's feigned retreat down the railroad. He withdrew his infantry to the breastworks begun by VI Corps at the end of June and prepared to resist. Wilcox's men stormed the entrenched Yankee picket line a few hundred yards west of the works, which ran north and south a few yards west of the tracks. He then sent forward two of his brigades to strike the breastworks. The Federals in the works blasted his men. For a couple of hours afterward, Confederate sharpshooters kept Unionist heads down and immobilized the Yankee cannon by picking off artillery horses.

Now Cooke's and MacRae's brigades from Heth's division and their accompanying artillery deployed. Hill posted the Virginia and Alabama Brigades to prevent any attack on his left flank by the Yanks at Globe Tavern, four miles north. Then he became too ill to continue. Command devolved upon Heth, who confined himself to positioning the artillery. He deferred to Wilcox on the infantry's placement because Wilcox had arrived first on the ground. The Virginians and Alabamians endured enemy shelling. Wilcox prepared to attack the Union earthworks west of the railroad again, once again with only two brigades. A Southern defeat akin to the previous Sunday's seemed in the making. The Confederate artillery opened at 5 p.m. Twenty minutes later Lane's brigade of Wilcox's division and Cooke's brigade of Heth's division advanced eastwardly into the tempest of Federal fire as a thunderstorm bore down on them from the west.

The Southern sharpshooters and artillery had cowed most of the enemy infantrymen. The remainder might have repulsed the first line of Secessionist foot soldiers, but the Yankee guns ran short of ammunition. One of the supporting Confederate brigades—MacRae's of Heth's division—advanced on the initiative of its commander just as part of Cooke's brigade recoiled. MacRae's brigade gave the attack new impetus and Union infantrymen began grounding their arms. A looming Southern disaster turned into a Northern catastrophe.[29]

One of Hill's staff officers rode up to the Mahone men.

---

29 Horn, *The Battles for the Weldon Railroad, August 1864*, 226-262.

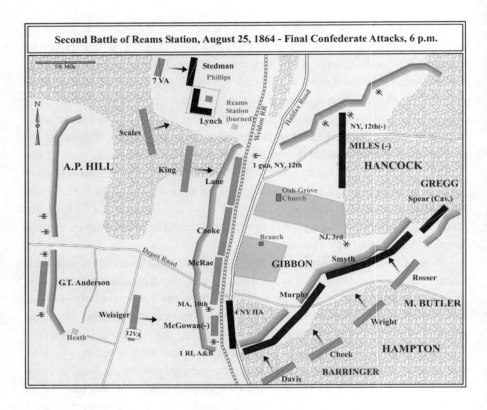

Second Battle of Reams Station, August 25, 1864 - Final Confederate Attacks, 6 p.m.

"The works have been carried and thousands of prisoners captured," he shouted.[30]

The Virginians and the Alabama Brigade reformed line of battle. The Alabamians hastened to the captured breastworks' extreme left. Weisiger's troops double-quicked towards the right for 700 yards across a flat, muddy field. Bird—back with the New Grays after his stint with the color guard— found himself heading toward an enemy cannon. "The muzzle looked as large as an ordinary flour barrel," he wrote.[31] A bullet killed the New Gray next to Bird—Sgt. Joseph R. Bell. He had just returned to the ranks from a wound suffered in the Wilderness.

The 12th's men, arriving within 200 yards of the earthwork, saw in its ditch hundreds of bluecoats. Most were coming in as prisoners. A few were running south along the ditch and escaping. The regiment's soldiers thought

30   Bernard Diary, August 27, 1864.

31   Henry Van Leuvenigh Bird to Margaret Randolph, October 15, 1864.

the fugitives were forming to sweep around the right flank of the Confederates in the captured breastworks. The Virginians hastened toward the works, which consisted of railroad iron and telegraph wire. The wire remained invisible until the troops came within a few feet. "We were too tired to mind trifles and it was laughable even in the midst of the fire to see men catch their feet in the wire and plunge headlong against the works," Bird wrote.[32]

Weisiger's brigade secured the works' southern end against counterattack. The Northerners running southward had nothing in mind other than escaping. "They did not fire a gun at us as well as I could see as we charged upon them," noted Bernard.[33] Like other Confederate infantrymen on this part of the field, Bird and about a dozen more of the 12th's men jumped over the works, dropped their rifles, turned a captured Napoleon on the retreating column and fired double charges of canister.[34] Bird and his comrades "did perhaps some of the wildest shooting of the war," Bernard observed.[35] Their first shot cut off the top of a nearby pine. The wild cannonade that followed did more than the Northerners to delay the Southern cavalry bearing down on the Federal left flank. Secessionist gunners arrived moments later and served the pieces more accurately.

The Unionists on the embankment's other side, the Corcoran Legion's 155th and 170th New York, briefly forced the Virginians to halt. Weisiger's men soon out-Yankeed the Yankees in ingenuity by tossing railroad ties over the embankment onto the bluecoats' heads. The Virginia Brigade resumed its advance against feeble resistance. The Virginians and Hampton's cavalry trapped the Northerners on this part of the battlefield. Most surrendered. The remaining Unionists skedaddled into the woods east of their works. Darkness made pursuit impossible.

The Confederates had inflicted 2,727 casualties, more than 2,000 of them prisoners. Nine cannon and 3,100 stand of small arms fell into Southern hands.[36] The victory cost the Secessionists 750 killed, wounded and missing. The 12th suffered two casualties. Bell alone perished. Hancock's men wounded one of the Herrings.[37]

32 Henry Van Leuvenigh Bird to Margaret Randolph, August 28, 1864.

33 Bernard Diary, August 27, 1864.

34 Bird to Randolph, August 28, 1864.

35 Bernard Diary, August 27, 1864.

36 Horn, *The Battles for the Weldon Railroad, August 1864*, 276.

37 Macon Daily *Telegraph*, September 3, 1864, p. 1, col. 3.

Late that night in a pouring rain, the Confederate infantrymen withdrew. They staggered through ankle deep mud toward Dinwiddie Court House, bedding down for the night five miles from the battlefield. At nine next morning, they resumed their tramp back to Petersburg. The column approached the city late in the afternoon. Hill and his staff led the triumphal procession. Behind them came seven stands of enemy colors. Nine captured guns followed. Next in line shambled the prisoners. Then came the Confederate troops, with the 12th at their head, passing other Southern soldiers massed above Butterworth's Bridge. The regiment's men were "cheering, yelling and raising a row generally," according to Bird.[38] They reached their camp at Walnut Hill an hour before sundown, "very much broken down by the travel," recorded Bernard.[39] Many of the Petersburg soldiers, including Bird, fell out and went home, a luxury available to few other men in the army. Bird reached home about dark. After a light meal, he lay down on the sofa, awakening at 10 a.m. next day.[40]

The Confederate victory at Second Reams Station halted Grant's fourth offensive at Petersburg. The Northerners had failed to capture Richmond or Atlanta. The presidential election approached. Southerners hoped the Union would elect a peace-at-any-price Democratic administration that would offer an armistice and independence. "All eyes are turned to the great Democratic Convention to assemble on Monday next in Chicago," Bernard observed on August 27.[41]

On August 31, the regiment went on picket with part of the 41st Virginia in weather "just cool enough to keep the mosquitoes quiet," according to Sale.[42] The Democrats fulfilled Confederate expectations, nominating McClellan for president on a platform that declared the war a failure. But a Federal push had begun in Georgia. While Mac composed his acceptance speech, Sherman compelled the Southerners to evacuate Atlanta. Its capture revived the flagging Union cause and brought a flood of volunteers. Lincoln postponed indefinitely the unpopular draft scheduled for early September.

---

38 Bird to Randolph, August 28, 1864.

39 Bernard Diary, August 27, 1864.

40 Bird to Randolph, August 28, 1864.

41 Bernard Diary, August 27, 1864.

42 Sale Diary, August 31, 1864.

Confirmation of the rumors about Atlanta's fall reached the regiment on September 6. "Cool, disagreeable & drizzly day, just such a one as is most calculated to produce the blues," Sale noted.[43] The weather summoned the prospect of an early, severe winter. This weighed heavily on the 90 men who remained with the 12th's colors. "If the campaign lasts much longer I will have to command my own company, and be my own company," wrote Bird.[44] His company, 119 strong before Seven Pines, took only six into action at Globe Tavern, losing two. A few days later at Second Reams Station, it lost another.[45]

Many of the 12th's men lacked blankets. Wood was becoming scarce. Rations had dwindled to a third of a pound of meat instead of a half, and a pound of meal rather than a pound and a half. Scroungers lost all sense of shame. Doncey Dunlop had earned promotion to sergeant. Phillips excused Dunlop from a picketing detail to see if he could get some food at his father's residence. Doncey found some fine mutton chops and stole them, leaving his family without any meat. He and his companions feasted on the mutton. "For some time Donald did not have any desire to go home to see the old father," Phillips remembered.[46]

The cool, clear weather of late August returned September 7. Next day Grant's military railroad began running between City Point and the Federal lines. The hungry, ill-clad Southern troops glumly listened to the cars hauling the comforts of home to their enemies. By now, visits to Petersburg had lost much of their charm for the Confederates. The city had deteriorated further under Yankee shellfire. "When this war shall have ended this City will ever remain a standing shame on our enemy who in spite of not being able to whip our armies try to kill poor innocent children & helpless women & old men," Sale recorded.[47] Bombardment had torn some portions of the town to pieces. Many homes stood vacant because their owners had departed for less dangerous places.

One of the empty houses belonged to the Waddells. Mrs. Waddell had left Petersburg to join her mother in Raleigh. But many others stayed, including

43 Ibid., September 6, 1864.

44 Henry Van Leuvenigh Bird to Margeret Randolph, August 29, 1864.

45 Ibid.

46 Phillips, "Sixth Corporal," 62.

47 Sale Diary, September 1, 1864.

the Banisters. Blair's brother Norborne died on his 16th birthday. Shells fell constantly, making it impossible to take Norborne's body to Blandford Cemetery. His family buried him in their garden. Nobody else was present but their slaves and Reverend Platt. This somber occasion earned the Banisters a visit the next day from Lee, whose father had been a friend of Blair's great-grandfather. From then until the campaign's end, Lee dined with the Banisters every Sunday that no fighting occurred.

The 12th got cheering news on September 18. "The regiment recd an addition of what is commonly known as food for gunpowder in the shape of 20 conscripts," Sale observed.[48] Reports of Southern success in the previous day's Beefsteak Raid arrived as well. By month's end, the 12th would have 242 effectives, 9 more than went into August's fighting.[49] But bad tidings also came. McClellan's repudiation of his party's peace plank had thrown the Democrats into disarray. "The whole North is jubilant over their recent military successes and there is much despondence in the South," noted Bernard.[50]

Whatever optimism the conscripts and the Beefsteak Raid engendered went up in smoke early on the morning of September 21. Union artillery opened thunderously. The men thought the Federals had sprung another mine. Next day the Secessionists learned that the cannonade celebrated Sheridan's whipping of Early at Winchester in the Shenandoah. "Our affairs are dark now much more gloomy than at any previous time and our men are much discouraged," Sale recorded. "Is it possible that after so many victories, so much suffering, and so hopeful a beginning we are to be finally conquered?"[51] Many assumed they would have to abandon Petersburg.

Another Yankee bombardment opened September 24, in honor of Sheridan's victory over Early at Fisher's Hill. An unusual quiet prevailed along the lines September 28. To the 12th's veterans, the silence indicated the approach of battle. Orders to drill strengthened the conviction of the men whom Sale called "our knowing prophets" that fighting would soon break out.[52]

---

48 Ibid., September 18, 1864.

49 Inspection Report, Mahone's Brigade, September 28, 1864, Record Group 109, Entry 15, Box 16, NA.

50 Bernard Diary, September 28, 1864.

51 Sale Diary, September 22, 1864.

52 Ibid., September 28, 1864.

The prophets proved correct next day as Grant launched another offensive—his fifth at Petersburg, to prevent Lee from reinforcing Early. Federal troops stormed Fort Harrison north of James River and threatened Richmond. Weisiger's brigade drilled and paraded all day, then ambled over to Rives Salient, where Jerusalem Plank Road entered the Dimmock line. The Virginians relieved Davis' brigade at night under a severe fire from the Union pickets.

"Mahone's beauties," as the soldiers of Porte's division now referred to themselves, did not participate on September 30 in the defeat suffered by the Southerners in their attempt to recover Fort Harrison or in the successful Confederate defense of the South Side Railroad at Peebles' farm southwest of Petersburg.[53] The Mahone men became acquainted with their sector of the fortifications. Many probably wished they were fighting. At Rives Salient the Norfolk Division renewed its acquaintance with trench warfare. The hideous landscape afforded a preview of World War I's Western Front. "There is a ditch cut for every possible want and over every portion of the ground," Sale observed.[54] Existence in the breastworks at Walnut Hill seemed idyllic by comparison. There the main lines stood more than a mile apart. "If we get behind the breastworks to shelter ourselves from the fire of artillery & Sharpshooters we are never at rest for fear of the mortar shelling which can reach us in almost any position we may take," Sale noted.[55]

Mahone's brigade did not participate in the unsuccessful Confederate counterattack along the Squirrel Level Road west of Globe Tavern on October 1. Torrential showers that day made the earthworks at Rives Salient even worse. "The trenches are one mass of yellow clay about ankle deep and our bed is of the same material," Sale recorded.[56] The 100 pickets furnished by the 12th that day reached an informal truce with their enemy counterparts to enable all of them to bail out their rifle pits. But the men in the main lines kept firing off their wet muskets, making the sentries jumpy. Occasionally they had to take a few shots at one another so that their officers would not

53 Ibid., October 3, 1864.

54 Ibid., October 2, 1864. For the Petersburg trenches' ugliness, see generally Earl J. Hess, *In the Trenches at Petersburg: Field Fortifications and Confederate Defeat* (Chapel Hill, NC, 2009).

55 Ibid., September 30, 1864.

56 Ibid., October 1, 1864.

order them to fire steadily. "It is astonishing with how much faith each side trusts the other in this arrangement, always giving notice when they will commence the firing," observed Sale.[57]

"Rats! To your holes!" was the warning cry in this sector.[58]

Just before dark on October 2, the Virginians shifted rightward. Sloshing about under enemy fire in ditches and covered ways full of mud brought the 12th to the most comfortable position it had yet found at Rives Salient. When Wise's brigade arrived next morning to relieve Weisiger's troops, they greeted it with groans and rambled off to an unknown destination expecting Porte to get them into a fight. To their relief, they halted in the pine grove at Walnut Hill and pitched their raghouses. The paymaster arrived to distribute their meager earnings. A month's pay for a private came to 18 dollars Confederate, amounting to a mere 75 cents at the unofficial exchange rate of 24 for one dollar of United States Currency. But 75 cents was better than nothing. "By the time it was fairly paid out the women from town with pies & such truck came out in a general rush to sell them and it was right amusing to see the anxiety to get to them," noted Sale.[59]

Quiet prevailed during the regiment's first few days back in the pine grove at Walnut Hill. On October 5, the Richmond Grays' Pvt. James Frank Hawkins received his second wound of 1864 in this seemingly safe place. A bullet that must have traveled about a mile glanced down from a tree and entered the fleshy part of his thigh.

The authorities had every available man in line the following day, even some considered seriously ill. Grant's fifth offensive had disrupted the Confederate defense lines north of the James, putting his men much closer to Richmond. Southside, the offensive had brought Federal forces a mile and a half closer to the South Side Railroad. Grant did not renew his fifth offensive at Petersburg. The Federals contented themselves with advancing their pickets on the morning of October 8 and setting fire to a house near Battery 45, a formidable five-gun work also known as Fort Lee or the Star Fort standing where Boydton Plank Road entered the works. The Northerner sentries then withdrew. Weisiger's brigade shuffled away from Wilcox's farm, bivouacking behind Battery 45.

57 Ibid., October 2, 1864.

58 Todd, "Reminiscences," 230.

59 Sale Diary, October 3, 1864.

The 12th suffered a shock next morning. The Riflemen's Pvt. Albert W. Hobbs died of a congestive chill. "He was an excellent old man & a fine soldier," recorded Bernard.[60] At midnight, the Virginians shifted pursuant to a rumor that the Yankees were preparing to charge the picket line. Near 3 a.m., Weisiger's men stacked arms in the bleak, cold ravine in front of the Wilcox house. The rumor that the Unionists planned to charge the Confederate picket line proved false. The Virginians lay in the ravine all day October 10, then returned to their camp in Wilcox's pine grove.

The ranks resumed swelling in mid-month. "All the old dead heads from the hospitals are beginning to come forth," noted Sale.[61] Bird, hearing of a battery strengthened by 56 supernumeraries from a single company, wrote, "Isn't it shameful to think how things have been conducted heretofore?"[62] Large numbers of conscripts arrived daily. By October 24, the 12th had received about 100 of these new men. Those from Petersburg included Pvt. James C. Riddle, a wealthy young farmer and tobacconist. Conscripted on October 14, he reached Camp Lee near Richmond next day. Along with some other Petersburg men, he elected to join the 12th. "I hear that we will only be wanted for six weeks but you can hear anything at this place," Riddle wrote to his wife, left alone to tend several small children.[63] Sent to the regiment on October 16, he was assigned to the Riflemen.

Thirty-five or 40 other men had come through enemy lines to join the Confederate ranks, many from Norfolk. There the Federals had declared that everyone between the ages of 16 and 55, male or female, must take the oath of loyalty to the United States by September 15 or be sent beyond Yankee lines. The refugees from Norfolk included someone Sale knew. Sale was sitting by a campfire with his head in his hands, lost in thought, when a youth touched him on the shoulder.

"Well, what will you have?" asked Sale.

The youth did not answer. Sale looked up and saw a stranger in a civilian suit. Sale bade him good day.

"Don't you know me?" the youth asked.

---

60   Bernard Diary, October 10, 1864.

61   Sale Diary, October 13, 1864; Ibid., October 14, 1864.

62   Bird to Randolph, October 15, 1864.

63   James C. Riddle to Wife, October 15, 1864, James C. Riddle Papers, VHS.

"No," said Sale, though he suspected his visitor was someone from Norfolk by his clothes.

Sale looked straight into his eyes and saw two big tears well up and roll down. Then Sale realized it was his cousin Charlie. Sale recalled,

> How on earth I did not recognize him I do not understand and hardened as I am as I thought I was, the sight of one whom I loved so much brought me very near to tears; maybe I did wipe one or two away. Had I all Norfolk to pick from I should least have expected him. He was so backward and was so much loved by his Mother & Father that great indeed must be their love for their country to offer their hearts' greatest treasure on its altar.[64]

Charlie wished to join the army. Sale insisted that Charlie should wait at least until next spring. Charlie wanted to stay with Sale. It took two days, but Sale finally persuaded his cousin that he was unfit for a soldier's duties. Disappointed, Charlie departed for Richmond, where other relatives found him a post in the Transportation Department. "God grant the war may end before he becomes old enough to take part in it," wrote Sale.[65]

A court-martial occurred after the August fighting. The New Grays' Pvt. John James Campbell had worked as a cashier for a Petersburg dry goods merchant before the war. In the words of his fellow New Gray, Sgt. Robert George Thompson, Campbell "would not fight."[66] Assignment to the Ordnance Department had prevented this incapacity from causing him any trouble in 1862 and 1863. He served in the Ordnance Department of Longstreet's Corps at Chickamauga. But in 1864 Campbell's detail ended. He returned to the 12th. On July 30, he disgraced himself by not going into the Crater battle. The court-martial sentenced him to wear a ball and chain. Lewellen had returned to the regiment from the recruiting duty that succeeded his wound at Crampton's Gap, moving up to lieutenant colonel as Feild advanced to colonel on Weisiger's promotion to brigadier general for his heroism at the Crater, while Jones filled Lewellen's billet as major. Lewellen interceded with Lee on Campbell's behalf. Lee promised Campbell a reprieve if he went into the next fight and behaved well. Lewellen asked Thompson to help get Campbell into the next fight.

64 John F. Sale to Aunt, December 31, 1864.

65 Ibid.

66 Statement of Robert George Thompson.

Other soldiers also looked forward to another battle, regarding Uncle Sam as their commissary and considering what they captured from him a tax. Bird wanted to reequip himself at the foe's expense with a blanket and an oil cloth, to find an overcoat that his sister might convert into a cloak and to obtain a present for his betrothed.

CHAPTER 19

Burgess Mill

Early on the cold, rainy morning of October 27, the men heard heavy firing from what Sale termed "that much dreaded right flank."[1] Manson was beginning a spiritual diary, writing, "It reminds me that I have business at the throne of Grace & that my soul's interests cannot be neglected."[2] Marching orders reached Weisiger's brigade about 9 a.m. The Virginians and their division's Alabama Brigade hurried west to Battery 45. There they waited for Harris' Mississippi Brigade to extricate itself from the trenches and join them. Word came that the enemy had taken possession of Vaughan Road on the extreme Confederate right. After an hour the Virginians and Alabamians resumed their tramp without the Mississippians. Mahone rode ahead to Burgess Mill, where Boydton Plank Road crossed Hatchers Run. He conferred with Heth, the Secessionist right's overall commander that day.

For the second time that autumn, Grant had launched an offensive to capitalize on a victory by Sheridan in the Shenandoah—this one at Cedar Creek on October 19. Grant's new offensive—his sixth at Petersburg—had the same objective south of the James as his previous offensive—the South Side Railroad. North of the James he expected Butler's army to feint against the Confederate left. Southwest of Petersburg, V and IX corps thrashed forward

---

1 Sale Diary, October 27, 1864.

2 Joseph R. Manson, "A Spiritual Diary," October 27, 1864, Joseph R. Manson Papers, VHS.

on the Petersburg side of Hatcher's Run toward the South Side Railroad's tracks. II Corps splashed across the run at Vaughan Road and shambled westward on Dabney Mill Road toward Boydton Plank Road. Gregg's cavalry division crossed the run at Monk's Neck Bridge and advanced on II Corps' left. II Corps and Gregg's division moved under Hancock.

Meade expected IX Corps or V Corps would find unfinished fortifications between the right of Petersburg's breastworks and Hatchers Run. But the Southerners had completed the extension of their fortifications to the run above Armstrong's Mill about a week earlier.

By the time of Mahone's conference with Heth, Confederate horse soldiers had contained II Corps and Gregg's division. Dearing's cavalry brigade held Boydton Plank Road's bridge over Hatchers Run. On White Oak Road, Butler's division of horsemen stood between the Northerners and the run's Claiborne Road crossing, two miles upstream. W. H. F. "Rooney" Lee's cavalry division occupied Boydton Plank Road south of Gravelly Run, barring the way to Dinwiddie Court House. Batteries with the three Southern mounted forces opened a crossfire on II Corps. The bluecoats prepared to cross Hatchers Run at Burgess Mill, roll up the Confederate earthworks that extended southwest from Petersburg to the run and seize the South Side Railroad. The time had come for the Secessionist Infantry to counterattack. Heth assigned this task to Mahone.

The Virginia and Alabama brigades followed Boydton Plank Road to the top of the hill west of Picture Branch, then filed off to the left past several guns. Rejoined by Porte, the Mahone men fell in behind MacRae's North Carolina Brigade. The column proceeded southwestward through the pines to one of Hampton's dams on Hatchers Run below the bridge at Burgess Mill, crossing the run on the dam. It would admit only two men abreast at a time. Little daylight remained on this overcast afternoon by the time Porte's force had finished crossing.

A short distance into the woods on the other side, Mahone shook out a skirmish line. His force had come close to the Yankees. Orders could not safely be shouted but had to be given by signal. Porte agreed on a sign with the officer in charge of the skirmish line, then ordered him to instruct each of his skirmishers not to say a word upon sighting the Unionists. Instead, they would give the sign to the general at the column's head directly behind the skirmish line.

The Confederates quietly struggled southwestward for a third of a mile, crossing marshy, overgrown terrain that made the Wilderness look hospitable. The column reached an oak wood with thick undergrowth. The Southern

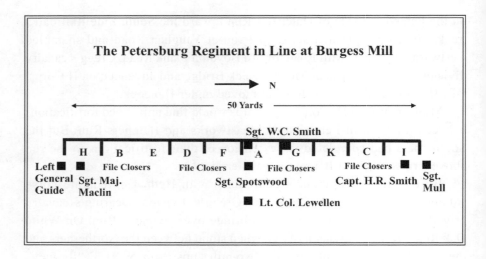

skirmishers halted, signaling that they had contacted the bluecoats. Mahone deployed his three brigades facing west, softly directing his men to fix bayonets, dress on the colors and push directly ahead as soon as their units had properly formed. MacRae's brigade advanced on the right, Weisiger's brigade on the left. King's Alabama Brigade moved behind the Virginians and North Carolinians in column of regiments, ready to provide support. The men learned that the Yankees occupied the timber ahead.

All the marching and countermarching put the 12th on the Virginia Brigade's left, instead of in the regiment's proper place on the right. Lewellen led the 12th. Campbell stood at his side. Up to this point the brigade's sharpshooters alone, posted about 20 paces apart, protected Mahone's left. Porte, reasoning that since II Corps had come by a country road not far from the Confederate left, more Yanks probably occupied the road, took skirmishers from the Juniors, who formed the 12th's extreme left, and ran them perpendicularly to the Virginia Brigade to avoid any surprise from the left flank.[3] Twenty picked men under Chappell further reinforced the flank guards, who received orders not to advance but to hold their ground and protect the left.[4]

Mahone did not know it, but advancing on his left was Crawford's division of V Corps. Orders had sent Crawford's division across Hatcher's Run after

3 Ibid.

4 "William H. Harrison, Southern Patriot," *The Progress-Index* (Petersburg, VA), April 30, 1961, p. 5, cols. 1-4.

the Confederate works on the run's other side had stymied the advance of V and IX corps. Crawford's division had little more than its name and those of its brigades in common with the unit Mahone had mauled on August 19. With Hofmann's brigade on the left, Bragg's brigade on the right and the Maryland Brigade in reserve, Crawford's division was floundering upstream along the right bank of Hatcher's Run to connect with II Corp's right.

Porte's battle line pushed through the thickets. Mahone passed down his line, quietly encouraging his soldiers to reserve their fire and rely on the bayonet. Lieutenant Colonel George Harney of Hofmann's brigade brought up his 147th New York Infantry to deploy as skirmishers to the Virginians' left. Harney mistook the Juniors for his own men. He rode up to the Juniors, who took him prisoner.[5] The Southern battle line inched forward. "It was a thick swampy piece of ground as much as we could do to get through the thick undergrowth," remembered Phillips.[6] The 12th had advanced less than 100 feet when skirmishers of Pierce's brigade, Mott's division, opened fire with repeating rifles on the Virginians. Some of the 12th's men returned fire though they could scarcely see their opponents in the shadowy, smoky woods. The blue coated pickets skedaddled. Plunging forward, the regiment's soldiers viewed the results of their shooting. "Some bad, some not so bad," recalled Phillips. "Here we picked up some small rifles called the Spencer gun, load in the butt with a spring and would shoot [seven] times."[7]

The sound of Mahone's attack signaled the rest of the Southern units surrounding Hancock's forces to join in the assault. Harris' Mississippi Brigade had finally arrived at Burgess Mill. Some of the Mississippians charged southward alongside Dearing's brigade, trying to cross Hatchers Run. Butler's division stormed eastward on White Oak Road. Rooney Lee's division drove northeastward on Boydton Plank Road.

Weisiger's brigade crashed into the right half of Pierce's brigade. The 105th Pennsylvania confronted the 12th Virginia. Richardson fired his musket, then made for a beautiful stand of state colors in front of the 105th. The color bearer tried to keep Richardson from taking him or his banner. A big red-headed Keystoner aimed his musket at Richardson. The Riflemen's Pvt.

5 Sale Diary, October 27, 1864.

6 Phillips, "Sixth Corporal," 64.

7 Ibid. Phillips mistakenly says "16" times. The Henry rifle had a capacity of sixteen rounds, the Spencer a capacity of seven.

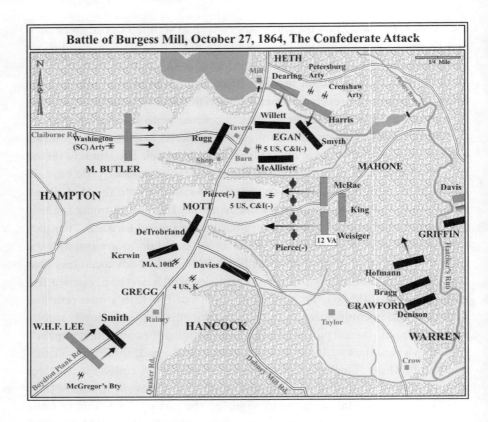

Battle of Burgess Mill, October 27, 1864, The Confederate Attack

Robert Atkinson, a former clerk, knocked down the redhead. Richardson captured the banner.

The Riflemen's Cpl. Robert "Bones" Hatcher, as fragile as Richardson was strong, seized another enemy color. Lewellen and Campbell took a third.[8] The banners seized included the 105th's national flag and a banner of the 63rd Pennsylvania, consolidated into the 105th.[9] MacRae's brigade overran a two-gun section of the 5th United States Battery and routed the left of Pierce's brigade. The Confederates captured about 400 Federals.

8 Statement of Robert George Thompson; Henry Van Leuvenigh Bird to Margaret Randolph, June 7, 1865; "Newsy Notes," *The Forest Republican* (Tionesta, PA), August 23, 1893, p. 3, col. 5; "Gets Back Its Colors," *The Star* (Reynoldsville, Pa.), September 20, 1893, p. 4, col. 4.

9 *OR* 40, 1:349.

The 12th's soldiers rushed forward from the deep woods into what Phillips described as "wood with very little undergrowth."[10] The men vaulted a fence at the timber's edge, 100 yards from where they had formed line of battle. They entered an open field. The brigade split in two. The smaller right wing continued straight west toward the Burgess house and Boydton Plank Road. The larger left wing wheeled to face part of De Trobriand's brigade of Mott's division, hastily deployed along a fence 200 yards southwest. Some of the bluecoats crouched behind the fence. A mounted Union officer motioned with a sword. The Virginians stood in the open field in fine spirits, banging away at De Trobriand's brigade and the other bodies of the enemy visible.

Tom Pollard, now the Old Grays' captain, found himself in the opening between the brigade's two wings. Encountering a Federal with a rifle in hand, Pollard ordered the Yankee to throw the weapon down. At first the Northerner mistook Pollard, who was wearing a captured blue cap and blue pants, for a Union officer. Quickly recognizing his error, the invader tried to bayonet Pollard, who caught the rifle between the first and second tail-bands. Shoving off the Federal, Pollard drew his revolver, put it against his opponent's temple and pulled the trigger. Only the cap exploded. Another Unionist 10 yards away stood loading his rifle, with his eyes directly on Pollard. "Will no one shoot that man?" Pollard thought. He adjusted the cap on his revolver, then heard a ball thud as it entered the body of the bluecoat preparing to shoot Pollard. A Confederate at the fence behind Pollard had killed the man. The Yankee struggling with Pollard still gripped the rifle. The Northerner did not let go until Pollard caught the small of the stock and jerked it across his knee. Pollard's prisoner then walked back toward the fence muttering something in a foreign language.

Pollard hurried on with the Virginia Brigade's right wing, charging along a branch toward the plank road. The North Carolinians and Virginians drove the remnants of Pierce's brigade across the road and into the trees beyond. Many Confederates followed the fleeing Unionists into the undergrowth on the far side of the bridge that carried the road over the branch.[11] Other Secessionists halted at the road and faced south to drive the bluecoats away

10 Phillips, "Sixth Corporal," 64.

11 George S. Bernard, "War Recollections, A Celebrated Engagement, The Battle of Burgess Mill, October 27, 1864—Interesting Narratives of Participants," Petersburg *Daily Index-Appeal*, June 14, 1895.

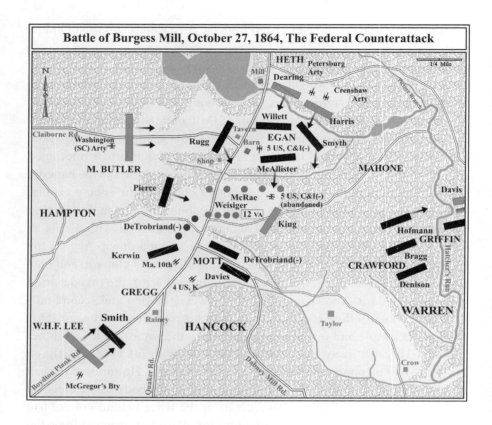

Battle of Burgess Mill, October 27, 1864, The Federal Counterattack

from Dabney Mill Road, Hancock's only direct link with the rest of Meade's army. Porte seemed about to cut off Hancock's command.

The Southerners' luck changed. An orchard hid four Yankee Infantry brigades facing north and west on high ground across the branch from the Confederates in the field. The attacks by Butler's division, Harris' brigade and Dearing's brigade failed to pin down all these Northerners. The biggest of the four Union brigades—McAllister's New Jersey Brigade of Egan's division—had more men than MacRae's and Weisiger's brigades combined and was preparing to cross Hatchers Run. When the Southerners burst out of the woods behind the brigade, the Jerseymen faced about. Together with a regiment from Smyth's brigade of Egan's division, they attacked southward across the branch's ravine into the field. These invaders struck the Secessionists near where the Tarheels had emerged from the woods. Most of the Yankees broke under Confederate fire and streamed back across the ravine. A few Unionists pressed on and engaged the Southerners in a hand-to-hand struggle for the two cannon lost by Pierce's brigade. The Secessionists quickly drove these Federals back across the ravine as well. There the Unionists rallied, repulsing the pursuing Confederates.

More bluecoats engaged Mahone's infantry. The Yankee brigade and division leaders used some of their men to fend off the surrounding Southerners and threw the rest against the Confederates in their midst. Part of Rugg's brigade of Egan's division, another of the Union brigades behind the Virginians and North Carolinians, charged southward along the plank road. Most of De Trobriand's brigade drove northward from Dabney Mill Road. Scattered survivors from Pierce's brigade joined one or the other of these pincers. They threatened to close at the Burgess house and cut off half the Virginians and Tarheels.

Pollard called this to Weisiger's attention. Weisiger ordered Pollard to the woods to inform Mahone. Pollard ran fifty yards. Weisiger called him back, then directed Pollard to form the disordered Virginia brigade. Hardly half a dozen men of any company remained together. Pollard stepped up on the embankment beside the plank road, calling on the Virginians to follow him into the field in fours regardless of companies. The troops formed line of battle in the field. At Weisiger's order the line charged back toward the woods. Men of both sides used bayonets and clubbed muskets in the confused fights that flared up from the plank road to the captured guns. The Northerners overwhelmed the soldiers of the Virginia and North Carolina brigades in the field, capturing two flags from MacRae's brigade and hundreds of Virginians and Tarheels. The prisoners included the wounded Scott, now the Huger Grays' captain, Riddle and Bird. The Federals retook the two guns lost by Pierce's brigade.

A bullet shattered Banister's right arm and ripped into his lung. The Riflemen's Sgt. Hartwell B. Harrison, a former store clerk, carried Banister to safety.

"Hartwell, if I die, tell my mother I am not afraid to die," pleaded Banister.[12]

Mahone deployed his Alabama Brigade along a fence at the woods' edge near the guns the Unionists had recaptured. The retreating Virginians and North Carolinians rallied on the Alabamians, helping them blast

---

12 Pryor, "A Child's Recollection Of War," *CV*, 39:56.

David Addison Weisiger, in a late-war photo
U. S. Army Military History Institute, Carlisle, PA

the pursuing bluecoats. "It was almost impossible to miss them as they were so thickly formed in mass," Phillips remembered.[13] Some Yankee guns on the high ground near the bridge turned from their duel with the

13 Phillips, "Sixth Corporal," 64.

Confederate artillery north of Hatchers Run and fired into the woods occupied by Porte's infantry.

Porte sat his horse amid the bursting shells, listening to the reports of his soldiers and assessing the situation. A shell exploded nearby, injuring his steed. Porte dismounted at once, sent the horse to the rear, obtained a new mount, then rode south to where the Virginians had emerged from the woods. From there he could see the Yankee Infantry opposite his right and the chaos of limber chests, caissons, ordnance wagons and ambulances confronting his left. He also observed Hancock and his staff sitting their horses under an oak tree near the Plank Road, 200 yards to the southwest.[14] Hampton's troopers continued to press their attacks along White Oak and Boydton Plank roads. Their bullets fell at Mahone's feet. Porte rode back to the remnant of his assault force, trying to find a way to strike the right rear of the Federals near Hatchers Run. The charges and countercharges back and forth across the branch that flowed between his men and the high ground had churned its bed into an impassible quagmire.

Waning light and a cold downpour persuaded him to order his troops back across Hatchers Run by the path they had taken into battle. That path proved elusive to soldiers unable to get their bearings in the woods because of the overcast. Many of Mahone's troops lost their way. Scattered bands of fugitives and stragglers from both sides roamed the forest, capturing and recapturing one another. They became prisoners for good upon stumbling into organized bodies of their enemies.

The Virginia Brigade's sharpshooters and their reinforcements did not get the word to retreat until long after the rest of Porte's force had departed. Then, recalled the City Guard's Cpl. William Henry Harrison, one of the men sent with Chappell to strengthen the sharpshooters, "we started for NOWHERE, for after forty minutes marching through huckleberry bushes and the like, we found ourselves just at the very spot from whence we started nearly an hour before—the whole party was lost."[15] After the group proceeded in a different direction in the drizzle, Harrison and some comrades captured three Federal cavalrymen, including an officer, and appropriated their overcoats and horses. Harrison then received orders to scout a path

14 Mahone thought he faced Grant and Meade, but they had left the field earlier. *OR* 42, 1:36, 231; Ibid., 3:405.

15 "William Henry Harrison, Southern Patriot," *The Progress-Index* (Petersburg, VA), April 30, 1961.

John R. Turner. *Virginia Historical Society*

back to Petersburg. Unsuccessful in that mission, he spied a train of Unionist ambulances and reported them to his party, which ambushed and captured the Northerners. The Virginians then devoted themselves to plundering the wagons and securing horses.

"Mr. Harrison," said the Herrings' Pvt. George W. Pollard, "it is getting dark and if you will take the lead I'll follow you and if we make a start all will join in."[16]

Harrison thought he headed southwest, toward Dinwiddie Court House, followed only by Pollard. Around nine p.m. they fell into the hands of the 7th Wisconsin of Bragg's brigade in Crawford's division.

Turner had been wounded in the knee during the regiment's initial charge. Hugh Smith lent his horse to Turner. The Riflemen's Pvt. Richard Henry May, brother of George William May, and another of Chappell's reinforcements for the sharpshooters, mounted the animal and took Turner up behind him. They tried to follow the path out of the woods. There was nothing to guide them that cloudy evening. They went astray in the brush. Riding a few 100 yards, they came to a field where a Federal battle line stood no more than 50 yards away. The pair turned back, recalled Turner, "but had not retraced our steps far before we halted, doubtful in what direction we could now safely go, the enemy seeming to be on all sides of us."[17] A mounted Northerner came riding from the direction of the Unionist line of battle, asking them for General Crawford's whereabouts. May, informing the Yankee that he was their

16   Ibid.

17   John R. Turner to George S. Bernard, n.d., George S. Bernard Papers, SHC.

prisoner, asked him to dismount. The Federal, seeing that May and Turner carried no weapons, hesitated to comply. Several armed Southern stragglers appeared. The Unionist dismounted. May took his horse and equipment and turned him over to the stragglers. Unlike many of their comrades, Turner and May made it back to Confederate lines that night.

The remnants of Mahone's force bivouacked on the slope of the hill east of Picture Branch. Weisiger's brigade and the 12th Virginia had suffered their heaviest losses of the war. The Virginians had 410 killed, wounded and missing.[18] Prisoners, including nearly all the brigade sharpshooters, accounted for most of the casualties. The 12th lost 43 men in the fight itself.[19] That number swelled to 105 during the withdrawal—3 killed, 13 wounded and 89 missing. Three of the wounded fell into enemy hands and three died of their injuries.[20]

Despite the statistics Burgess Mill failed to impress itself deeply on the 12th's collective memory. The men had shed less blood than in more than a dozen other fights. Most of the prisoners had fallen into enemy hands not on the battlefield but during the retreat. Conscripts not yet fully assimilated into the regiment accounted for half the losses.

The battle's positive aspects drew some of the sting of its negatives. Porte's force had dashed the last Unionist hope of seizing Richmond before the election.[21] Had Lincoln lost the coming election and the North abandoned the war, Burgess Mill and the related fighting north of the James might rank among the world's decisive battles. The 12th took 3 enemy flags, the only Federal colors captured in the fight. The conscripts' performance pleasantly surprised the regiment's veterans. Campbell received his reprieve from Lee.

That night the Confederate high command rushed reinforcements to the battlefield to smash Hancock's command in the morning. The Yanks had run low on ammunition. Porte's attack had mauled them. They withdrew from the Plank Road during the hours of darkness.

October 28 dawned clear and cool. "It is difficult to fix my heart upon my eternal interests in times of such excitement," noted Manson. "We are

18 Bernard Diary, October 31, 1864.

19 Ibid.

20 Rolls 514-534, M324, Record Group 109, NA; Henderson, *12VI*, 106-167.

21 *OR* 42, 2:373, proves that Hancock was preparing to cross Hatcher's Run and take the Confederates north of the run from behind before Mahone attacked.

looking for another battle today."[22] Harris' brigade and Hampton's cavalry trudged forward. They found that the Northerners had abandoned about 300 of their wounded. The Confederate pursuers plodded down Dabney Mill Road to the Armstrong's Mill and Vaughan Road crossings of Hatchers Run, meeting only Federal rear guards.

Weisiger's brigade dashed back toward the Dimmock Line. Miles' division of II Corps had feinted against the Confederate fortifications just south of the Crater. Hill worried that the bluecoats were preparing to assault Petersburg. The Virginians staggered into their camp in the pine grove on Walnut Hill at 2 p.m. Little rest awaited them. At dark they tramped off to the breastworks near Battery 45. "So ends another 'On to Richmond,'" Sale observed.[23]

Outside Petersburg the wounded lay in long tents each holding thirty on mattresses on either side of a middle aisle. Mrs. Banister went all the way through the tent she had heard sheltered her Blair without finding him.

"Maybe it is a mistake," she said.

"Mother, don't you know me?" said a ghastly looking fellow in a weak voice.

Mrs. Banister recognized her once handsome son. She remained at the hospital to nurse him. "My old mammy and I went out every day to help her," Blair's sister Anne recalled.[24] Thinking himself in battle, he would try to drag himself up, cheering and hurrahing. Three nights later, he died. His family brought his body back to their home, intending to bury him in the garden with his younger brother. But profound quiet prevailed along the lines. The surviving Banisters took up Norborne's body from the garden, burying him with Blair in the same grave in Blandford Cemetery.

The Virginians liked their new position near Battery 45, though they had to furnish what Sale termed "a tremendous picket."[25] The veterans had learned to feel more at ease on the picket line than in reserve. Being in reserve often meant going into battle. Their enlarged picket detail amounted to half the brigade, allowing the sharpshooters of their division's other

---

22   Manson, "A Spiritual Diary," October 28, 1864.

23   Sale Diary, October 28, 1864.

24   Pryor, "A Child's Recollection of War," *CV*, 39:56.

25   Sale Diary, October 29, 1864.

brigades to take advantage of information garnered from deserters about the Yankee sentries' routine.

On the night of October 29, Mahone inflicted a lopsided defeat on the invaders. His marksmen infiltrated the enemy picket line wearing captured Federal uniforms, seizing 230 sentinels of II Corps without firing a shot or losing a soldier. Todd remembered that "it was considered a very clever trick, and a good joke on 'our friend, the enemy.'"[26]

The prisoners taken at Burgess Mill by the Unionists reached Point Lookout, Maryland and began settling in there. "I arrived here yesterday, all safe, and have been most fortunate in getting quite comfortably fixed," Riddle wrote home on November 1. Peacetime acquaintances in the prison "most kindly took me into their house where I enjoy many kind advantages," he explained. He asked for a box of clothing and tobacco. "Tobacco will buy anything here," he declared.[27]

The resumption of desertion among the Confederates heralded winter's approach. Two men scuttled away on the night of November 2, three more the next evening, leaving as usual from the picket line. Some thought material deprivations accounted for the problem. The government had replaced neither blankets and overcoats abandoned at Burgess Mill nor worn out shoes. Short rations and low pay condemned the troops to a tantalizing position amid plenty. Despite a local bumper crop of sorghum molasses, the commodity sold for the astronomical price of $40 a barrel. Others believed more was involved. Sale thought the deserters tired of fighting. "We have some recruits which have been assigned to us who were very tired of the war before they took any active part in it," he added.[28] The men who deserted around this time included the Richmond Grays' Pvt. Augustus F. Rogers. He had suffered wounds at Malvern Hill, Second Manassas, Gettysburg, the North Anna and Globe Tavern. Now he had endured enough. He made his way over to the Unionists, took the loyalty oath and received transportation to Baltimore. The loss of such a soldier boded ill for the Southern cause.

On November 4, the natural consequence of their virtual annihilation twice within three months—at the Crater and at Burgess Mill—visited itself on the sharpshooter battalion of Weisiger's brigade. Orders disbanded the

26 Todd, "Reminiscences," 252.

27 James C. Riddle to Wife, November 1, 1864.

28 John F. Sale to Aunt, November 29, 1864.

battalion. For the war's remainder, the Virginians did without this useful infantry unit.

Election Day approached in Yankee land. Many believed Northern polling booths would decide the Confederacy's future. "The boys here are about equally divided between little Mac & old Abe," noted Sale.[29] McClellan stood for war conducted in a civilized fashion, Lincoln for what Sale described as war "in a savage manner with destruction and ruin following in the track of their army."[30] Those who wanted Abe reelected argued that this would keep the South united. They thought Mac's election would divide Dixie into a party favoring reconstruction and another insisting on war until independence was established.

Drumming and marching among the Northerners disturbed the peace prevailing on the rainy, unpleasant election eve. The fanfare and foul weather continued November 8, as the bluecoats voted. The 12th's men cut poles and began erecting houses for themselves. On the quiet day after the election, they put chimneys on their houses. November 11 saw the troops deprived of their labors' fruits. Mahone's division shifted its camp to Mayfield, a plantation about four miles west of Petersburg. Porte's troops immediately began building winter quarters again. The same day brought the news that Lincoln had won reelection.

This was the time of year when boards convened to examine officers. Sale had been elected second lieutenant of his company to replace an officer killed at Globe Tavern and passed the examination for the position. Todd passed the examination for his post as acting ordnance officer of Weisiger's brigade but was denied promotion. "The paper went up approved through the regular channel, but was returned by General [Josiah] Gorgas, Chief of Ordnance, with the endorsement that President Davis declined to commission any more Ordnance Officers from Virginia, her quota being full," Todd recalled.[31]

Before the end of the first week of December, the 12th's men had resumed the routine of drills and dress parades they had known since 1861. Reinforcements swelled the regiment's effectives to 298 and the aggregate

---

29 Sale Diary, October 29, 1864.

30 Ibid., November 8, 1864.

31 Todd, "Reminiscences," 261.

present and absent totaled 691.[32] "Prepare to move!" came the cry on December 7. The 12th broke camp at sundown. In high wind and cold rain, the soldiers set out southwestward with the rest of Hill's Corps on Boydton Plank Road. The rain let up as they slogged along. The regiment bivouacked at Burgess Mill. The downpour resumed while the men slept.

The troops rose early next morning, taking up the line of march at seven. "Rumor says the enemy are near Belfield with 2 corps of infantry & 1 division of cavalry," Bernard recorded.[33] Rumor had it largely right. Meade had sent southward under Warren the infantry of V Corps and Mott's II Corps division along with Gregg's cavalry division. Their mission was to finish destroying the Weldon Railroad south to Hicksford on Meherrin River. Once again Hill drew the task of stopping the Yankees with his own corps and Hampton's horsemen. This time Hill's orders called for him to head off the invaders at Belfield on the Meherrin's north bank, opposite Hicksford.

The regiment drew rations on the fly. "The meal was issued to us but nothing to cook it in," remembered Phillips. "During the day on the march we would take it in our hands and lick it like a calf."[34] The troops hiked until 4 p.m. "The roads were as muddy as they could well be, the artillery & wagons were constantly stalling & the men had frequently to lift the cannon & caissons by main strength out of the mud," recalled Whitehorne. "The horses were poor and broken down and were not able to pull them."[35] The 12th's soldiers encamped at Hawkings Church, about four miles south of Dinwiddie Court House. During a frigid nightfall, they built fires of oak and hickory to cook their suppers, burning a lot of wood to prepare ashes for the baking of ash cakes.

Cooks rose at four on December 9, shaping their cornmeal on oilcloths and stacking the cakes by the fire to have breakfast ready when their comrades awoke. The trek resumed at the break of an unusually cold day. Snow began falling while the men traipsed along that afternoon. They crossed Nottoway River at Wyatt's Mill. Ahead they could hear cannon fire. Just beyond the river the column's head reached a fork in the road. One way veered right,

32 Inspection Report, Mahone's Brigade, November 28, 1864, Record Group 109, Entry 15, Box 18, NA.

33 Bernard Diary, December 8, 1864.

34 Phillips, "Sixth Corporal," 66. Phillips confused this march with one of late January 1865.

35 Elmore, *Diary of J. E. Whitehorne*, 57.

southeastward toward Belfield about seven miles away. The other bore left, eastward toward Jarratt's Station. The column camped at the intersection. Soldiers like Whitehorne who had homes nearby took French leave. Others attended to urgent needs.

To survive in any army, a man needs to scrounge. Todd's brother George belonged to the 6th Virginia. That night George came to Todd's wagons in distress. The sole of one of George's shoes had become detached and he had walked all day with it that way. Todd thought of a soldier with a wallet of shoemaker's tools he employed to pick up "smart sums of money."[36] Todd promised to pay him well and to carry the wallet in an ordnance wagon. The shoemaker put George on his feet again.

Mahone conferred with his superior.

"General Hill, if you will allow me, sir, I would suggest that you take one half of the command and go one way, that is to Belfield," said Porte. "I will take the other half and go towards Jarratt's Station and cut them off and we are compelled to capture them all—there is no possible escape."

"No," said Hill. "I have orders to go to Belfield."[37]

Next morning another conference took place among the Southern generals. The Northerners had apprehended the approach of the Confederate infantry and were retreating. Hampton persuaded Hill to adopt a modified version of Porte's plan. Hill would seek to cut off the Federals below Jarratt's Station with his infantry. The cavalry would dog the tracks of Yankee rear guards withdrawing from Belfield.

The Norfolk Division headed for Jarratt's Station and at the Merry Oaks turned south, crossed Three Creeks and struck the Weldon Railroad north of Belfield. The Federals had already escaped to the north. Hill's infantry recrossed Three Creeks and skirmished with the Unionist rear guard of a few cavalrymen who fled precipitously before Mahone's Georgia and Florida brigades in the miserable weather. "The wind howled through the trees, and the rain froze as it fell, glazing everything it touched," recalled Todd.[38] Mahone's beauties followed the Northerners on Surry Court House Road for six miles, then bivouacked at nightfall a few miles east of Lebanon Church. The Virginians pitched their raghouses in the swirling snow, built

36 Todd, "Reminiscences," 266.

37 Phillips, "Sixth Corporal," 66.

38 Todd, "Reminiscences," 266.

fires and ate supper. Exhausted, most of the 12th's troops bundled under their blankets and oil cloths. "When we made fires at night, in a pine woods, the heat of the fires melted the sleet on the trees and we got thoroughly wet," recorded Whitehorne, who had rejoined the column that morning. "We slept but little, and I think it was one of the worst nights I ever experienced."[39]

Next day the Mahone men slogged toward Jarratt's Station in overcast and rain. The final stretch took the 12th along Halifax Road, then across a field, past a dead Confederate soldier. "As the barefooted men crossed the field on the icy snow you could see the blood in their tracks," remembered Phillips.[40] Mahone's beauties found Jarratt's Station burned to the ground, the rails torn up, the cross ties incinerated. The bluecoats had wrecked the railroad from Stony Creek Station to the outskirts of Belfield. "On every side ruin & destruction are visible, not even the negro quarters were spared," Sale recorded.[41] After resting at Jarratt's Station, Hill's Corps shuffled back toward Dinwiddie Court House. "Roads in awful condition," Phillips observed.[42] Several times the nearly starved artillery horses became mired in the mud. The famished infantry pulled the cannon. More of the 12th's soldiers left the column to visit friends and relatives in the surrounding countryside. Those remaining with the colors recrossed the Nottoway at Wyatt's Mill. Two miles beyond they bedded down for another bitterly cold night.

The next day's frigid hike took them to Dinwiddie Court House. Men straggled in from sundown until after nightfall. They built fires then cooked dinner, if they had something to eat. To keep warm they slept two together as they had since 1862. Ice and snow covered the frozen ground. Soldiers and their chums scraped the precipitation away with their feet. Spreading one of their Yankee oil cloths then one of their overcoats, the pair would cover up head and heels with their two blankets and the other overcoat.[43]

The 12th's men slouched back into their Mayfield camp at 1 p.m. December 13. A whiskey ration warmed them, but the liquor cheered them little. The lack of results from their ordeal angered the regiment's soldiers, though the 12th had suffered no casualties. Like the rest of the army, they

39 Elmore, *Diary of J. E. Whitehorne*, 57.

40 Phillips, "Sixth Corporal," 67.

41 Sale Diary, December 10, 1864.

42 Phillips Diary, December 11, 1864.

43 Phillips, "Sixth Corporal," 67.

blamed Hill for the failure to trap the invaders. "Had General Mahone's suggestion been accepted by General Hill, the whole of the raiders would have been captured as easy as eating," concluded Phillips.[44]

The Yankees enlivened the morning of December 18 with a sunrise cannonade. Next day the Confederates learned why. The Northerners were celebrating the victory of Maj. Gen. George C. Thomas over Hood at Nashville.

As usual, happiness at Christmas time depended largely on the degree a fellow had access to friends and family. The men from Petersburg fared best. For the soldiers reliant on the kindness of strangers, luck made the difference between a big eat or the cornbread and middling that camp offered.

Todd and Dr. Baker met William Jarvis as they entered Petersburg to attend Christmas services. The former Lafayette Guards captain now served as major in the 3rd Battalion, Virginia State Reserves. Jarvis invited Todd and Baker to dine with him at his residence on Old Street. "We accepted, and after church enjoyed a capital dinner at the major's hospitable board," recalled Todd.[45]

Sale, who had gotten in trouble for taking thirty-six hours of French leave visiting a cousin near Jarratt's Station, had to remain in camp and endure its meager fare.

Captives from the 12th huddling in Federal prison camps had it worse than the men in camp. "It is only since I have been a prisoner that I have been brought to understand fully that 'hope long deferred maketh the heart sick,'" Riddle wrote home. "I . . . so long to hear from you and the children."[46] He had not received word from his wife since his capture, though he had written her twice and inserted a personal in the New York *News*. Otherwise, Riddle had fared well, gaining an appointment as a surgeon's clerk. He had "a plenty of good wholesome fare a comfortable home and every thing that a prisoner has a right to expect."[47]

One of the lucky fellows who had his request for a furlough granted, Phillips left camp at 10 a.m. on December 23, arriving in Richmond five hours later. News greeted him of Savannah's capitulation to Sherman's army. Phillips spent the next few days going about town visiting his betrothed

---

44 Ibid.

45 Todd, "Reminiscences," 275.

46 James C. Riddle to Wife, December 16, 1864.

47 Ibid.

and his friends. At 7 a.m. on December 28, he boarded the Richmond, Fredericksburg & Potomac for Guinea Station. From there he walked twelve miles to Spotsylvania Court House. Picking up a barrel stave, he carved his dead brother's name into the wood. At 3 p.m., Phillips entered the trees near where the 12th had fought the Yankees on May 12. Soon he found his dead comrades lying on their backs on the slope of Heth's Salient. They had on all their clothing but their hats. Storms had blown these away. They possessed all their equipment except their muskets, which details from the Confederate Ordnance Department had collected. Phillips identified his brother Bob and their fellow Richmond Grays, Sgt. Charles W. Granger and Cpl. James Moreland. Phillips also recognized the Juniors' Cpl. James D. Scribner, the Riflemen's Cpl. (Dr.) Israel F. Disoway, and others.

Phillips confirmed his identification of his brother by checking Bob's haversack and finding the ivy root pipe he had made for Bob at Chancellorsville. Phillips went back to a small home near the court house. Two old ladies lived there. He asked them for a pick and shovel, which they gave him. Thanking them, he hurried back and dug a shallow grave by his brother's side. Laying Bob's corpse in the grave, Jim filled it in and put the marked board at the dead man's head. Phillips did his best to cover Granger with earth. Looking at the others again, Phillips knelt and prayed for them. "I was alone and you can imagine what a feeling I had come over me," he recalled. "Not a soul nearby but those dear dead men, men I had known so long & had been in battle many times."[48]

Night was coming on. Phillips returned the pick and shovel to the old ladies. "They gave me a half dozen nice winesap apples which was little tiny things when we were here fighting 12th May," he remembered.[49] Walking to an outpost, he asked the sergeant in charge of it for permission to spend the night. In the morning Phillips woke early and walked the 12 miles to Guinea Station, barely catching the train back to Richmond. "I have always wished that I violated my leave of absence and remained long enough to have buried all of the dead from our regiment," he recalled.[50]

The remains of many another of the 12th's soldiers lay in an arc running from the Wilderness through Spotsylvania, across the North Anna, past Cold

48 Phillips, "Sixth Corporal," 51.

49 Ibid.

50 Ibid., 51-52.

Harbor and into the woods and fields south of Petersburg. 1864 had proven the regiment's worst in terms of battle deaths. Seventy-nine of its members had perished from combat. The reason for this stood out clearly. On several occasions, the men had fought the enemy hand-to-hand.

One hundred and twelve men joined the 12th, an improvement over 1863. But 177 soldiers left the regiment for good. No change took place in the regiment's structure other than the formation of a company of sharpshooters from its ranks, and this company disbanded before year's end. The 12th's official aggregate strength had dwindled to 677 on December 28.[51] But no more than 631 belonged on the rolls.[52] Clerical errors, a common occurrence, probably accounted for the difference.

51 Inspection Report, Mahone's Brigade, December 28, 1864, Record Group 109, Entry 15, Box 21, NA.

52 Rolls 514-534, M324, Record Group 109, NA; Confederate Rosters, 2:1-56, LV; Henderson, *12VI*, 106-167.

CHAPTER 20

Hatchers Run

During the Christmas holidays the significance of Lincoln's reelection sank in for the 12th's soldiers. The prospect of four more years of hard war weighed heavily on them. "I fear all our suffering, our many privations & sacrifices have been for naught," wrote Sale. "Our rulers have been insufficient in knowledge suitable to their positions or else they have willfully neglected to have their whole attention to them."[1] Bernard observed. "Our prospects look very gloomy, more so than ever before."[2]

As the Continental Army had embodied the American colonies' cause in the War for Independence, so the Confederate Army manifested the South's cause in the Civil War. Usually Sale kept a stiff upper lip in his letters to relatives in enemy-occupied Norfolk, to preserve their morale, but now he leveled with them: "As long as the army kept in good spirits and acted well I could hope for a successful issue but to hear so frequently of the desertion of men who have been among the best soldiers serves to unnerve me."[3] Only two men had deserted from his company since 1862, but desertion had increased in other units. "The army is much dispirited and desertion is not an exceptional affair," Sale wrote. "One night last week 40 North

---

1 John F. Sale to Aunt, January 6, 1865.

2 Bernard Diary, January 1, 1865.

3 John F. Sale to Aunt, January 6, 1865.

Carolinians went off together from one division."[4] These Tarheel deserters had threatened to fire on any force that attempted to stop them. The incident demonstrated the deterioration of Lee's army. Sale became so pessimistic about the prospect of Southern victory that he advised Norfolk families, whose sons had swelled Lee's army that autumn, to keep them home.

While the Confederacy's fortunes plummeted, a notion previously considered taboo became the subject of editorials in the South's newspapers. "Another thing which makes matters worse….is that there is considerable talk in the papers &c about putting an army of negroes in the field," wrote Sale. "Many men who are willing to serve the country still longer are not willing to be placed on an equality with negroes which would not be helped were they placed as soldiers."[5] A rumor circulated about conscripting 30,000 slaves into the Confederate Army and inducing them to fight by offering a land grant and their freedom. Sale, a skeptic, wrote, "nothing will make a soldier of the negro."[6] But Sale had not seen the African-Americans fight.

The veterans welcomed the prevailing sleet and rain, which eliminated any danger of action. Precipitation turned the roads into quagmires making the movement of artillery and wagon trains impossible. The troops cut wood, drew stationery and clothing and tried to keep warm. Whenever possible, they went into town, got drunk, or traded newspapers with the Yankees. The routine of picket duty and dress parades prevailed with one new activity added—patrolling for brigands and deserters. These miscreants made it unsafe at night for anyone near the army. "A large force is kept patrolling for a distance of 15 miles but with every precaution none of the rascals can be caught," Sale wrote.[7]

By mid-January the 12th's ranks were filling. Federal policy on the exchange of prisoners had thawed. The Northerners first released the sick, the old and the very young. Before month's end the Unionists had begun to exchange the able-bodied. But many of the regiment's soldiers in captivity were still waiting their turn to board the truce boat when Yankee maneuvers rousted their comrades at Petersburg from winter quarters.

---

4 Ibid.

5 John F. Sale to Aunt, December 31, 1864.

6 John F. Sale to Aunt, January 6, 1865.

7 Ibid.

On January 15, the Unionists captured Fort Fisher and thus closed Wilmington, North Carolina, the Confederacy's last major port, at the other end of a railroad that ran southeast from Weldon, North Carolina. Most of the Federal Navy's James River Squadron participated in Wilmington's capture, leaving City Point lightly guarded and inviting a sortie of the Confederate Navy's James River Squadron.

Marching orders arrived on the night of January 24, in the middle of a frigid spell deeper than December's, with that squadron on a mission to bombard the Federal supply dump at City Point. The ground froze hard in the intense, dry cold. "As I rode across the pontoon bridge over the Appomattox I felt as if I had not a particle of clothing on me," remembered Todd, who wore a very heavy Federal overcoat.[8] The following afternoon, with the Confederate Navy already having failed in its mission, the 12th left camp heading southwestwardly on Boydton Plank Road in anticipation of an enemy raid on Weldon.

With Mahone on leave the Norfolk Division moved under its senior brigadier, Finegan, nicknamed "Barney."[9] Weisiger had also gone on leave. The 61st's Col. Virginius Groner led the Virginia Brigade. The 12th, commanded by Lewellen, reached Burgess Mill at dusk. The Virginians bivouacked in the woods where they had charged Pierce's brigade the previous October.

After daylight on January 26, Mahone's beauties set out again on Boydton Plank Road. The officers drove the rank and file hard. The intervals between rest halts grew unusually long. Finally permitted to halt, the men became so cold that the officers allowed them for the only time during the war to build fires of Virginia fence rails. The shivering soldiers traipsed through Dinwiddie Court House and across Nottoway River into Brunswick County. "Roads stiff frozen making it very disagreeable to march," Sale recorded.[10] The men left a trail of bloody footprints that stopped at the junction of Boydton and Lawrenceville plank roads, where the regiment bivouacked.

Next day the tramp resumed about sunrise. The route took the hungry soldiers through a countryside teeming with livestock, full of produce and flowing with apple brandy. As the day wore on, causes for celebration developed. The weather moderated. Word spread that the anticipated Federal

8 Todd, "Reminiscences," 267.

9 Ibid., 281.

10 Sale Diary, January 26, 1865.

Joseph Richard Manson, Late in the War
Richard Cheatham, Richmond, VA

raid on Weldon, as Sale noted, had proven "a fizz."[11] Men lucky enough to have relatives along the way went absent without leave to visit them. Manson, the Herrings' captain since July, had recently returned to the regiment from a furlough spent at home with his family. Now he repaired to his farm in Greensville County, just east of the Brunswick border. Bernard, a cousin of Manson's wife, descended upon the Mansons accompanied by Bones Hatcher. After dinner with the Mansons, Bernard and Hatcher had their haversacks and canteens filled by Mrs. Manson.

Even soldiers without connections had little trouble supplementing their rations where pigs ran wild and every farm had a stash of applejack. About sunset the troops staggered into camp in an oak grove on the spread of Dr. George Mason of Greensville County, three miles past the Manson farm. They built rousing fires and pooled their hams, spare ribs and brandy. Combined with their rations of coffee, sugar, beans and bread, the foraging's fruits furnished what Todd termed "a royal repast."[12] The grove echoed with laughter and song far into the night.

The Mahone men spent January 28 awaiting orders, resting and foraging in the bounteous landscape. Applejack kept flowing, eroding discipline.

Next morning dawned bitter cold. The column headed for Petersburg. By now nearly everyone had a canteen full of applejack. "Brandy flowed in large quantities & soon more were under its influence than at any time since commencing active service," Sale recorded.[13] More of the Virginia

11 Ibid., January 27, 1865.

12 Todd, "Reminiscences," 268.

13 Sale Diary, January 31, 1865.

Brigade's soldiers took French leave and proceeded toward their homes. A battalion of cavalry sent to prevent the infantrymen from going absent without leave accomplished little. The first day's return march took the dwindling column to a point on Lawrenceville Plank Road four miles from Nottoway Bridge.

Bernard and Hatcher got posted as guards at the Manson farm until the morning of January 30, when the column and most of the scrounging stragglers had passed. The troops crossed the Nottoway back into Dinwiddie County, bivouacking that night a mile north of Dinwiddie Court House.

January's last day saw the 12th's numb and nearly played out soldiers shamble back into their winter quarters near Petersburg. That afternoon three distinguished Southern commissioners passed through the lines on their way to confer with Lincoln at Hampton Roads. Word had it the Yankees proposed recognition of Confederate independence, restoration of all Secessionist territory, reimbursement for damages done and an alliance to enforce the Monroe Doctrine against the French foray into Mexico. The conference took place at Fort Monroe on February 3. Lincoln offered the commissioners nothing but unconditional surrender, which they could not accept. They began their trip back to Confederate lines the following day.

On February 5, their fellow Southerners still awaited news of the conference's outcome. Grant attempted to catch the Secessionists off guard. Before first light Meade's army advanced westward. II Corps, now under Maj. Gen. Andrew A. Humphreys, slipped along the Petersburg side of Hatchers Run to Armstrong's Mill. Gregg's cavalry division trotted through Reams Station to Boydton Plank Road to intercept the wagon trains reported moving along that route. V Corps slogged along the far side of Hatchers Run to a point halfway between Armstrong's Mill and Dinwiddie Court House, to support the cavalry if necessary. The Yanks easily reached their objectives, but their horsemen captured only a handful of vehicles.

Late that afternoon orders to move out reached the 12th's men. The Virginians hustled to their right, passing over the works north of Hatchers Run, then stumbling through the thickets toward II Corps. Heth was again directing affairs on the Confederate right. He employed Mahone's division to hold II Corps back from Boydton Plank Road. Heth tried to drive his own division down behind the right of II Corps to cut it off from the rest of Meade's army. As the sun set on this clear, windy day, the Mahone men had what Phillips called "a very sharp engagement" with II Corps.[14] Fire from Smyth's division wounded several of the 12th's soldiers and McAllister's brigade repulsed Heth's division.[15] Mahone's beauties did not return to the Petersburg lines until after nightfall.

The Mahone men lay in the lines until noon, then tramped back toward camp. Before they arrived instructions came to head for Burgess Mill at a run. V Corps had withdrawn to the vicinity of Armstrong's Mill the previous evening. Now it had advanced again, striking northwestward on Dabney Mill Road toward the steam sawmill giving the road its name. Near a pile of sawdust so big the Federals thought it a fort, they broke Pegram's division of Gordon's Corps, killing Brig. Gen. John Pegram. Major General John Brown Gordon, a lawyer and mine owner who had risen from the Raccoon Roughs' captain in the 6th Alabama to command of Jackson's old corps, threw Evans' division into the gap and called for reinforcements.

The Norfolk Division's men hastened several miles southwestward to Burgess Mill. The Dabney Mill Road led them eastwardly into the woods where the fighting raged. Rain was falling. The fight was going badly for the Confederates. After initially driving the Northerners, Evans' division had fallen back. Gordon directed Mahone's beauties to form behind Pegram's and Evans' divisions. Barney, still leading Mahone's division in Porte's absence, asked Gordon how his troops would get past the troops in front of them.

"Don't shoot into our men, but run over them if they do not go ahead," said Gordon, who had suffered a wound at Malvern Hill, five at Sharpsburg and another at Shepherdstown.[16]

To plug the hole in the Confederate lines, Finegan used his two leading brigades—the Virginia and Alabama brigades. Weisiger's brigade, still under Groner, filed off by the right flank to the road's right. The Alabama Brigade filed off to the left. The 12th's soldiers double-timed into line across a field. Their left flank came under enemy fire. Yankee bullets hit several men, including Leslie Spence. A partially spent bullet struck him, making a loud sound and turning him half around. He fell into the arms of Phillips.

---

14 Phillips, "Sixth Corporal," 68.

15 Ibid.

16 "Battle of Hatcher's Run," *Weekly Intelligencer* (Atlanta), April 12, 1865, page 1, cols. 5-6.

"You are not hurt, go on," said Phillips.[17]

Spence got up and went into line.

The Virginians and Alabamians finally formed line, facing left and letting pass through their ranks the broken Second Corps troops streaming out of the woods. The 12th's men found themselves under Finegan's eyes. He sat mounted on his handsome chestnut sorrel. Barney wore a peculiar uniform that day—a civilian coat and a beaver hat. He also brandished a walking stick. Hot on the Second Corps men's heels, the enemy appeared—V Corps soldiers from Pearson's brigade of Griffin's division and Baxter's brigade of Crawford's division. The Virginia and Alabama brigades of Mahone's division gave the invaders a volley. Finegan guided his horse forward to lead the Alabamians and Virginians, then ordered a charge.

"On ye go you brave lads," Barney cheered.[18]

With a yell the two brigades crashed forward through the woods. Yankee bullets dropped soldiers right and left. A minnie broke Sale's right arm and burrowed deep into his right side. Private George A. Spence, conscripted in Richmond in 1863 and assigned to the Norfolk Juniors, fell with a bullet in his head. His brother Leslie ran to his side.

The Northerners broke and fled, trying without success to rally on the crests between Dabney's Mill and the Federal earthworks at Armstrong's Mill. The fugitives swept away a VI Corps brigade sent to reinforce them. Mahone's beauties pursued, with the division's other brigades going into line as they arrived. The Mahone men shot down numerous skedaddling Unionists. Finegan, still with the Virginia Brigade, became flushed with excitement.

"Pursue them, me brave Virginny boys, they run like deer," he shouted in his rich Irish brogue.[19]

Undergrowth and trees disordered the Confederate ranks. Barney halted his men to reform their lines, then advanced again. The Secessionists found the Federals gaining the shelter of their earthworks near Armstrong's Mill, their starting point. In the gathering darkness Finegan deployed a picket line. The rest of his soldiers withdrew, some to attend the dead and wounded. The wounded included Ello Daniel—exchanged the previous autumn out

17 Phillips, "Sixth Corporal," 68.

18 Ibid.

19 Todd, "Reminiscences," 282.

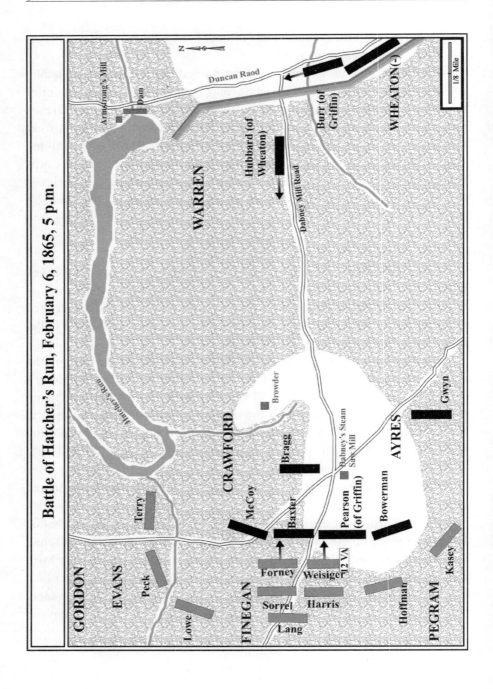

Battle of Hatcher's Run, February 6, 1865, 5 p.m.

of the captivity that began at Bradshaw's farm—as well as Doncey Dunlop and Bernard. "I . . . received a slight scratch on the cheek, the position of my head only saving me from a dreadful wound or perhaps death," Bernard recorded.[20]

Leslie Spence recognized that his brother George was mortally wounded. Leslie asked Phillips for permission to get George off the battlefield. "I could not give it," lamented Phillips, though perhaps no man in the regiment could have sympathized more.[21] Leslie then approached Groner, who also denied permission. Returning to George, Leslie found him still breathing. Leslie took matters into his own hands, calling upon his fellow Richmond Grays for help. Two of them assisted him in carrying George rearward. As they trudged in that direction, George died.

Many of the 12th's survivors were stripping dead Northerners. "Left their manly form stretched out on the cold icy ground without a stitch of garment to hide or shelter their nakedness," complained Phillips, who tried in vain to stop them. "They were sometime or other some dear womans darling who thought the world of them yet this was their end and those people who loved them never saw them again."[22]

The rain became sleet. By the time the exhausted soldiers tottered out of the woods on Dabney Mill Road, ice covered everything. "The smallest limb on a tree as large as your arm was about four times as large covered with ice," Phillips remembered. "So much weight as to break them off and we was uneasy because of these great limbs falling upon us."[23] The troops reached Boydton Plank Road and entered a piece of scrub pine. Scraping away the ice and snow until they got down to solid ground, they spread their wet blankets. The men lacked the means to make fires, but across the plank road the Alabama Brigade's fires blazed in a pine grove. The Alabamians slept so soundly that the Virginians walked over, picked up their axes and firewood and took them back across the road. The 12th's soldiers constructed brush shelters, built fires, then wrapped themselves in their wet blankets and went to sleep. The Alabamians "lay there asleep until they became cold, fire had gone out, all dark, no axe and no nothing," Phillips remembered.

---

20   Bernard Diary, February 9, 1865.

21   Phillips, "Sixth Corporal," 69.

22   Ibid.

23   Ibid.

"We had all and was warm & nicely fixed."[24] About 2 a.m., food arrived. The men had not eaten in more than twenty-four hours. Now they received three days' rations, consisting of, Phillips recalled, "a small piece of corn bread about half as large as an ordinary hand and about four tablespoons of so called corn beef (nothing but corned mule)."[25]

Rain and sleet continued falling after daybreak. "One could scarcely walk without falling," remembered Whitehorne. The men who had not already wolfed down their rations cooked them up, some on frying pans fashioned from half a Federal canteen. Cooking proved an ordeal on this windy day. "It seemed to make no difference on which side the fire one might be the smoke went straight to him," recalled Whitehorne.[26] After breakfast the men built fortifications. Musketry crackled in the woods to the east. The bluecoats advanced across the previous day's battlefields and drove the Confederate pickets back to their main lines. Before dusk the Unionists unsuccessfully charged Weisiger's brigade. An enemy bullet wounded yet another of the 12th's men.

The Northerners remained inactive on February 8. At 1 p.m., the regiment's soldiers left the line, returning to their camp at 4 p.m. to cut wood. Next day they drew a whiskey ration. Manson voiced the thoughts of many comrades, writing, "I bless God for the mercy which has spared my life through another conflict."[27]

The butcher bill for the 12th Virginia came to six killed or dead of wounds, seventeen otherwise wounded and two captured.[28] The enemy had mortally wounded Sale. The ball that had broken his right arm had passed through his right lung and lodged in his bowels. engendering the peritonitis that the doctors of those days, in the absence of antibiotics, could not cure. Cousin Charlie traveled from Richmond to visit Sale at the Fair Ground Hospital on February 11. Charlie found Sale suffering terribly. Next day a Roman Catholic priest administered the last sacrament. Then Sale died. Before nightfall the Juniors accompanied his remains to Petersburg's Catholic Cemetery. "Though brave and chivalrous, his tenderness to others

24 Ibid., 70

25 Ibid.

26 Elmore, *Diary of J. E. Whitehorne*, 58.

27 Manson, "A Spiritual Diary," February 8, 1865.

28 Bernard Diary, February 9, 1865; Henderson, *12VI*, 106-167.

was that of a woman, and his intercourse with all was marked by a suavity of manner which never failed to inspire regard," wrote Owens, a friend of Sale's father, in Johnny's obituary.[29]

Weak from many months of imprisonment, the exchanged soldiers now returning to the ranks could not truly replace the losses for months more. But a new source of troops lay at hand. The Confederates were finally confronting the question of whether to tap their last reserve of manpower—slaves.

The Secessionists reacted to the peace conference's failure by digging in their heels. "We have all resolved to fight them to the bitter end," Whitehorne wrote.[30] The extent of their resolve soon become apparent. Confederates saw themselves as following the path their forefathers had trodden during the War for Independence. One of the steps taken by their forefathers had been to arm some of their slaves and free them in return for fighting the common enemy. But in a conflict in which the very existence of slavery was at issue, such a step seemed anathema. Not until January 1864 was the subject broached. As 1864 passed the Confederacy steadily shrank. Support for such a measure spread. The bravery of blue uniformed blacks provided the idea's proponents with powerful arguments. The prospect of four more years of the Lincoln administration's hard war policy settled the issue. By early 1865 most Southerners stood ready to free and arm slaves to fill the thinning ranks of their armies.

Legislation was introduced in the Confederate Congress. Davis and Lee pressured the Congress to pass the legislation in time for the South to organize and train a substantial force of blacks. Lee encouraged his army's regiments to voice their opinions. In mid-February Lee's regiments held mass meetings to decide whether they would approve a policy of recruiting and arming blacks. The 12th held its meeting on February 15. Jones chaired, appointing a commission to express the regiment's sentiments. The New Grays' Sgt. Lewis Lunsford, Jr., and the Juniors' Pvt. Albert A. Delbridge served on the commission with Jones. They saw the Confederacy left with little choice. By "the cruel and barbarous manner" in which the "public enemy" had conducted the war, the foe had "evinced an unwavering determination" to strip Southerners of "all their rights and privileges as freemen and citizens" and subjugate if not exterminate them. The Lincoln

29 O., "In Memoriam," Sale Papers.

30 James E. Whitehorne to Sister, February 11, 1865.

administration had rejected all Davis' efforts to negotiate an honorable peace. The Federals offered the Confederates "no conditions save those of abject vassals to Northern power & fanaticism." The Yankees had demonstrated to Southerners that they could entertain no hopes of peace save in the maintenance of their cause by force of arms.

The commissioners concurred that the Confederacy should meet "the fierce war spirit of the foe" with "a feeling of stern defiance." They believed the Secessionists justified "in using all the means which Providence" had given them for winning the war. Professing themselves "ready to make all necessary sacrifices in defense of liberty, the right to choose our own rulers, make our own laws and control our own institutions," they proposed cheerful acquiescence if their civil and military leaders deemed "the policy of enlisting and arming negroes as soldiers in the common defense" advisable.[31]

The regiment enacted the resolution with only one dissenting voice out of more than 200 present and voting. The rest of the brigade voted similarly. Such resolutions passed throughout the army. The Confederate Congress heeded the army's voice, ignored the cries of zealots that such a measure was inconsistent with the Confederacy's theoretical underpinnings and finally chose to follow the practical path taken by the colonists in the War for Independence. On February 20, the House of Representatives authorized the enlistment of blacks for service in the South's armies. The Senate followed suit on March 8. Five days later the bill reached Davis' desk. He signed it despite its failure to authorize the government to conscript slaves and emancipate them in return for their services.

The measure came too late. Only two weeks remained before the spring campaign would open. The Secessionists outfitted and trained only two companies of African-American troops. They drilled in Richmond's Capitol Square under the Virginia State Reserves' First Lt. Virginius Bossieux, who had served as a private in the Richmond Grays until February 1862.

Another change that occurred in the Confederacy concerned the Commissary Department. Its failure to provide adequate rations to the soldiers on the field of Hatchers Run outraged the Confederate Congress, leading to the ouster of Commissary Lucius B. Northrop and the department's reorganization. His successor established a new system for collecting supplies, set up depots and improved delivery of rations to the combat troops.

---

31 47-V-1865, M474, Letters Received by Adjutant Inspector General, Record Group 109, NA.

By February's end many of the regiment's prisoners of war had been exchanged—including Edwards, Riddle and Gunn. But many remained in Federal custody, including Bird. Numerous friends and relatives nearby sent him stamps and money. He had sufficient leisure to study Spanish and German. "I would rather die than stay here one single year," he nonetheless complained. "If ever I see a bird encaged at home I shall release it, I can now fully appreciate one's feelings when it beats its breast in vain against the bars of its cage."[32] The 12th's official aggregate strength stood at 30 officers and 624 men.[33] Regiment, brigade and division had participated in nearly all the fighting around Petersburg. They needed a rest.

At March's beginning Feild returned to the regiment, attempting to take charge. But fragments of bone continued to work their way out of his Spotsylvania wound. He returned home on a thirty-day leave of absence. Lewellen had gone into the hospital. Command devolved upon Jones.

Marching orders arrived on March 3's cloudy evening. Amendments came at midnight, directing the regiment to prepare to move out at daylight. Daylight came and the troops did not budge. The clear, warm skies turned rainy and dismal. Speculation ran rampant. Some thought Petersburg and Richmond about to be evacuated. News had just arrived of Sheridan's rout of Early at Waynesboro two days before, prompting others to suppose their destination the South Side Railroad to entrain for High Bridge or Lynchburg.

The 12th left camp at seven that evening. Mahone's division headed for the Howlett Line, the Confederate fortifications across the Bermuda Hundred peninsula's neck. The Mahone men went to relieve Pickett's division. Crossing the Appomattox in a cold rain, they entered a forest. "The march through the woods was terrible," recorded Bernard, one of the many who fell out during the trek.[34] On March 5, Weisiger's brigade took over the formidable earthworks about a mile south of the James. Pickett's division plodded into the Confederate lines north of the river. Stragglers from Mahone's division stumbled into the trenches throughout the day.

The famished, frazzled, threadbare appearance of Mahone's beauties, particularly in the Florida Brigade, shocked the troops in Pickett's division. Nobody called Weisiger's brigade General Lee's Regulars now. But morale

---

32 Henry Van Leuvenigh Bird to Margaret Randolph, February 12, 1865.

33 Inspection Report, Mahone's Brigade, February 28, 1865, Record Group 109, Entry 15, Box 23, NA.

34 Bernard Diary, March 7, 1865.

in the Norfolk Division remained good. "Our men have been so killed out that the division is the smallest in the army, but they can yet whip any one Corps the invaders may throw against us," noted Whitehorne.[35] Pickett's All Virginia Division had benefited from nearly a year in this quiet sector. "Pickett's Division had recruited wonderfully and had become by large odds the largest division in the army," remembered Phillips.[36] But many of the division's soldiers had developed a bad attitude, grumbling that they had done all the hard fighting for Richmond in 1864. They regarded any further strenuous duty as an imposition. Little sympathy existed for them among the Mahone men, who had done far more of 1864's hard fighting. "I fear dissatisfaction has seeped down from its commander and I don't think they can hold the line," observed Whitehorne.[37]

The 12th shifted farther left on the evening of March 6, billeting near Mrs. Howlett's house, where a Confederate battery covered the obstructions in Trent's Reach. The new quarters brought the men within range of the enemy gunboats on the James. The 12th had its first taste of trench warfare since the previous October. Only sixty yards separated the picket lines. About 400 yards lay between the main trenches. Four of the regiment's soldiers took advantage of their proximity to the enemy to desert.

Nightly firing at deserters gave picket duty on the Howlett Line an aspect absent from the rifle pits southwest of Petersburg. Later in March one deserting Floridian was killed and another captured by an officer who lay in wait for them outside the picket line. The departure of the division's faint-hearted for enemy lines represented nothing new. Such migrations had occurred every year since 1862 as the spring campaign's opening approached. However badly desertion affected the "Gophers" (the division's new nickname for the Floridians), the number of deserters from the 12th had decreased annually since 1862. 1865 would prove no exception. Those of Mahone's beauties who did not desert settled quickly into the routine so beneficial to Pickett's division, which included furloughs of twelve hours and upwards when the soldiers could walk to Petersburg or hop trains to Richmond to visit friends and relations. The troops had decent huts, good water and plenty of time for reflection. Phillips resumed work on his company's history, which he

---

35 James E. Whitehorne Diary, March 30, 1865, SHC.

36 Phillips, "Sixth Corporal," 71.

37 Whitehorne Diary, March 30, 1865.

had begun earlier. Manson brought his spiritual diary to a close, observing, "May the terrible scourge of war soon be removed."[38]

Sheridan's cavalry corps was coming down from the Shenandoah. On March 12, the blue coated horsemen reached Louisa County, near enough to Richmond to frighten its citizens. On the Howlett Line, the Mahone men reached an accommodation with the Federals opposite them. Johnny Reb would swap tobacco for Jimmie Yank's sugar, coffee, chocolate, soap, newspapers, chickens and hardtack. They exchanged commodities by throwing them to each other or by depositing them at a log which lay midway between the lines. This commerce generated considerable correspondence. More notes seemed to fly back and forth between the sentries than bullets. The arrangement became so cozy that officers interfered and forbade trading and any other kind of fraternization "in imitation of our respective Governments," wrote Riddle. "I hope very much that we will not get to pickett firing as it accomplishes nothing whatever as a general rule and is only a dangerous annoyance."[39]

On March 18, Petersburg's citizens awarded Mahone a sword, belt and sash in recognition of his services in the city's defense. The presentation occurred near his headquarters in Chesterfield County, where officers, soldiers, citizens and ladies had gathered. As many of the troops as could safely withdraw from the trenches witnessed the event. David Fitzhugh May made the presentation.

The Cockade City could not have selected anyone more appropriate than the father of the City Guard's five "Brave Mays." He bestowed the sword after a short speech, "which was delivered with a depth of emotion not unbecoming a 'noble old Roman,' three of whose sons were 'dead on the field of battle' and a fourth disabled for life," recalled Todd.[40] Unpracticed in public speaking, Mahone replied creditably, releasing from his official report the statistics compiled by his division from his assumption of command until Burgess Mill. The Norfolk Division had captured 6,704 prisoners, fifteen pieces of artillery, forty-two colors, 4,867 small arms, 235 horses, forty-nine wagons and ambulances and 537 slaves. According to enemy sources, the losses in killed and wounded in those commands facing the division totaled 11,000. Mahone maintained that he had inflicted upon the Northerners a

38 Manson, "A Spiritual Diary," March 9, 1865.

39 James C. Riddle to Wife, March 17, 1865.

40 Todd, "Reminiscences," 285.

loss of 17,704 soldiers at the cost of 5,248 killed, wounded and missing.[41] Few if any could claim to have equaled this record.

Porte's record did not please everyone. Corporal John M. Mason of Company A in the 9th Alabama remembered,

> Billey Mahone was allways voluntering to charge. Some place or other he wanted to get his name up for promotion. but he didant think of us poor fellows lives so he came out all right we didant like him anyhow. we didant want a virginian over us. for when we done the fighting he would give the prase to his old Va. brigade that couldant show a good fight. but they were ready to be praised for what other brigades done.[42]

Two days later Lee won one of his least known victories, triumphing on behalf of Virginia over the Davis Administration's quota system. This was denying promotion to many Virginians who had passed the examination for commissions as ordnance officers. Lee circumvented the Confederate version of reverse discrimination by appointing the aggrieved Virginians acting ordnance officers with the rank and pay of second lieutenants of artillery. The 12th had a beneficiary of Lee's maneuver—Todd, still a sergeant though acting ordnance officer of Weisiger's brigade. "I drew back pay for about eight months, about $700.00, and thought myself wealthy, not having had any money scarcely during that time," he remembered. "I immediately bought a breakfast in Petersburg, which cost me twenty dollars."[43]

Lee, recently appointed the Confederate armies' general-in-chief, had restored Johnston to command in the Carolinas. Word arrived that Johnston had battled Sherman at Bentonville in North Carolina. Johnston withdrew to Smithfield in the Old North State. Sherman pushed on to Goldsboro. There Sherman rendezvoused with Maj. Gen. John M. Schofield's army. They paused to regroup and prepare for the journey northward's next stage. Some expected great things of Johnston. Others thought the Bentonville fight meant nothing. Even if Johnston halted Sherman's relentless northward progress, Sherman could still send Grant enough soldiers by sea to compel Lee to abandon Petersburg and Richmond. The Yankee steamboats would get Sherman's troops to Grant long before Johnston's army could join Lee.

---

41 "Presentation of a Sword to Major-General Mahone," Richmond Daily *Dispatch*, March 22, 1865, p. 3, col. 2; Bernard Diary, March 21, 1865.

42 John M. Mason, Jr., ed., *Three Years in the Army or the Life and Adventures of a Rebel Soldier* (Warren, Oh, 1950), 3, 24.

43 Todd, "Reminiscences," 262.

CHAPTER 21

The Appomattox Campaign

On March 24, Grant issued orders launching his ninth offensive at Petersburg. But Lee, not Grant, opened the spring campaign. Like thousands of other Confederates, he realized that Sherman's approach—whether by land or by sea—would soon make Petersburg and Richmond untenable. Lee hoped to slip away from Grant when the roads dried and join Johnston in North Carolina. To keep Grant from starting an offensive and force him to withdraw the Yankee left, making a retreat to the southwest easier, Lee struck at Fort Stedman near the Appomattox on March 25. The attack failed, costing him more men than he could afford. The Federal counterattack critically weakened the Confederate right between Petersburg and Hatchers Run.

Grant aimed his offensive at the South Side Railroad. It commenced on schedule March 27. Two days later the Unionists effected their left's first permanent extension beyond Boydton Plank Road. Sheridan's cavalry slopped through the mud toward Dinwiddie Court House, the key to the entire Southern position. Once the invaders occupied Dinwiddie Court House, they would pose such a threat to the Confederate line of retreat that Lee would have to abandon Petersburg and Richmond.

The regiment's soldiers could hear the fighting Southside that day. Their own situation remained comfortable. Provisions from friends and relatives relieved the monotony of cornbread and bacon. Forty-eight hour passes remained available.

Pickett's division drew the assignment of guarding the Confederate right against Grant's onslaught. Reinforced by part of Bushrod Johnson's division and almost every cavalryman available to Lee, the All Virginia Division splashed out to Five Forks in the rain on March 30. Quiet prevailed on the Howlett Line. Phillips proceeded with the history of his company. Whitehorne began a new volume of his diary on some blank pages in his roll book.

Next day Maj. Gen. George E. Pickett's reinforced division failed to drive Sheridan and his troopers from Dinwiddie Court House. But it looked like Pickett's command would finish the job in the morning. On the Howlett line the 12th engaged in battalion drill and drew sugar, coffee, meal, peas and ham fat. In a picket affair the Confederates left of Weisiger's brigade captured six bluecoats carrying repeating rifles. Recruited in Europe the previous winter, none spoke English. "No wonder Lincoln can give Grant a new army every time we bust his old one," observed Whitehorne.[1]

April 1 dawned cloudy, but the sky soon cleared. Word of the previous day's battle of Dinwiddie Court House reached Mahone's division. Some of the 12th's men received passes. Others visited friends and relatives in nearby units, or entertained visitors from neighboring formations and home. That evening dinner cooked in spiders set over the fires.

"Boom," Whitehorne recorded, "three or four big guns opened at once."[2] Stunned, the regiment's soldiers dashed out of their huts, dugouts and bombproofs and hurried to the breastworks. From there they saw the Federal gunners less than 500 yards distant, blasting away. Fifteen enemy cannon plastered the 12th's houses. Shells knocked corners off some and penetrated the walls of others, exploding inside and tearing things apart. Short of ammunition, the Southern artillery did not reply.

The bombardment ceased after an hour. Quiet returned to the Bermuda Hundred front. One by one, the soldiers ducked back into their houses to assess the damage. Some found their huts wrecked. Others confronted burnt dinners seasoned with dirt and clay. The 12th's men bedded down with orders to be up and in the trenches by daylight, gun in hand. "I reckon Mahone expects a charge from the invaders," noted Whitehorne, who went to sleep with an unexploded shell under his bunk. "Let them come—it takes us to welt them!"[3] Fearing the enemy would open fire again that night after they had gone to bed, some men remained dressed.

1 Whitehorne, Diary, April 1, 1865.

2 Ibid.

3 Ibid.

These fellows proved prescient. They included Whitehorne. His hut provided shelter for himself, his cousin Sgt. William Shelton Davis and Cpl. Algernon Allen. Davis and Allen donned their nightshirts. Whitehorne had just rolled into bed when, he recorded, "Bang! went a big gun which burst over us, but did no damage."[4] He leapt up with his comrades, who ran out barefoot in their nightclothes. When Davis reached the ditch, he jumped in, landing up to his knees in mud and water. Whitehorne remained in their hut to save their blankets, canteens and other belongings. Finally, he got his shoes on, picked up his jacket and sprinted headlong into the ditch, remaining there for about an hour with Allen and Davis.

After the shelling the Virginians prepared to edge rightward. Harris' Mississippi Brigade had held the works in that direction but had departed for Petersburg. About daylight the 12th sidled right a quarter mile and occupied the 6th Virginia's former quarters—cabins which the enemy had not shelled at all. The 12th's men counted noses and discovered that the two bombardments had injured no one. "We have no rations, but can keep from thinking about it by sleeping to make up for the time we lost last night," Whitehorne noted.[5] The troops drawing picket duty found themselves charged and driven in by the Unionists on this previously quiet sector, but the regiment again suffered no casualties. Those who remained awake could only wonder what was happening.

Todd dressed with unusual care that morning, intending to call at Mahone's headquarters, which occupied a comfortable farm house. Mrs. Mahone and Miss Susie Hipkins were paying Porte a visit. Despite the distant roar of artillery around Petersburg, quiet had returned to Bermuda Hundred.

At headquarters Todd encountered Capt. Robertson Taylor, a member of Mahone's staff. Porte, Taylor and Todd stood in the yard talking. A courier galloped up on a lathered horse and swung out of the saddle. Grabbing the courier's dispatch, Mahone read it. His demeanor conveyed the communication's importance.

Calling his own messenger, Mahone ordered an ambulance hitched up to take the ladies to Richmond. Then he entered the house, followed by Taylor. A few minutes later Taylor emerged and gave Todd the news. The

4 Ibid.

5 Ibid.

Yankees had broken through the Confederate lines southwest of Petersburg and killed Hill. Mahone's division had orders to march.

Late on the afternoon of April 1, Sheridan's horsemen—reinforced by a corps of infantry—had crushed Pickett's division and the cavalry of Lee's army at Five Forks, opening the way to the South Side Railroad. Grant feared that Lee would strip his lines to deal Sheridan's force a blow of the sort that had smashed II Corps at Second Reams Station the previous August. The Federal general-in-chief initiated an assault all along the lines for early the following morning. The Union onslaught had the desired effect, breaking through the Confederate lines between Fort Gregg and Hatchers Run and cutting Lee's army in two. Lee ordered the evacuation of Petersburg and Richmond.

Todd mounted up and galloped to Weisiger's headquarters. The news Todd brought did not surprise Weisiger, who had just returned from Petersburg after witnessing the fighting there. Todd hitched his horse at headquarters and ran down the works a short distance to tell his brother George to prepare to move. Returning to headquarters, Todd did not wait long before Mahone's courier arrived with orders for Weisiger's brigade to evacuate the line that night. The artillery would lead the way, pulling out quietly at 8 p.m.

The 12th's men awoke throughout the afternoon and evening into an atmosphere rife with rumors running the gamut from a Federal breakthrough to a Confederate victory. Not until 11 p.m., after the moon had risen clear and calm, did they receive instructions to pack up and prepare to march at 2 a.m. Reports came that the Northerners had annihilated Harris' brigade at Fort Gregg. Mr. May arrived from Petersburg bringing word that the authorities there were burning the warehouses and tobacco barns containing military stores. The veterans tried to get some more sleep before they evacuated the Howlett Line—those not detailed to bury cannon.

Officers and sergeants shook the slumberers awake shortly before 2 a.m. The regiment exited Bermuda Hundred. Abandoning cooking utensils, surplus baggage and company papers, the troops moved by the right flank down the breastworks about half a mile, then filed off westward at a right angle. They halted at Richmond & Petersburg Turnpike. Only the pickets— the Richmond Grays under Phillips—covered the retreat. They had orders to withdraw at 3 a.m., when the moon set, then proceed to Chester Station and act as the column's rear guard.

The 12th rested 15 minutes on the turnpike, then headed for Half Way House. The men had gone a short distance when an explosion stunned them.

The Confederate admiral in command at Drewry's Bluff had fired the magazine there. Another blast followed when the 12th got within a mile of Half Way House. Southern sailors at Rocketts Landing, a few miles upstream, had blown up *Patrick Henry*. The troops passed many ladies standing in their yards crying. The gridiron floated above Richmond and Petersburg for the first time in almost four years.

The regiment reached Half Way House at daybreak. At Chester Station, a few miles west, mounds of clothing and tobacco were burning when the 12th arrived. Horse Taylor snatched 33 undamaged trousers and a jacket from the flames but became so warm, had such a heavy load on his back and got hustled along so fast by the rear guard, that he threw away all but six pairs of pants and the jacket. Giving the jacket to Whitehorne, Horse kept one pair of trousers for himself and distributed the others to his comrades.

The soldiers expected to make a stand at Chesterfield Court House but passed it without halting. Speculation then focused on Burke's Station as a possible rallying point. The roads remained in bad condition, the teams poor and weak. The prospects of making it to Burke's Station looked dim. The troops camped in a chestnut grove. After stacking arms, some went to a nearby creek, washed and bathed their feet. The 12th's soldiers devoured such supper as they had brought with them, then pitched their raghouses and bedded down.

Back at Chester Station, the pickets stood rear guard for Mahone's division until a wagon train passed. Phillips then led his men westward toward Chesterfield Court House, arriving in the afternoon and forming line of battle to meet an expected enemy dash that never materialized. Assigned to protect the trains of Mahone's division, the company headed toward Richmond and later turned west on Genito Road toward Powhatan Station. Phillips' men hiked until 9 p.m.

The Norfolk Division's body broke camp early on April 4. The Mahone men plodded westward through Chesterfield County, passing broken down wagons, ambulances, caissons and cannons. Baggage, papers, clothing, blankets and utensils littered the road. "Once in a while we would come to an Ordinance wagon broken down or mired so deep it could not be moved, with the shells lying on the ground, the powder all poured or thrown out in the mud or water," noted Whitehorne.[6] Weisiger's brigade, at the column's

6 Ibid., April 5, 1865.

end, crossed the Appomattox at Goode's Ford on a pontoon bridge at 4 p.m. Engineers stood by to burn the bridge as soon as the rear guard caught up and stragglers finished passing. Two miles beyond, the Virginians camped in a pine grove.

The Richmond Grays rejoined the 12th there. Awakening at three that morning, the Grays shambled along behind the wagon train. "Caissons were abandoned & we set fire to them & blowed them up," remembered Phillips. "Shot & shell we scattered in every direction."[7] Within two miles of Powhatan Station, the Grays left the wagons and took the road to the left, which eventually led them back to Mahone's division. Phillips' company lost at least 10 soldiers to straggling and desertion. The Federals wounded but a single man.

The Virginia Brigade drew one day's ration of bacon and cornmeal. Lacking their spiders, the soldiers made up and baked their meal in their frying pans. The companies had no more meal on hand. "This will be out tomorrow night and where we are to get any more heaven only knows," recorded Whitehorne.[8] The 12th's men went to sleep footsore and exhausted. Though they had tramped 23 miles, they had orders to move by 3 a.m.

Rising half an hour earlier, they trudged the nine remaining miles to Amelia Court House without a rest. In a field near the county building, they found their wagons and cannon parked. Lee had massed most of his army at Amelia Court House the previous day. He could not proceed farther because the rations he had ordered shipped there on the Richmond & Danville did not arrive. The forces that had arrived at Amelia Court House on April 4 had spent that day foraging, allowing the invaders to block the way to Burke's Station.

The 12th's soldiers halted. The Mahone men each drew a small piece of meat. An hour later they staggered toward Painesville in response to a report that the enemy had captured 300 Southern wagons. After four miles the division returned to Amelia Court House. Cutting across a farm on a little lane, Mahone's beauties then trekked westward on Deatonsville Road. Two miles from Amelia Court House, the column's van encountered Union cavalry videttes. Skirmishers from the Georgia Brigade advanced and cleared the road, capturing 25 enemy troopers. The column resumed its hike.

7 Phillips, "Sixth Corporal," 72.

8 Whitehorne, Diary, April 4, 1865.

Resting occasionally, the ravenous soldiers shuffled along until night fell. Those with the foresight and forbearance to have saved some of the pones cooked the previous evening gobbled them. Scarcely had they finished when they took to the terrible roads again, rambling all night across Flat Creek's bridge and past fire-gutted Amelia Springs Resort. Indications of demoralization multiplied. If a wagon stalled, its occupants threw part of its contents on the roadside. The officers' slaves loaded themselves with this plunder until they broke down and threw it all away. Some of the exhausted, hungry troops "fell down on the road & remained all night & were picked up by the enemy," recalled Phillips. His company lost two more men that night.[9]

Before daybreak on April 6, a little rain fell. At sunup near Deatonsville, the Mahone men halted to shake what crumbs they could from their haversacks. They had eaten everything they had left by the time they fell in again. The soldiers marched without another rest until 3 p.m., when they reached Rice's Station and heard heavy picket firing ahead. Heth's and Wilcox's divisions, shattered in the fighting of April 2, stood in line of battle across Burke's Station Road. Yankees blocked the way, forcing Lee's army to turn west toward Lynchburg instead of southwest toward Danville and a junction with Johnston's army in North Carolina. The Norfolk Division took up a supporting position, with Weisiger's brigade occupying a hillside. Soon the musketry got hot and the artillery quickened. The Virginians had to hug the clay to avoid the shells.

Their wagons lumbered along far behind on Burke's Station Road. Yankee cavalrymen nipped at the column's flanks. Roadside skirmishes had become common. Todd received instructions to send for his wagons by a road which forked to the right, and to follow in person with one wagon the soldiers who kept to Burke's Station Road. Just as his wagon reached the hill's brow, overlooking the valley of Big Sailor's Creek, a strong force of enemy cavalry attacked an artillery battalion in front of him. The remnant of Pickett's division and part of Bushrod Johnson's division engaged the bluecoats. The fighting grew severe.

Todd left his wagon on the hill. Riding forward across the creek to ascertain the situation, he found "great excitement and disorder." Whipped men were coming to the rear saying, as usual, that everything was "cut to

9 Phillips, "Sixth Corporal," 73.

pieces."[10] He met some acquaintances who informed him that the enemy had captured the artillery battalion and taken possession of Burke Station Road. Todd returned to his wagon and ordered the driver to turn around and dash for the other road. The wagon had nearly reached it when a courier galloped up with an order from Ewell, now the Department of Richmond's commander, directing Todd to come forward to supply ammunition to the remnant of Pickett's division, which had lost its ordnance wagons at Five Forks. Todd recalled, "I immediately returned, crossed the 'creek,' ascended the hill, and soon found myself in a trap—for, instead of wanting ammunition, the men whom I saw would have prized seven league boots more than any other commodity."[11]

While the Federal cavalry blocked the column, VI Corps pressed the Confederates from behind. Anderson, commanding the Secessionist column's van, attempted to break through the Northern cavalry while Ewell at the column's tail tried to halt VI Corps. Anderson's attack allowed his staff and some stragglers to escape but did not help the trains. The wagons in front of Todd remained immobile. He could not proceed. The Confederate troops engaged with the Unionist cavalry broke and came running back. One of their officers asked Todd to help him rally his men, which Todd attempted in vain, finding the Secessionist line shattered and the enemy in hot pursuit. "The minnie balls were 'zipping' by us with unpleasant frequency," he remembered.[12] He spurred back to his wagon. From there he could see approaching bluecoats who had overwhelmed Ewell's command. Todd told his driver to abandon the wagon and try to make his escape. Leaving the main road on his left, Todd galloped into the forest and attempted to steer between the enemy's two lines.

In the woods he joined the surgeon of Harris' brigade and the ordnance officer of Bushrod Johnson's division. None of them had a weapon. They did not get far. As they emerged from the woods into a field, a Yankee cavalry lieutenant 20 feet away cocked a revolver, demanding their surrender. Spying a dismounted Unionist cavalryman nearby with rifle ready, the Southerners complied. The enemy lieutenant, whom Todd described as "a red-headed, red-bearded and red-faced rascal," took hold of their horses' reins and robbed

10   Todd, "Reminiscences," 296.

11   Ibid.

12   Ibid., 297.

Todd's fellow ordnance officer of his watch.[13] A Confederate color bearer emerged from the woods with his banner. The Federal lieutenant ordered the color bearer to bring in his flag.

"Damn you, come and take it," replied the color bearer, simultaneously directing a color guard to fire.[14] The Yankee lieutenant's horse fell dead. Quickly picking himself up, the lieutenant "ran like the devil was after him," Todd recollected. "His sabre got between his legs and tumbled him over as he reached a slight declivity, and disappeared, leaving us free again."[15] Todd and his companions remounted and entered a skirt of woods on their right. Emerging from the trees, "we ran plumb into a whole regiment of Federal cavalry," Todd remembered. "[Its] Colonel could not help laughing at our astonishment."[16] He sent Todd and his comrades to the prisoner rendezvous guarded by several cavalrymen who joined the captives in nipping at the surgeon's canteen of medicinal brandy.

After two hours on the hillside near Rice's Station, the Virginia Brigade withdrew to Burke's Station Road under heavy fire. Weisiger's troops headed to the rear for a short distance, then took a lane to the right. Soon they heard heavy firing. The Norfolk Division formed line across the lane on the high ground overlooking Big Sailor's Creek to prevent the enemy from capturing the rest of the army's trains. Porte's troops opened ranks to allow the rabble who had escaped to pass. The Northerners did not advance. The Mahone men remained until 10 p.m., then departed, leaving nothing behind but a few cavalry pickets.

The battle of Sailor's Creek struck Mahone's beauties as a disgraceful affair on the parts of Anderson's and Ewell's commands. Mahone's division lost all its wagons and ambulances. The 12th had one man wounded—Pvt. Edward Shefferson, detached from the Archer Rifles to serve as a teamster. The enemy captured Todd, Shefferson, some other troops on detached duty with the trains and a few stragglers. The Unionists may have taken captive as many as 17 of the regiment's men.[17]

---

13 Ibid., 298.

14 Ibid.

15 Ibid., 299.

16 Ibid.

17 Ibid.; Phillips, "Sixth Corporal, 73; Henderson, *12VI*, 106-167; Elmore, *Diary of J. E. Whitehorne*, 78-79, 82-84.

The Norfolk Division reached High Bridge around midnight, now acting as rear guard for Lee's army. Deploying to wait until everyone else crossed, Mahone's beauties tried to snatch such sleep as they could. They crossed the Appomattox on High Bridge in a drizzle at 2:30 a.m. Such transportation as remained to the division crossed on a nearby pontoon bridge. Porte allowed his soldiers to rest about a mile north of the crossings. He returned to oversee the bridges' destruction, which would slow the Yankee pursuit and arrived at the spans at 7 a.m. They remained intact with enemy skirmishers rushing toward them. The engineers fired the bridges. Some pickets and a few pieces of artillery remained on a hill north of the river to annoy the invaders. The pickets included a squad from the 12th's New Grays.

Prodded by a few shells from the approaching Federals of II Corps, Mahone's division resumed its tramp northwestward on Jamestown Road behind the wagon train. "We could not move fast owing to the want of good teams," Whitehorne recorded. "Our mules are broken down and travel slowly and we could not go before the wagons."[18] Behind this column the Unionists extinguished the fires on the bridges. The flames had not done their work. By 9 a.m., the Northerners had repaired the pontoon bridge and began crossing the Appomattox. Scattering the Confederate pickets west of the bridges, the bluecoats resumed pursuit of Lee's army while the Unionists south of the river kept trying to head off the Secessionists. The pickets from the New Grays who escaped at the bridges included Robert Thompson, busted to private since Burgess Mill.

Four miles west Mahone's division was approaching Cumberland Church and the intersection of Jamestown and Cumberland Court House roads. Secessionist cavalry rode back toward the bridges to reconnoiter and reported that the Federals had crossed the river in force and would soon attack Porte's column. Lee ordered Mahone to occupy a line across Cumberland Court House Road at Cumberland Church, facing north and east. The church stood on a hill southwest of Jamestown Road and north of the track that the wagon train would take westward. The cannon of Poague's battalion unlimbered behind and to the right of Mahone's division. When Lee's order arrived Mahone was already forming line of battle in anticipation of such instructions. His men needed another 20 minutes to fashion with bare hands and bayonets what Whitehorne termed "a tolerable

18 Whitehorne Diary, April 7, 1865.

breastworks."[19] Porte covered his front with skirmishers. One company from each of the Virginia Brigade's regiments advanced as pickets. In the 12th this duty fell to the Riflemen, directed to come in if pushed hard.

The pickets driven from High Bridge by II Corps sought their commands. Thompson followed the South Side Railroad southwestward. By 1 p.m., he had recrossed the Appomattox to Farmville. There he found men unloading food from a railroad car and he obtained some bacon. Soon he encountered Maj. Henry E. Young, Lee's Judge Advocate General, who stopped Thompson.

"Where are you going?" asked Young.

"To my command," said Thompson.

"Where is your gun?" Young asked.

"I threw it away at High Bridge where the Yankees got up to me while I was left on picket line," Thompson said.

"You go over there," said Young, gesturing toward a motley collection of soldiers nearby. "There are a lot of stragglers that we are going to try and arm."

"I have always gone into a fight with my command and I mean to join them," said Thompson.

"I will shoot you if you do not go," said Young.

Thompson picked up a musket on the roadside. Young rode in front of Thompson.

"Are you going to stay here?" asked Thompson.

"I am going to make you join that command," Young said.

"If you stop me here I mean to shoot you," Thompson said.

Previously "very rude & abusive," recalled Thompson, Young became polite.

"Are you going to your command?" Young asked. "All right, go ahead."[20]

Thompson went his way. In minutes the stragglers swept by him on the run with Young leading them. Bursting Yankee shells tracked the crowd. Wagons drove by in what Thompson called "a regular stampede" with their occupants tossing out their contents.[21] He crossed the Appomattox again at Farmville and headed northward to rejoin the 12th. Enemy troopers occupied Farmville shortly afterward.

---

19 Ibid.

20 Statement of Robert George Thompson.

21 Ibid.

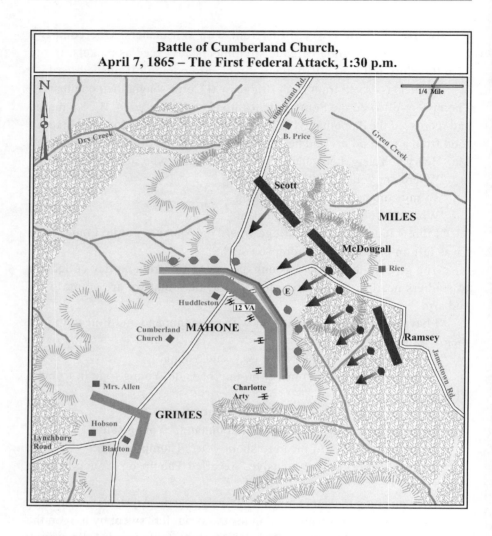

Firing commenced at Cumberland Church about three miles north of Thompson as the Confederate rear guard tried to stop II Corps. Skirmishers from Miles' division drove in the Riflemen. An enemy bullet nicked Tayleure. The Riflemen tumbled in over the breastworks. Southern cannon opened on the enemy, visible at the woods' edge around 400 yards distant. But the Federals did not press the Confederate line at this point. Their attack focused to the 12th's right. There the Northerners got in among the unsupported Charlotte Artillery's fieldpieces. Mahone summoned Grimes' division of Gordon's Corps from its post near the junction of the wagon

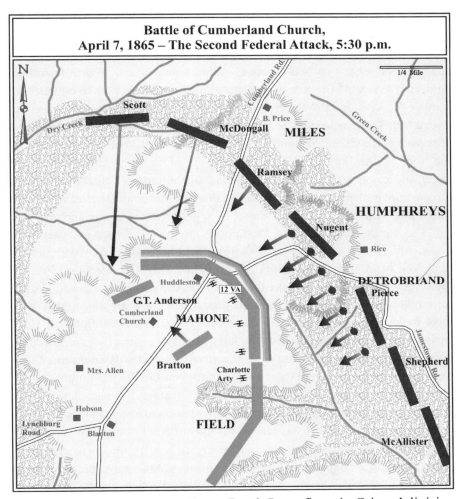

track and Cumberland Court House Road. Porte flung in Grimes' division and drove back the Unionists. Field's division of Longstreet's Corps arrived and relieved Grimes' division, which returned to its previous position.

A lull followed, broken only by an occasional exchange of shots with skirmishers from Miles' division. Thompson arrived, rejoining the regiment in time to witness a shell from a Confederate cannon kill a lieutenant in the 41st Virginia. "We were lying down in front supporting the battery," remembered Thompson.[22] The shell exploded at the cannon's mouth.

22 Ibid.

At 4 p.m., the 12th's men saw a Unionist battle line appear about a mile beyond the Confederate left. The Federals swung around in the rolling countryside trying to turn Mahone's flank. "The quick eye of General Mahone saw at once what they were about," Whitehorne noted.[23] Porte borrowed Anderson's Georgia Brigade from Field's division and posted it to outflank the Yankee flankers. In minutes the 12th's soldiers saw the blue battle line come over a hill. The Northerners received a fire which cut many down. Numerous survivors surrendered. Simultaneously, another Federal column advanced up the slope against the Confederate brigades left of the Virginians "in beautiful order and came on yelling like demons," according to Whitehorne.[24] Well directed fire pushed the bluecoats back in disorder and confusion, leaving many killed and wounded. The Confederates jumped over the works and charged.

The Yanks called it a day. "I suppose the invaders were satisfied they could not run over Mahone," Whitehorne observed.[25] At dark pickets deployed beyond the breastworks to prevent a surprise. Weisiger directed the troops in the works to make themselves as comfortable as possible until midnight. Then they would have to depart. "We are all thoroughly wet, have had scarcely any sleep for three days, have had nothing to eat since early yesterday morning and now he tells us to make ourselves comfortable, how absurd, maybe he intend[s] it as a joke," recorded Whitehorne.[26] The regiment's soldiers spread their rubber cloths on the miry ground.

For the eighth time in 11 months, Mahone's beauties had locked horns with II Corps—the most pugnacious corps in the Union army.[27] On this occasion the Federals suffered 571 casualties, no fewer than 171 of them captives.[28] The Southerners had relieved of its flag the 5th New Hampshire, which had given the 12th its baptism of fire at Seven Pines. Mahone's forces suffered fewer than 200 casualties.[29] They included only Tayleure in the 12th.[30]

23 Whitehorne Diary, April 7, 1865.

24 Ibid.

25 Ibid.

26 Ibid.

27 Fox, *Regimental Losses*, 3, 8, 10-14, 115-116, 122-424.

28 Chris Calkins, *The Appomattox Campaign: March 29–April 9, 1865* (Conshohocken, PA, 1997), 202.

29 "CWSAC Battle Summary," National Park Service, Washington D.C.

30 Henderson, *12VI*, 106-167.

The Virginians departed Cumberland Church on schedule at midnight on April 8. Rain was still falling. The men slogged along on terribly muddy roads. Their route took them north and west through Curdville toward New Store, past hundreds of wagons broken down or stuck. The weary soldiers, who had eaten nothing except a little parched corn all day, halted only for the wagon trains to catch up. In the evening enemy cavalry charged the wagons. Stragglers including Horse Taylor repulsed the Yankees. Taylor suffered a serious wound but fought until the wagons were safe. During the trek to Amelia Court House four days earlier, the usually pleasant Allen had turned on Taylor, telling him that the war was closing without him having ever done anything to help the South. Allen's remark hurt Taylor and he put up a stiff fight just to show Allen. "Bitter words made a coward fight like a wild man," observed Whitehorne.[31]

The regiment bivouacked at 6 p.m. near Holiday Creek, beyond New Store. To their joy the famished troops drew a day's ration of meal and bacon. They made up the flour in oilcloths, baked it on hot rocks, then tucked in to what some of them considered the best supper of their lives. Men who had thought themselves finished now felt ready for more marching and fighting. Cannonading resounded ahead. Rumor had it that the enemy had gotten in front of them again. The Virginians bedded down expecting plenty of action on the morrow.

The Norfolk Division broke camp before sunrise on April 9. Fighting still raged far ahead. The Mahone men traipsed three miles, halting at daylight. Resting 15 minutes, Mahone's beauties crept forward another three miles, past New Hope Church and a farm called Pleasant Retreat. Arriving within a mile and a half of Appomattox Court House, they could hear firing on several sides.

The firing ceased. The column halted. "All the men were jubilant as we concluded we had whipped the enemy and put their guns out of commission," recorded Whitehorne. "The road seemed clear."[32] Stacking arms, most of the troops tried to snatch some sleep. Wagons kept rolling past them toward the court house.

At 10 a.m., the wagons finished passing. The troops fell in again and took up arms. Instead of going to the front, the Mahone men retraced their steps for a mile to Pleasant Retreat. Forming line of battle facing north in

---

31 Whitehorne Diary, April 7, 1865.

32 Ibid., April 9, 1865.

an open field, the soldiers stacked arms once more. Reflexively, they began erecting breastworks. The men remained full of spirit and eager to have a go at Sheridan and the Yankee cavalry.

Several Federal officers had ridden in and out of camp under flags of truce that morning. The 12th's soldiers attached no significance to them. Soon Mahone came up and told the men to stop building breastworks, their digging was unnecessary. This puzzled some. "We did not know what to think," remembered Whitehorne.[33] Others became suspicious. "We began to smell a mice," recalled Phillips.[34] One of the regiment's lads came running toward to his comrades at a dog trot.

"The jig is up," he cried.[35]

Whispers spread the report that Lee had surrendered the army. The troops were thunderstruck. "We were profoundly convinced that Lee would ultimately triumph in spite of all odds," remembered Tayleure.[36] But Weisiger confirmed the report's truth.

"All the officers cried and most of the privates broke down and wept like little children and Oh, Lord! I cried too," Whitehorne recorded.[37] Officers pushed the blades of their swords into the ground and broke them. The rank and file did the same with their bayonets. Rather than surrender the 12th's old rag, Phillips and William Smith tore up that bullet-riddled banner while the Old Grays' Pvt. James Cook Birdsong, an apprentice printer captured at Chancellorsville and wounded at Cold Harbor, watched. Taking a star and a part of the red and white colors for his own, Phillips distributed the rest to anyone else who wished a scrap, and Cpl. Francis Charles Stainback of the City Guard received the portion of the flag that read "12th. Va."[38] The scene became too much for Mahone. He rode away.

Soon the soldiers learned the details. Lee had held a council of war the previous night. The Yankees confronted the remnant of his army on three

---

33 Ibid.

34 Phillips, "Sixth Corporal," Private Collection of Elise Phillips Atkins, 74.

35 "A Brooklyn Man Got It: The Sword Which Was Made For Jefferson Davis," Brooklyn *Eagle*, November 30, 1890, p. 17, cols. 5-6.

36 Ibid.

37 Whitehorne Diary, April 9, 1865.

38 See John Horn, "The Last Battle Flag of the Petersburg Regiment," petersburgcampaign@ blogspot.com, May 6, 2018.

Phillips Flag Fragment. The inscription reads: "This portion of a star is the center of star from the Battle Flag of the 12th Va Infantry, which I with my own hands tore it up at Appomattox when we surrendered on the 9th of April 1865. I divided it out to those who wished a portion of it. I have cut off four of the points from time to time one piece to D. M. Dunlop, one to Leroy S. Edwards & others. I also have my sword which I had on and the dirt has never been wiped off since I returned. J. E. Phillips, Capt Richmond Grays". *Elise Phillips Atkins, Arlington Heights, IL*

sides. The council decided to try breaking through the enemy's line near Appomattox Court House at daybreak. They would surrender the army if the attack failed. The army's cavalry and the foot soldiers of Gordon's Corps charged the Northerners at the appointed time, at first making headway against Sheridan's horsemen. Then the Southerners ran up against infantry and retired.

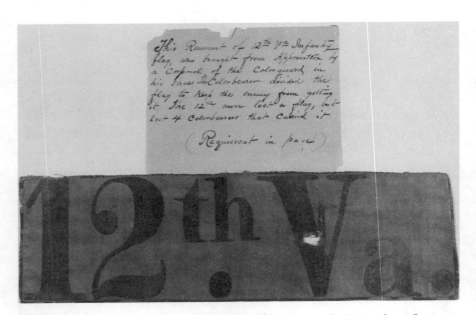

Stainback Flag Fragment. The inscription reads: "This Remnant of 12th Va Infantry flag, was brought from Appomattox by a Corporal of the colorguard in his shoe. The colorbearer divided the flag to keep the enemy from getting it. The 12th never lost a flag, but lost 4 colorbearers that carried it (*Requiescat in pace*)". *Francis Charles Stainback Collection, Virginia Military Institute Museum, Virginia Military Institute*

The surrender humiliated Whitehorne. "I have a feeling we are not being true or loyal to our countless comrades who gave up their lives during this four years," he noted. "What would Jackson, or Stuart, or—any of them say about us?"[39] His fellow Mahone men raged that the rest of the army, except for Field's division, had let them down. "I wish General Lee had called on Mahone's Division to make that attack this morning," Whitehorne recorded.[40] Mahone's beauties told themselves that Lee knew best.

The 12th's lads pitched their raghouses in the open field at Pleasant Retreat. That night Weisiger's brigade formed line and visited the remnant of Harris' brigade to bid the Mississippians good-bye. Often adjacent to one another in the division's order of march, the two brigades had fought side by side on many fields. A special bond existed between them. Jones made a speech thanking the Mississippians for their heroism, fortitude and gallantry.

39 Whitehorne Diary, April 9, 1865.

40 Ibid.

Brigadier General Nathaniel Harrison Harris responded with an address of his own thanking the Virginians for the high opinion expressed of his men. By the time the Virginians returned to their camp, a pale watery moon had risen. "Last night we were free soldiers of the Southern States," wrote Whitehorne, "tonight we are defeated men, prisoners of the Northern States."[41]

The men of Mahone's division first contacted their captors on April 10. That the enemy had not whipped them on the battlefield recently made the division's soldiers doubly hostile to the Federals. "They were remarkably respectful," Whitehorne wrote of Yankee officers he had seen that day. "They look mean and sheepish and will not look at our men boldly."[42] The speech Mahone made that rainy day reinforced the defiant attitude of some of his soldiers. He told them that the blame for Lee's surrender did not lie with them—they had done their duty like brave men. Porte also announced the surrender's terms. The troops would get paroles rather than go into Northern prison camps. They would go home carrying their private property. Officers would retain their side arms. These terms met with approval.

Later that day Mahone's beauties drew rations from the Unionists. "Nothing so well became the conquerors as their generous treatment of their late adversaries," remembered Tayleure. "Rations were promptly and freely issued to our starving men, and in many instances money was given them to help on their way homeward."[43] The pickings varied among the 12th's men. Some drew only crackers while others got beef, sugar and coffee as well.

The division's soldiers remained at Pleasant Retreat the following day awaiting paroles that did not come. Persistent rain kept everything wet and muddy. The men received small pieces of beef and remained hungry unless lucky enough to have acquaintances in this desolate part of the state.

The regiment's troops experienced a degree of reconciliation with the Federals that day. A Northern officer who had attended school with Jones visited him that day. "We saw him come up and hold out his hand—the Major did nothing for so long it was painful," recalled Whitehorne. "Then he took the offered hand and I had a feeling the war was really over."[44]

41 Ibid.

42 Ibid., April 10, 1865.

43 "Bad Effect of Lincoln's Assassination," Vicksburg *Evening Post*, January 7, 1885, p. 2, col. 3.

44 Whitehorne Diary, April 11, 1865.

The rain continued and the bluecoats failed to provide the 12th's soldiers with any food at all on April 12. On that day, the old Norfolk Division gave up its arms.

Falling in that morning, the Mahone men waded through two miles of mud to Appomattox Court House. With Porte ill, they marched under his senior brigadier, Harris. At the court house they found V Corps assembled under Maj. Gen. Samuel Wylie Crawford, a former doctor whose division they had helped destroy at Globe Tavern the previous August. The invaders stood in two columns facing each other 40 paces apart. Mahone's beauties passed in review between the lines of Federals, then closed in to the left and halted. Facing the front, the Southerners dressed to the right, fixed such bayonets as survived and stacked arms. "They did not look at us, did not look defiant, did not make disrespectful remarks," remembered Whitehorne. "Our men marched up boldly and stacked arms and did not seem to mind any more than if they had been going on dress parade."[45] Then the Confederates faced right again and countermarched by file from between the columns of Yankees and back to camp at Pleasant Retreat. "Such a disagreeable day I never spent before," recalled Phillips.[46]

The paroles arrived at 9 p.m. that evening. Company commanders and first sergeants who had retired for the night jumped up, borrowed pens and ink, scrounged scraps of tallow candle and improvised candlesticks by jabbing old bayonets in the soft soil. Within an hour they prepared the paroles, had Jones sign them and distributed them. The troops could leave for home next morning as early as they chose. Whitehorne, who had scarcely eaten anything since the 10th, helped prepare the paroles for the Huger Grays. "Two signatures on a piece of paper—one in the spring of 1861 which made me a soldier—the other in the spring of 1865 which makes me----," he wrote. "I feel very weak and pale."[47]

Like the rest of the regiment's soldiers, he wanted to head homeward as early as possible next morning.[48]

45 Ibid., April 12, 1865.

46 Phillips, "Sixth Corporal," VHS, 75.

47 Whitehorne Diary, April 12, 1865.

48 For some of their journeys home, see John Horn, "Even a Stranger to My Children," petersburgcampaign@blogspot.com, March 22, 2018.

CHAPTER 22

The River of Men

T h e river of men flowing through the 12th had reached its journey's end. The regiment's last campaign had seen four of its soldiers wounded. One of them, Shefferson, fell into enemy hands. The 12th lost to capture, desertion or straggling 98 other officers and men of around 296 present when Petersburg's evacuation began. Twenty-one officers and 180 men ended the war at Appomattox. Sixteen of those officers and all those men surrendered with the colors, five officers with other formations.[1] Only about 24 of the approximately 200 infantry regiments in Lee's army reached Appomattox with as many soldiers.[2]

The regiment's field and staff who surrendered included Jones, commander of the 12th in most of the battles during the war's last years; Hugh Smith, the regiment's last adjutant; Surgeon Claiborne, still accompanied by his mare despite minnies and horse thieves; Stevens, the regiment's quartermaster; and Quartermaster Sergeant Spottswood, one of the few who had fought at Sharpsburg.

Members of the Petersburg City Guard who reached Appomattox included Cogbill, wounded carrying the colors at Malvern Hill; Ivey, captured at Chancellorsville; George W. May, co-captor of 27 Federals at Globe

---

1 "Paroles of the Army of Northern Virginia," *SHSP* (1887), 15:303, 347-348, 350-352; Todd, "Reminiscences," 299; John H. Claiborne, "Last Days of Lee and His Paladins, an Address Delivered before A. P. Hill Camp of Confederate Veterans, of Petersburg, Va., on the Evening of the 6th of March, 1890," *War Talks*, 266; Bernard, Appendix, *War Talks*, 323-324; Elmore, *Diary of J. E. Whitehorne*, 78-79, 82-84; Phillips, "Sixth Corporal," 71-76; Henderson, *41st Virginia Infantry*, 107; Henderson, *12VI*, 106-167.

2 "Paroles of the Army of Northern Virginia," 15:1-487.

Private Henry T. Booker of the City Guard, a former clerk wounded and captured at Crampton's Gap, made it to Appomattox despite a buttock wound at Heth's Salient that caused a serious rectal infection.

U. S. Army Historical Education Center

Tavern; William Harrison, captured after Burgess Mill; and David Fitzhugh May, Jr., the last of the company's five brothers from the wealthy May family—three brothers dead and a fourth crippled gave the lie to the notion of a rich man's war and a poor man's fight. Waddell, on leave at the time of Petersburg's fall, would apply for his parole on May 14 in Raleigh, where he had joined his family.

The Petersburg Old or "A" Grays numbered among those who surrendered Tom Pollard, who led the 12th out of the pocket at Burgess Mill; Sam Brown, who saved Chase at the Crater; Simmons, who recovered Dean's body after the Crater; and William Smith, the regiment's last color bearer.

Soldiers of the Petersburg New or "B" Grays making it to Appomattox included Campbell, who helped capture a flag at Burgess Mill; Lunsford, who assisted drafting the resolution in favor of recruiting slaves; Thompson, who prevailed in his argument at Farmville with Lee's Judge Advocate General; and two soldiers joining the regiment more than once—Cpl. James M. D. Tatum, who reenlisted in 1862 after a medical discharge in 1861; and Pvt. William B. Donnan, conscripted in 1864 after a medical discharge in 1862 and paroled after a transfer to the Invalid Corps on March 23, 1865.[3] Private Charles David "Charley" Blanks and Magee, by then a first lieutenant, laid down their arms with this company after returning from furloughs but did not receive paroles.[4]

The Lafayette Guards surrendered Tyler, who commanded the brigade's sharpshooter battalion; Laughton, wounded seven times during the war; Erastus Ferguson, formerly of the Herrings, wounded in the Wilderness and

3 Henderson, *12VI*, 159. If Donnan had still belonged to the Invalid Corps, he would have been paroled with the Invalid Corps, as five other former 12th Virginia soldiers were. William G. Nine and Ronald G. Wilson, *The Appomattox Paroles: April 9-15, 1865* (Lynchburg, VA, 1989), 247.

4 Allen W. Magee to James M. Quicke, n.d., *War Talks*, Appendix, 322-324.

Private Joseph R. Gray of the Huger Grays, captured at Gettysburg's Bliss farm, and wounded and captured at Burgess Mill, made it to Appomattox. *Otis Historical Archives, Armed Forces Medical Museum, Armed Forces Institute of Pathology, Washington, D.C*

at Cold Harbor, now a first lieutenant; and Pvt. James Skelton Gilliam, Jr., who had transferred to the 41st Virginia in 1862 but transferred back to the 12th before the its last campaign's beginning.

Members of the Petersburg Riflemen giving up the struggle at Appomattox included Charles Walsh, the literacy class' teacher during the harsh winter of 1863–1864; Robbins, who with Walsh and George Bernard escaped captivity at Bradshaw's Farm; Daniel, captured at Bradshaw's Farm; Dick Davis, who lost the flag he captured at the Crater; Turner, who made it wounded through the woods to safety after Burgess Mill; Richard May, who assisted Turner that night; Bones Hatcher, captor of an enemy banner at Burgess Mill; Hartwell Harrison, who helped the mortally wounded Banister off the field at Burgess Mill; Riddle, captured at Burgess Mill and subsequently exchanged; and Tayleure, the only one of the regiment's soldiers wounded at Cumberland Church.

From the Huger Grays, those surrendering included Whitehorne, twice wounded and always grumbling; his cousin, William Davis; Allen, who had shared their hut; and Horse Taylor, the regiment's last man to take a bullet.

Soldiers from the Richmond Grays ending the war at Appomattox included the compassionate Phillips; Mayo, survivor of the bloodbath east of Heth's Salient and now a sergeant: and Gunn, who joined the regiment more than once and was captured at Cold Harbor.

Among those who surrendered with the Norfolk Juniors stood Owens, the head of the brigade's Masonic Lodge; and Albert Delbridge, another member of the commission framing the resolution in favor of recruiting Confederate States Colored Troops.

Members of the Meherrin Grays or Herrings, making it to Appomattox included Manson, who carried Bernard off the field at Crampton's Gap; Welton, whom Richardson saved at the Crater; and George Pollard, captured with William Harrison after Burgess Mill.

The Archer Rifles surrendered among others the fearless, hard-swearing Chappell, the pious Hayes, and two soldiers who had stepped into the river twice. Private Robert McLemore received a special discharge in 1861 to do government factory work but reenlisted in 1862. Private Louis K. Wagner, discharged because of his Russian citizenship in 1861, enlisted as a substitute in 1862.

Five officers ended the war at Appomattox while absent on duty with higher military organizations. Crippled at Crampton's Gap, the Riflemen's Morgan surrendered as a lieutenant keeping the medical records at Lee's headquarters. The Riflemen's Patterson, now a captain, was paroled as Acting Assistant Inspector General of Mahone's division. Weisiger, the regiment's original commanding officer, surrendered in command of his brigade. Cameron, another joining the 12th more than once, surrendered as Assistant Adjutant General of Weisiger's brigade. Former courier Jimmy Blakemore surrendered as a second lieutenant and Ordnance Officer of Ransom's brigade in Bushrod Johnson's division.

The rank and file the regiment surrendered exceeded in number the muskets they carried. Severely wounded Horse Taylor and at least 26 support personnel or men knocked loose from soft spots in the rear left no more than 153 likely musket bearers.

Just one of those who probably lacked muskets belonged to the 12th's only company originally enlisting for the duration, the Herrings, who may have carried thirty muskets, nearly a fifth—two average companies' worth—of the regiment's likely maximum of 153. They had more soldiers in their ranks at the surrender, lost fewer men on the retreat to Appomattox and shed fewer deserters during the war than any other company of the 12th. Well-educated outfits like the Riflemen made outstanding contributions to the officer corps and the Confederate administrative apparatus, but Lee's command was defeated for want of more companies like the Herrings.

With 10 companies like the Herrings, the regiment would have surrendered 300 rank and file, all but 10 of them bearing muskets. At Appomattox Lee had only two infantry regiments that strong. Weisiger's brigade, if composed of companies like the Herrings, would have ended the war with 1,410 men, all but 47 carrying muskets.[5] Only one of Lee's 39 infantry brigades surrendered that strong.[6]

During the 12th's existence, 1,538 officers and men belonged to the regiment. What had become of the 1,337 who did not surrender at Appomattox? Death accounted for 279. The Federals killed or mortally wounded 159. Many regiments on both sides suffered more deaths from enemy action than the 12th, including the 5th New Hampshire, which the 12th opposed on its first and last days of land combat and which of the more than 2,000 infantry regiments in Union service lost more killed and mortally wounded than any other.[7] Some Federal heavy artillery regiments lost more killed or mortally wounded in a single day than the 12th suffered throughout the entire war.[8]

But with more than 10 percent of its soldiers killed or mortally wounded, the 12th suffered a higher percentage of killed and dead from wounds than the "nearly 10 per cent" that the Confederate armies generally lost.[9] Had the 12th fought for the Union, it would have merited a place among the United States Army's "Three Hundred Fighting Regiments," where the criteria for inclusion required a loss of at least 130 killed or mortally wounded, or 10 percent of the unit's total enrollment.[10] On most of its battlefields, the regiment faced one or more of the Union's "Three Hundred Fighting Regiments."[11]

The 12th's losses of more than 57 percent at Crampton's Gap and more than 41 percent at Globe Tavern number among "Remarkable Percentages Of Loss In Confederate Regiments In Particular Engagements."[12] This represents a surprising result for a formation which fellow Southerners claimed "never stood a charge," or "couldant show a good fight," or ought to have given its muskets to men who would fight.[13] Even the regiment's

<hr>

5 The 16th Virginia had only seven companies by this time, and Weisiger's brigade thus only 47. Trask, *16th Virginia Infantry*, 8-9.

6 "Paroles of the Army of Northern Virginia," *SHSP*, 15:144. Bratton's South Carolina Brigade of Field's division in Longstreet's Corps had 1,549 officers and men at Appomattox. Ibid.

7 Fox, *Regimental Losses*, 3, 15.

8 Ibid., 17.

9 Ibid., 555. "The average loss in the Union Armies was 5 per cent," writes Fox. Ibid. See Table 1. This table is illustrative rather than definitive.

10 Ibid., 122.

11 See Table 2. This table is illustrative rather than definitive.

12 Ibid., 556-558. See Table 3. This table is illustrative rather than definitive.

13 Waters and Edmonds, *A Small but Spartan Band*, 144.

Table 1:   The 12th Virginia's Losses Compared with Other Confederate Regiments

REGIMENT	DIVISION	KILLED OR DIED OF WOUNDS	PERCENTAGE LOST DURING WAR
6th Alabama	Rodes'	373*	17.6%*
8th Alabama	Mahone's	300*	21.1%*
14th Alabama	Mahone's	281*	19.4%*
5th Alabama	Rodes'	276*	16.0%*
10th Alabama	Mahone's	268*	18.7%*
15th Alabama	Field's	257*	15.7%*
3rd Alabama	Rodes'	251*	15.2%*
6th Georgia	Hoke's	239*	18.4%*
12th Alabama	Rodes'	234*	16.5%*
11th Alabama	Mahone's	222*	21.9%*
4th Alabama	Field's	229*	16.1%*
3rd Georgia	Mahone's	221*	14.9%*
18th Mississippi	McLaws'	214*	14.9%*
21st Mississippi	McLaws'	210*	17.0%*
16th Tennessee#	Cheatham's	209*	16.7%*
48th Georgia	Mahone's	200*	14.3%*
9th Alabama	Mahone's	192*	16.8%*
18th Georgia	McLaws'	184*	14.8%*
7th North Carolina	Wilcox's	184*	12.6%*
8th Georgia	Hood's	168*	13.3%*
22nd Georgia	Mahone's	164*	13.2%*
33rd Virginia	E. Johnson's	164*	11.8%*
60th Georgia	Early's	162*	12.2%*
12th Virginia	**Mahone's**	**159***	**10.3%***
23rd Georgia	Hoke's	153*	13.5%*
49th Virginia	Early's	153*	12.3%*
42nd Mississippi	Heth's	150*	15.1%*
20th Tennessee#	Breckenridge's	147*	12.3%*
48th Alabama	Field's	146*	13.9%*
49th Georgia	Wilcox's	142*	12.2%*
55th North Carolina	Heth's	140*	10.7%*
59th Alabama	B. Johnson's	139*	9.4%
14th Georgia	Wilcox's	138*	12.5%*

Table 1 (continued)

REGIMENT	DIVISION	KILLED OR DIED OF WOUNDS	PERCENTAGE LOST DURING WAR
13th Alabama	Heth's	138*	11.0%*
34th Virginia	B. Johnson's	138*	7.1%
44th Alabama	Field's	135*	12.3%*
47th Alabama	Field's	131*	12.2%*
35th Georgia	Wilcox's	128	10.0%*
6th Virginia	Mahone's	124	7.5%
57th Virginia	Pickett's	112	6.2%
60th Virginia	Wharton's	109	5.8%
41st Virginia	Mahone's	105	7.0%
27th Georgia	Hoke's	104	9.0%
41st Alabama	B. Johnson's	102	7.0%
3rd Virginia	Pickett's	101	9.3%
23rd Virginia	E. Johnson's	99	9.0%
8th Virginia	Pickett's	99	7.7%
48th Virginia	E. Johnson's	96	7.3%
16th Virginia	Mahone's	92	7.5%
60th Alabama	B. Johnson's	92	7.4%
58th North Carolina#	Stevenson's	91	4.5%
1st Virginia	Pickett's	89	7.9%
30th Georgia#	Walker's	85	7.3%
43rd Alabama	B. Johnson's	83	7.3%
54th Virginia#	Stevenson's	83	4.5%
59th Virginia	B. Johnson's	81	3.3%
61st Virginia	Mahone's	76	6.5%
9th Virginia	Pickett's	76	4.5%
61st Alabama	Rodes'	71	7.9%
63rd Virginia#	Stevenson's	68	4.4%
Average Confederate Regiment			Almost 10%

* Meets criterion for Fox's Fighting 300 Regiments (130 or 10% killed or died of wounds).
\# Army of Tennessee.

own members underestimated it, calling it "a Saratoga trunk regiment," and styling themselves the "Kid Glove Boys."

One hundred and sixteen of the regiment's soldiers perished of disease. Their predominantly urban origins accounted for the low ratio of deaths by

Table 2:   The 12th Virginia's Losses Compared with Union Regiments

REGIMENT	BATTLES INVOLVING 12TH VIRGINIA	KILLED OR DIED OF WOUNDS DURING WAR	PERCENTAGE LOST DURING WAR
5th New Hampshire	Seven Pines	295*	11.8%*
20th Indiana	King's School House	201*	14.3%*
87th New York	"	29	2.8%
1st United States Sharpshooters	Malvern Hill	153*	10.9%*
18th New York	Crampton's Gap	39	3.5%
31st New York	"	71	7.6%
32nd New York	"	45	4.3%
8th Pennsylvania Cavalry	Chancellorsville	60	1.8%
1st Delaware	Gettysburg	158*	7.6%
12th New Jersey	"	177*	9.5%
106th Pennsylvania	"	104	9.7%
140th Pennsylvania	Bradshaw's Farm	198*	17.4%*
51st Pennsylvania#	Spotsylvania	177*	8.6%
12th Massachusetts	North Anna	193*	12.6%*
35th Massachusetts	"	148*	9.8%
2nd New York Heavy Artillery	Cold Harbor	214*	4.2%
1st Vermont Heavy Artillery	Gurley House	164*	7.1%
62nd New York	"	98	6.9%
14th New York Heavy Artillery	Globe Tavern	226*	9.0%
155th New York	Second Reams Station	115	13.8%*
170th New York	"	129	12.8%*
63rd Pennsylvania#	Burgess Mill	186*	13.8%*
105th Pennsylvania+	"	245*	12.2%*
12th Virginia		**159***	**10.3%***
Average Union Regiment			5.0%

* Meets criterion for inclusion in Fox's Fighting 300 Regiments (130 or 10% killed or died of wounds).
\# Lost a flag to the 12th Virginia that day.
\+ Lost two flags to the 12th Virginia that day.

disease to deaths in combat because of the immunities developed by urban soldiers. Deaths by disease often amounted to double the deaths in combat in more rural units.

Besides the victims of enemy action and disease, one man was executed and three more died accidentally.

Less drastic forms of honorable separation took their toll, such as transfer, purchasing a substitute, resigning, refusing to stand for reelection, or other lawful forms of discharge. They accounted for the absence of 510 more soldiers from the 12th's last bivouac. Dishonorable forms of separation, such as desertion, discharge for absence without leave, taking the loyalty oath while in captivity and getting cashiered, accounted for the absence of another 137 officers and men at Appomattox.

Besides these 909 soldiers lost to the 12th, 428 more had become separated. Captivity accounted for the absence of 181 of the regiment's officers and men.[14] As of Lee's surrender, this many were in or on their way to Federal prison camps. Though lost to the 12th for good, they would have appeared on an official return as, "Absent With Leave or Prisoners." Another 120 went on detail, detached duty or furlough never to come back. Official returns listed them as absent on detached service or absent with leave. The balance of 127 soldiers unaccounted for at Appomattox probably died, deserted or failed to recover from their wounds or illnesses.

In early April 1865, the allegation arose that 60,000 Virginians deserted or were absent without leave.[15] The 12th lost at least 127 soldiers to desertion during the war. Thirty-one of the regiment's men were absent without leave on February 28, 1865, the last time a count was taken. If all Virginia's other infantry, cavalry and artillery units suffered proportionate losses to desertion and absence without leave, the total would have fallen far short of 60,000—even assuming all 127 of the 12th's men unaccounted for at the war's end had deserted. But Virginia fielded few other units as well-fed, well-disciplined and highly motivated as the Petersburg Regiment.[16]

---

14 Nine hundred and nine soldiers accounted for 926 separations because some joined the regiment twice or thrice.

15 J. B. Jones, *A Rebel War Clerk's Diary at the Confederate States Capital*, 2 vols. (Philadelphia, 1866) 2:464.

16 Savas Beatie intends to publish a roster online at www.savasbeatie.com.

Table 3:   A Comparison of the 12th Virginia's Losses

REGIMENT	BATTLE	DIVISION	PRESENT	LOSS	PERCENT
1st Texas	Sharpsburg	Hood's	226	186	82.3
21st Georgia	Second Manassas	Ewell's	242	184	76.0
26th North Carolina	Gettysburg	Heth's	820	588	71.7
6th Mississippi	Shiloh	Hardee's	425	300	70.5
8th Tennessee	Murfreesboro	Cheatham's	444	306	68.2
10th Tennessee	Chickamauga	Johnson's	328	224	68.0
Palmetto S'shooters	Frayser's Farm	Longstreet's	375	254	67.7
17th South Carolina	Second Manassas	Evans'	284	190	66.9
23rd South Carolina	Second Manassas	Evans'	225	149	66.2
44th Georgia	*Mechanicsville*	*D. H. Hill's*	*514*	*335*	*65.1*
1 Ala. Battalion	Chickamauga	Preston's	260	168	64.6
2nd N. C. Bn.	Gettysburg	Rodes'	240	153	63.7
16th Mississippi	Sharpsburg	Anderson's	228	144	63.1
27th North Carolina	Sharpsburg	Walker's	325	199	61.2
5th Georgia	Chickamauga	Cheatham's	317	194	61.1
2nd Tennessee	Chickamauga	Cleburne's	264	159	60.2
15th and 37th Tenn.	Chickamauga	Stewart's	202	121	59.9
6th Alabama	Seven Pines	D. H. Hill's	632	373	59.0
20th Tennessee	*Chickamauga*	*Stewart's*	*183*	*108*	*59.0*
16th Alabama	Chickamauga	Cleburne's	414	243	58.6
15th Virginia	Sharpsburg	McLaws'	128	75	58.5
6th and 9th Tenn.	Chickamauga	Cheatham's	335	194	57.9
18th Georgia	Sharpsburg	Hood's	176	105	57.3
12th Virginia	**Crampton's Gap**	**Anderson's**	**150**	**86**	**57.3**
1st S. C. Rifles	Gaines' Mill	A. P. Hill's	537	306	56.9
10th Georgia	Sharpsburg	McLaws'	148	84	56.7

Table 3 (continued)

REGIMENT	BATTLE	DIVISION	PRESENT	LOSS	PERCENT
18th North Carolina	Seven Days	A. P. Hill's	396	224	56.5
3rd Alabama	Malvern Hill	D. H. Hill's	354	200	56.4
18th Alabama	Chickamauga	Stewart's	527	297	56.3
17th Virginia	Sharpsburg	Pickett's	55	31	56.3
7th North Carolina	Seven Days	A. P. Hill's	450	253	56.2
12th Tennessee	Murfreesboro	Cheatham's	292	164	56.1
22nd Alabama	Chickamauga	Hindman's	371	205	55.2
9th Georgia	Gettysburg	Hood's	340	189	55.0
16th Tennessee	Murfreesboro	Cheatham's	377	207	54.9
4th North Carolina	Seven Pines	D. H. Hill's	678	369	54.4
20th Tennessee	*Murfreesboro*	*Breckenridge's*	*300*	*163*	*54.3*
27th Tennessee	*Shiloh*	*Hardee's*	*350*	*190*	*54.2*
23rd Tennessee	Chickamauga	Buckner's	181	98	54.1
12th South Carolina	Second Manassas	A. P. Hill's	270	146	54.0
4th Virginia	*Second Manassas*	*Jackson's*	*180*	*97*	*53.8*
8th Georgia	Gettysburg	Hood's	312	168	53.8
4th Texas	Sharpsburg	Hood's	200	107	53.5
27th Tennessee	*Perryville*	*Cleburne's*	*210*	*112*	*53.3*
1st South Carolina	Second Manassas	A. P. Hill's	283	151	53.3
49th Virginia	Seven Pines	D. H. Hill's	424	224	52.8
29th Mississippi	Chickamauga	Liddell's	368	194	52.7
12th Alabama	Seven Pines	D. H. Hill's	408	215	52.6
7th South Carolina	Sharpsburg	McLaws'	268	140	52.2
58th Alabama	Chickamauga	Stewart's	288	149	51.7
7th Texas	Raymond	John Gregg's	306	158	51.6
6th South Carolina	Seven Pines	D. H. Hill's	521	269	51.6
15th Georgia	Gettysburg	Hood's	335	171	51.0

Cont. ...

Table 3 (continued)

REGIMENT	BATTLE	DIVISION	PRESENT	LOSS	PERCENT
11th Alabama	Frayser's Farm	Longstreet's	357	181	50.7
17th Georgia	Second Manassas	Hood's	200	101	50.5
37th Georgia	Chickamauga	Stewart's	391	194	50.1
3rd North Carolina	Gettysburg	Johnson's	312	156	50.0
63rd Tennessee	Chickamauga	Preston's	402	200	49.7
41st Alabama	Chickamauga	Breckenridge's	325	158	48.6
4th Virginia	*Chancellorsville*	*Trimble's*	*355*	*172*	*48.4*
32nd Tennessee	Chickamauga	Stewart's	341	165	48.3
1st Maryland	Gettysburg	Johnson's	400	192	48.0
8th Mississippi	Murfreesboro	Breckenridge's	282	133	47.1
44th Georgia	*Malvern Hill*	*D. H. Hill's*	*142*	*65*	*45.7*
32nd Virginia	Sharpsburg	McLaws'	158	72	45.5
1st Arkansas	Chickamauga	Cleburne's	430	194	45.1
18th Mississippi	Sharpsburg	McLaws'	186	83	44.6
9th Kentucky	Chickamauga	Breckenridge's	230	102	44.3
14th South Carolina	Gaines' Mill	A. P. Hill's	500	215	43.0
20th Tennessee	*Shiloh*	*Breckenridge's*	*380*	*159*	*41.8*
39th North Carolina	Chickamauga	B. Johnson's	247	103	41.7
33rd North Carolina	Chancellorsville	A. P. Hill's	480	199	41.4
12th Virginia	**Globe Tavern**	**Mahone's**	**94**	**39**	**41.4**
5th Alabama	Malvern Hill	D. H. Hill's	225	92	40.8
Hampton Legion	Seven Pines	Hood's	350	141	40.2
26th Alabama	Malvern Hill	D. H. Hill's	218	86	40.0

This table is illustrative rather than definitive. The 12th Virginia is in **bold**. Italics mark the other regiments with more than one documented remarkable loss: the 20th and 27th Tennessee, the 4th Virginia and the 44th Georgia. The chart is based on Fox, *Regimental Losses*, 556-558; McMurray, *Twentieth Tennessee*, 365; John W. Busey and David G. Martin, *Regimental Strengths and Losses at Gettysburg* (Hightstown, N. J., 2005), 280; and Clark, *North Carolina Regiments*, 2:719. I have accepted McMurray's figures on the 20th Tennessee's losses at Chickamauga (108 of 183) over Fox's (88 of 183).

Epilogue: A. P. Hill Camp, United Confederate Veterans

Eddie Whitehorne may have put best a question in the minds of all the regiment's survivors:

> Lord! The war has been going on so long I can't realize what a man would do now it's over. All I know is to drill, and march, and fight. How can we get interested in farming or working in a store or warehouse when we have been interested day and night for years in keeping alive, whipping the invaders, and preparing for the next fight?[1]

For almost all the 12th's survivors, the need to feed themselves and their families provided sufficient motivation for a quick return to civilian pursuits. Though many of the Petersburg Regiment's soldiers joined militia units after Reconstruction, only one emigrated after the Civil War. The Huger Grays' George T. Mason, educated in Europe, obtained a commission in the French Army and died in Tonkin, French Indo-China— now known as Vietnam.

James Edward "Eddie" Whitehorne. *Fletcher L. Elmore, Louisville, KY*

1 Whitehorne Diary, April 9, 1865.

Everard Meade Feild. *Virginia Historical Society*

Mahone returned to the Norfolk & Petersburg's presidency. After expanding it into the predecessor of today's Norfolk Southern Railway, he led a coalition of Republicans, Readjusters and blacks to victory in Virginia's 1881 elections and became a United States Senator. By his term's end, the tide had turned in the Democrats' favor. When he died in 1895, his victory at the Crater had come to symbolize the South's triumph over Reconstruction and reformers such as himself.

Weisiger returned to business in Petersburg and later moved to Richmond. Feild, who unsuccessfully attempted to return to the regiment during its retreat to Appomattox, relocated from Greensville County to Petersburg, becoming active in business, politics and veterans' affairs. Lewellen moved to Danville and edited the *Danville Register*. Jones became a prominent educator, teaching mathematics at Randolph-Macon College.

The City Guard's Cameron studied law and edited several newspapers. William Harrison served as Petersburg's collector of Internal Revenue for the United States government. Francis Stainback walked home to the Cockade City with the portion of the regiment's flag reading "12th. Va." in his shoe.

The Old Grays' William Smith returned to construction in Nashville, Tennessee. He would die in the Philippines in 1899 as colonel of the 1st Tennessee Infantry, United States Volunteers. Birdsong moved to North Carolina, becoming its state librarian.

When the New Grays' Bird got out of the prison camp at Point Lookout, he returned to Petersburg, married his sweetheart and entered business. Brown managed hotels in Richmond and later, in the Blue Ridge. Magee became a tobacconist. Marks resumed life as a Petersburg merchant. Hugh Smith manufactured soap and candles. Doncey Dunlop moved to Baltimore.

Philip Francis Brown. *Virginia Historical Society*

The Riflemen's George Bernard tried unsuccessfully to return from furlough to the 12th during the retreat to Appomattox. Afterward, as he rode down the Shenandoah Valley toward home, he encountered a wagon train rolling in the opposite direction, "as if nothing had happened," remembered Bernard, who

> often recalled the appearance of this organized party of Confederates—the last I ever saw—quartermaster, or wagon-master, and teamsters, still in the faithful discharge of their duty, solemnly and slowly moving to their point of destination in obedience to the orders of some superior officer whose commands had, when they were issued, the bayonets of the once powerful Army of Northern Virginia, to enforce them, but which now was a thing of the past.[2]

Bernard returned to law practice in Petersburg, as did his half-brother, Meade. Todd, after his release from prison on Johnson's Island in Lake Erie, practiced law in Norfolk. Edwards became a prominent educator. Richard May served as superintendent of schools in Lunenburg County. Turner established himself in Petersburg as a merchant in dry goods. Dick Davis studied law and became a prominent attorney, as did Robert Henry who had suffered a severe wound while serving on Mahone's staff at Burgess Mill. Blakemore relocated to New York. Keiley founded the Petersburg *Index*. James Claiborne worked as the medical agent for several civic and business concerns in Petersburg. John Claiborne's reunification with his wife and children probably typified the experiences of his fellow family men:

> Four years before, almost to the day, at my home in Petersburg, I had taken them in my arms, and giving a last kiss and "God bless you" I had gone out

---

2 George S. Bernard, ed., in Claiborne, "Last Days of Lee and His Paladins," *War Talks*, 284.

William Hodges Mann. *Virginia Historical Society*

with my comrades and compatriots to the war, with brilliant uniforms and flying banner, with heart full of hope . . . and now, alone, ragged, unaccompanied by one single comrade, unheralded, without country, without home, without faith and without bread, I was before them, even a stranger to my children.[3]

He resumed the practice of medicine in Petersburg. William Hodges Mann, who had served as a scout behind enemy lines after his Seven Pines wound disabled him, studied law. Morgan moved to Baltimore and entered the grain and mining businesses. Shepard taught chemistry at Randolph-Macon College. Stith went into hotel management. Tayleure, who noticed a distinct chill in relations between North and South after Booth's assassination of Lincoln, moved back to New York and managed public housing in South Brooklyn. There he may have rubbed shoulders with his old comrades from the 7th New York National Guard.

The Huger Grays' Whitehorne relocated from Pleasant Shade in Greensville County to Petersburg and went into the dry goods business. Scott departed Virginia for Texas—perhaps embarrassed by his granduncle, Old Fuss and Feathers. One of General Scott's Dinwiddie County nephews deposited the old man's portrait in a millpond after the war.

The Richmond Grays' Jim Phillips married his girl soon after returning to Richmond. He eventually resumed work as a tinsmith. Two points of the star he took from the 12th's old rag at Appomattox went to Dunlop and Edwards. Miles Phillips returned to work as a wall paper hanger and upholsterer and became a leader in Richmond's Volunteer Fire Association. Laughton became active in veterans' affairs. Spence became a successful businessman and helped reorganize the Richmond Grays to participate in Grant's funeral and Grover Cleveland's inauguration. Mayo became a prominent Richmond

---

3 Claiborne, "Last Days of Lee and His Paladins," *War Talks,* 272.

George Smith Bernard. *Virginia Historical Society*

lawyer and businessman. Commanding the 25th Battalion, Virginia State Reserves, Elliott had played a minor role in the conspiracy to kidnap Lincoln that led to his assassination by Booth. Elliott returned to civilian life as a Richmond newspaper editor. Whitlock helped establish Richmond as a major tobacco center.

The Juniors' Owens returned to Norfolk, where he founded another Masonic Lodge.

Robust in health and strong of intellect, the Herrings' Manson repaired to his Brunswick County spread.

Fletcher Archer, who had raised the Archer Rifles, resumed law practice. Chappell returned to bartending.

Some of the 12th Virginia's veterans grew prominent politically. George Bernard became Petersburg's Commonwealth Attorney. Meade Bernard became Commonwealth Attorney of Brunswick County. Robert Henry served as Commonwealth Attorney of Wise County. Meade Bernard and Mann ascended to the bench. George Bernard, Brown, Dick Davis, Elliott, Keiley, Mann, Hugh Smith and Charles Walsh served as state legislators. Cameron and Fletcher Archer became majors of Petersburg, while Keiley served as mayor of Richmond and Shepard became mayor of Ashland, Virginia. Cameron and Mann served as governors of Virginia. Keiley received an appointment as the International Court's President. He died under the hooves of runaway horses in Paris in 1905.

The regiment's soldiers formed veterans' groups soon after the cessation of hostilities. The A. P. Hill Camp became Petersburg's United Confederate Veterans chapter. Richmond veterans joined the R. E. Lee Camp and Norfolk veterans the Pickett-Buchanan Camp, both of which with the A. P. Hill Camp and the Stonewell Camp of Portsmouth formed the Grand Camp Confederate Veterans, Department of Virginia. Within the A. P. Hill Camp, the 12th's members predominated, developing their own style of writing history. They published addresses on the war's various battles in newspapers and in the Southern Historical Society's papers, then circulated the articles among their comrades, soliciting comments. In 1892, the A. P. Hill Camp published the results of these round robins in *War Talks of Confederate Veterans*, compiled and edited by George Bernard. He had another volume ready for publication in 1896, but it disappeared, reappearing at a flea market in 2004. Purchased for 50 dollars, it sold for $15,000 to the History Museum of Western Virginia and in 2012 was published as *Civil War Talks: Further Reminiscences of George S. Bernard and His Fellow Veterans*.[4]

4 Newsome, Horn and Selby, eds., (Charlottesville, Va., 2012).

Bibliography

Manuscripts

Alabama Department of Archives and History, Confederate Regimental History Files, 8th Alabama Infantry.

E. P. Alexander Papers, Southern Historical Collection, University of North Carolina at Chapel Hill, Chapel Hill, North Carolina.

Alexander Whitworth Archer, "Recollections of a Private Soldier--1B61," Papers of R. E. Lee Camp, United Confederate Veterans, Virginia Historical Society, Richmond, Virginia.

Fletcher H. Archer Letters, Historic Petersburg Foundation, Petersburg, Virginia.

George S. Bernard Papers, Alderman Library, University of Virginia, Charlottesville, Virginia.

George S. Bernard Papers, Perkins Library, Duke University, Durham, North Carolina.

George S. Bernard Papers, Southern Historical Collection, University of North Carolina at Chapel Hill, Chapel Hill, North Carolina.

Dorsey N. Binion Letters, Michael F. Musick Collection, U. S. Army Military History Institute, Carlisle Barracks, Pennsylvania.

Henry van Leuvenigh Bird Letters, Bird Family Papers, Virginia Historical Society, Richmond, Virginia.

Jerome Bliss Diary, New York State Military Museum and Veterans Research Center, Saratoga Springs, New York.

Burgess Family Memoir, Petersburg National Battlefield Park, Petersburg, Virginia.

Notes of St. George Tucker Coalter Bryan, Grinnan Family Papers, Virginia Historical Society, Richmond, Virginia.

William E. Cameron Papers, Alderman Library, University of Virginia, Charlottesville, Virginia.

Charles Campbell Diary, Manuscripts and Rare Book Department, Earl Gregg Swem Library, College of William and Mary, Williamsburg, Virginia.

Ezra Carman, "The Maryland Campaign," Manuscript Division, Library Of Congress.

John H. Claiborne Papers, Alderman Library, University Of Virginia, Charlottesville, Virginia.

John H. Claiborne Papers, Virginia Historical Society, Richmond, Virginia.

Compiled Records Showing Service of Military Units in Confederate Organizations, Record Group 109, M861, Record Group 109, National Archives, Washington, D.C.

Compiled Service Records of Confederate General and Staff Officers and Non-Regimental Enlisted Men, M331, Record Group 109, National Archives, Washington, D.C.

Compiled Service Records of Confederate Soldiers Who Served in Organizations From the state of Virginia, M 324, Record Group 109, National Archives, Washington, D.C.

Confederate Service Records Of Virginia Soldiers, 1861-1865, Confederate Rosters, Vol. 2, Library of Virginia, Richmond, Virginia.

Crater Collection, American Civil War Museum, Richmond, Virginia.

Letter, Theophilas Daniel to "my Dear wife," April 3, 1862, Private Collection of John Horn, Oak Forest, Illinois.

Thomas E. Darden Letter, Rowley-Gifford-Clegg Papers, Filson Club, Louisville, Kentucky.

Department of Military Affairs, Adjutant General's Office, Military Records, 12th Virginia Infantry, Box 38, Archives Division, Library of Virginia, Richmond, Virginia.

Leroy Summerfield Edwards Letters, Hargrett Rare Book and Manuscript Library, The University of Georgia, Athens, Georgia.

Leroy Summerfield Edwards Papers, McGraw-Page Library, Randolph-Macon College, Ashland, Virginia.

Letter, Archibald B. Goodwyn to "Dr. Crawford," December 18, 1861, Private Collection of John Horn, Oak Forest, Illinois.

Henry Heth Papers, American Civil War Museum, Richmond, Virginia.

Francis W. Knowles Diary, East Carolina University, Greenville, North Carolina.

James H. Lane, "Incidents of Individual Gallantry," Military Collection, North Carolina Department of Archives and History, Raleigh, North Carolina.

James H. Lane Papers, Auburn University Special Collections & Archives Department, Auburn University, Auburn, Alabama.

Lee Headquarters Papers, Virginia Historical Society, Richmond, Virginia.

Letters Received by Adjutant Inspector General, Record Group 109, M474, National Archives, Washington, D.C.

James Longstreet Papers, Southern Historical Collection, University of North Carolina at Chapel Hill, Chapel Hill, North Carolina.

William Mahone Papers, Preston Library, Virginia Military Institute, Lexington, Virginia.

William Mahone Papers, Library of Virginia, Richmond, Virginia.

William Mahone Report, Civil War Times Illustrated Collection, U. S. Army Military History Institute, Carlisle Barracks, Pennsylvania.

Mahone Family Papers, David M. Rubenstein & Rare Manuscript Library, Duke University, Durham, North Carolina.

Joseph R. Manson Papers, Private Collection of William T. Zielinski, Havertown, Pennsylvania.

Joseph R. Manson Papers, Private Collection of Richard Cheatham, Richmond, Virginia.

Joseph R. Manson Papers, The Lewis Leigh Collection, U. S. Army Historical Education Center, Carlisle Barracks, Pennsylvania.

Joseph R. Manson Papers, Virginia Historical Society, Richmond, Virginia.

John Pegram May Letters, Private Collection of James G. Thayer, Richmond, Virginia.

McGill-Mahone Family Papers, Special Collections, University of Virginia Library, Charlottesville, Virginia.

William McWillie Notebook and Diary, Mississippi Department of Archives and History, Jackson, Mississippi.

Military Historical Society of Massachusetts Collection, Mugar Library, Boston University, Boston, Massachusetts.

William T. Morgan Letter, The Lewis Leigh Collection, U. S. Army Military History Institute, Carlisle Barracks, Pennsylvania.

Letter, William T. Morgan to Fletcher H. Archer, July, 1861, William T. Morgan Papers, Navarro College Archives, Navarro College, Corsicana, Texas.

Oscar O. Mull Diary, Virginia Historical Society, Richmond, Virginia.

Claudius Walke Murdaugh Papers, Virginia Historical Society, Richmond, Virginia.

Office Of The Adjutant Inspector General, Inspection Reports, Mahone's Brigade, Record Group 109, National Archives.

Letter, H. L. Patten to "Dear Col.," July 10, 1864. Association of Officers of the 20th Massachusetts Volunteer Infantry, "Reports, letters & papers appertaining to 20th Mass. Vol. Inf. (Boston, Mass.: Boston Public Library, 1868), 234-235.

Pearsall Letters, North Carolina Department of Archives and History, Raleigh, North Carolina.

James Eldred Phillips Papers, Private Collection of Elise Phillips Atkins, Arlington Heights, Illinois.

James Eldred Phillips Papers, Virginia Historical Society, Richmond, Virginia.

James C. Riddle Papers, Virginia Historical Society, Richmond, Virginia.

John F. Sale Papers, Library of Virginia, Richmond, Virginia.

John Simmons Shipp Diary, Virginia Historical Society, Richmond, Virginia.

Francis Charles Stainback Collection, Virginia Military Institute Museum, Virginia Military Institute, Lexington, Virginia.

John M. Stone Papers, Mississippi Department of Archives and History, Jackson, Mississippi.

Westwood A. Todd, "Reminiscences of the War Between the States April 1861-July 1865," Southern Historical Collection, University of North Carolina at Chapel Hill, Chapel Hill, North Carolina.

United Daughters Of The Confederacy Applications, United Daughters of the Confederacy Hall, Richmond, Virginia.

John Bell Vincent Diary, Virginia Historical Society, Richmond, Virginia.

Mrs. Charles Waddell Diary, Papers of Miss Georgia Hicks, Collection of the United Daughters of the Confederacy, North Carolina Division, North Carolina Department of Archives and History, Raleigh, North Carolina.

Charles E. Waddell Diary, American Civil War Museum, Richmond, Virginia.

Samuel Hoey Walkup Diary, Southern Historical Collection, University of North Carolina at chapel Hill, Chapel Hill, North Carolina.

Charles M. Walsh Diary, U. S. Army Historical Educational Center, Carlisle Barracks, Pennsylvania.

David A. Weisiger Letters, Weisiger Family Papers, Virginia Historical Society, Richmond, Virginia.

James E. Whitehorne Papers, Library of Virginia, Richmond, Virginia.

James E. Whitehorne Diary, Southern Historical Collection, University of North Carolina at Chapel Hill, Chapel Hill, North Carolina.

Reuben Lovett Whitehurst Commonplace Book, Virginia Historical Society, Richmond, Virginia.

Phillip Whitlock, "The Life of Phillip Whitlock, Written by Himself," Beth Ahabah Museum and Archives Trust, Richmond, Virginia.

Cadmus M. Wilcox, Report of Operations, Lee Headquarters Papers, Virginia Historical Society, Richmond, Virginia.

Unpublished Studies

Bearss, Edwin C., "The Battle Of Hatcher's Run, February 5-7, 1865," United States Department of the Interior, National Park Service, 1966.

Calkins, Christopher M. "With The 12th Virginia On Its Final March To Appomattox April 2-12, 1865," Petersburg National Battlefield Park, n.d.

"CWSAC Battle Summary," National Park Service, Washington, D. C.

McDaid, William Kelsey, "Four Years Of Arduous Service": The History Of The Branch-Lane Brigade In The Civil War," Michigan State University, 1987.

Suderow, Bryce A. "Confederate Casualties During The Siege Of Petersburg, June 13-Aug. 25, 1864," Private Collection of Bryce A. Suderow, Washington, D.C., 1984.

_____. "Casualties at Burgess Mill." Private Collection of Bryce A. Suderow, Washington, D.C.

_____. "October 27, 1864: Burgess Mill." Private Collection of Bryce A. Suderow, Washington, D.C.

White, David D. "History of the 14th Alabama." Private Collection of David D. White.

Books

A Committee of the Regimental Association. *History of the Thirty-Fifth Regiment Massachusetts Volunteers, 1862-1865.* Boston: Mills, Knight & Co., Printers, 1884.

Archer, John M. *Fury on the Bliss Farm at Gettysburg.* U.S.A.: Maury Books, 2015.

Aubery, James. *The Thirty-Sixth Wisconsin Volunteer Infantry, 1st Brigade, 2nd Division, 2nd Army Corps, Army of the Potomac, An Authentic Record of the Regiment from Its Organization to Its Muster out, a Complete Roster of Its Officers and Men with Their Record; Full List of Casualties, in Detail, Dates and Places; Its Itinerary from Place of Muster to Muster out; Maps Showing Its Movements; a Copy of Every Official Paper in the War Department Pertaining to the Regiment, and Others Pertaining Indirectly to the Command; Illustrations of Events, Biography, Etc.; Statistics; With Reminiscences from the Author's Private Journal.* Milwaukee: n.p., 1900.

Baltz, Louis J., III. *The Battle Of Cold Harbor: May 27-June 13, 1864.* Lynchburg, Va.: H. E. Howard, Inc., 1994.

Barnes, Charles H. *History of the Philadelphia Brigade, Sixty-Sixth, Seventy-First, Seventy-Second and One Hundred and Sixth Pennsylvania Volunteers.* Philadelphia: J. B. Lippincott & Co., 1876.

Bates, Samuel P. *History of Pennsylvania Volunteers, 1861-5, Prepared in Compliance with Acts of the Legislature.* 5 Volumes. Harrisburg: B. Singerly, State Printer, 1869.

Bearss, Edwin C., with Suderow, Bryce A. *The Petersburg Campaign.* 2 Vols. El Dorado Hills, Ca.: Savas Beatie, 2012.

Benedict, George C. *Vermont in the Civil War.* 2 Vols. Burlington, Vt.: The Free Press Association, 1886.

Beringer, Richard E., Hattaway, Herman, Jones, Archer, and Still, William, W., Jr. *Why The South Lost The Civil War.* Athens, Ga.: The University Of Georgia Press, 1986.

Bernard, George S., ed. *War Talks Of Confederate Veterans: Addresses delivered before A.P. Hill Camp of Confederate Veterans, of Petersburg, Va., with ADDENDA giving*

Statements of Participants, Eye-Witnesses and others, in respect to Campaigns, Battles, Prison Life and other War Experiences. Petersburg: Fenn & Owen, 1892.

Bigelow, John. *The Campaign Of Chancellorsville.* New Haven: Yale University Press, 1910.

Billings, John D. *The Tenth Massachussetts Battery.* Boston: Hall & Whiting, 1881.

Blake, Nelson M. *William Mahone Of Virginia, Soldier and Political Insurgent.* Richmond: Garrett & Massie, 1935.

Bond, Natalie J., and Coward, Osmun L., eds. *The South Carolinians.* New York: Vantage Press, 1958.

Brown, Henry LeFevrer, comp. *History Of The Third Regiment Excelsior Brigade 72d New York Volunteer Infantry 1861-1865.* Jamestown, N.Y.: Journal Printing Co., 1902.

Brown, Philip F. *Reminiscences of the War of 1861-1865.* Richmond: Whittet and Shepperson, 1917.

Busey, John W., and Martin, David G. *Regimental Strengths and Losses at Gettysburg.* Hightstown, N. J.: Longstreet House, 2005.

Calkins, Christopher M. *Thirty-Six Hours Before Appomattox: The Battles of Sayler's Creek, High Bridge, Farmville and Cumberland Church, April 6 and 7, 1865.* Farmville, Va.: Farmville Herald, 1989.

_____. *The Appomattox Campaign, March 29-April 9, 1865.* Conshohocken, Pa.: Combined Books, Inc., 1997.

Campbell, R. Thomas. *Academy on the James: The Confederate Naval School.* Shippensburg, Pa.: Burd Street Press, 1998.

_____, and Flanders, Alan B. *Confederate Phoenix: The CSS Virginia.* Shippensburg, Pa.: Burd Street Press, 2001.

Cavanaugh, Michael A. *6th Virginia Infantry.* Lynchburg, Va.: H. E. Howard, Inc., 1988.

_____, and Marvel, William. *The Battle Of The Crater: "The Horrid Pit," June 25-August 6, 1864.* Lynchburg, Va.: H. E. Howard, Inc., 1987.

Chamberlaine, William W. *Memoirs of the Civil War Between the Northern and the Southern Sections of the United States of America 1861 to 1865.* Washington, D.C.: Press of Byron S. Adams, 1912.

Chapla, John D. *48th Virginia Infantry.* Lynchburg, Va.: H. E. Howard, Inc., 1989.

Child, William. *A History Of The Fifth Regiment New Hampshire Volunteers in the American Civil War 1861-65.* 2 Vols. Bristol, N.H.: R. W. Musgrove, Printer, 1893.

Christ, Elwood W. *"Over A Wide, Hot,.... Crimson Plain:" The Struggle For The Bliss Farm At Gettysburg, July 2nd and 3rd, 1863.* Baltimore: Butternut and Blue, 1994.

Claiborne, John Herbert. *Seventy-five Years in Old Virginia.* Neale Publishing Co.: New York, 1904.

Clark, Walter, ed. *Histories of the Several Regiments and Battalions from North Carolina in the Great War 1861-'65*. Goldsboro, N.C.: Nash Brothers, Book and Job Printers, 1901.

Cockrell, Monroe, ed. *Gunner with Stonewall: Reminiscences of William Thomas Poague, Lieutenant, Captain, Major, and Lieutenant Colonel of Artillery, Army of Northern Virginia, C.S.A.; A Memoir Written for his Children in 1903*. Jackson, Tenn.: McCowat-Mercer Press, 1957.

Cockrell, Thomas D. and Ballard, Michael B., eds. *A Mississippi Rebel In The Army Of Northern Virginia: The Civil War Memoirs of Private David Holt*. Baton Rouge: Louisiana State University Press, 1995.

Coddington, Edwin H. *The Gettysburg Campaign: A Study in Command*. New York: Charles Scribner's Sons, 1968.

Cook, Benjamin F. *History of the Twelfth Massachusetts Infantry (Webster Regiment)*. Boston: Twelfth (Webster) Regiment Association, 1882.

Couture, Richard T., ed. *Charlie's Letters: The Correspondence Of Charles E. DeNoon*. Collingswood, N. J.: C. W. Historicals, 1982.

Cross, David F. *A Melancholy Affair at the Weldon Railroad: The Vermont Brigade, June 23, 2864*. Shippensburg, Pa.: White Mane Publishing Co., Inc., 2003.

Crotty, D. G. *Four Years Campaigning in the Army of the Potomac*. Grand Rapids, Mi.: Dygert Bros. & Co., 1874.

Dabney, Virginius. *Virginia: The New Dominion*. Charlottesville, Va.: The University Press of Virginia, 1971.

Divine, John E. *8th Virginia Infantry*. Lynchburg, Va.: H. E. Howard, Inc., 1983.

Dobbins, Austin C., ed. *Grandfather's Journal: Company B, Sixteenth Infantry Volunteers, Harris' Brigade, Mahone's Division, Hill's Corps, A.N.V., May 27, 1861-July 15, 1865*. Dayton, Oh.: Morningside House, Inc., 1988.

Dunlop, William S. *Lee's Sharpshooters; or, The Forefront of Battle: A Story of Southern Valor That Never Has Been Told*. Little Rock: Tunnah & Pittard, 1899.

Dupuy, T. N. *The Evolution of Weapons and Warfare*. Indianapolis: The Bobbs-Merrill Company, Inc., 1980.

Eanes, Greg. *'Destroy The Junction,' The Wilson-Kautz Raid & The Battle for the Staunton River Bridge: June 21, 1864 to July 1, 1864*. Lynchburg, Va.: H. E. Howard, Inc., 1999.

Early, Jubal A. *War Memoirs: Autobiographical Sketch And Narrative Of The War Between The States*. Bloomington, Ind.: Indiana University Press, 1960.

Elliot, Joseph Cantey. *Lieutenant General Richard Heron Anderson: Lee's Noble Soldier*. Dayton, Oh.: Morningside Press, 1985.

Elmore, Fletcher L., Jr., comp. *Diary Of J. E. Whitehorne, 1st Sergt., Co. "F," 12th Va. Infantry, A. P. Hill's 3rd Corps, A. N. Va.* Utica, Ky.: McDowell Publications, 1995.

Evans, Clement E., ed. *Confederate Military History.* 12 Vols. Atlanta: Confederate Publishing Company, 1899.

Evans, Robert G., comp. and ed. *The 16th Mississippi Infantry, Civil War Letters and Reminiscences.* Jackson: University Press of Mississippi, 2002.

Folsom, James M. *Heroes and Martyrs of Georgia, Georgia's Record in the Revolution of 1861.* Macon, Ga.: Burke, Boykin & Company, 1864.

Fox, William F. *Regimental Losses in the American Civil War,* 1861-1865. Albany, N.Y.: Albany Publishing Company, 1889.

Frederick, Gilbert. *The Story Of A Regiment, Being A Record Of The Military Services Of The Fifty-Seventh New York State Volunteer Infantry In The War Of The Rebellion 1861-1865.* Chicago: Fifty-seventh veteran association, 1895.

Freeman, Douglas Southall. *R. E. Lee.* 4 Vols. New York: Charles Scribner's Sons, 1935.

_____. *Lee's Lieutenants.* 3 Vols. Charles Scribner's Sons: New York, 1944.

_____, ed. *Lee's Dispatches.* Baton Rouge: Louisiana State University Press, 1957.

Freminville, Christophe-Paulin de la Poix, Chevalier de. *Le Combat des Trente, Poeme du XIV.e Siecle, Transcrit sur le Manuscrit Original, Conserve a la Bibliotheque du ROI, et Accompagne de Notes Historiques.* Brest: LeFournier et DePeriers, 1819).

Fuller, Charles A. *Personal Recollections of the War of 1861.* Sherburne, N.Y.: News Job Printing House, 1906.

Fuller, J. F. C. *The Generalship Of Ulysses S. Grant.* London: J. Murray, 1929.

Furguson, Ernest B. *Chancellorsville 1863: The Souls of the Brave.* New York: Alfred A. Knopf, 1992.

Gallagher, Gary W., ed. *Lee The Soldier.* Lincoln, Neb.: University Of Nebraska Press, 1996.

_____, ed. *The Wilderness Campaign.* Chapel Hill: The University of North Carolina Press, 1997.

Galwey, Thomas Francis. *The Valiant Hours.* Harrisburg: The Stackpole Company, 1961.

Girvan, Jeffrey M. *The 55th North Carolina in the Civil War: A History and Roster.* Jefferson, N.C.: McFarland & Company, Publishers, 2006).

Graham, Martin, and Skoch, George. *Mine Run: A Campaign of Lost Opportunities, Oct. 21--May 1, 1864.* Lynchburg, Va.: H. E. Howard, Inc., 1988.

Grand Army Of The Republic, Massachusetts Department, John A. Andrew Post No. 15. *The Old Stars And Stripes Of The Richmond Grays And The "Grays" in the Confederate Army.* Boston: n.p. , 1887.

Green, Linda L. *First, for the Duration: The Story of the Eighth Alabama Infantry, C.S.A.* Westminster, Md.: Heritage Books Inc., 2008.

Greene, A. Wilson. *A Campaign of Giants, The Battle for Petersburg: From the Crossing of the James to the Crater*. Vol. 1 of a projected 3. Chapel Hill, N.C.: The University of North Carolina Press, 2018.

Grimes, Bryan. *Extracts of Letters of Major-General Bryan Grimes to His Wife*. Raleigh: Edwards, Broughton, 1883.

Haines, William P. *History of the Men of Company F With Description of the Marches and Battles of the 12th New Jersey Volunteers*. Camden, N.J.: C. S. Magrath, 1897.

Hardee, William H. *Rifle And Light Infantry Tactics, For The Exercise And Manoeuvres Of Troups When Acting As Light Infantry or Riflemen*. Philadelphia: Lippincott, Crawford & Co., 1855.

Hardin, Martin D. *History of the Twelfth Regiment Pennsylvania Reserve Volunteer Corps (41st Regiment of the Line) from its Muster into the United States Service, August 10th, 1861, to its Muster Out, June 11th, 1864, together with Biographical Sketches of Officers and Men and a Complete Muster-Out Roll*. New York: Martin D. Hardin, 1890.

Hardy, Michael C. *The Fifty-Eighth North Carolina Troops, Tar Heels in the Army of Tennessee*. Jefferson, N.C.: McFarland & Company, Inc., Publishers, 2010.

Harris, J. S. *Historical Sketches of the Seventh Regiment North Carolina Troops, 1861-'65*. Mooresville, N.C.: Mooresville Printing Co., 1893.

Harrison, Noel G. *Chancellorsville Battlefield Sites*. Lynchburg, Va.: H. E. Howard, Inc., 1993.

Haynes, Martin A. *History of the Second Regiment New Hampshire Volunteers*. Manchester, N.H.: Charles F. Livingston, Printer, 1865.

_____. *A History Of The Second Regiment New Hampshire Volunteer Infantry In The War Of The Rebellion*. Concord, N.H.: Republican Press Association, 1896.

Hays, Gilbert Adams. *Under the Red Patch; Story of the Sixty-Third Regiment, Pennsylvania Volunteers, 1861-1864*. Pittsburgh: Sixty-third Pennsylvania Volunteers Regimental Association, 1908.

Head, Thomas A. Head. *Campaigns and Battles of the Sixteenth Regiment, Tennessee Volunteers, in the War between the States, with Incidental Sketches of the Part Performed by other Tennessee Troops in the same War, 1861-1865*. Nashville: Cumberland Presbyterian Publishing House, 1885.

Henderson, G. F. R. *Stonewall Jackson and the American Civil War*. 2 Vols. London: Longmans, Green, and Co., 1902.

Henderson, William D. *12th Virginia Infantry*. Lynchburg, Va.: H. E. Howard, Inc., 1984.

_____. *41st Virginia Infantry*. Lynchburg, Va.: H. E. Howard, Inc., 1986.

_____. *The Road To Bristoe Station: Campaigning with Lee and Meade, Aug. 1-Oct. 20, 1863*. Lynchburg, Va.: H. E. Howard, Inc. 1984.

Hennessey, John J. *Return To Bull Run: The Campaign And Battle Of Second Manassas.*
New York: Simon & Schuster, 1993.

_____. *Second Manassas Map Study.* Lynchburg, Va.: H. E. Howard, Inc., 1986.

Hess, Earl J. *Pickett's Charge—The Last Attack at Gettysburg.* Chapel Hill: The University
of North Carolina Press, 2001.

_____. *Into the Crater: The Mine Attack at Petersburg.* Columbia, S.C.: University of
South Carolina Press, 2010.

_____. *In the Trenches at Petersburg: Field Fortifications and Confederate Defeat.*
Chapel Hill, N.C.: University of North Carolina Press, 2009.

Hewett, Janet B., et al., eds., *Supplement to the Official Records of the Union and
Confederate Armies.* 100 Vols. Wilmington, N.C.: Broadfoot Publishing Company,
1994-2001.

*Historical Sketch of the Quitman Guards, Company E, Sixteenth Mississippi Regiment,
Harris' Brigade, by One of the Quitman Guards.* New Orleans: Isaac T. Hinton,
Printer, 1888.

Horn, John. *The Petersburg Campaign: June 1864-April 1865.* Conshohocken, Pa.:
Combined Books, Inc., 1993.

_____. *The Siege of Petersburg: The Battles for the Weldon Railroad, August 1864.* El
Dorado Hills, Ca.: Savas Beatie, 2015.

Howe, Thomas H. *Wasted Valor: The Petersburg Campaign: June 15-18, 1864.* Lynchburg,
Va.: H. E. Howard, Inc., 1988.

Humphreys, Andrew A. *The Virginia Campaign of '64 and '65.* New York: Charles
Scribner's Sons, 1883.

Hutchinson, Gustavus B. *A Narrative Of The Formation And Services Of The Eleventh
Massachusetts Volunteers.* Boston: Alfred Mudge & Son, Printers, 1893.

Johnson, Robert Underwood, and Buel, Clarence Clough, eds. *Battles and Leaders of
the American Civil War.* 4 Vols. New York: Thomas Yoseloff, 1956.

Jones, John Beauchamp. *A Rebel War Clerk's Diary at the Confederate States Capital.*
2 Vols. Philadelphia: J. B. Lippincott and Company, 1866.

Jordan, Ervin L. *Black Confederates and Afro-Yankees in Civil War Virginia.* Charlottesville:
The University Press of Virginia, 1995.

Keiley, Anthony M. *In Vinculis; or, The Prisoner of War.* New York: Blelock and
Company, 1866.

Kepler, William. *History of the Three Months and Three Years of Service from April 16,
1861, to June 22, 1864, of the Fourth Regiment, Ohio Volunteer Infantry in the War
for the Union.* Cleveland: Leader Printing Company, 1886.

Kleese, Richard B. *49th Virginia Infantry.* Lynchburg, Va.: H. E. Howard, Inc., 2002.

Krick, Robert E. L. *Staff Officers in Gray: A Biographical Register of the Staff Officers in the Army of Northern Virginia.* Chapel Hill: The University of North Carolina Press, 2003.

Krick, Robert K. *Lee's Colonels: A Biographical Register Of The Field Officers Of The Army of Northern Virginia.* Dayton: Morningside Bookshop, 1979.

La Bree, Ben, ed. *Campfires of the Confederacy.* Louisville: Courier Journal Job Printing Company, 1898.

Levin, Kevin M. *Remembering the Battle of the Crater: War as Murder.* Lexington, Ky.: University Press of Kentucky, 2012.

Livermore, Thomas L. *Numbers and Losses in the Civil War in America, 1861-1865.* Boston: Houghton Mifflin and Company, 1900.

Locke, William Henry. *The Story of the Regiment.* Philadelphia: J. B. Lippincott, 1868.

Loehr, Charles T. *War History of the Old First Virginia Infantry Regiment,* Army of Northern Virginia. Richmond: Wm. Ellis Jones, Book and Job Printer, 1884.

Longstreet, James. *From Manassas to Appomattox: Memoirs of the Civil War in America.* Philadelphia: J. P. Lippincott Co., 1896.

Macnamara, Daniel G. *The History of the Ninth Regiment Massachusetts Volunteer Infantry.* Boston: E. B. Stillings & Co., Printers, 1899.

Macnamara, M. H. *The Irish Ninth In Bivouac And Battle.* Boston: Lee And Shepard, 1867.

Mackowski, Chris. *Strike Them a Blow: Battle along the North Anna River, May 21-25, 1864.* El Dorado Hills, Ca.: Savas Beatie, 2015.

_____, and White, Kristopher D. *A Season of Slaughter: The Battle of Spotsylvania Court House, May 8-21, 1864.* El Dorado Hills, Ca.: Savas Beatie, 2013.

_____, and White, Kristopher D. *Chancellorsville's Forgotten Front: The Battles of Second Fredericksburg and Salem Church, May 3, 1863.* El Dorado Hills, Ca.: Savas Beatie, 2013.

Macrae, David. *The Americans At Home.* New York: E. P. Dutton and Co., 1952.

Mahone, William. *The Crater.* Petersburg: The Franklin Press Co., n.d.

Manarin, Louis H. *Henrico County Field of Honor.* 2 Volumes. Henrico County, Virginia, 2004.

Martin, James. M., comp. *History Of The Fifty-Seventh Regiment Pennsylvania Veteran Volunteer Infantry.* Meadville, Pa.: McCoy & Calvin, Printers, 1904.

Mason, John M., Jr., ed. *Three Years in the Army; or, The Life and Adventures of a Rebel Soldier.* Warren, Oh.: n.p., 1950.

Matter, William D. *If It Takes All Summer: The Battle Of Spotsylvania.* Chapel Hill: University of North Carolina Press, 1988.

McMurray, W. J., M.D. *History of the Twentieth Tennessee Volunteer Infantry, C.S.A.* Nashville: The Publishing Committee, 1904.

Miller, Francis Trevelyan, and Lanier, Richard Sampson, eds. *Poetry and eloquence of Blue and Gray*. New York: The Review of Reviews Co., 1911.

Miller, J. Michael. *The North Anna Campaign: "Even to Hell Itself," May 21-26, 1864*. Lynchburg, Va.: H. E. Howard, Inc., 1989.

Mixson, Frank M. *Reminiscences of a Private*. Columbia, S.C.: The State Company, 1910.

Moore, John W. *Roster of North Carolina Troops in the War between the States*. 5 Vols. Raleigh: Ashe & Gatling, State Printers and Binders, 1882

Mulholland, St. Clair A. *The Story of the 116th Regiment, Pennsylvania Volunteers in the War of the Rebellion, the Record of a Gallant Command*. Philadelphia: F. McManus, Jr. & Co., 1903.

Murfin, James V. *The Gleam of Bayonets: The Battle Of Antietam And The Maryland Campaign*. New York: Thomas Yoseloff, 1965.

Neale, Gay. *Brunswick County, Virginia, 1720-1975*. Richmond: Whittet and Shepperson, 1975.

Nevins, Allan. *Ordeal of the Union*. 8 Vols. Charles Scribner's Sons: New York, 1947.

Newsome, Hampton, Horn, John and Selby, John, eds. *Civil War Talks: Further Reminiscences of George S. Bernard and His Fellow Veterans*. Charlottesville, Va.: University Press of Virginia, 2012.

Newsome, Hampton. *Richmond Must Fall: The Richmond-Petersburg Campaign, October 1864*. Kent, Oh.: The Kent State University Press, 2013.

Newton, Steven. *The Battle of Seven Pines, May 31-June 1, 1862*. Lynchburg, Va.: H. E. Howard, Inc., 1993.

Nine, William G., and Wilson, Ronald G. *The Appomattox Paroles: April 9-15, 1865*. Lynchburg, Va.: H. E. Howard, Inc., 1989.

Oldaker, Glenn C., comp. *Centennial Tales: Memoirs of Colonel "Chester" S. Bassett French, Extra Aide-de-camp to Generals Lee and Jackson, the Army of Northern Virginia, 1861- 1865*. New York: Carleton Press, 1962.

Osborne, Charles C. *Jubal: The Life and Times of General Jubal A. Early, CSA*. Chapel Hill, N.C.: Algonquin Books, 1992.

Parker, Thomas H. *History of the 51st Regiment of P.V. and V.V. from Its Organization at Camp Curtin, Harrisburg, Pa., in 1861, to Its Being Mustered Out of the United States Service at Alexandria, Va., July 27th, 1865*. Philadelphia: King & Baird, 1869.

Pfanz, Donald C. *War So Terrible: A Popular History of the Battle of Fredericksburg*. Richmond: Page One History Publications, 2003.

Pfanz, Harry W. *Gettysburg: The First Day*. Chapel Hill: The University of North Carolina Press, 2001.

_____. *Gettysburg: The Second Day*. Chapel Hill: The University of North Carolina Press, 1987.

_____. *Gettysburg—Culp's Hill and Cemetery Hill.*. Chapel Hill: The University of North Carolina Press, 1993.

Phisterer, Frederick. *New York in the War of the Rebellion.* 5 Volumes. Albany: J. B. Lyon Company, 1912.

Porter, John W. H. *A Record of Events in Norfolk County, Virginia from April 10, 1861 to May 10, 1862, with a History of the Soldiers and Sailors of Norfolk County, Norfolk City, and Portsmouth who served in the Confederate States Army or Navy.* Portsmouth, Va.: W. A. Fiske, Printer, 1892.

Priest, John Michael. *Before Antietam: The Battle for South Mountain.* Shippensburg, Pa.: White Mane Publishing Company, Inc., 1992.

_____. *Antietam: The Soldiers' Battle.* New York: Oxford University Press, 1993.

_____. *Victory Without Triumph: The Wilderness, May 6th & 7th, 1864.* Shippensburg, Pa.: White Mane Publishing Company, Inc., 1996.

_____. *Into the Fight: Pickett's Charge at Gettysburg.* Shippensburg, Pa.: White Mane Publishing Company, Inc., 1998.

Rankin, Thomas M. *23rd Virginia Infantry.* Lynchburg, Va.: H. E. Howard, Inc., 1985.

Reidenbaugh, Lowell. *33rd Virginia Infantry.* Lynchburg, Va.: H. E. Howard, Inc., 1987.

Rhea, Gordon C. *The Battle of the Wilderness, May 5-6, 1864.* Baton Rouge: Louisiana State University Press, 1994.

_____. *The Battles for Spotsylvania Court House and the Road to Yellow Tavern.* Baton Rouge: Louisiana State University Press, 1997.

_____. *To the North Anna River: Grant and Lee, May 13-25, 1864.* Baton Rouge: Louisiana State University Press, 2000.

_____. *Cold Harbor: Grant and Lee, May 26-June 3, 1864.* Baton Rouge: Louisiana State University Press, 2002.

_____. *On to Petersburg: Grant and Lee, June 4-15, 1864.* Baton Rouge: Louisiana State University Press, 2017.

Rhoades, Jeffrey L. *Scapegoat General: The Story of Major General Benjamin Huger, C.S.A.* Archon Books: Hamden, Ct., 1985.

Rigdon, John C. *Historical Sketch and Roster of the Georgia 8th Infantry Regiment.* Cartersville, Ga.: Eastern Digital Resources, 2003.

_____. *Historical Sketch and Roster of the Georgia 22nd Infantry Regiment.* Cartersville, Ga.: Eastern Digital Resources, 2003.

_____. *Historical Sketch and Roster of the Georgia 30th Infantry Regiment.* Cartersville, Ga.: Eastern Digital Resources, 2004.

_____. *Historical Sketch and Roster of the Georgia 48th Infantry Regiment.* Cartersville, Ga.: Eastern Digital Resources, 2003.

_____. *Historical Sketch and Roster of the Georgia 60th Infantry Regiment.* Cartersville, Ga.: Eastern Digital Resources, 2004.

Robertson, James I., Jr. *General A. P. Hill: The Story of a Confederate Warrior.* New York: Random House, Inc., 1987.

Robertson, William G. *The First Battle for Petersburg: The Attack and Defense of the Cockade City, June 9, 1864.* El Dorado Hills, Ca.: Savas Beatie, 2015.

Rowland, Dunbar. *Military History of Mississippi, 1803—1898.* Spartanburg, S.C.: The Reprint Company, Publishers, 1998.

Sawyer, Franklin. *A Military History of the 8th Regiment, Ohio Volunteer Infantry—Its Battles, Marches, and Army Movements.* Cleveland: Fairbanks & Co., Printers, 1881.

Schmutz, John F. *The Battle of the Crater: A Complete History.* Jefferson, N.C.: McFarland & Company, Inc., Publishers, 2009.

Scott, J. L. *60th Virginia Infantry.* Lynchburg, Va.: H. E. Howard, Inc., 1997.

Scott, James G., and Wyatt, Edward A. *Petersburg's Story: A History.* Petersburg: Titmus Optical Co., 1960.

Scott, Johnny L. *34th Virginia Infantry.* Lynchburg, Va.: H. E. Howard, Inc., 1999.

Scott, Kate M. *History of the One hundred and Fifth Regiment of Pennsylvania Volunteers.* Philadelphia: New-World Publishing Company, 1877.

Scott, Robert Garth. *Into the Wilderness with the Army of the Potomac.* Bloomington: Indiana University Press, 1985.

Sears, Stephen W. *Chancellorsville.* New York: Ticknor & Fields, 1996.

_____. *Gettysburg.* New York: Ticknor & Fields, 2004.

_____. *Landscape Turned Red: The Battle of Antietam.* New York: Ticknor & Fields, 1983.

_____. *To The Gates of Richmond: The Peninsula Campaign.* New York: Ticknor & Fields, 1992.

Slotkin, Richard. *No Quarter: The Battle of the Crater, 1864.* New York: Random House, 2009.

Smith, Gustavus Woodson. *The Battle Of Seven Pines.* New York: C. G. Crawford, Printer, 1891.

Smith, John D. *The History of the Nineteenth Regiment of Maine Volunteer Infantry, 1862-1865.* Minneapolis: Great Western Printing Co., 1909.

Sommers, Richard J. *Richmond Redeemed: The Siege at Petersburg.* Garden City, N.Y: Doubleday & Company, Inc., 1981.

_____. *Challenges of Command in the Civil War, Generalship, Leadership and Strategy at Gettysburg, Petersburg and Beyond: Generals and Generalship.* Vol. 1 of a projected 2. El Dorado, Ca.: Savas Beatie, 2018.

Sorrel, G. Moxley. *Recollections of A Confederate Staff Officer.* Dayton, Ohio: Morningside Bookshop, 1978.

Stackpole, Edward J. *The Fredericksburg Campaign*. Harrisburg: Military Services Publishing Co., 1957.

Steere, Edward. *The Wilderness Campaign, The Meeting of Grant and Lee*. Mechanicsburg, Pa.: Stackpole Books, 1960.

Stewart, George R. *Pickett's Charge: A Microhistory of the Final Attack at Gettysburg, July 3rd, 1863*. Boston: Houghton Mifflin Co-r 1957.

Stewart, William H. *A Pair Of Blankets: War-Time History in Letters to the Young People of the South*. Wilmington, N. C.: Broadfoot Publishing Company, 1990. [61st Virginia Infantry]

Sublett, Charles W. *57th Virginia Infantry*. Lynchburg, Va.: H. E. Howard, Inc., 1985.

Swinton, William. *History of the Seventh Regiment National Guard, State Of New York, During The War Of The Rebellion*. New York: Fields, Osgood, & Co., 1870.

Trask, Benjamin H. *9th Virginia Infantry*. Lynchburg, Va.: H. E. Howard, 1984.

_____. *16th Virginia Infantry*. Lynchburg, Va.: H. E. Howard, Inc., 1986.

_____. *61st Virginia Infantry*. Lynchburg, Va.: H. E. Howard, Inc., 1988.

Trinity Hymnal. Atlanta: Great Commission Publishers, 1990.

Trudeau, Noah Andre. *Bloody Roads South: The Wilderness to Cold Harbor, May-June, 1864*. New York: Little, Brown and Company, 1989.

_____. *The Last Citadel: Petersburg, Virginia, June 1864- April, 1865*. El Dorado Hills, Ca.: Savas Beatie, 2014.

_____. *Out of the Storm: The End of the Civil War, April- June, 1865*. New York: Little, Brown and Company, 1994.

The Union army: a history of military affairs in the loyal states, 1861-1865 – records of the regiments in the Union army – cyclopedia of battles – memoirs of commanders and soldiers. 8 Vols. Madison, Wis.: Federal Pub Co., 1908.

United States War Department. *The War of the Rebellion: A Compilation of the Official Records of the Union and Confederate Armies*. 128 Vols. Washington, D.C.: U. S. Government Printing Office, 1880-1901.

Vickers, George Morley. *Under Both Flags: A Panorama of the Great Civil War, As represented in Story, Anecdote, Adventure, and the Romance of Reality, Written by Both Sides; the Men and Women Who Created the Greatest Epoch in our Nation's History*. DesMoines: Mutual Books Concern, 1896.

Underwood, Wille Bruce, comp. *Isaac W. Underwood: His Ancestors and Descendants*. Baltimore: Gateway Press, Inc., 1988.

Wallace, Lee A, Jr. *A Guide to Virginia Military Organizations, 1861-1865*. Richmond: Virginia Civil War Commission, 1964.

_____. *3rd Virginia Infantry*. Lynchburg, Va.: H. E. Howard, Inc., 1986.

Warner, Ezra. *Generals In Gray*. Baton Rouge: Louisiana University Press, 1959.

Waters, Zack C., and Edmonds, James D. *A Small but Spartan Band: The Florida Brigade in Lee's Army of Northern Virginia*. Tuscaloosa: University of Alabama Press, 2010).

Washburn, George H. *A Complete Military History and Record of the 108th Regiment, New York Volunteers*. Rochester, N.Y.: E. R. Andrews, 1894.

Webb, Alexander S. *The Peninsula*. New York: Charles Scribner's Sons, 1881.

Weaver, Jeffrey C. *63rd Virginia Infantry*. Lynchburg, Va.: H. E. Howard, Inc., 1991.

_____, and Sherwood, George L. *54th Virginia Infantry*. Lynchburg, Va.: H. E. Howard, Inc., 1993.

_____, and Sherwood, George L. *59th Virginia Infantry*. Lynchburg, Va.: H. E. Howard, Inc., 1994.

Wert, Jeffrey D. *Gettysburg: Day Three*. New York: Simon & Schuster, 2003.

Wheeler, Richard. *Sword over Richmond*. New York: Harper & Row, 1986.

Wiggins, Clyde G., III, ed. *My Dear Friend: The Civil War Letters of Alva Benjamin Spencer, 3rd Georgia Regiment, Company C*. Macon, Ga.: Mercer University Press, 2007.

Williamson, Warren. *Mother May You Never See The Sights I Have Seen: The Fifty-seventh Massachusetts Veteran Volunteers in the Last Year of the Civil War*. New York: Harper & Row, Publishers, 1990.

Wise, Jennings C. *The Military History of the Virginia Military Institute, 1839 to 18___65*. Lynchburg, Va.: J. P. Bell Company, Inc., 1915.

Wise, John Sergeant. *The End of an Era*. Cambridge, Ma.: Houghton, Mifflin and Company, 1899.

Yeary, Mamie, comp. *Reminiscences of the Boys in Gray, 1861-1865*. Dallas: Smith & Lamar, 1912.

Young, Alfred C., III. *Lee's Army*. Baton Rouge: Louisiana State University Press, 2013.

Articles

Armstrong, Michael J., and Soderbergh, Steven E. "Refighting Pickett's Charge: mathematical modeling of the Civil War battlefield," *Social Science Quarterly* 96, No. 4 (May 14, 2015), 1153-1168.

"The Battle of the Crater: Roster of the Members of the 12th Virginia Infantry, Mahone's Brigade, Who Were Engaged." *Southern Historical Society Papers* XXXI (1893), 271-274.

Bernard, George S. "Malvern Hill: Recollections of the Fight by one who was there." *Southern Historical Society Papers* XVIII (1890), 56-71.

_____. "Great Battle Of The Crater: The Work Of Mahone And Weisiger At The Fight." *Southern Historical Society Papers* XXVIII (1900), 65-71.

Birdsong, James C. "The Petersburg Grays." *Southern Historical Society Papers* XXXVI (1908), 360-362.

Brown, Philip F. "Vivid Memories Of The War In Virginia." *Confederate Veteran* XVIII (1910), 64.

Bryan, Goode. "Report of General Goode Bryan." *Southern Historical Society Papers* VI (1878), 83.

Cameron, William E. "Historic Waters of Virginia: The Battle in Hampton Roads as Viewed by an Eye witness, The Achievements Of The Virginia; An Interesting Paper—The Improvised Confederate Naval Fleet." *Southern Historical Society Papers* XXXII (1904), 347-354. [12th Virginia Infantry]

Confederate Veteran XVI, 1908.

Deaton, W. E., comp. "Seventeen Days Of Sunset: The Diary Of J. E. Whitehorne, Sergeant, Company F, 12th Virginia, Infantry, C. S. A." *The Military Engineer* XXXI, No. 177 (1939), 182-186.

De Peyster, John W. "A Military Memoir Of William Mahone, Major General In The Confederate Army." *The Historical Magazine* VII, Second Series (1870): 390-406.

Gottfried, Bradley M. "Mahone's Brigade: Insubordination or Miscommunication," *Gettysburg Magazine*, No. 18, July 1998,

Herbert, Hilary A. "History of the Eighth Alabama Volunteer Regiment, C.S.A." Edited by Maurice S. Fortin. *Alabama Historical Quarterly* 39 (1977): 5-321.

Jones, Charles R. "Historical Sketch," *Our Living and Our Dead*, April 15, 1874.

Kershaw, Joseph B. Kershaw. "Operations of Kershaw's Division" *Southern Historical Society Papers* VI (1878), 81.

Lane, James H. "History of Lane's North Carolina Brigade: Battle Of Spotsylvania Court-House—Report Of General Lane." *Southern Historical Society Papers* IX (1881), 145-156.

Laughton, John E. "The Sharpshooters Of Mahone's Brigade: A Paper Read by Captain John E. Laughton, Jr., Before Pickett Camp, Confederate Veterans, Richmond, Va." *Southern Historical Society Papers* XXII (1894), 98-105.

Libby, George W. "John Brown And John Wilkes Booth." *Confederate Veteran* XXXVIII (1930), 138-139.

Northen, Robert N. "The Raw Confederate of April 1861." *Southern Historical Society Papers* XXI (1893), 346-352.

"The Old Guard Of Richmond, Va." *Confederate Veteran* V (1897), 484-485. [12th Virginia Infantry]

Owen, Thomas M. "The Work of William Henry Fowler as Superintendent of Army Records, 1863-1865." *Transactions of the Alabama Historical Society*, Vol. II, 1897-1898, 171-198.

"Paroles of the Army of Northern Virginia, R. E. Lee, Gen., C.S.A., Commanding, Surrendered at Appomattox, C. H., Va., April 9, 1865." *Southern Historical Society Papers* XV (1886).

Perry, William F. "Reminiscences of the Campaign of 1864 in Virginia," *Southern Historical Society Papers* VII (1879), 49-63.

Pryor, Anne Banister. "A Child's Recollections Of War." *Confederate Veteran* XXXIX (1931), 54-57.

Rollins, Richard. "The Second Wave of Pickett's Charge," *Gettysburg Magazine*, No. 18, July 1998.

Smythe, Angela. "Has He Been Hiding in Plain Sight? John Wilkes Booth and the Richmond Grays. https://www.scribd.com. May 10, 2010.

Stewart, William H., and White, Whitman V. "The No Name Battle," *Blue and Gray*, vol. 5, no. 1 (Jan., 1895), 29-35.

Wallace, William. "Operations of the Second South Carolina Regiment in the Campaigns of 1864 and 1865." *Southern Historical Society Papers* VII (1879), 128-131.

Zachry, Alfred. "Fighting with the 3d Georgia." (Part 1). *Civil War Times Illustrated* 33 (September/October 1994): 26, 66-77.

_____. (Part II). *Civil War Times Illustrated* 33 (November/December 1994: 32, 100-112.

Newspapers

The Daily Asheville (N.C.) *Citizen*

Atlanta *Southern Confederacy*

(Atlanta) *The Sunny South*

Atlanta Weekly *Intelligencer*

Augusta (Ga.) Daily *Chronicle & Sentinel*

The Baltimore *Sun*

Brooklyn *Eagle*

The Carolina Spartan (Spartanburg, S.C.)

Charleston (S.C.) Daily *Courier*

The Daily Chattanooga *Rebel* (Griffin, Ga.)

Clarksville *Chronicle* (Clarksville, Tenn.)

Clinch Valley News (Jeffersonville, Va.)

The Daily *Phoenix* (Columbia, S.C.)

The Commonwealth (Scotland Neck, N.C.)

The Forest Republican (Tionesta, Pa.)

Greensboro (N.C.) Daily *News*

Keowee *Courier* (Pickens, S.C.)

Kingsport *Times* (Kingsport, Tenn.)

Macon Daily *Telegraph*

Memphis Daily *Appeal*

National *Tribune*

New Haven Morning *Journal and Courier*

New Orleans *Times*

New York *Times*

Norfolk *Ledger*

Norfolk *Pilot-Virginian*

Petersburg Daily *Express*

Petersburg *Enterprise*

Petersburg Daily *Index-Appeal*

Petersburg Daily *Register*

The Progress-Index (Petersburg, Va.)

The Daily Confederate (Raleigh, N.C.)

Raleigh (N.C.) *Register*

The Star (Reynoldsville, Pa.)

Richmond Daily *Dispatch*

Richmond *Enquirer*

Daily Richmond *Examiner*

Richmond *News Leader*

Richmond *Sentinel*

Richmond *Times-Dispatch*

Richmond *Whig*

Spirit of the Age (Raleigh, N.C)

Staunton *Spectator*

Vicksburg Evening *Post*

The (Washington, D.C.) *Evening Star*

Winston-Salem *Journal* (Winston-Salem, N.C.)

Yorkville (S.C.) *Enquirer*

Map Collections and Miscellaneous Maps

Antietam Battlefield Board. *Atlas of the Battlefield of Antietam*. Washington, D.C.: War Department, Chief of Engineers, 1904.

Bachelder, John B. *Map of the Battle Field of Gettysburg, Second Day's Battle*. Office of the Chief of Engineers, U.S. Army, 1876.

Civil Works Map File. Virginia. Records of the Office of the Chief of Engineers. Record Group 77. National Archives. Washington, D.C.

Confederate Engineer Bureau, Virginia Historical Society, Richmond, Virginia.

Cowles, Calvin D., comp. *The Official Military Atlas of the Civil War*. New York: Gramercy Press, 1983.

Esposito, Vincent J. *The West Point Atlas of American Wars*. New York: Frederick A. Praeger, 1959.

McElfresh, Earl B. *Chancellorsville Battlefield, Spotsylvania County, Virginia, 1863*. Olean, N.Y.: McElfresh Map. Co., 1996.

United States Geological Survey. Virginia 7.5 Minute Series. Brokenburg, Carson, Chancellorsville, Dutch Gap, Petersburg, Salem Church, Seven Pines, Spotsylvania and Sutherland Quadrangles. Reston, Va.: United States Department of the Interior, 1974-1987.

_____. Virginia. Farmville Sheet (1891), Petersburg Sheet (1894), Richmond Sheet (1895), Spotsylvania Sheet (1892).

Virginia Historical Society, Richmond, Virginia.

John Willian Papers, Map of the Battle of the Jerusalem Plank Road, June 22, 1864, Private Collection of John Horn, Oak Forest, Illinois.

Websites

ahec.armywarcollege.edu

www.archives.alabama.gov/referenc/alamilor/8thinf.html

beta.worldcat.org/archivegrid

www.beyondthecrater.com

chroniclingamerica.loc.gov

Civil War Richmond

www.civil-war-soldiers.mooseroots.com

www.dmna.ny.

www.findagrave.com

www.history.navy.mil

www.jewish-history.com/civilwar/

www.loc.gov

www.merriam-webster.com/dictionary

www.newspapers.com/

www.nps.gov/civilwar/soldiers-and-sailors-database.htm

www.pa-roots.com

www.petersburgcampaign@blogspot.com

www.petersburgproject.org

rmccivilwar.blogspot.com/2012/09/joseph-richard-manson-student-1846-1849.html

www.scribd.com

thomaslegion.net/7thnorthcarolinainfantryregimentstatistics.html

Acknowledgments

It takes a village to produce a book of non-fiction.

I am particularly indebted to Hampton Newsome, Ralph Peters, Edwin C. Bearss, Chris Calkins, Chris Daw, Elizabeth Parham Horn, Chris Mackowski, Darlene O'Keefe, Gordon Rhea, William Glenn Robertson, Dr. Richard J. Sommers, Bryce Suderow, Noah Andre Trudeau, and George Zelenack.

I am also grateful to Elise Phillips Atkins, Joann Buckmaster, Michael A. Cavanaugh, Jr., Richard A. Cheatham, Herbert Coons, Dr. David F. Cross, Bob Dietz, Fletcher Elmore, Thomas L. Elmore, Jerry Gibbs, A. Wilson Greene, Lowell Griffin, Randy Hackenburg, Mrs. Alexander Hamilton, Robert Hancock, Noel G. Harrison, William D. Henderson, the late Dr. John T. Hendron, Harold Jacobson, Helen M. Kelley, Robert E. L. Krick, Robert K. Krick, Don Lauter, Ted Linton, Dr. Richard McMurry, Nancy B. Nevins, Forrest Pedlar, John Michael Priest, John Reynolds, Rebecca Rice, Suzanne Savery, Dr. Richard Shrader, Mrs. Joseph Schweidler, Gary Simpson, Brooke Sporleder, Jeffrey Stocker, James G. Thayer, William Turner, Zack Waters, David White, Dr. John White, Col. Julian Whitehorne, Lamar Williams, Alfred Young, William T. Zielinski, the staffs at Alderman Library (University of Virginia), the American Genealogical Lending Library, the Armed Forces Medical Museum, Chicago Heights Stake (United Church of Christ), Hargrett Rare Books Library (University of Georgia), the Library Of Congress, the Mississippi Department of Archives and History, the Museum of the Confederacy, Mugar Library (Boston University), the National Archives, the Newberry Library, Orland Stake (United Church of Christ), Perkins Library (Duke University), Preston Library (Virginia Military Institute), Swem Library (College of William and Mary), the Tinley Park Public Library, the United States Army Military History Institute (Carlisle Barracks), the Virginia Historical Society, Virginia Military Institute Museum, Virginia State Library, and Wilson Library (University of North Carolina at Chapel Hill).

I would also like to thank my publisher Savas Beatie, including but not limited to Managing Editor Theodore P. Savas, Marketing Director Sarah Keeney, and Media Specialist Renee Morehouse.

Finally I thank my wife and children for their patience.

If I missed anyone, *mea maxima culpa*! It is all my fault.

Index

Bernard, Pvt. Richard F., 103

Bird, Pvt. Henry V. L. "Birdie," Norfolk, 30; Seven Days battles, 68; Second Manassas, 85, 87; to Petersburg, 259, 263; Jerusalem Plank Road, 282; The Crater, 289, 297, 300-301, 305; Globe Tavern, 316-317; Second Reams Station, 322-325, 329, 331; Hatcher's Run, 365; post war, 402; *photo*, 283

Birdsong, Pvt. James C., 384, 402

Blakemore, Pvt. James H., 274-276, 403

Blandford Cemetery, 287, 326, 344

Blanks, Pvt. Charles D. "Charley," 390

Bolling, Col. Robert B., 91, 93, 195

Bolling, 2Lt. William N., 91

Bond, Capt. Thomas H., 6

Booker, Pvt. Henry T., *photo*, 390

Booth, John Wilkes, 8, 22, 346, 404-405; *photo*, 23

Bossieux, 1Lt Virginius, 364

Bounty and Furlough Act, The, 38-41

Bowden, Capt. Robert R., 196, 199, 201

Boydton Plank Road, 319, 328, 332-333, 335, 337, 341, 347, 355, 357, 361, 369

Branch, Capt. Edwin W. "Ned," 170, 177, 199-200, 202

Branch, Capt. James R., 24

Branch, Thomas, 7

Brandy Station, 164, 176

Brandy Station, Second battle of, 199-201

Bristoe Station, 208, 210-211, 213

Broadbent, Capt. William W., 299

Brockett, Col. Edgar L., 6, 21, 41

Brown, John, 5-6, 8, 22-23

Brown, Pvt. Philip F., 18, 20, 64, 67, 72, 76, 82-83, 89, 92, 100, 108, 112-113, 120, 219; *photo*, 403

Brown, Pvt. Samuel E., 299

Burgess Mill, 332-343, 345, 347, 355, 358, 367, 390-392, 403

Burke's Station, 373-374, 376-377, 301, 303

Cameron, Capt. William E., 177, 237; Peninsula Campaign, 34-35, 40-41; Seven Pines, 50, 55-57; Second Manassas, 92, 95; Maryland Campaign, 103; Chancellorsville, 140, 144; Gettysburg, 172, 179, 185-186, 189, 195-

196; Brandy Station, Second battle of, 197, 199-202; post war, 392, 402, 405; *photo*, 172

Campbell, Pvt. John J., 330, 334, 336, 343, 390

Chancellorsville, 138-139, 144-145, 148, 150, 152-154, 157-159, 161, 166, 178, 196, 223, 389

Chancellorsville, Virginia, 136, 139-140

Chappell, 1Lt. George D., 24, 105, 187, 200, 261, 334, 342, 392, 405

Chase, Pvt. Henry E., 296, 299, 390

City Point, 307, 325, 355

Claiborne, Dr.. James W.; 5-6, 8-9, 16, 21-22, 27, 56, 59, 195-196, 200, 238, 302, 389, 403

Claiborne, Dr. John H., 21-22, 403, *photo* 6

Clarke, Pvt. Samuel S., 260

Clingman, Brig. Gen. Thomas L. and his brigade, 294, 308-309, 311-313, 317

Cockade Barracks, 26-27, 36, 43, 45, 64

Cogbill, Color Sgt. George W., 79, 389

Cold Harbor, 265, 267, 289, 391

Colquitt, Brig. Gen. Alfred H. and his brigade, 308-312, 317, 259

Crampton's Gap, 104-106, 108, 110-114, 119, 121, 133, 137, 159, 392-393

Crater, The, 285-290, 293-294, 296-309, 313, 317, 330, 344-345, 390-392, 402

Crawford, 1Lt. Jacob V., 40

Critz, Capt. James P., 40

Crow, Cpl. John E., 102-103, 108, 110, 286, 294-296

Culpeper Court House, 136-138, 163-164, 166, 197, 201, 203, 206-207, 211-213

Cumberland Church, 380-383, 391

Custer, Brig. Gen. George A., 223

Dahlgren Raid, 223-224

Daniel, Pvt. Ello K., 242-244, 359, 391

Davis, President Jefferson, 33, 40, 121, 162, 205, 214, 346, 363-364, 368

Davis, Pvt. Richard B., 291, 297, 299, 302-303, 391, 403, 405; *photo*, 290

Davis, Sgt. William S., 371, 391

Dawson, Pvt. Nicholas, 79

Dean, Pvt. Leonidas H., 249, 261, 289, 291, 296, 306, 390

Delaware Military Unit; 1st Infantry, 180

About the author

A native of the Chicago area, John Horn received a B.A. in English and Latin from New College (Sarasota, Florida) in 1973 and a J.D. from Columbia Law School in 1976. He has practiced law around Chicago since graduation, held local public office, and lived in Oak Forest with his wife and law partner, H. Elizabeth Kelley, a native of Richmond, Virginia. They have three children. He and his wife have often traveled to the Old Dominion to visit relatives, battlefields, and various archives.

John has published articles in *Civil War Times, Illus.*, *America's Civil War*, and elsewhere, and is the author of several books including *The Siege of Petersburg: The Battles for the Weldon Railroad, August 1864* (El Dorado Hills, CA: Savas Beatie, 2015). You can read John's blog posts at www.petersburgcampaign.blogspot.com.